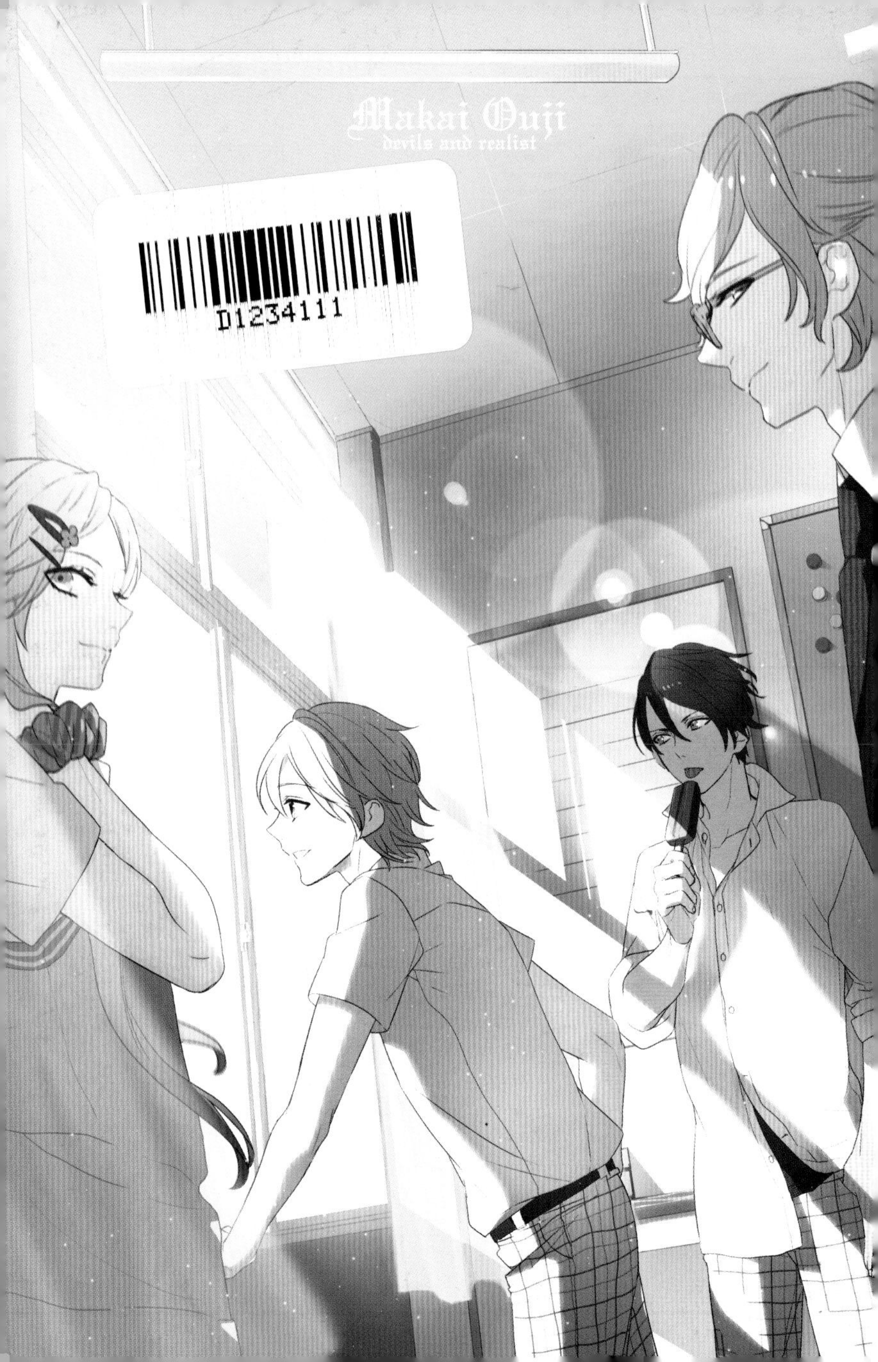
Makai Ouji
devils and realist

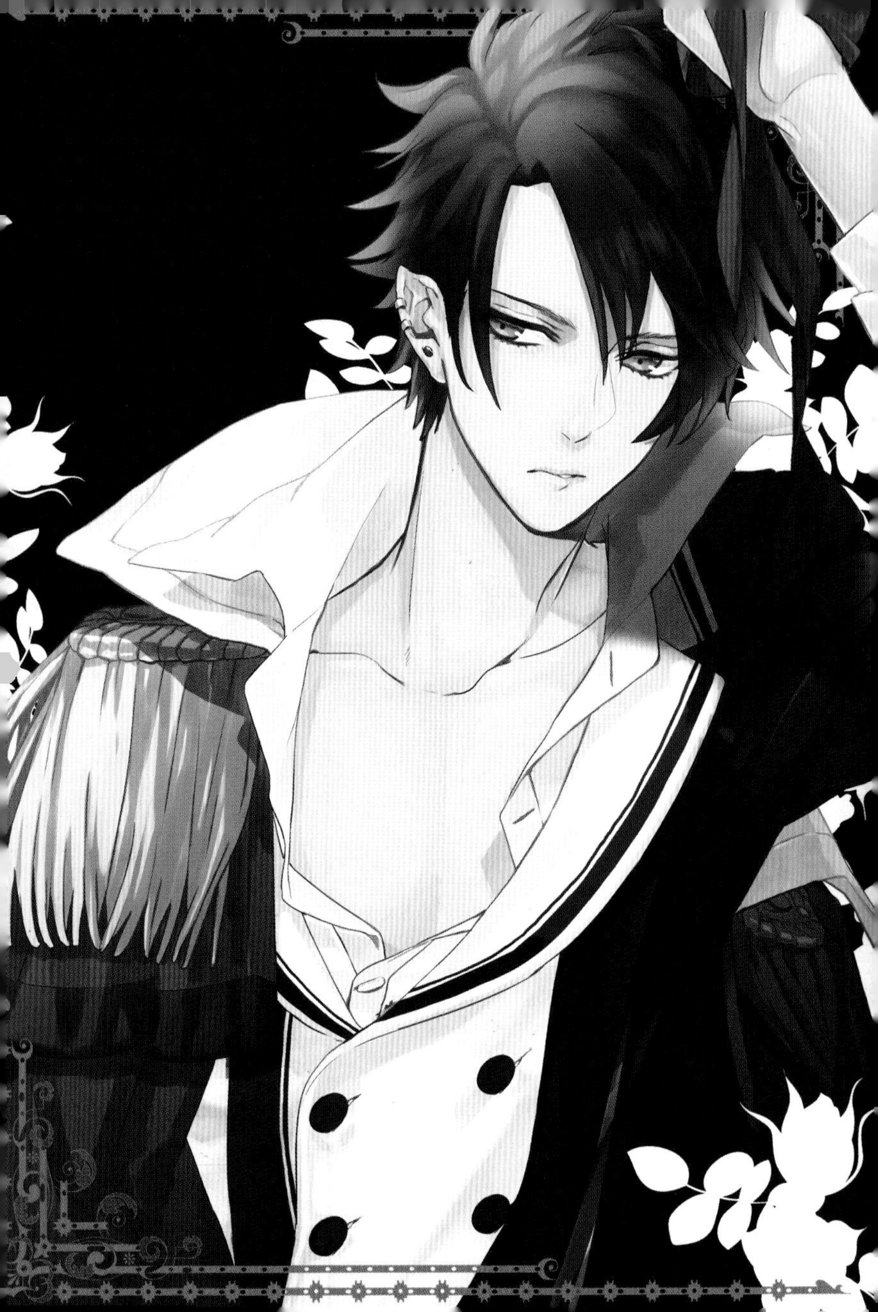

Devils and Realist
vol.10

story by Madoka Takadono
art by Utako Yukihiro

Cast of Characters

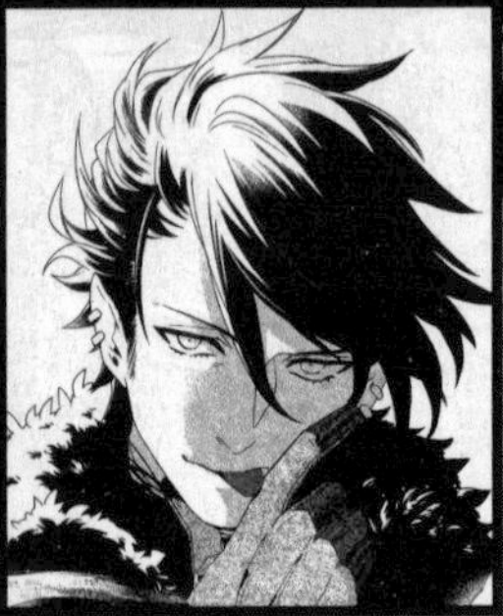

Dantalion

71st pillar and commander of 36 armies of Hell, he is Grand Duke of the Underworld. He is one of the candidates for representative king and is relied on at school as a jock.

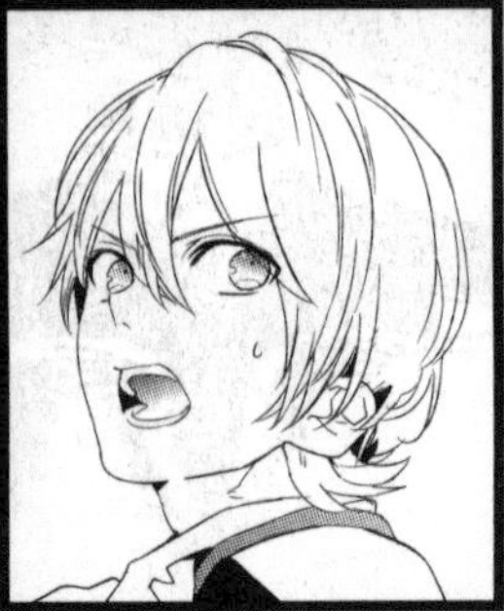

William

A brilliant realist from a famous noble family. As the descendant of King Solomon, he is the Elector with the authority to choose the representative of the king of Hell. He is slowly beginning to accept this role.

Kevin

William's capable yet gambling-addicted butler who is also a pastor at the academy. In truth, he is the angel Uriel who has been dispatched from Heaven.

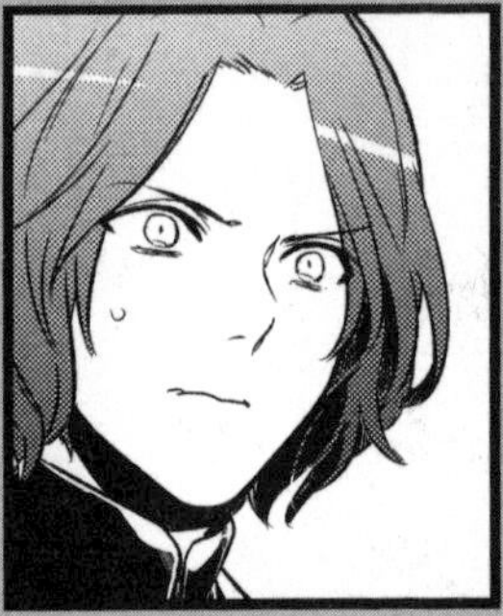

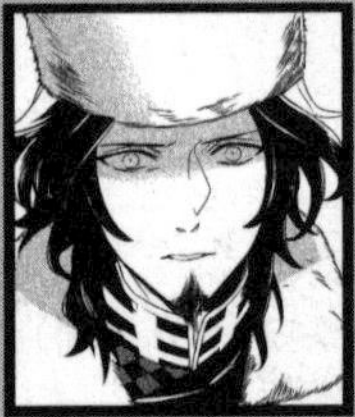

Baphomet

Dantalion's butler and lone retainer, who is also an excellent cook.

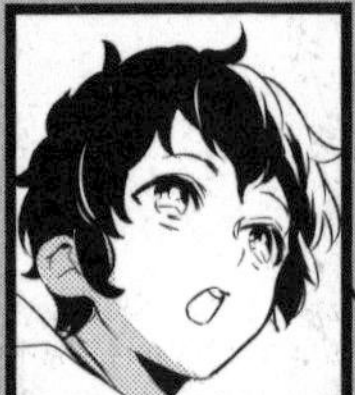

Metatron

An angel with enormous power. He encourages Uriel to join him in a heavenly conspiracy to convince Michael to go to sleep.

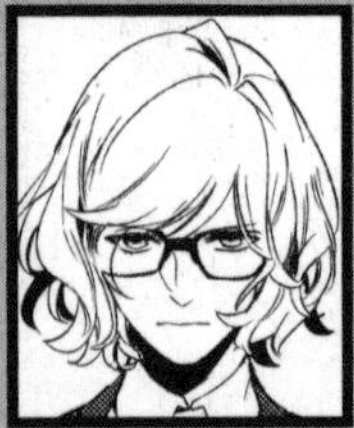

Camio

A candidate for representative king, Camio is Solomon's 53rd pillar and a Great President of Hell. He is an excellent student at school and serves as class representative.

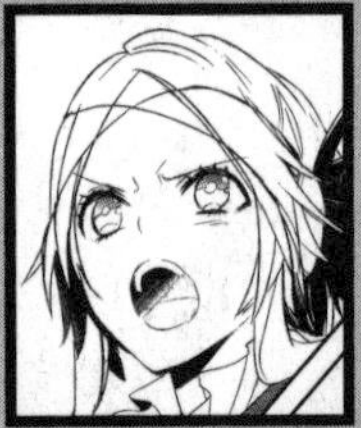

Sytry

Twelfth Pillar of Hell who leads 60 armies. Sytry is Prince of Hell and a candidate to represent the king. He is treated like a princess at school because of his beautiful appearance.

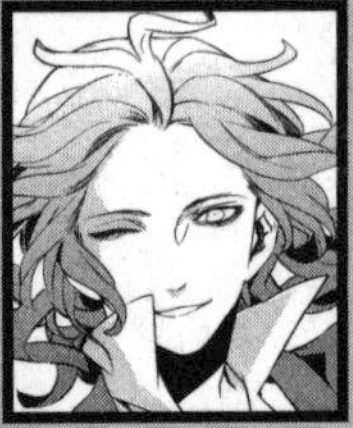

Mathers

Having left the Church of England, he calls himself Count Glenstrae and is an instructor at the school.

The Story So Far

The demons Dantalion and Sytry appear suddenly before impoverished noble William to tell him that he is the Elector who will decide the representative king of Hell. The pair join him at school as students, and William lives a life more and more entangled with the doings of Hell. While all this is going on, Dantalion's retainer, Baphomet, is preparing to go to sleep. In search of a new retainer to support him while Baphomet sleeps, Dantalion reaches out to Mathers, who is knowledgeable about many demonic matters. Meanwhile, Baphomet welcomes William into the manor in his master's absence, and begins to explain how he came to serve Dantalion...

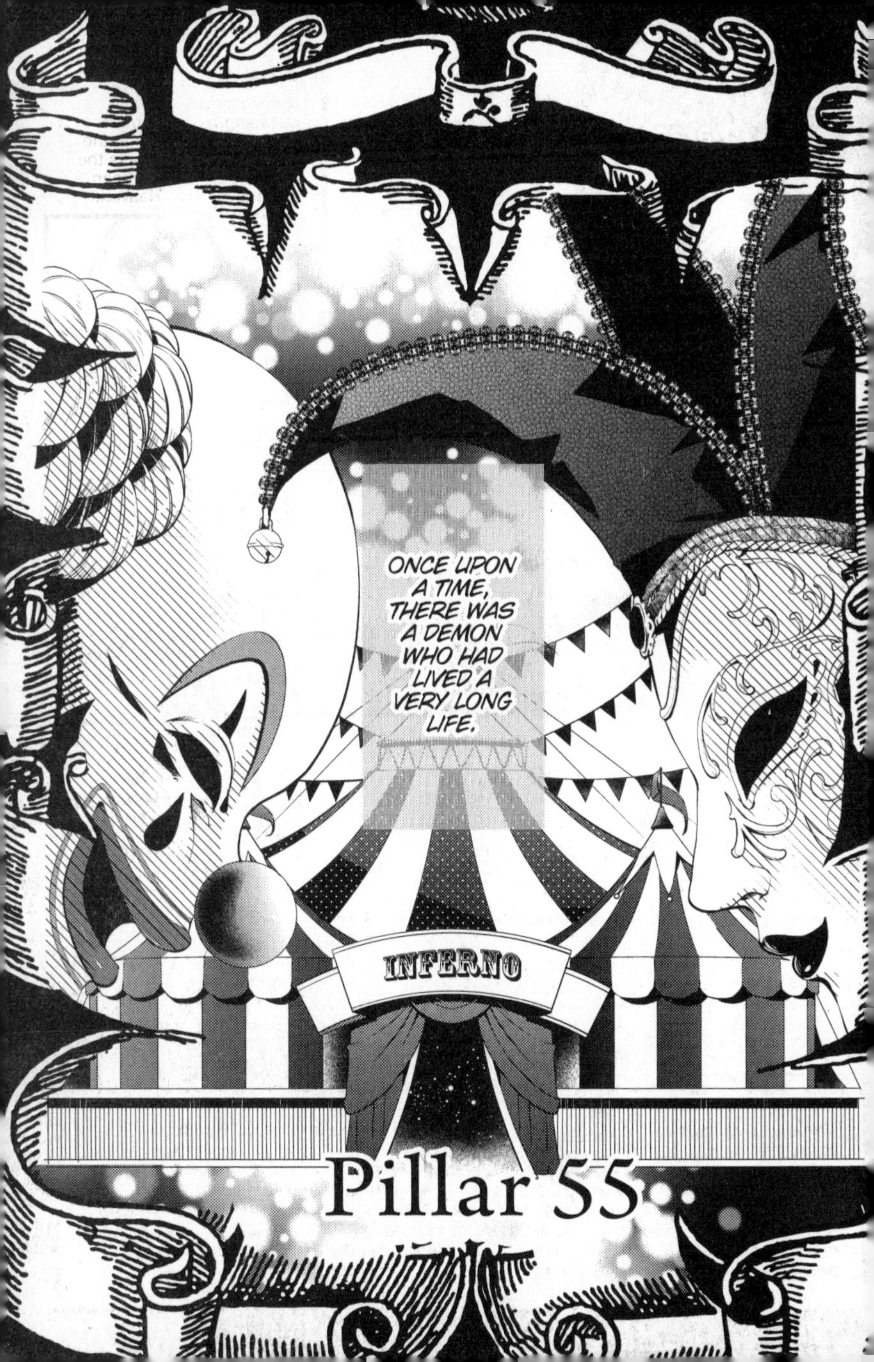
ONCE UPON A TIME, THERE WAS A DEMON WHO HAD LIVED A VERY LONG LIFE.
INFERNO
Pillar 55

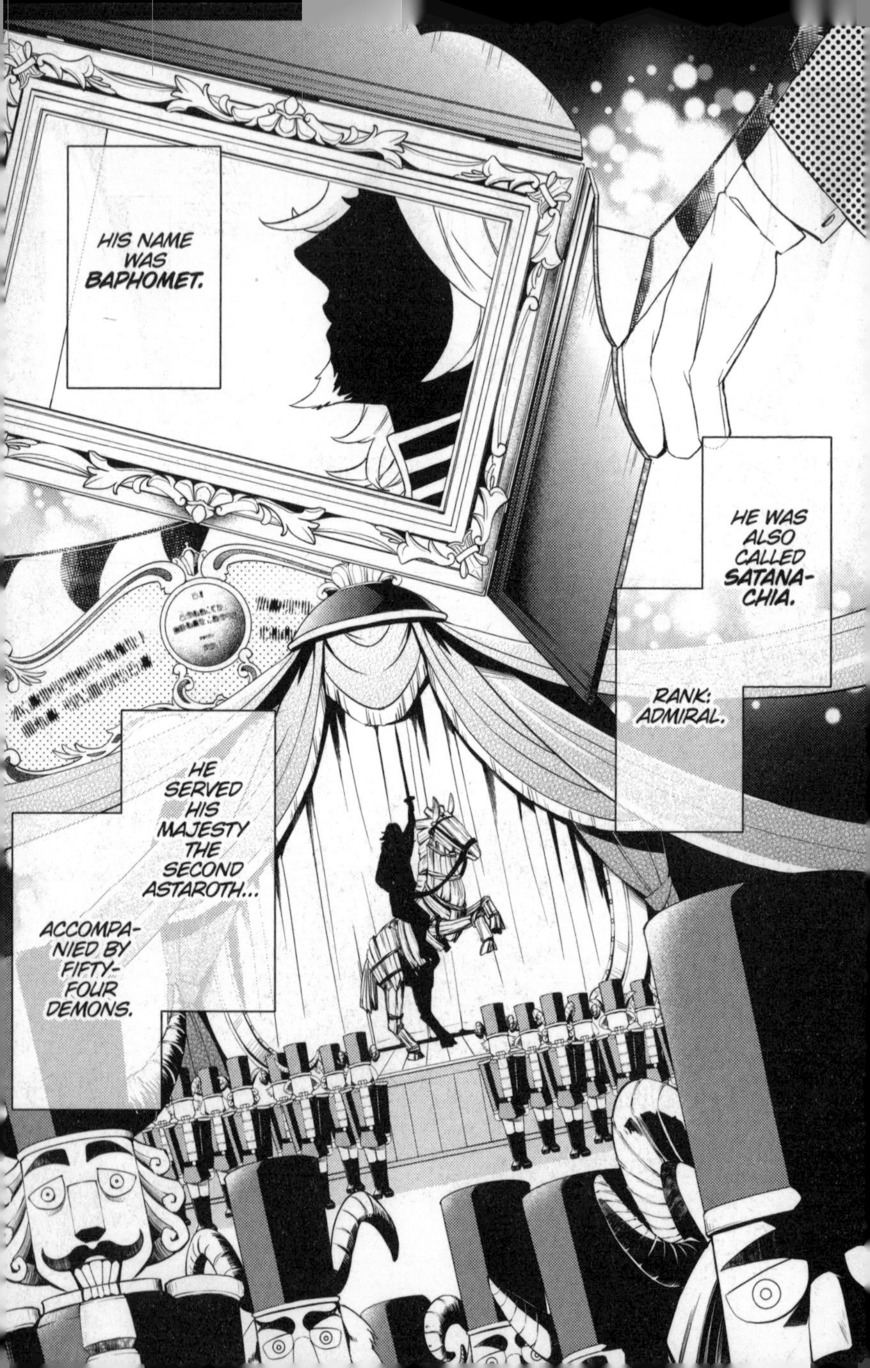
HIS NAME WAS BAPHOMET.
HE WAS ALSO CALLED SATANACHIA.
RANK: ADMIRAL.
HE SERVED HIS MAJESTY THE SECOND ASTAROTH...
ACCOMPANIED BY FIFTY-FOUR DEMONS.

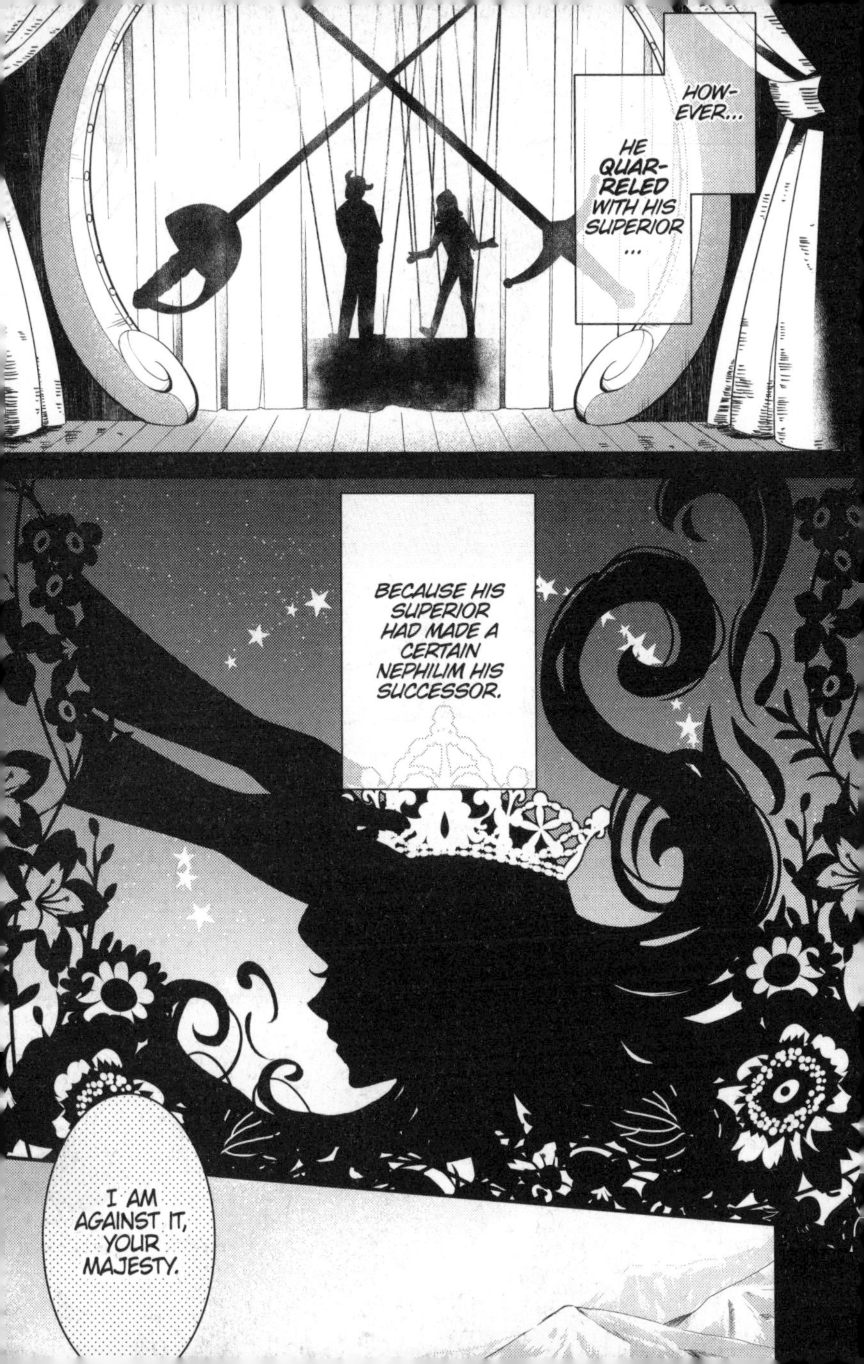
HOW-EVER...
HE QUARRELED WITH HIS SUPERIOR ...
BECAUSE HIS SUPERIOR HAD MADE A CERTAIN NEPHILIM HIS SUCCESSOR.
I AM AGAINST IT, YOUR MAJESTY.

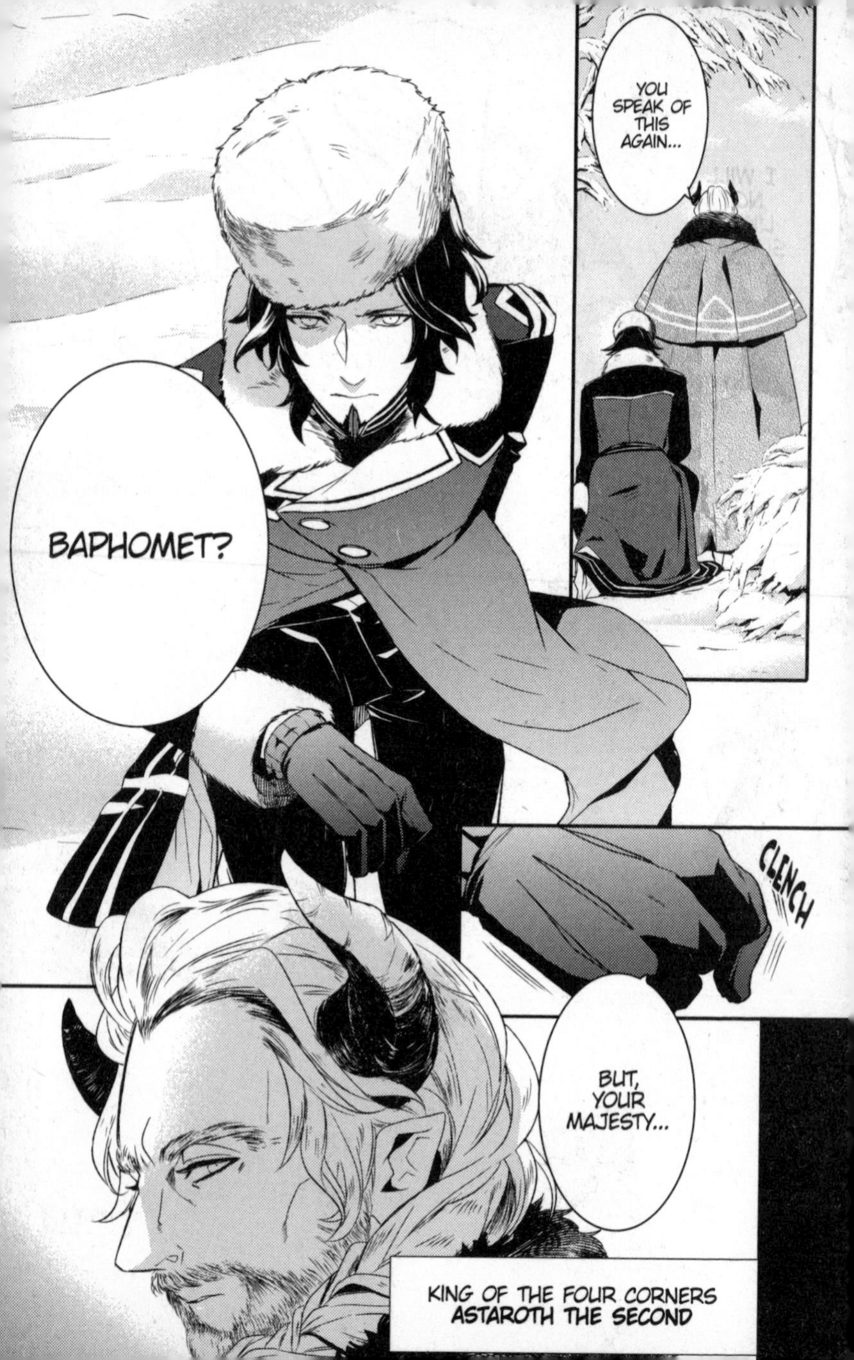
YOU SPEAK OF THIS AGAIN...
BAPHOMET?
CLENCH
BUT, YOUR MAJESTY...
KING OF THE FOUR CORNERS ASTAROTH THE SECOND

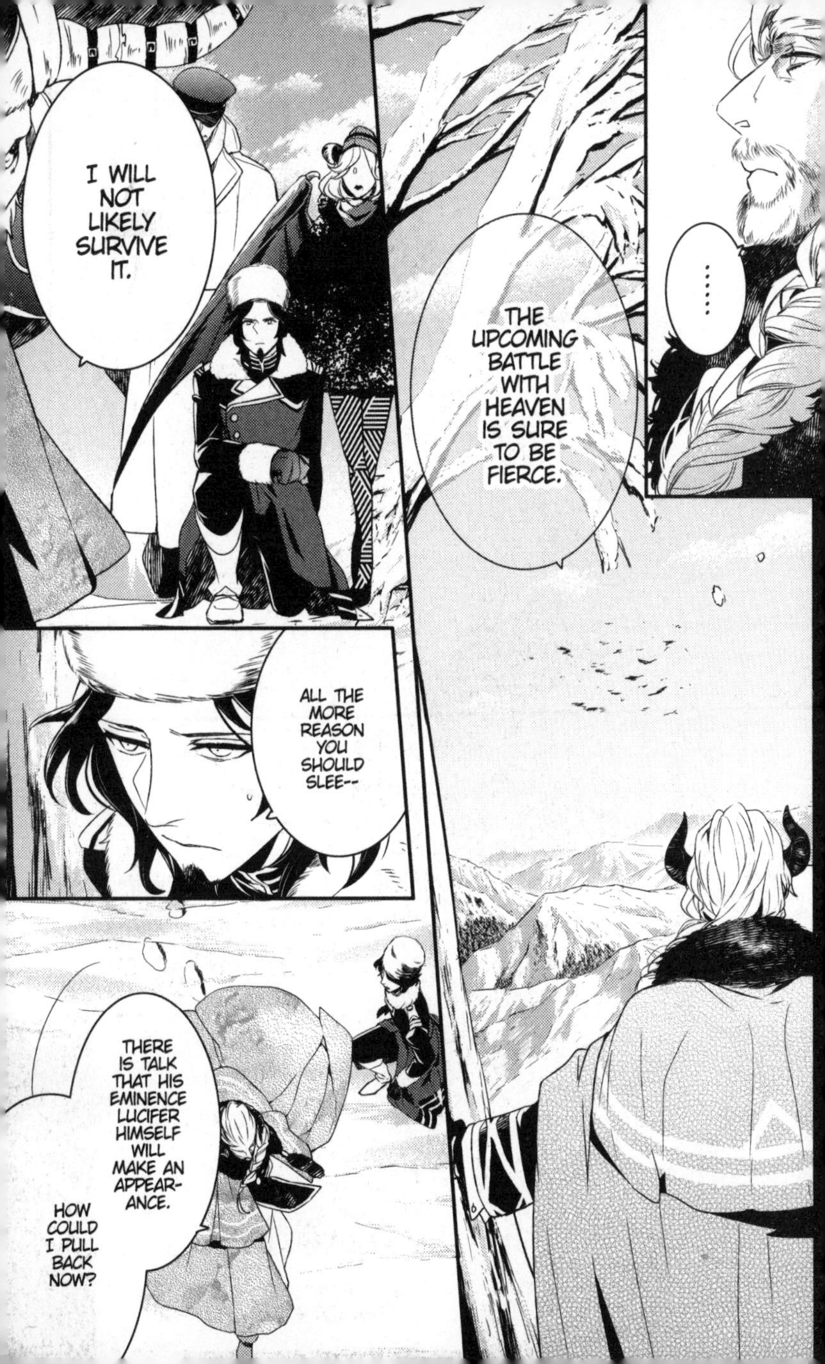
......
THE UPCOMING BATTLE WITH HEAVEN IS SURE TO BE FIERCE.
I WILL NOT LIKELY SURVIVE IT.
ALL THE MORE REASON YOU SHOULD SLEE--
THERE IS TALK THAT HIS EMINENCE LUCIFER HIMSELF WILL MAKE AN APPEAR-ANCE.
HOW COULD I PULL BACK NOW?

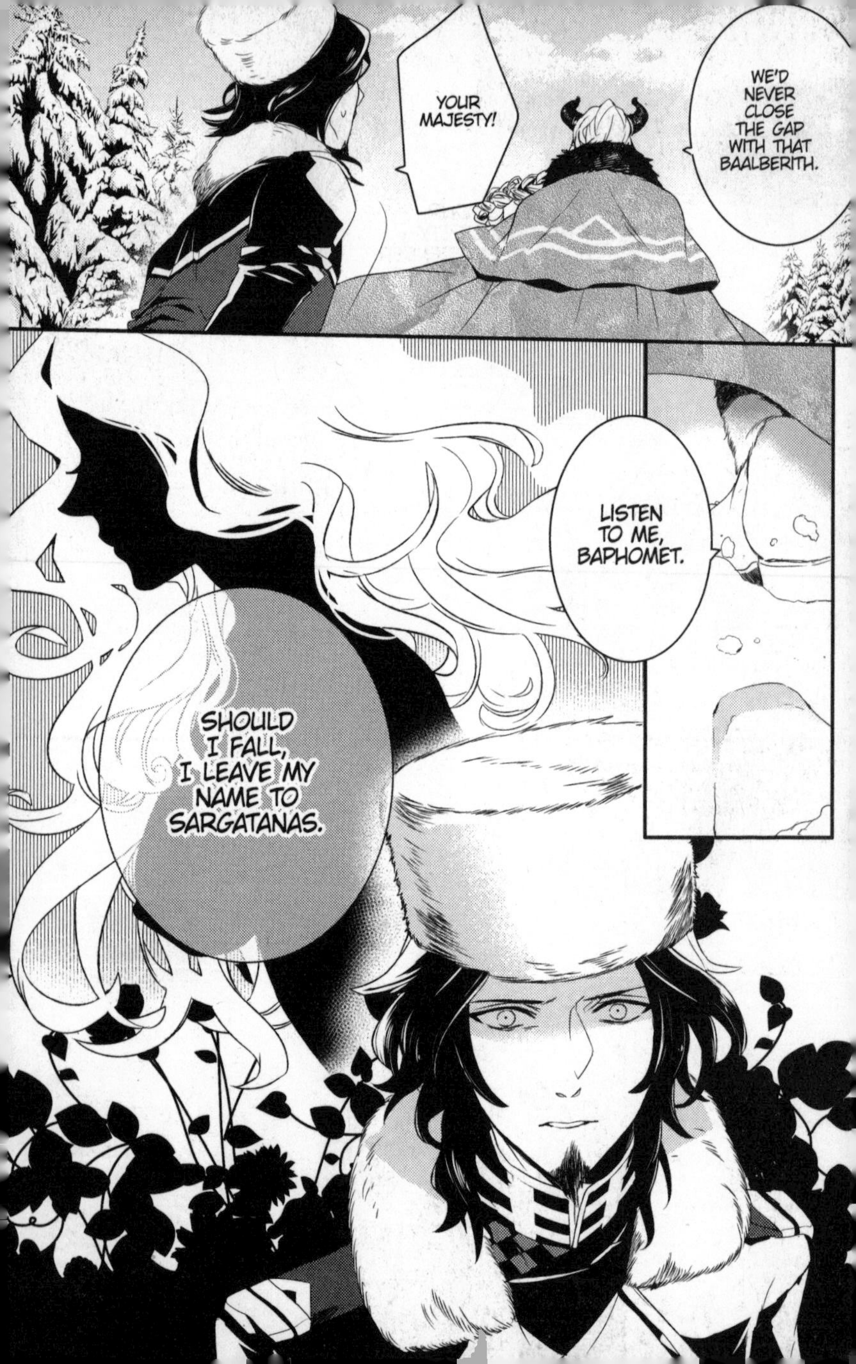
WE'D NEVER CLOSE THE GAP WITH THAT BAALBERITH.
YOUR MAJESTY!
LISTEN TO ME, BAPHOMET.
SHOULD I FALL, I LEAVE MY NAME TO SARGATANAS.

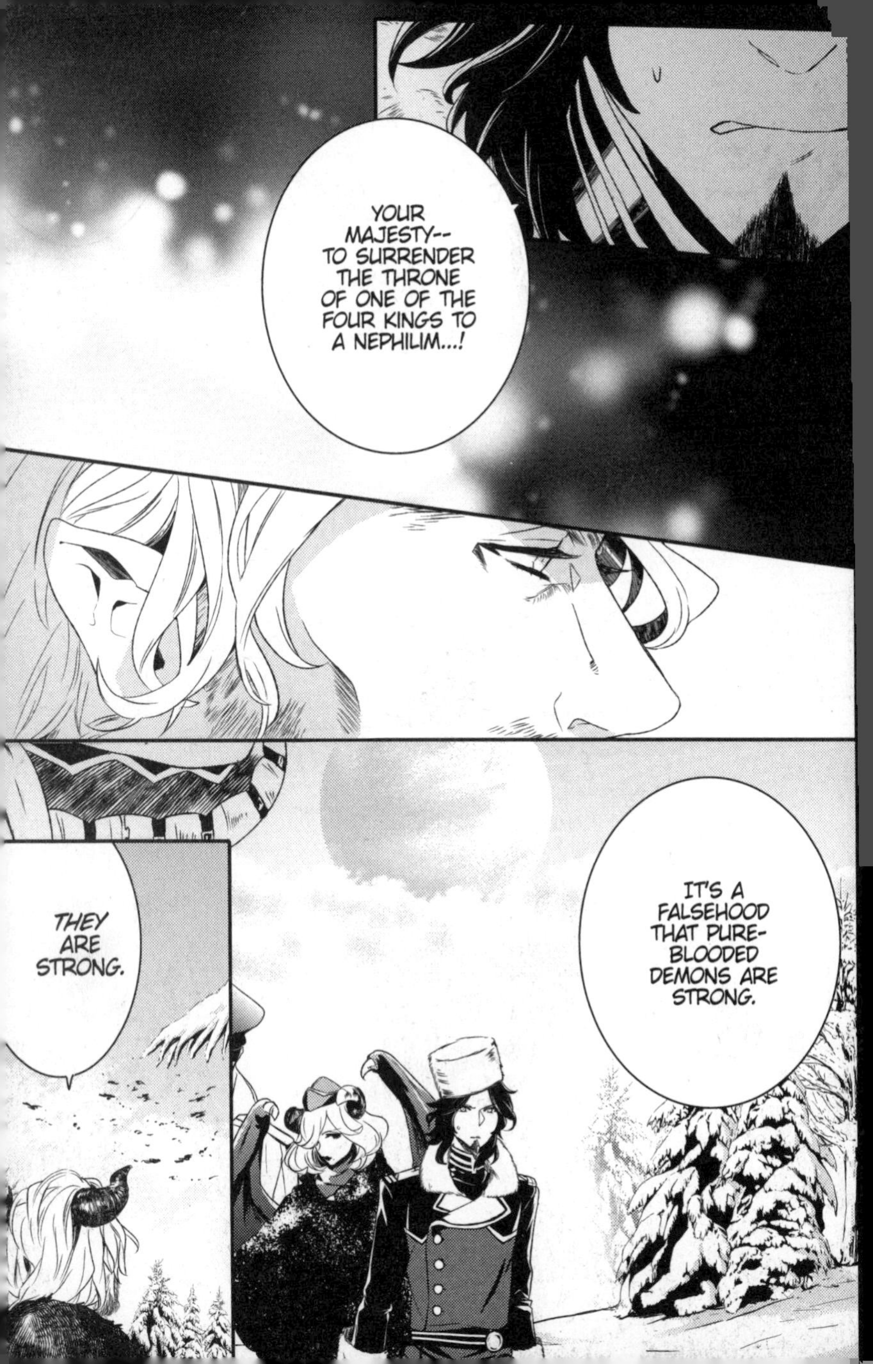
YOUR MAJESTY-- TO SURRENDER THE THRONE OF ONE OF THE FOUR KINGS TO A NEPHILIM...!
IT'S A FALSEHOOD THAT PURE-BLOODED DEMONS ARE STRONG.
THEY ARE STRONG.

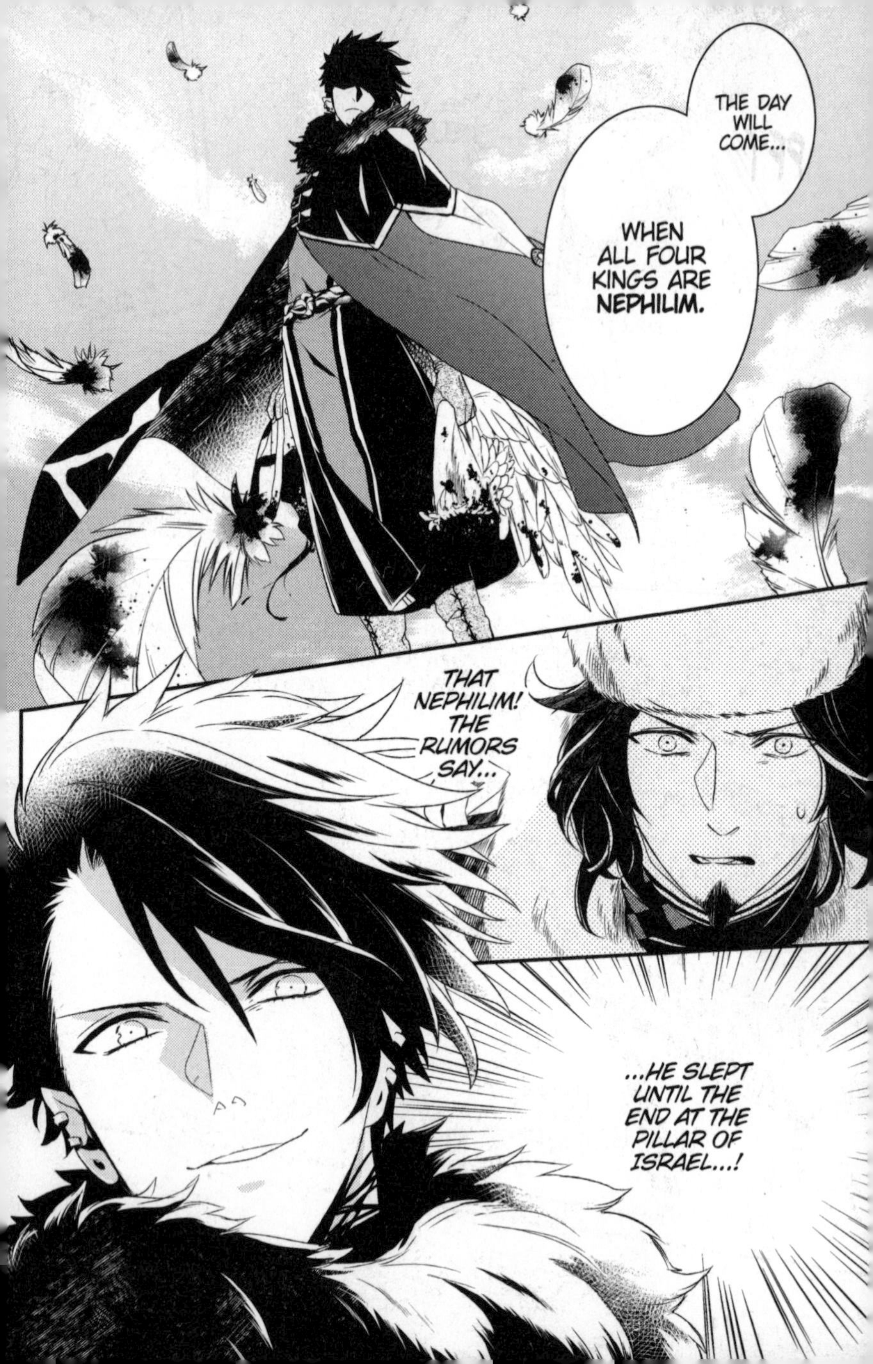
THE DAY WILL COME...
WHEN ALL FOUR KINGS ARE NEPHILIM.
THAT NEPHILIM! THE RUMORS SAY...
...HE SLEPT UNTIL THE END AT THE PILLAR OF ISRAEL...!

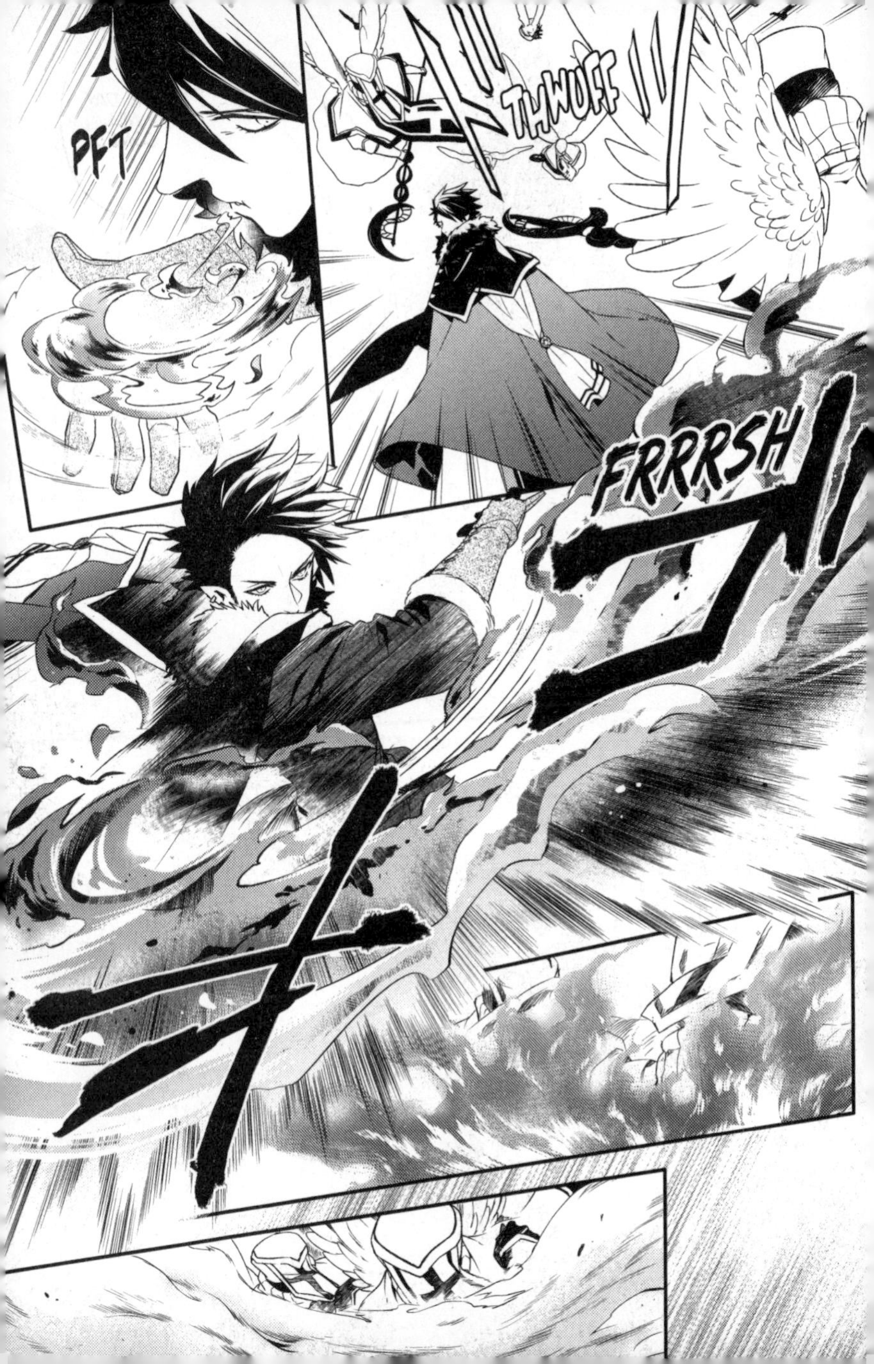
THWUFF
PFT
FRRRSH

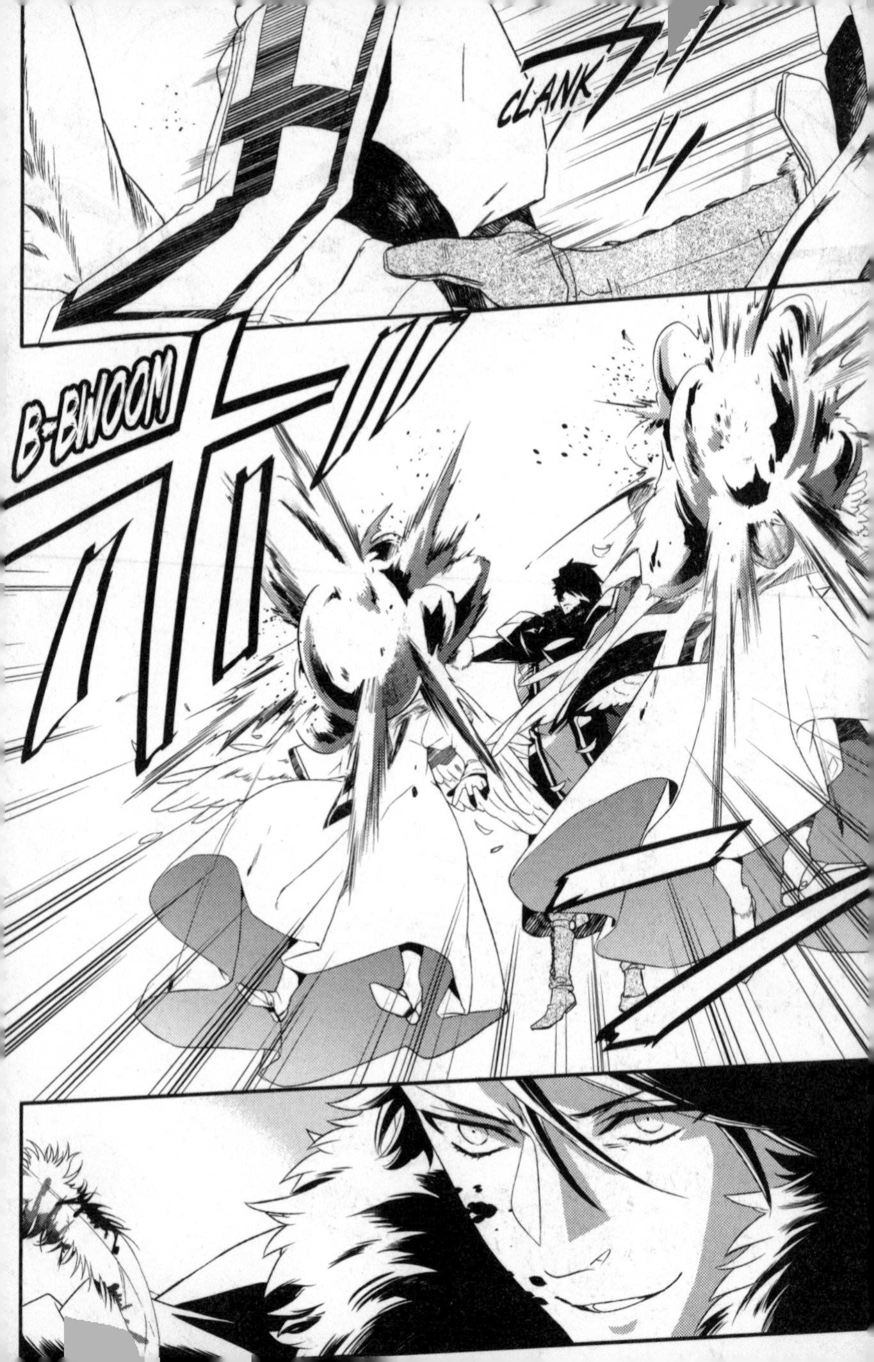
CLANK
B-BWOOM

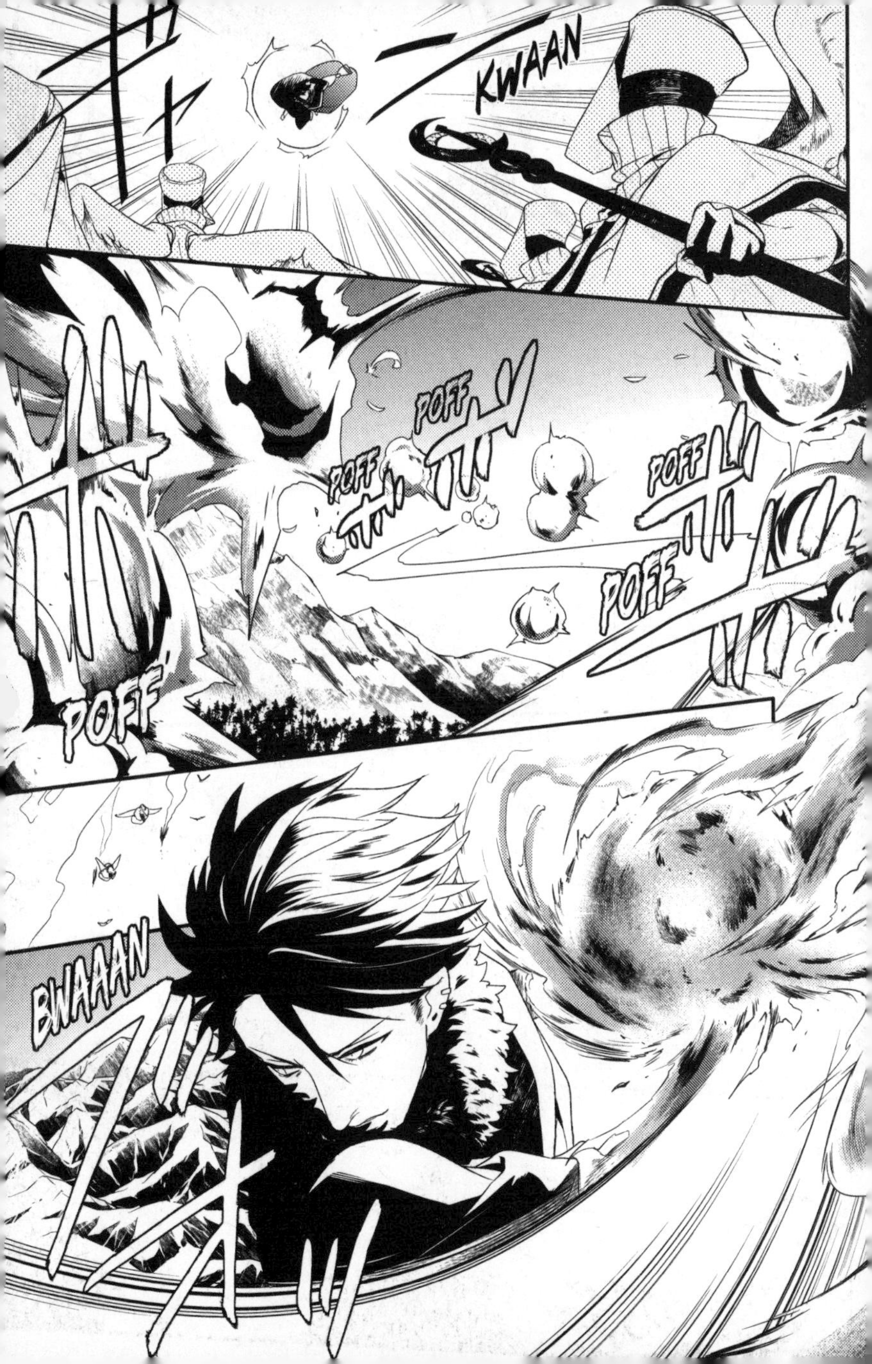
KWAAN
POFF
POFF
POFF
POFF
POFF
BWAAAN

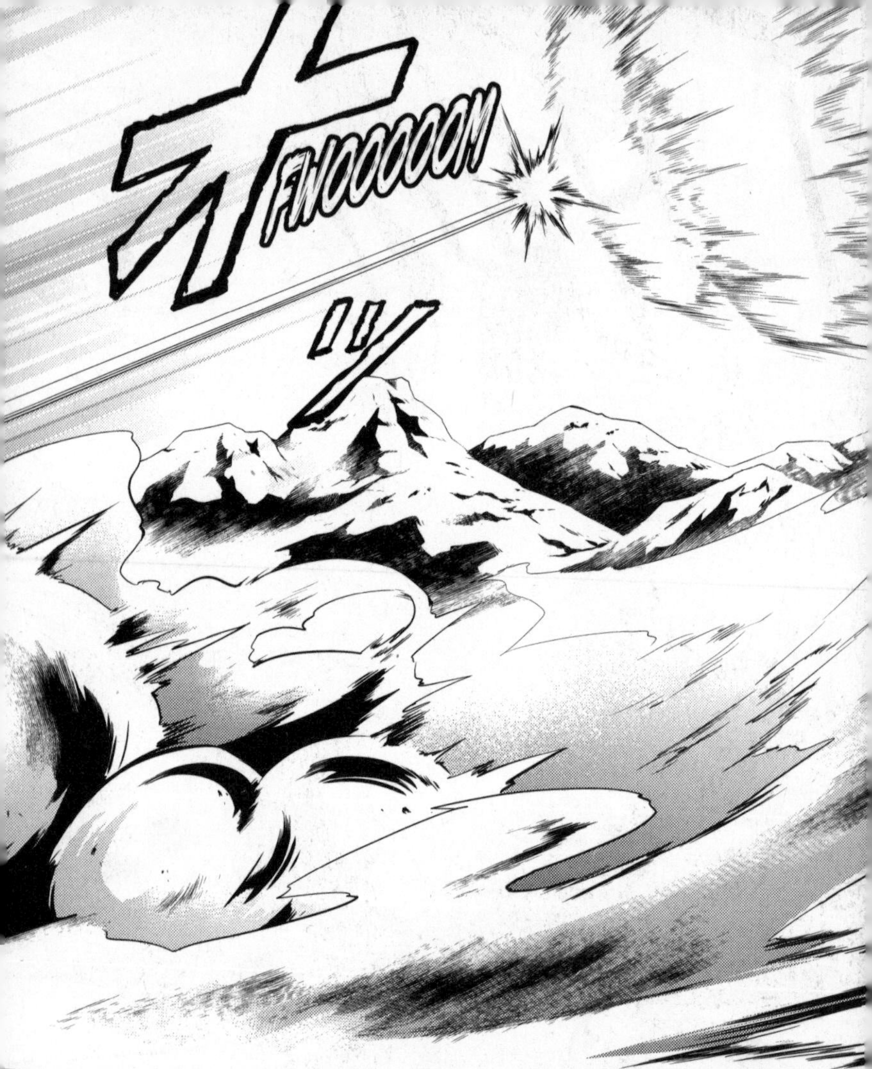
FWOOOOOM

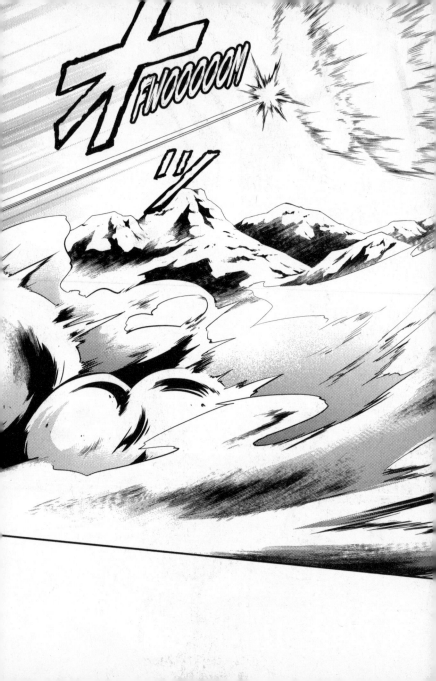

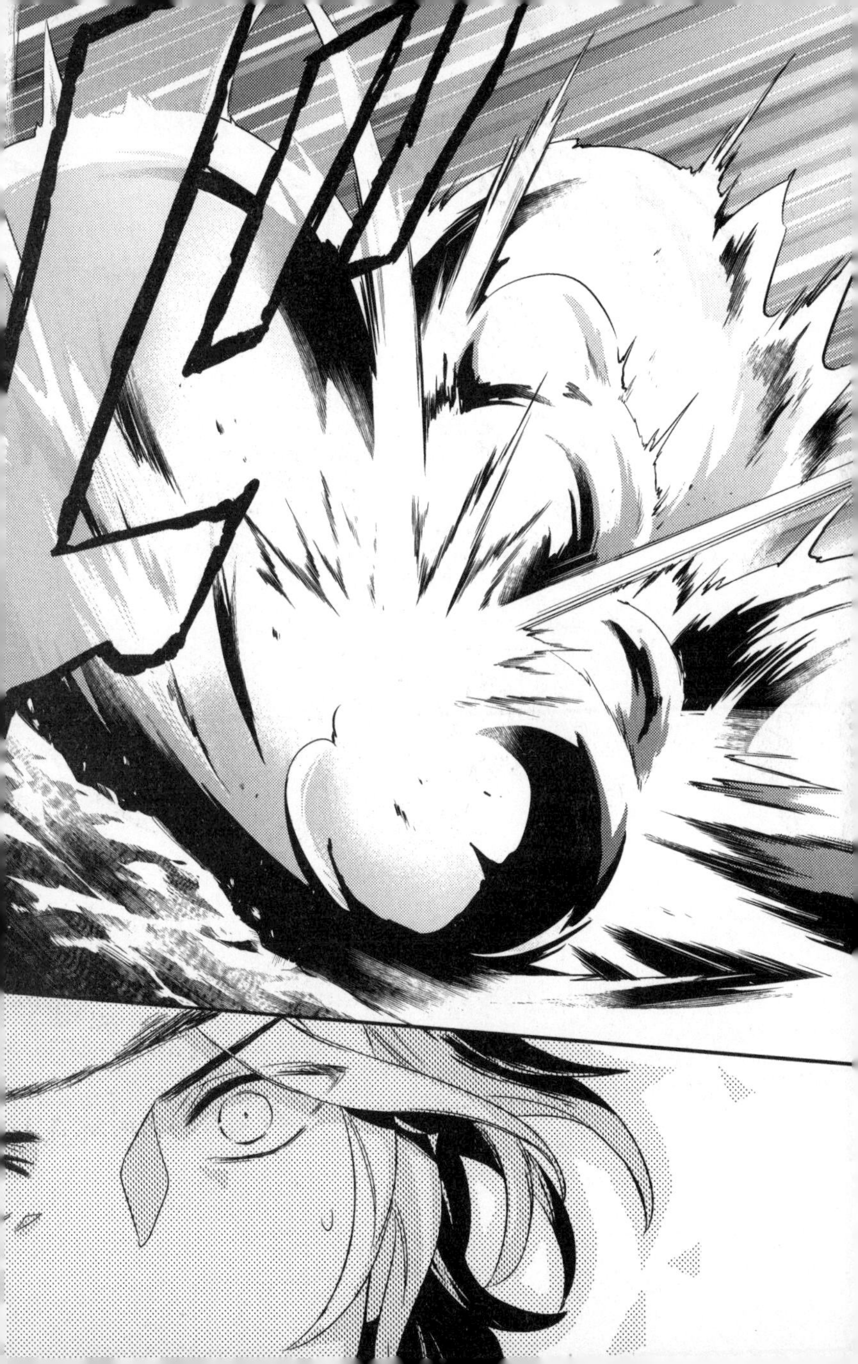

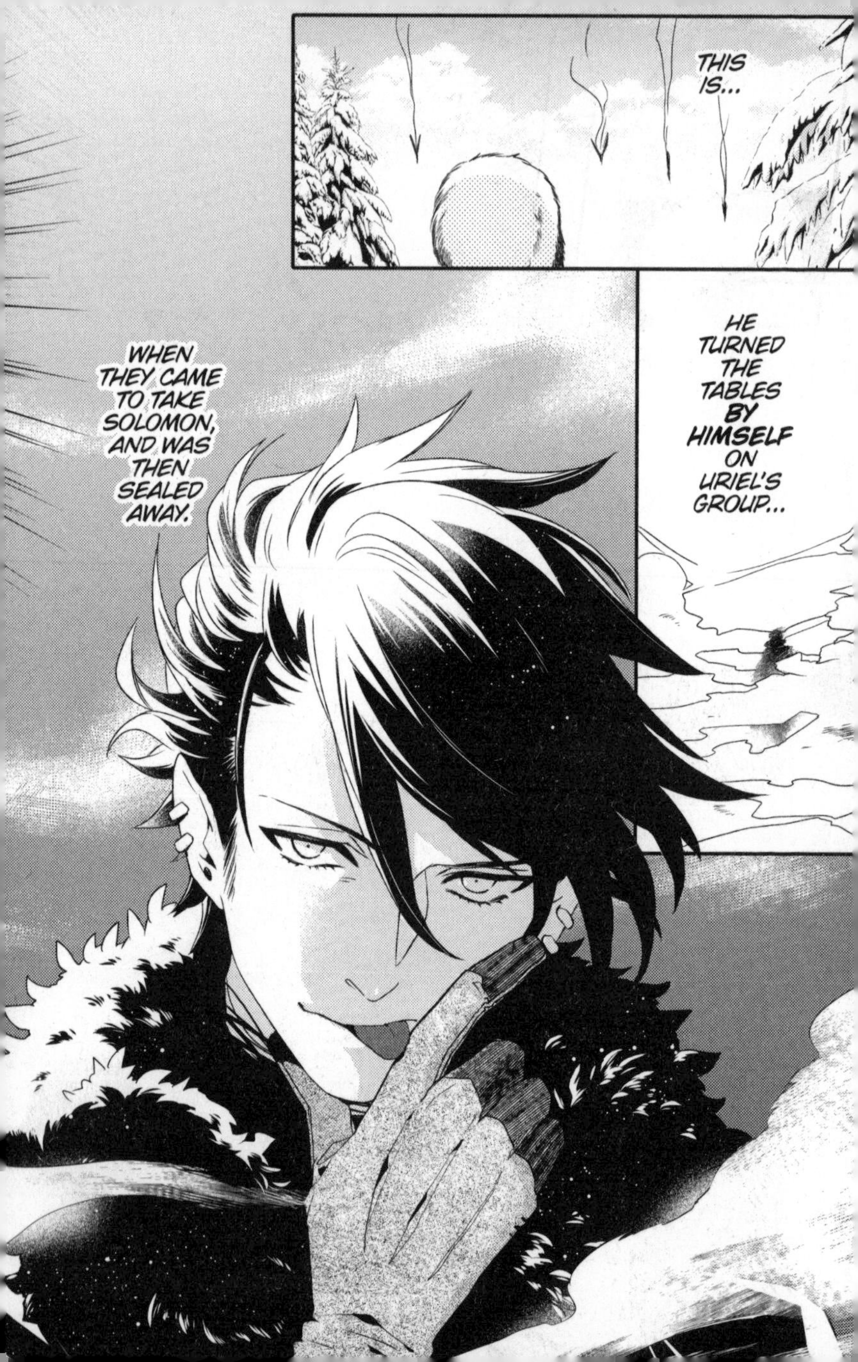
THIS IS...
HE TURNED THE TABLES BY HIMSELF ON URIEL'S GROUP...
WHEN THEY CAME TO TAKE SOLOMON, AND WAS THEN SEALED AWAY.

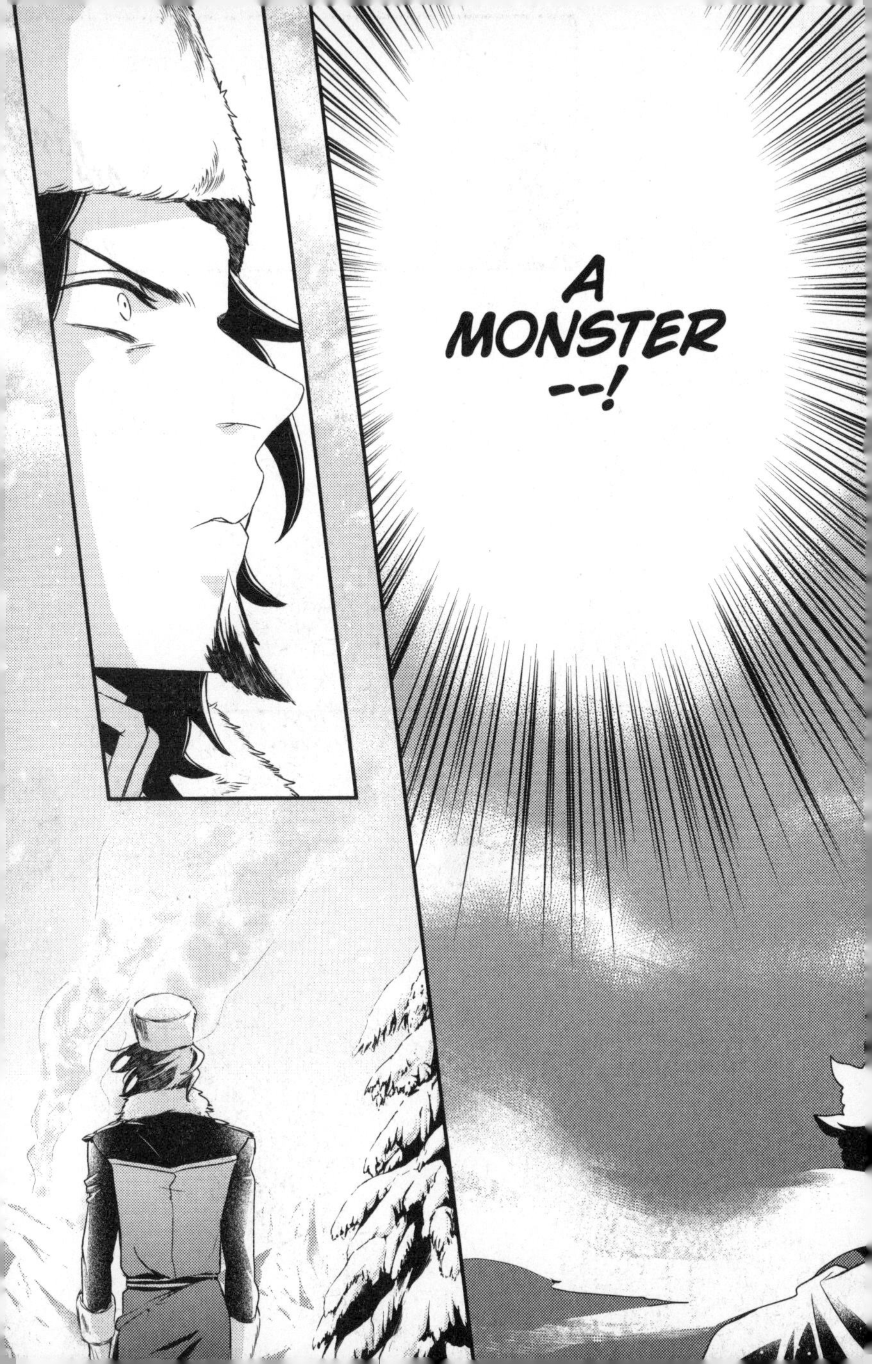
A MONSTER --!

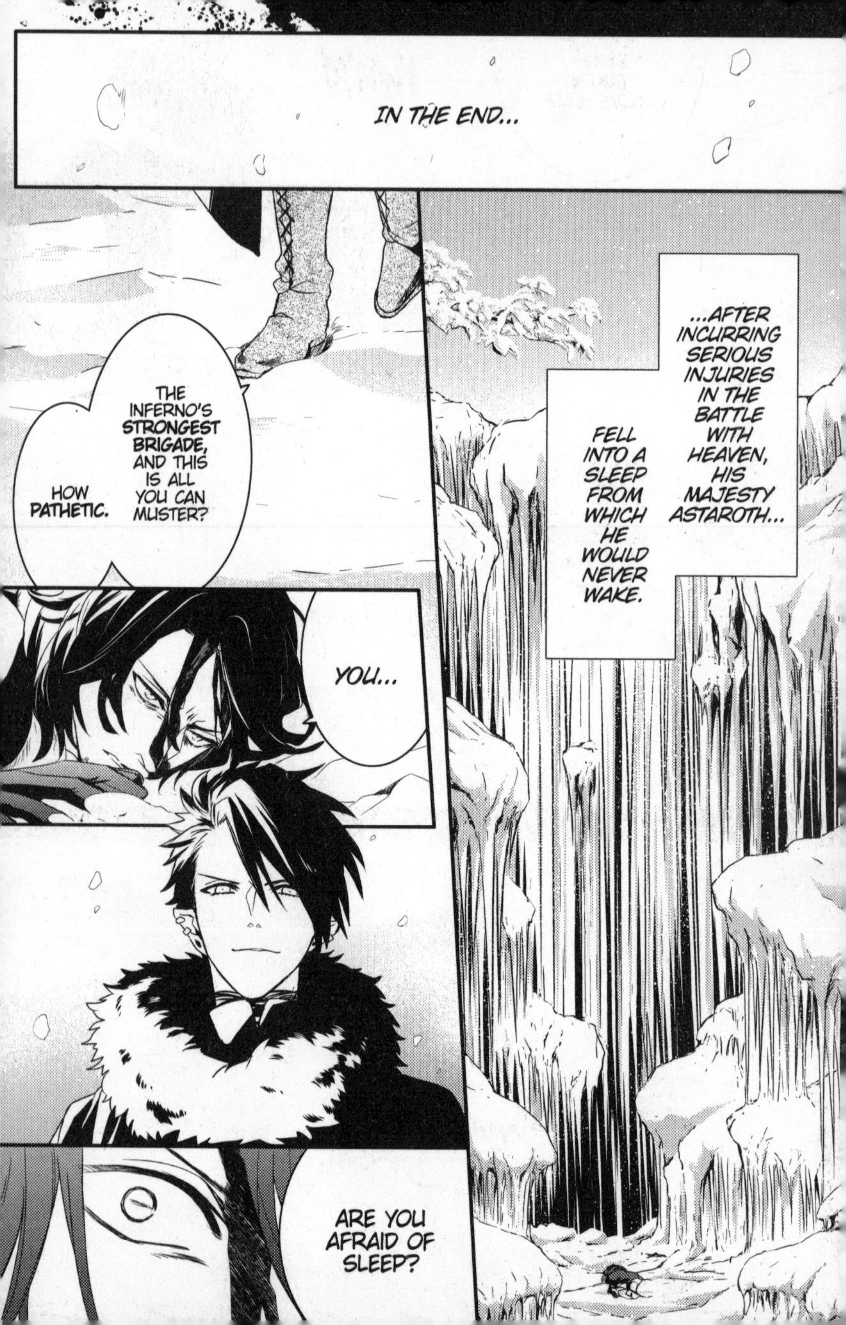
IN THE END...
...AFTER INCURRING SERIOUS INJURIES IN THE BATTLE WITH HEAVEN, HIS MAJESTY ASTAROTH...
FELL INTO A SLEEP FROM WHICH HE WOULD NEVER WAKE.
THE INFERNO'S STRONGEST BRIGADE, AND THIS IS ALL YOU CAN MUSTER?
HOW PATHETIC.
YOU...
ARE YOU AFRAID OF SLEEP?

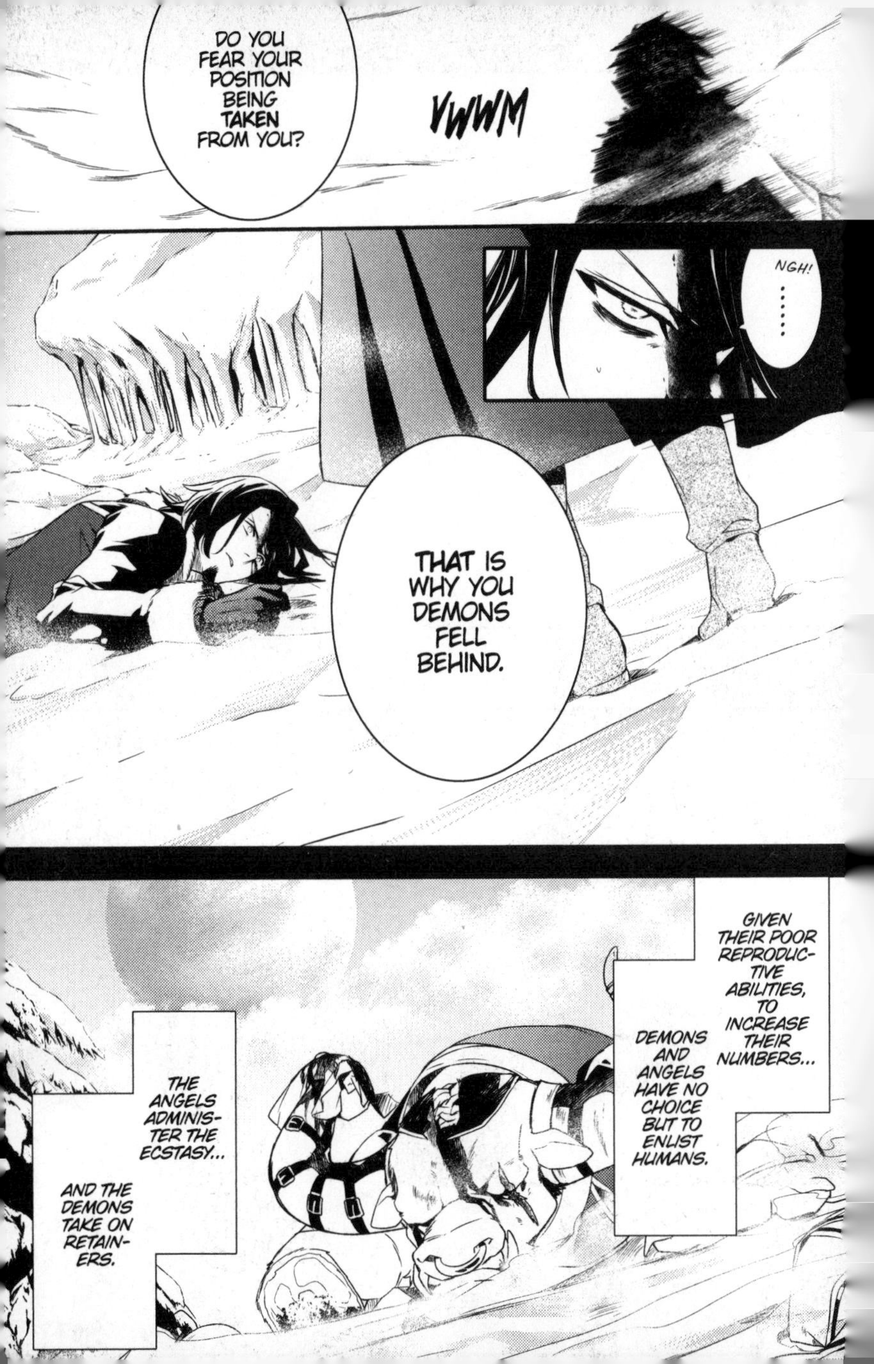
DO YOU FEAR YOUR POSITION BEING TAKEN FROM YOU?
VWWM
NGH!
......
THAT IS WHY YOU DEMONS FELL BEHIND.
GIVEN THEIR POOR REPRODUCTIVE ABILITIES, TO INCREASE THEIR NUMBERS...
DEMONS AND ANGELS HAVE NO CHOICE BUT TO ENLIST HUMANS.
THE ANGELS ADMINISTER THE ECSTASY...
AND THE DEMONS TAKE ON RETAINERS.

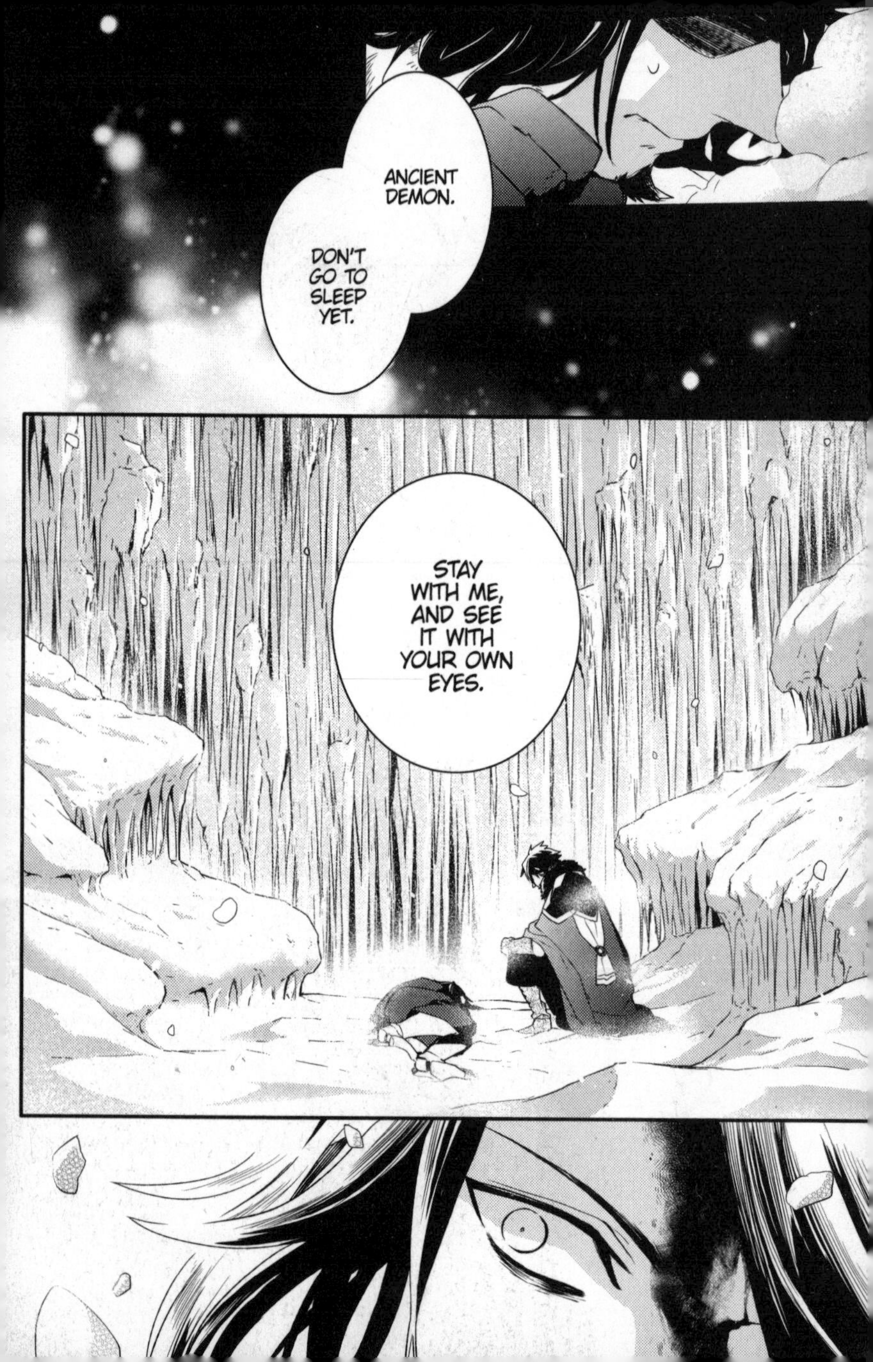
ANCIENT DEMON.
DON'T GO TO SLEEP YET.
STAY WITH ME, AND SEE IT WITH YOUR OWN EYES.

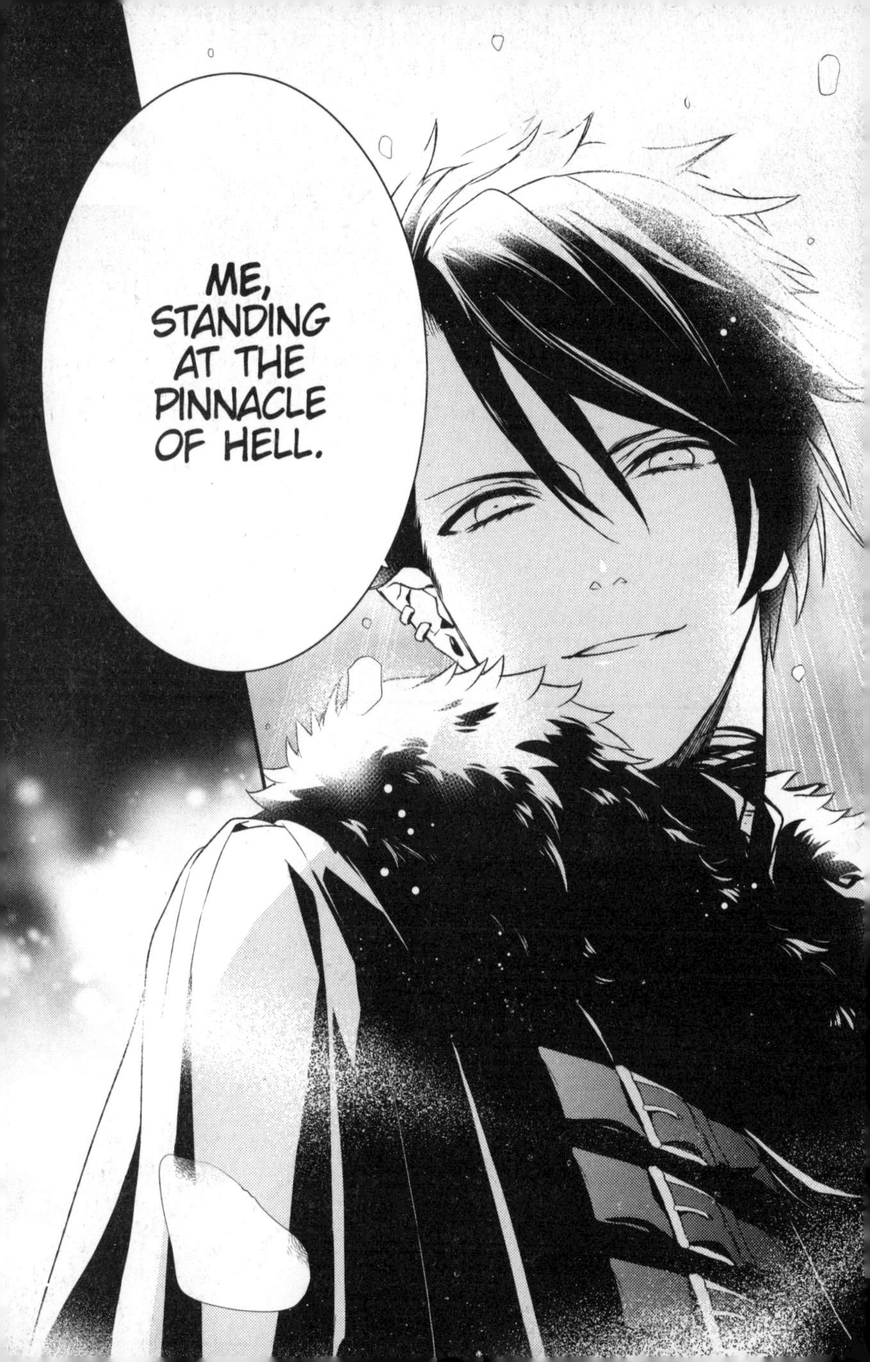
ME, STANDING AT THE PINNACLE OF HELL.

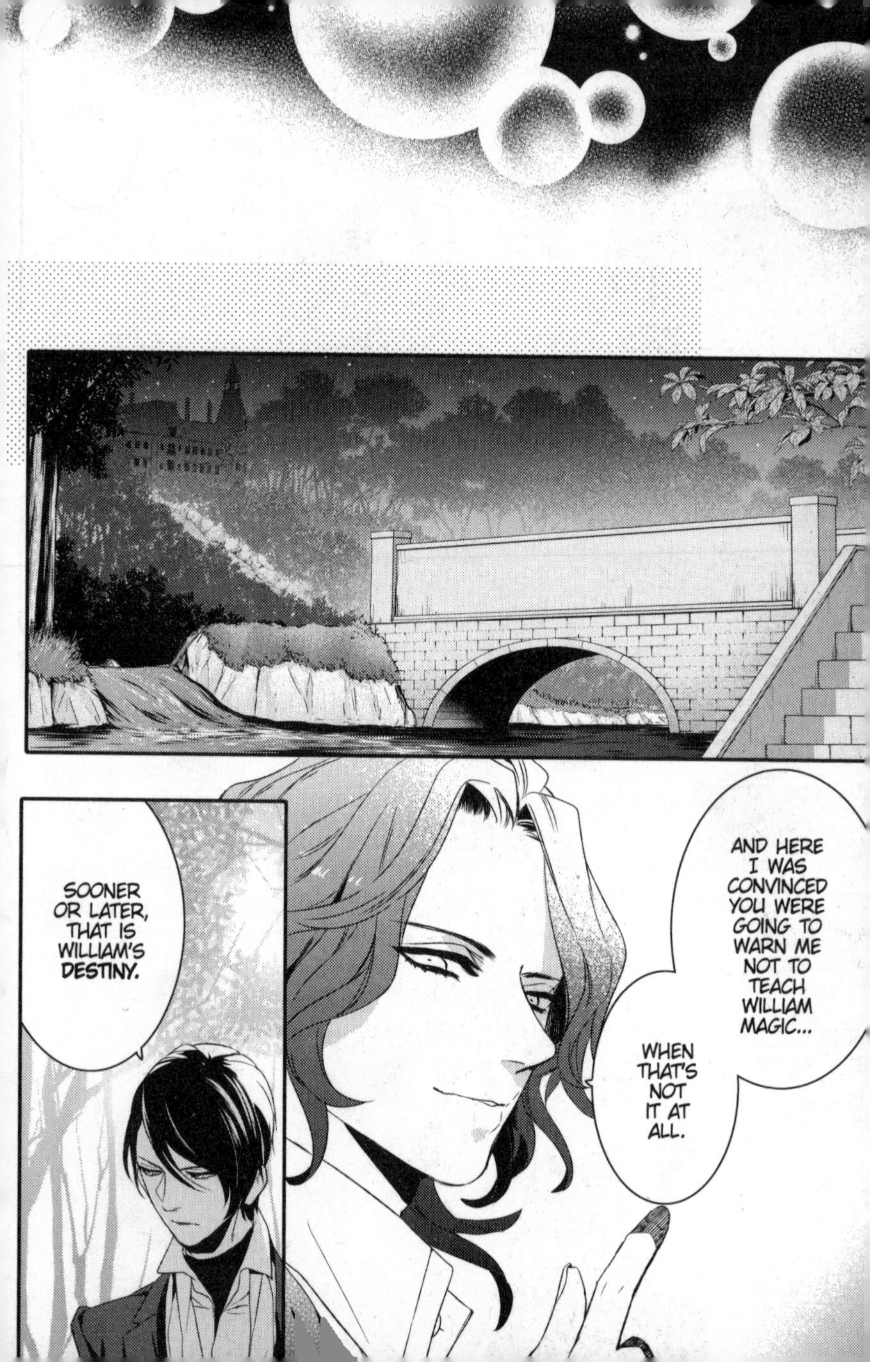
AND HERE I WAS CONVINCED YOU WERE GOING TO WARN ME NOT TO TEACH WILLIAM MAGIC...
WHEN THAT'S NOT IT AT ALL.
SOONER OR LATER, THAT IS WILLIAM'S DESTINY.

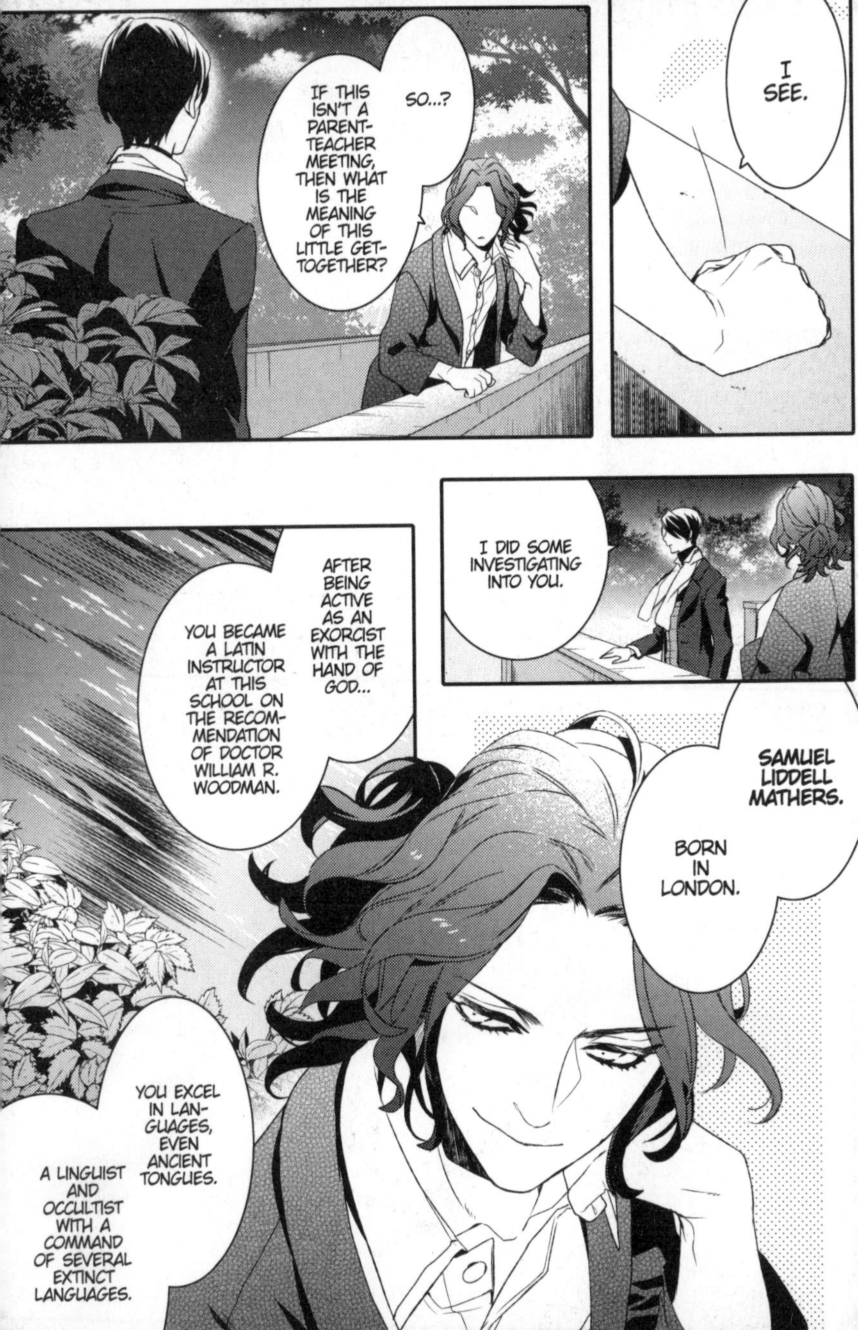
I SEE.
SO...?
IF THIS ISN'T A PARENT-TEACHER MEETING, THEN WHAT IS THE MEANING OF THIS LITTLE GET-TOGETHER?
I DID SOME INVESTIGATING INTO YOU.
SAMUEL LIDDELL MATHERS.
BORN IN LONDON.
AFTER BEING ACTIVE AS AN EXORCIST WITH THE HAND OF GOD...
YOU BECAME A LATIN INSTRUCTOR AT THIS SCHOOL ON THE RECOMMENDATION OF DOCTOR WILLIAM R. WOODMAN.
YOU EXCEL IN LANGUAGES, EVEN ANCIENT TONGUES.
A LINGUIST AND OCCULTIST WITH A COMMAND OF SEVERAL EXTINCT LANGUAGES.

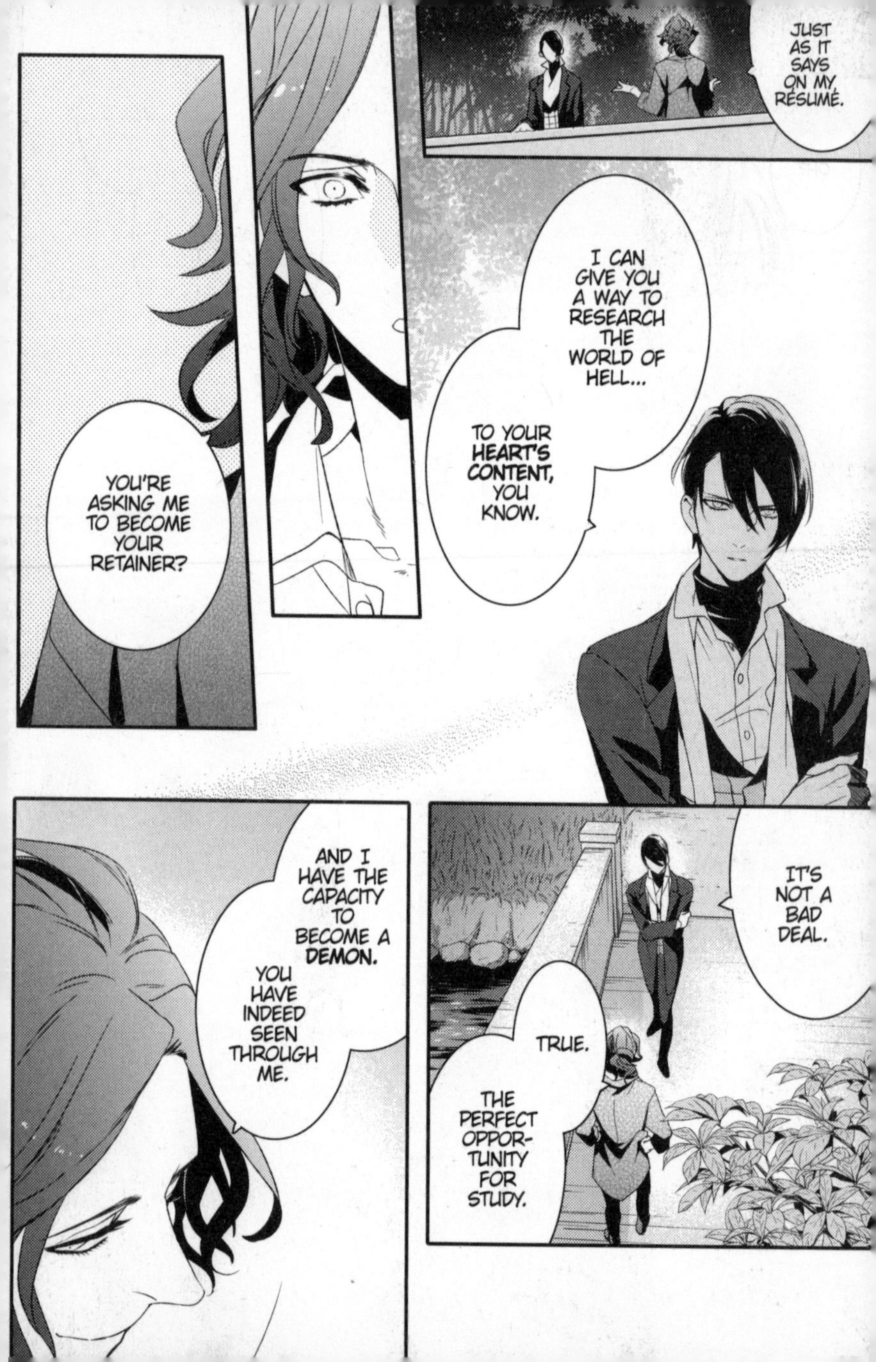
JUST AS IT SAYS ON MY RÉSUMÉ.
I CAN GIVE YOU A WAY TO RESEARCH THE WORLD OF HELL...
TO YOUR HEART'S CONTENT, YOU KNOW.
YOU'RE ASKING ME TO BECOME YOUR RETAINER?
IT'S NOT A BAD DEAL.
TRUE.
THE PERFECT OPPORTUNITY FOR STUDY.
AND I HAVE THE CAPACITY TO BECOME A DEMON.
YOU HAVE INDEED SEEN THROUGH ME.

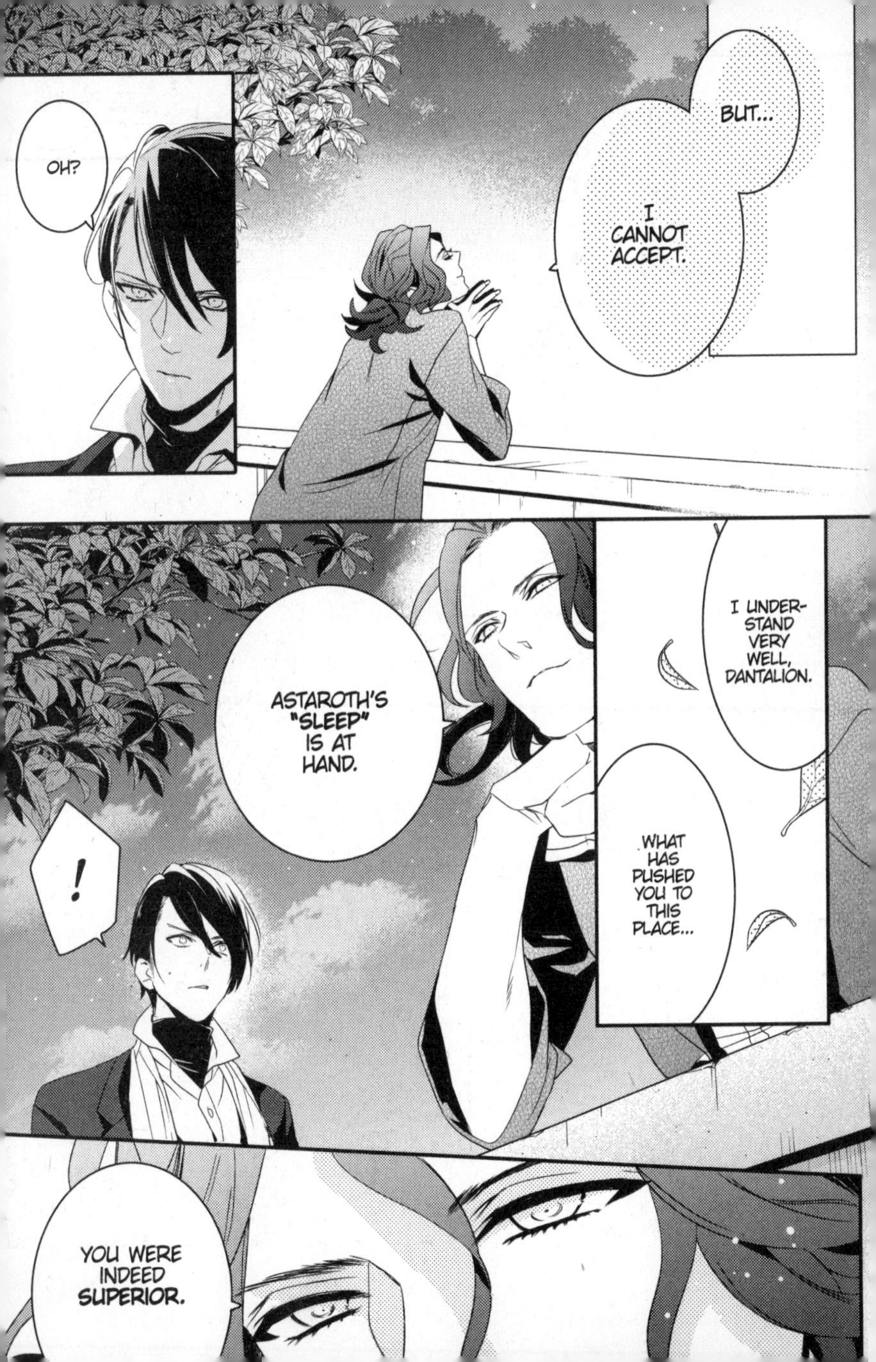
BUT...
I CANNOT ACCEPT.
OH?
I UNDER-STAND VERY WELL, DANTALION.
WHAT HAS PUSHED YOU TO THIS PLACE...
ASTAROTH'S "SLEEP" IS AT HAND.
!
YOU WERE INDEED SUPERIOR.

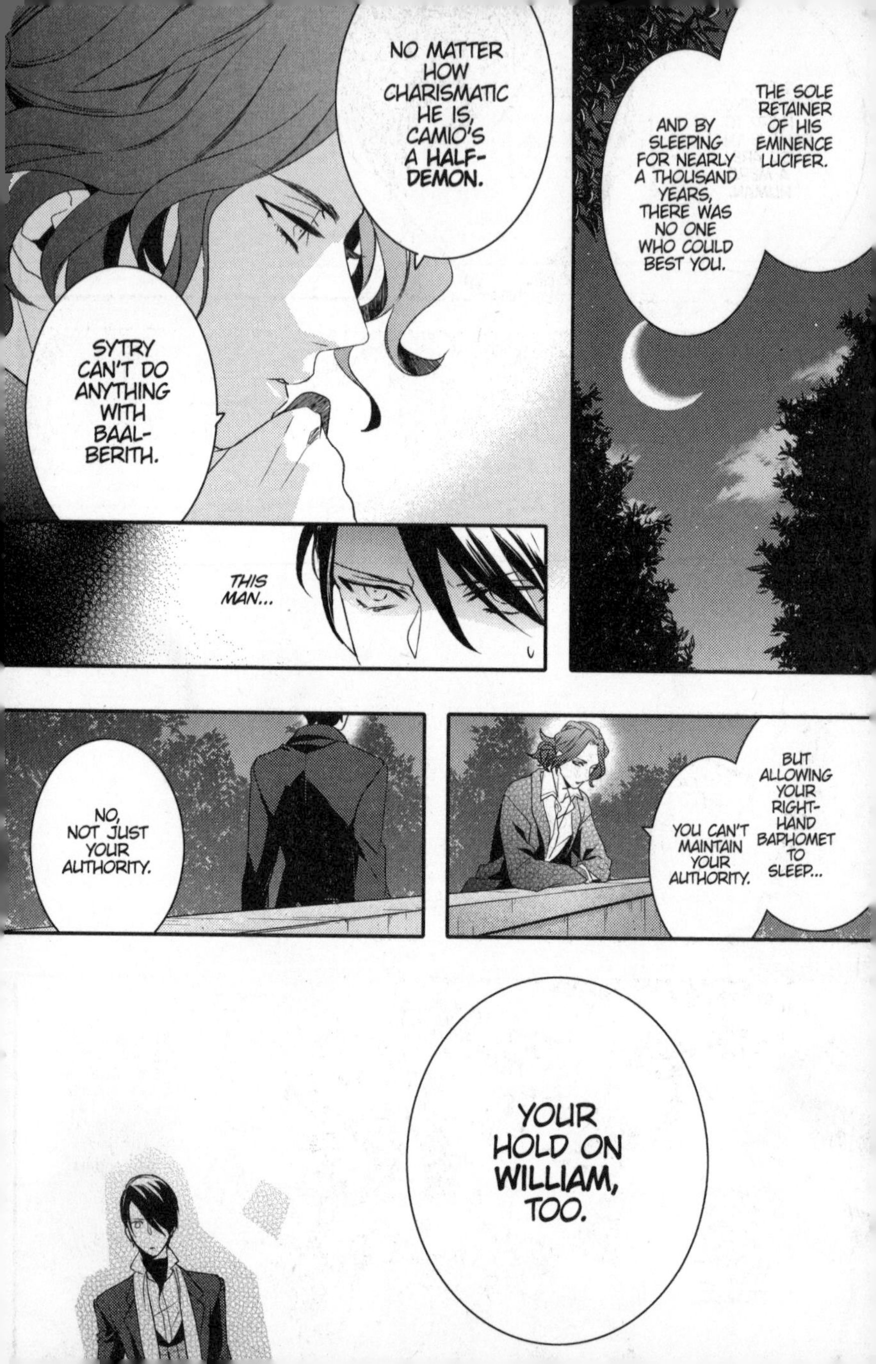
THE SOLE RETAINER OF HIS EMINENCE LUCIFER.
AND BY SLEEPING FOR NEARLY A THOUSAND YEARS, THERE WAS NO ONE WHO COULD BEST YOU.
NO MATTER HOW CHARISMATIC HE IS, CAMIO'S A HALF-DEMON.
SYTRY CAN'T DO ANYTHING WITH BAAL-BERITH.
THIS MAN...
BUT ALLOWING YOUR RIGHT-HAND BAPHOMET TO SLEEP...
YOU CAN'T MAINTAIN YOUR AUTHORITY.
NO, NOT JUST YOUR AUTHORITY.
YOUR HOLD ON WILLIAM, TOO.

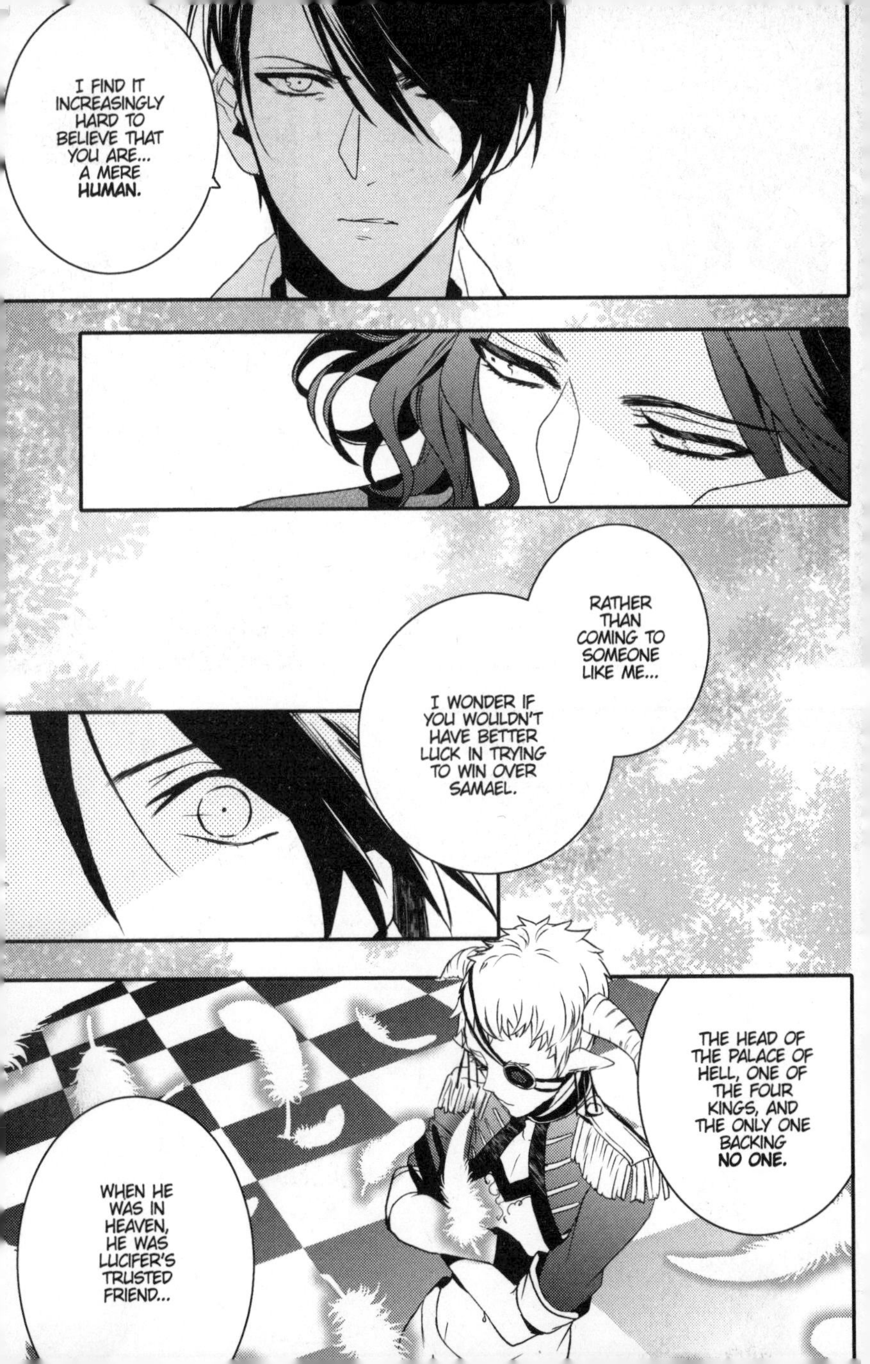
I FIND IT INCREASINGLY HARD TO BELIEVE THAT YOU ARE... A MERE **HUMAN.**
RATHER THAN COMING TO SOMEONE LIKE ME...
I WONDER IF YOU WOULDN'T HAVE BETTER LUCK IN TRYING TO WIN OVER SAMAEL.
THE HEAD OF THE PALACE OF HELL, ONE OF THE FOUR KINGS, AND THE ONLY ONE BACKING **NO ONE.**
WHEN HE WAS IN HEAVEN, HE WAS LUCIFER'S TRUSTED FRIEND...

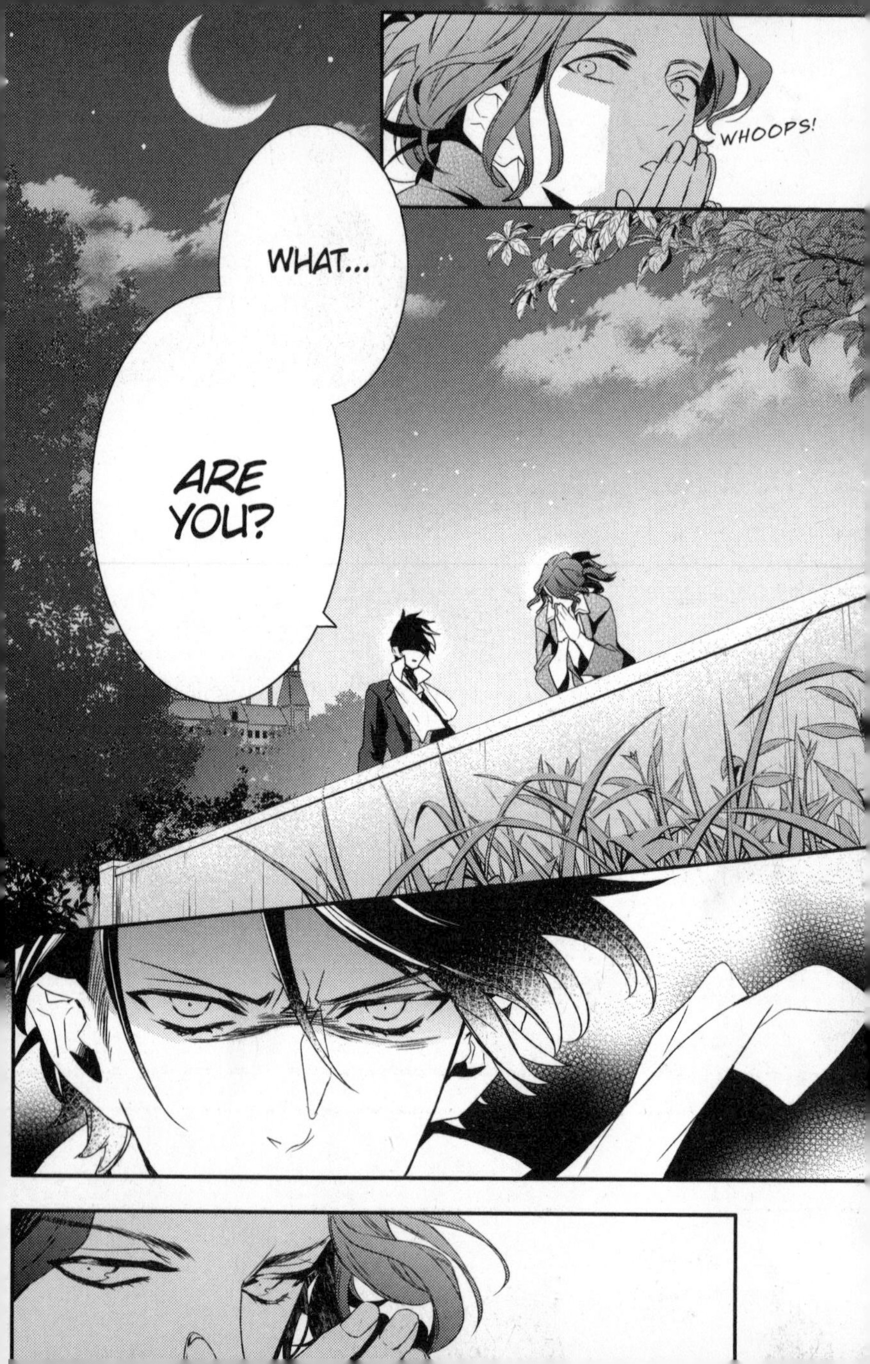
WHOOPS!
WHAT...
ARE YOU?

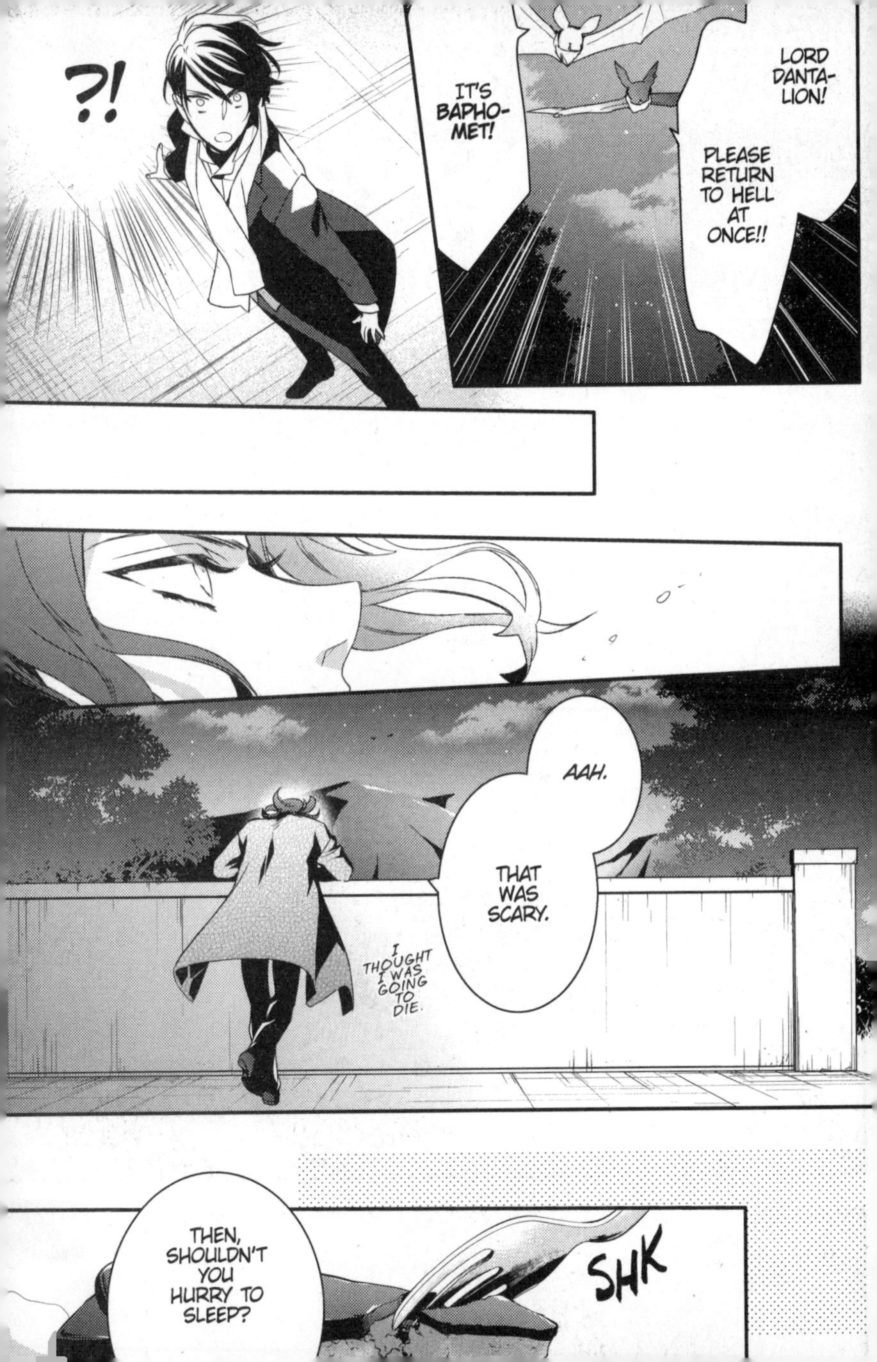
LORD DANTA-LION!
PLEASE RETURN TO HELL AT ONCE!!
IT'S BAPHO-MET!
?!
AAH.
THAT WAS SCARY.
I THOUGHT I WAS GOING TO DIE.
SHK
THEN, SHOULDN'T YOU HURRY TO SLEEP?

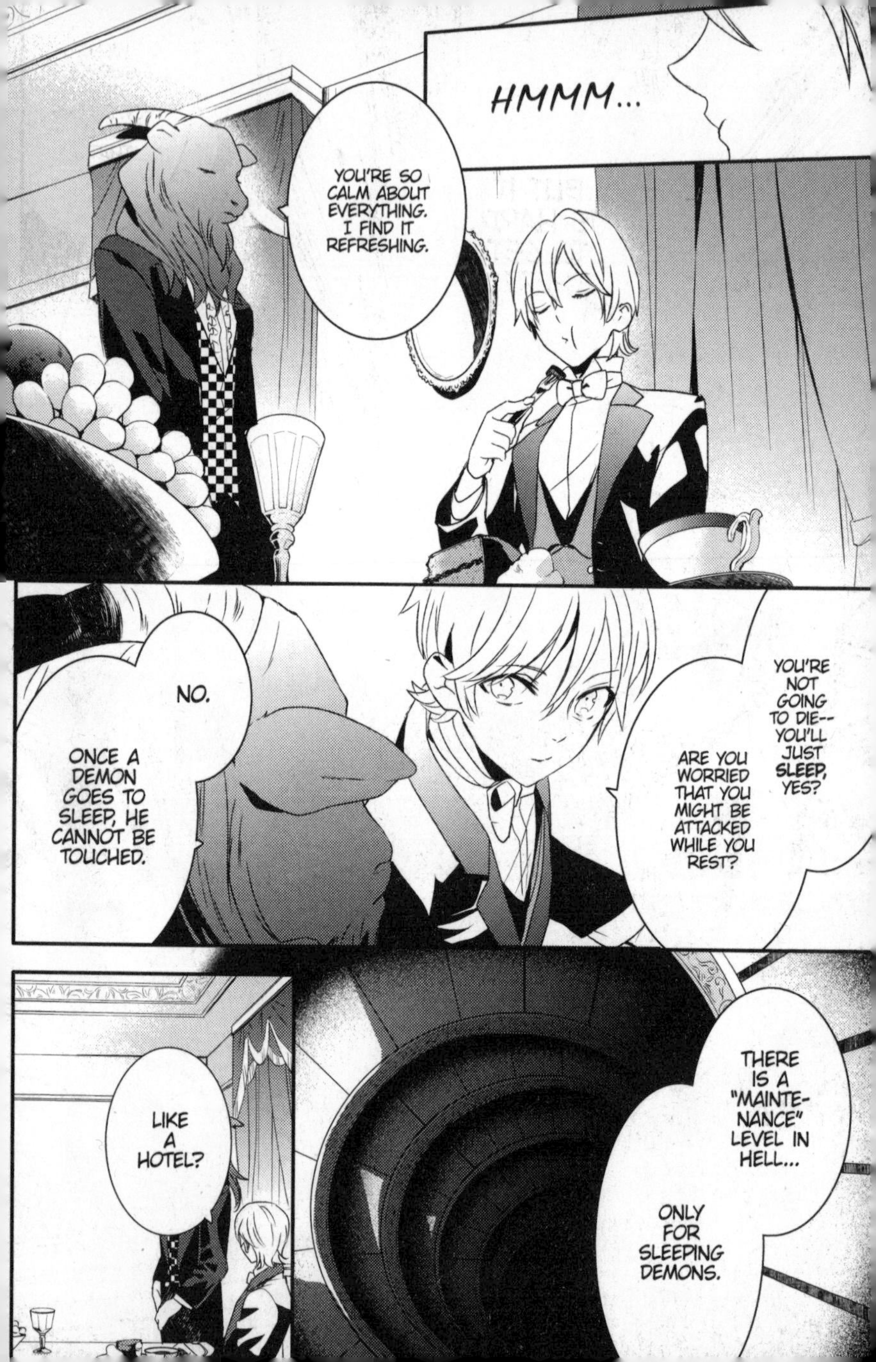
HMMM...
YOU'RE SO CALM ABOUT EVERYTHING. I FIND IT REFRESHING.
YOU'RE NOT GOING TO DIE-- YOU'LL JUST SLEEP, YES?
ARE YOU WORRIED THAT YOU MIGHT BE ATTACKED WHILE YOU REST?
NO.
ONCE A DEMON GOES TO SLEEP, HE CANNOT BE TOUCHED.
THERE IS A "MAINTE-NANCE" LEVEL IN HELL...
ONLY FOR SLEEPING DEMONS.
LIKE A HOTEL?

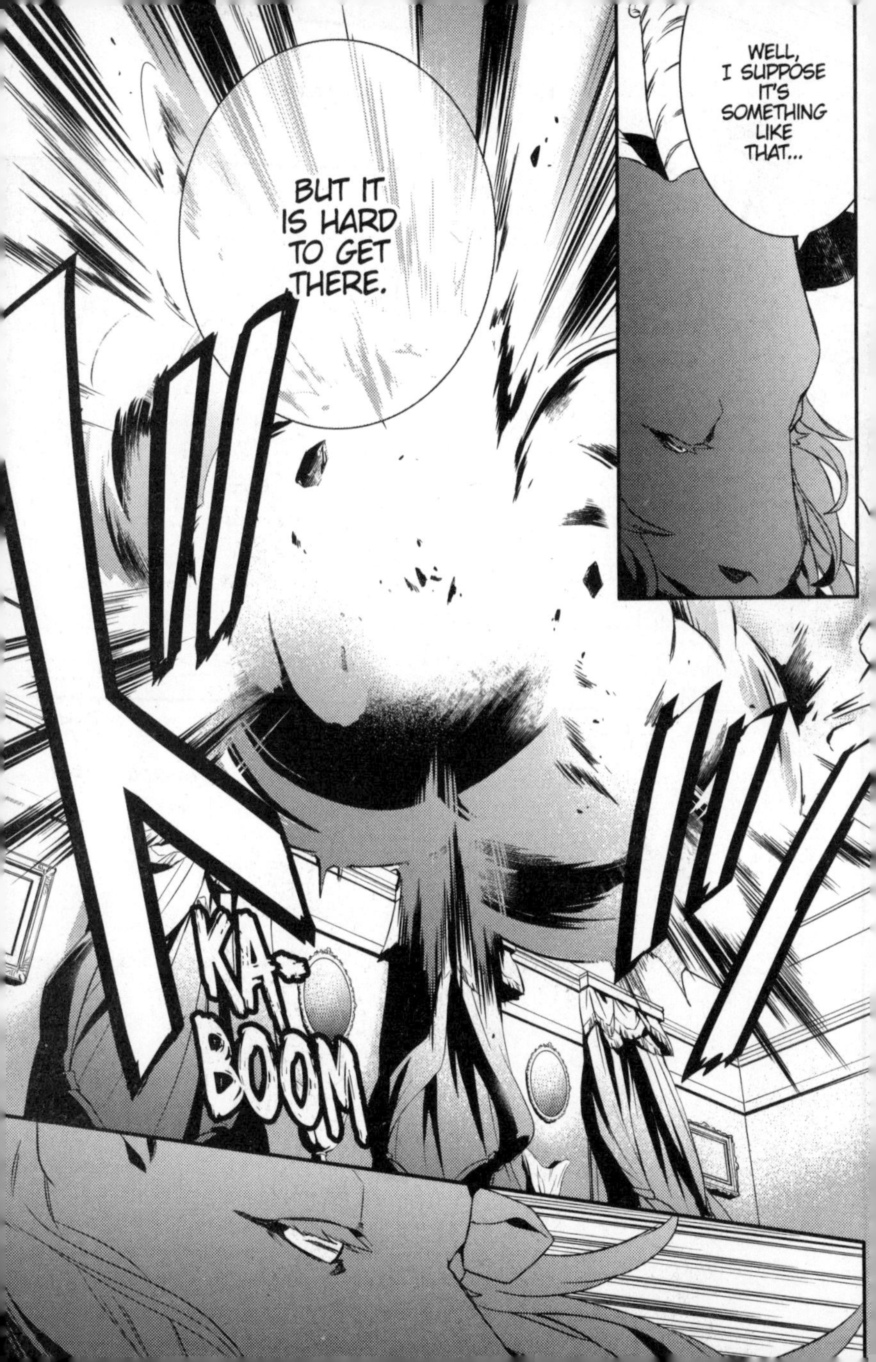
WELL, I SUPPOSE IT'S SOMETHING LIKE THAT...
BUT IT IS HARD TO GET THERE.
KA-BOOM

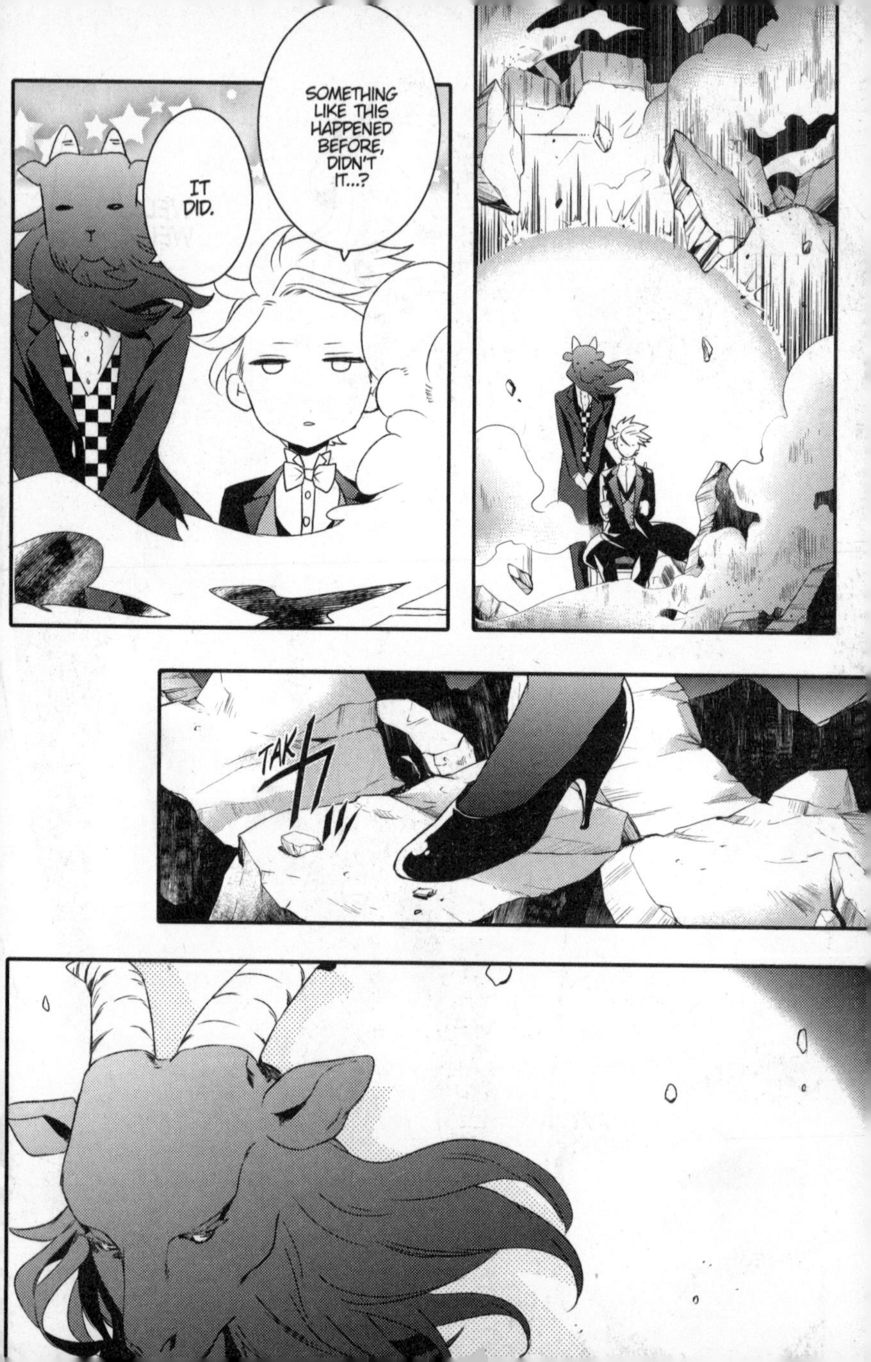
SOMETHING LIKE THIS HAPPENED BEFORE, DIDN'T IT...?
IT DID.
TAK

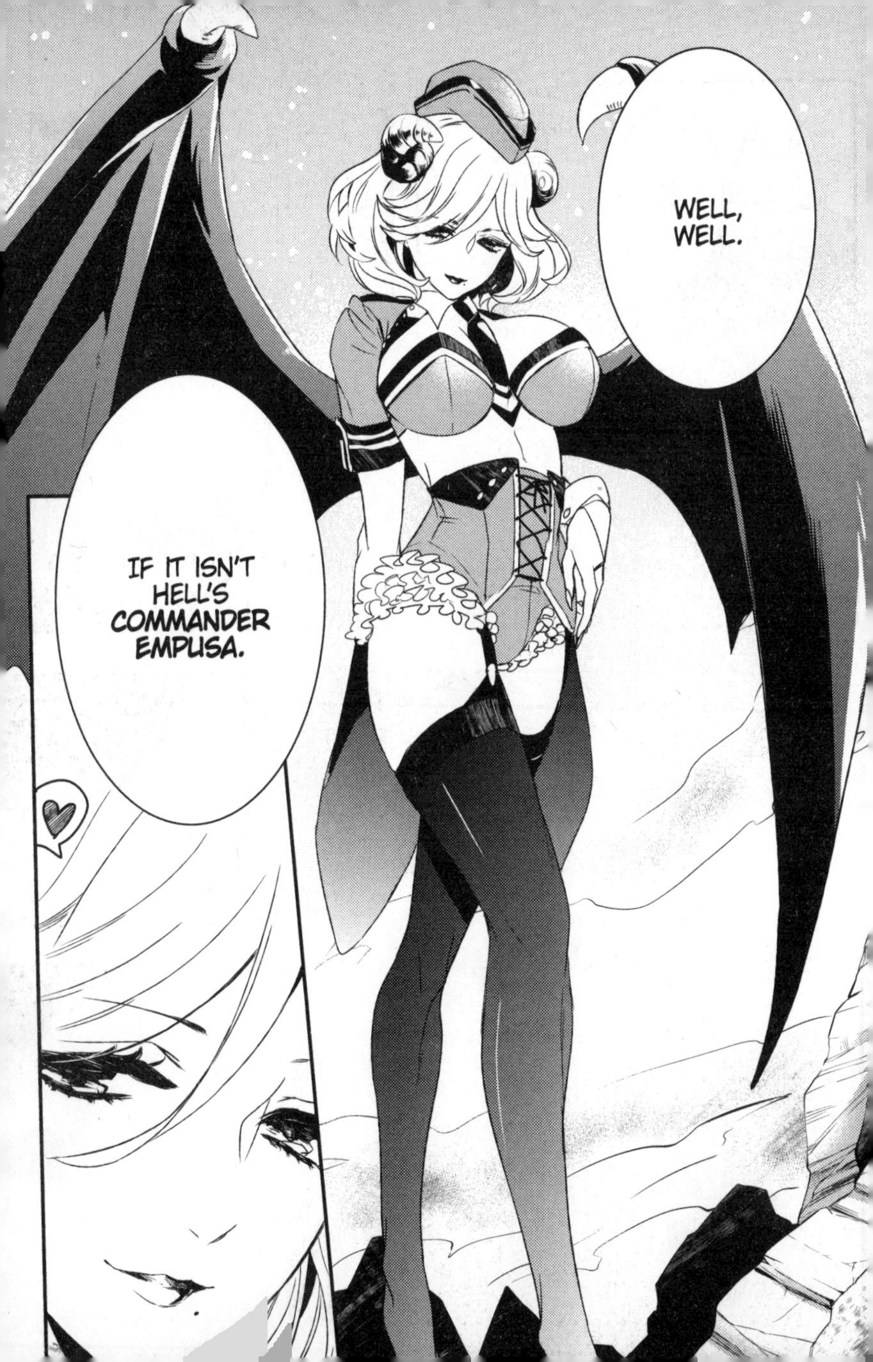
WELL, WELL.
IF IT ISN'T HELL'S COMMANDER EMPUSA.

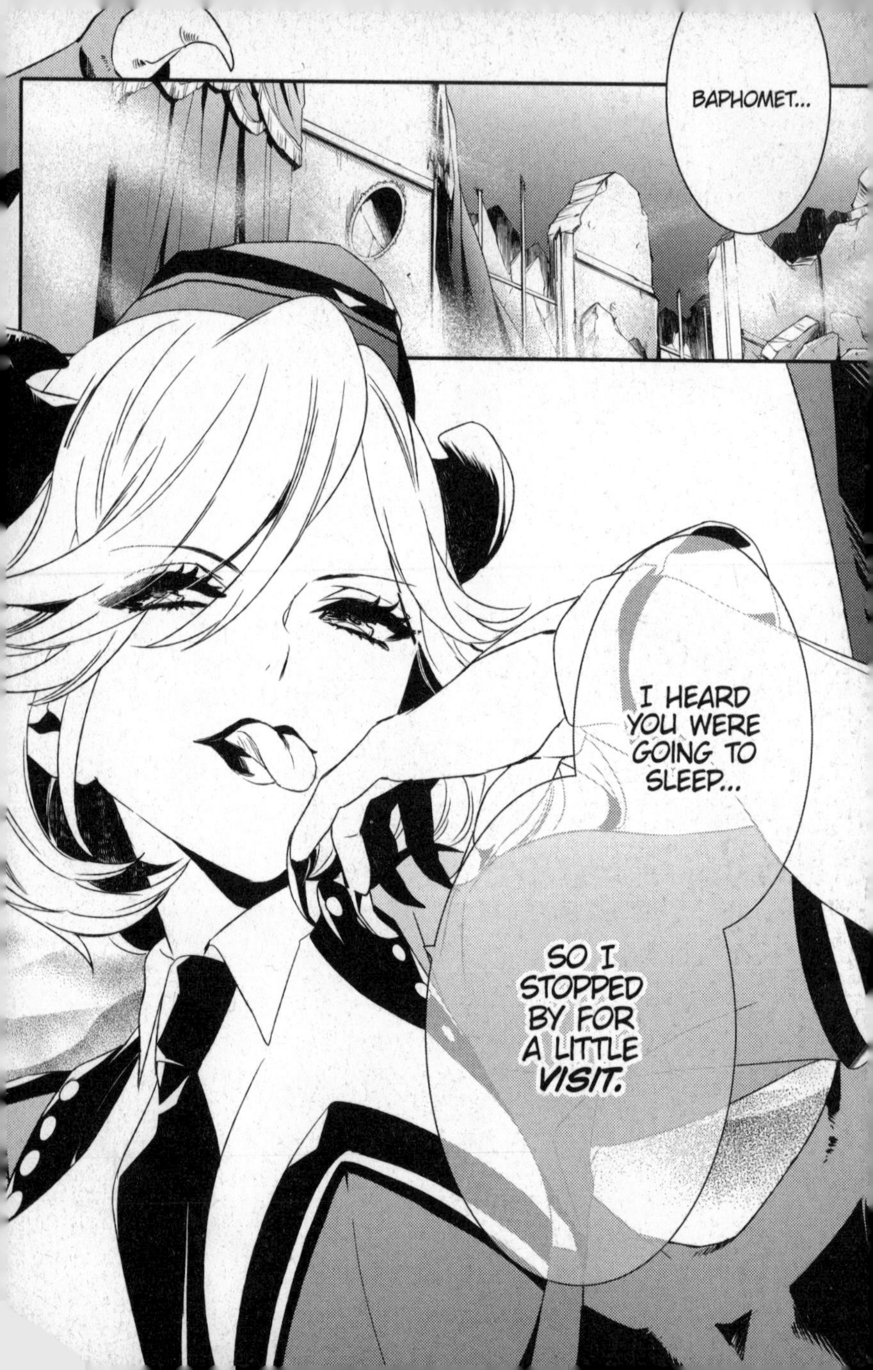
BAPHOMET...
I HEARD YOU WERE GOING TO SLEEP...
SO I STOPPED BY FOR A LITTLE *VISIT.*

魔界王子
devils and realist

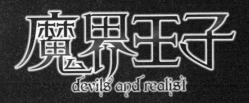

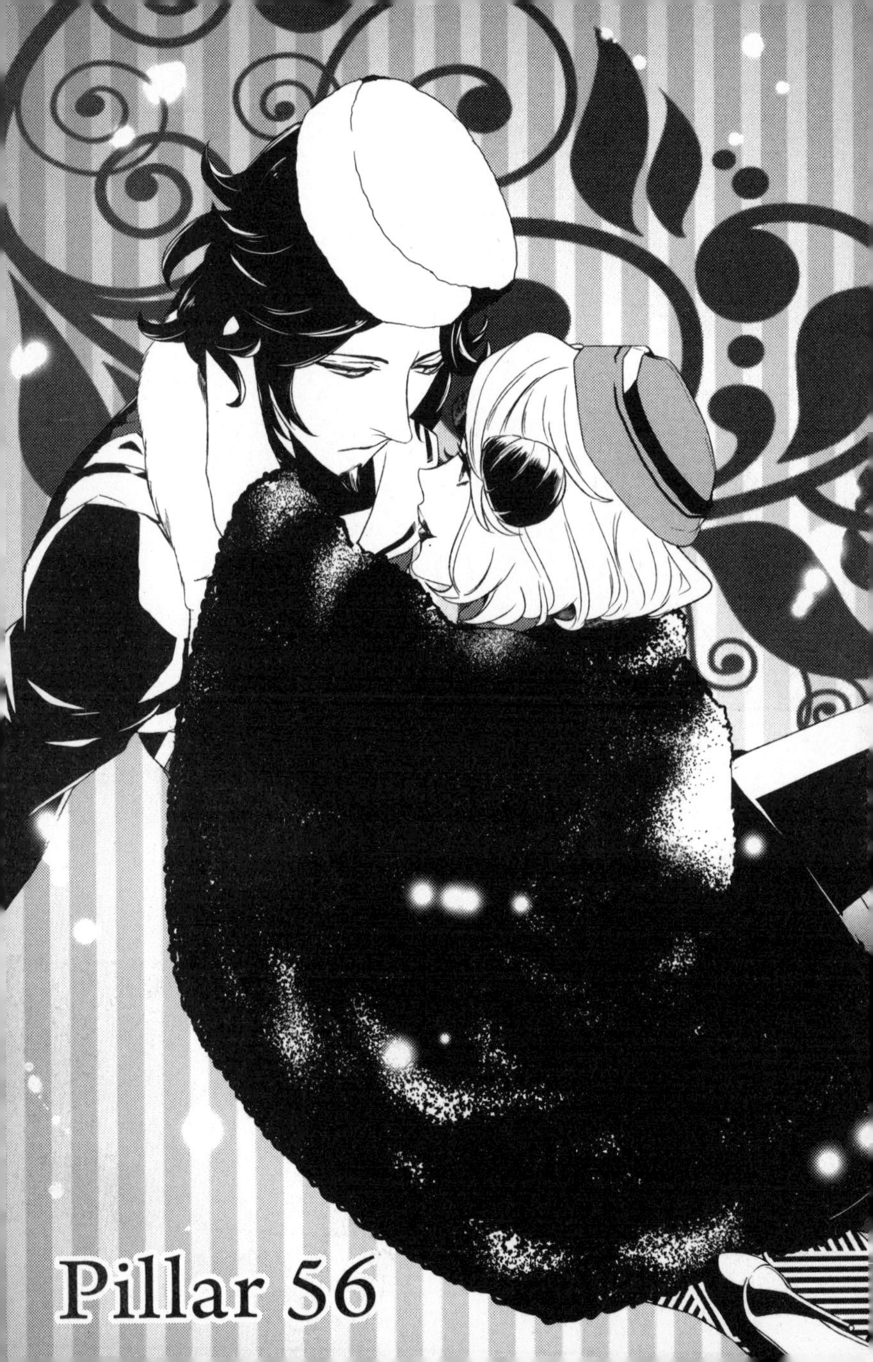

Pillar 56

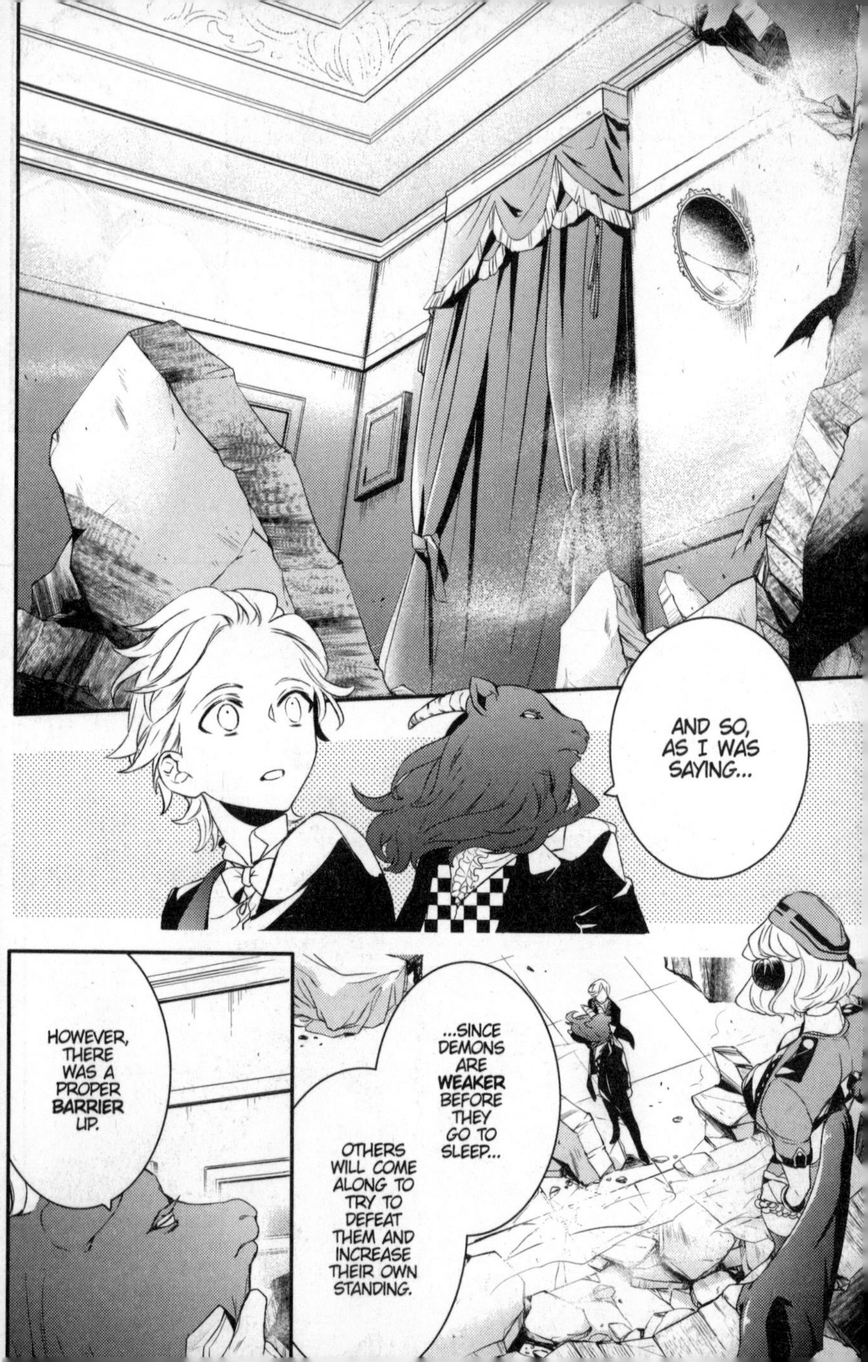
AND SO, AS I WAS SAYING...
...SINCE DEMONS ARE **WEAKER** BEFORE THEY GO TO SLEEP...
OTHERS WILL COME ALONG TO TRY TO DEFEAT THEM AND INCREASE THEIR OWN STANDING.
HOWEVER, THERE WAS A PROPER **BARRIER** UP.

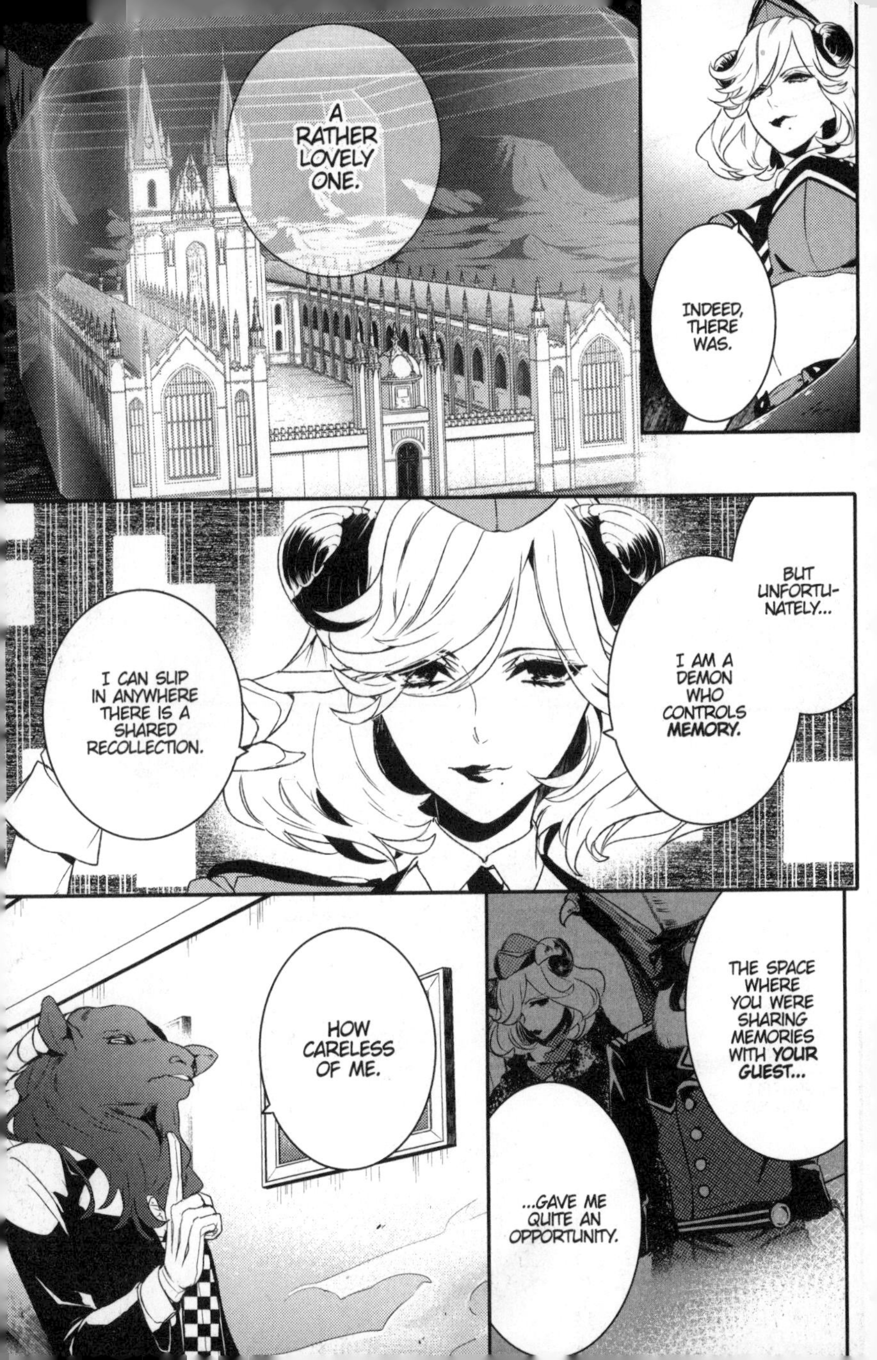
INDEED, THERE WAS.
A RATHER LOVELY ONE.
BUT UNFORTUNATELY...
I AM A DEMON WHO CONTROLS MEMORY.
I CAN SLIP IN ANYWHERE THERE IS A SHARED RECOLLECTION.
THE SPACE WHERE YOU WERE SHARING MEMORIES WITH YOUR GUEST...
...GAVE ME QUITE AN OPPORTUNITY.
HOW CARELESS OF ME.

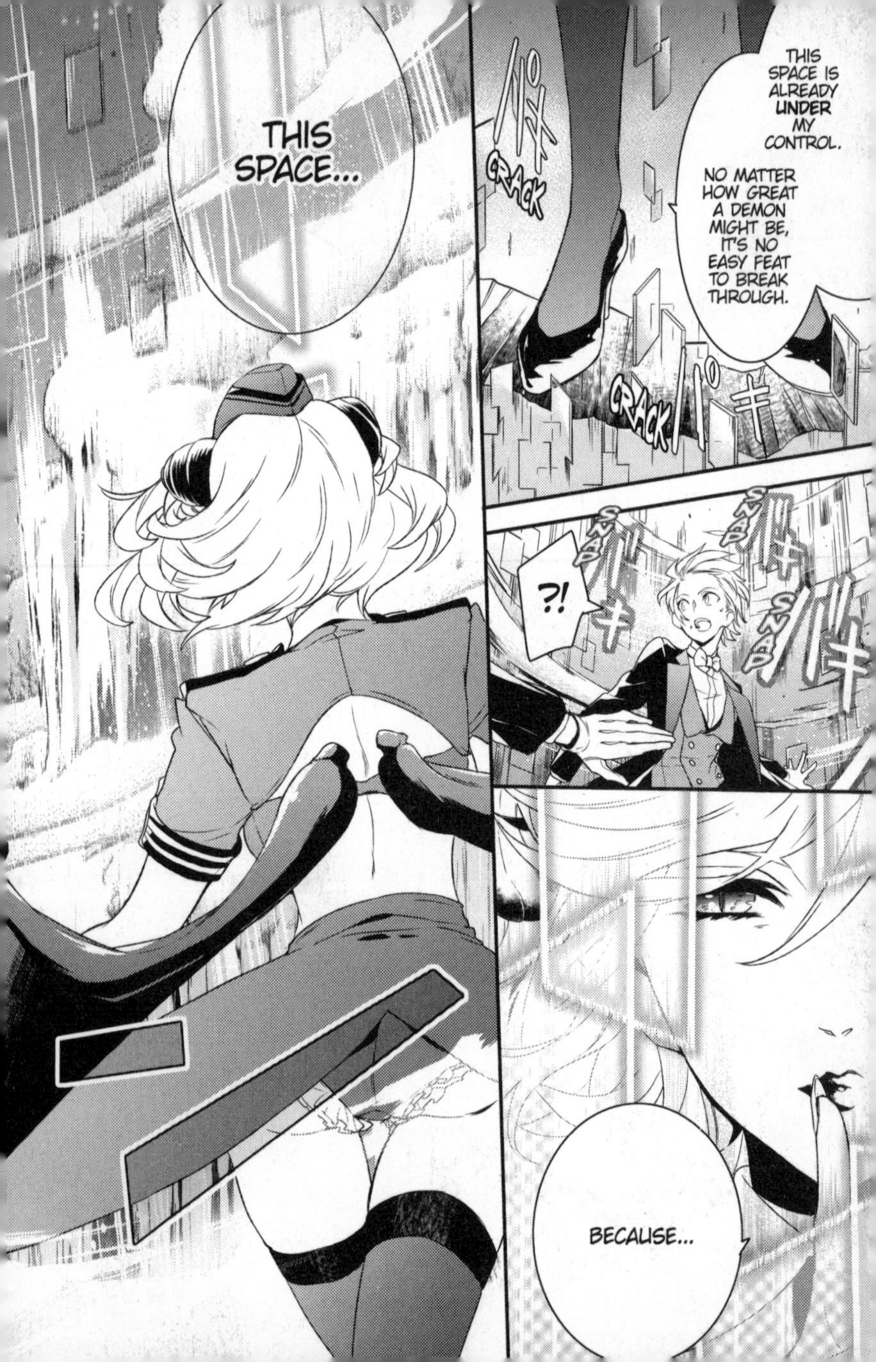
CRACK
THIS SPACE IS ALREADY UNDER MY CONTROL.
NO MATTER HOW GREAT A DEMON MIGHT BE, IT'S NO EASY FEAT TO BREAK THROUGH.
CRACK
SNAP
SNAP
SNAP
?!
BECAUSE...
THIS SPACE...

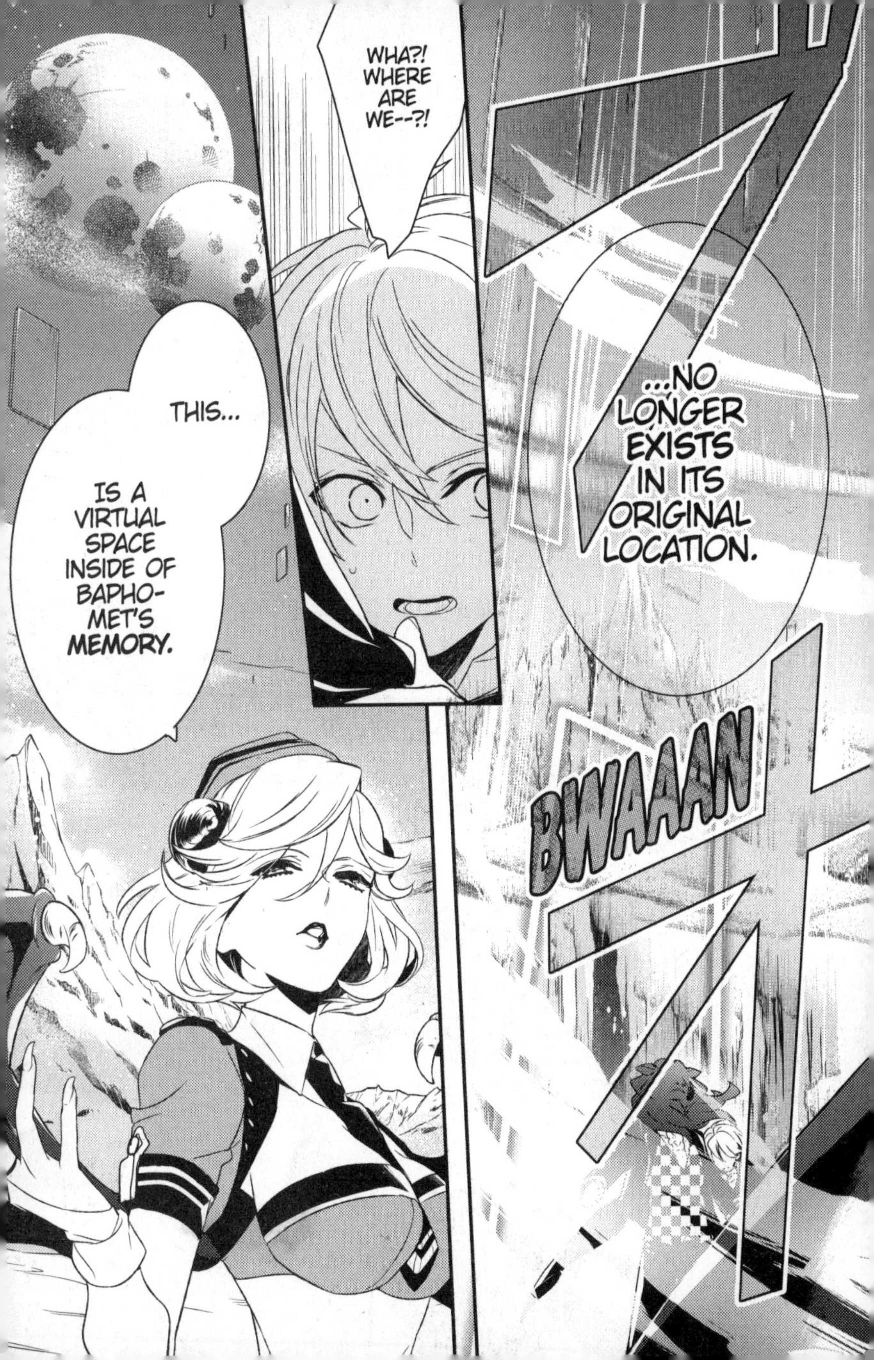
...NO LONGER EXISTS IN ITS ORIGINAL LOCATION.
BWAAAN
WHA?! WHERE ARE WE--?!
THIS...
IS A VIRTUAL SPACE INSIDE OF BAPHO-MET'S MEMORY.

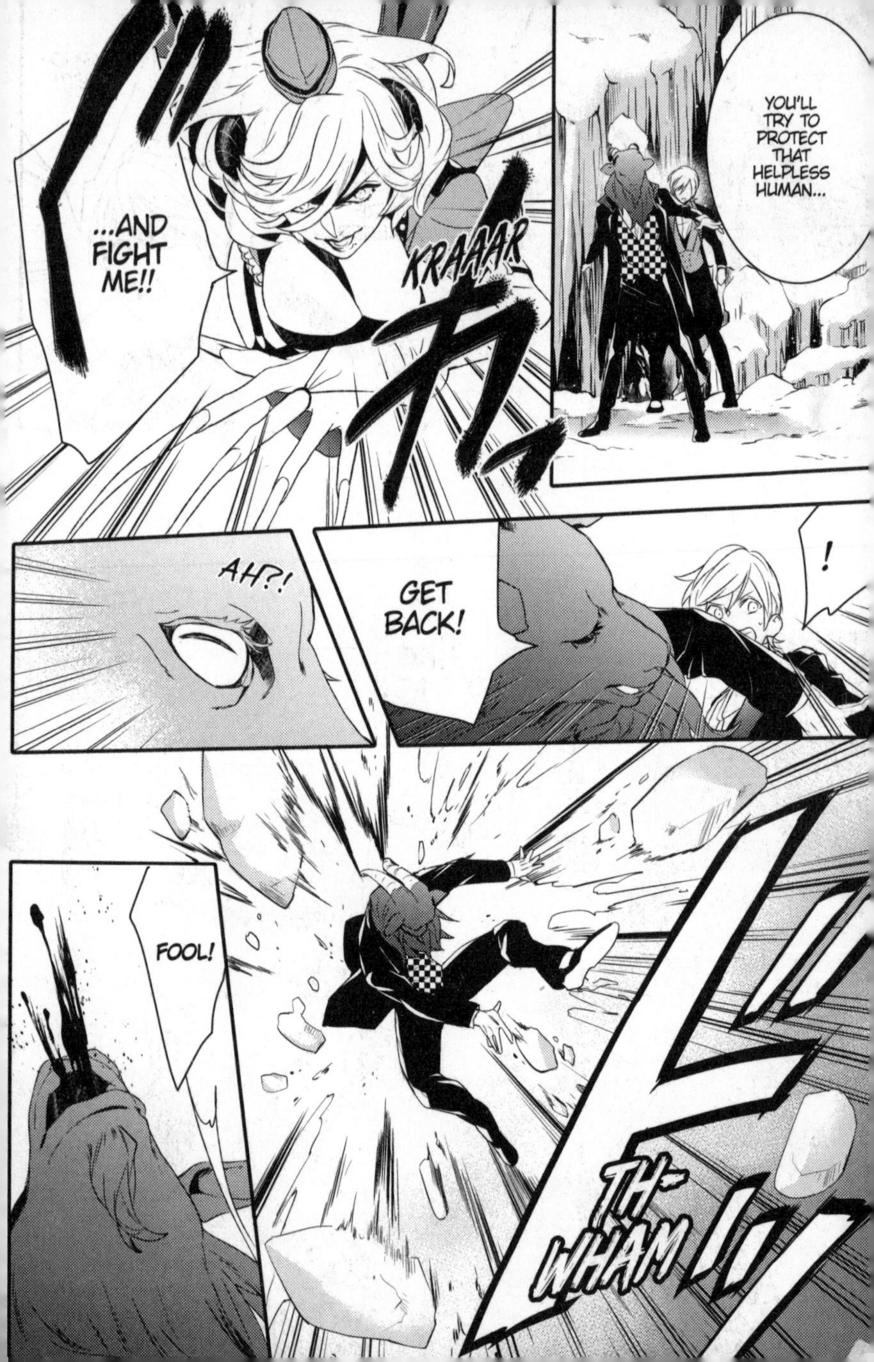
YOU'LL TRY TO PROTECT THAT HELPLESS HUMAN...
...AND FIGHT ME!!
KRAAAR
!
GET BACK!
AH?!
TH-WHAM
FOOL!

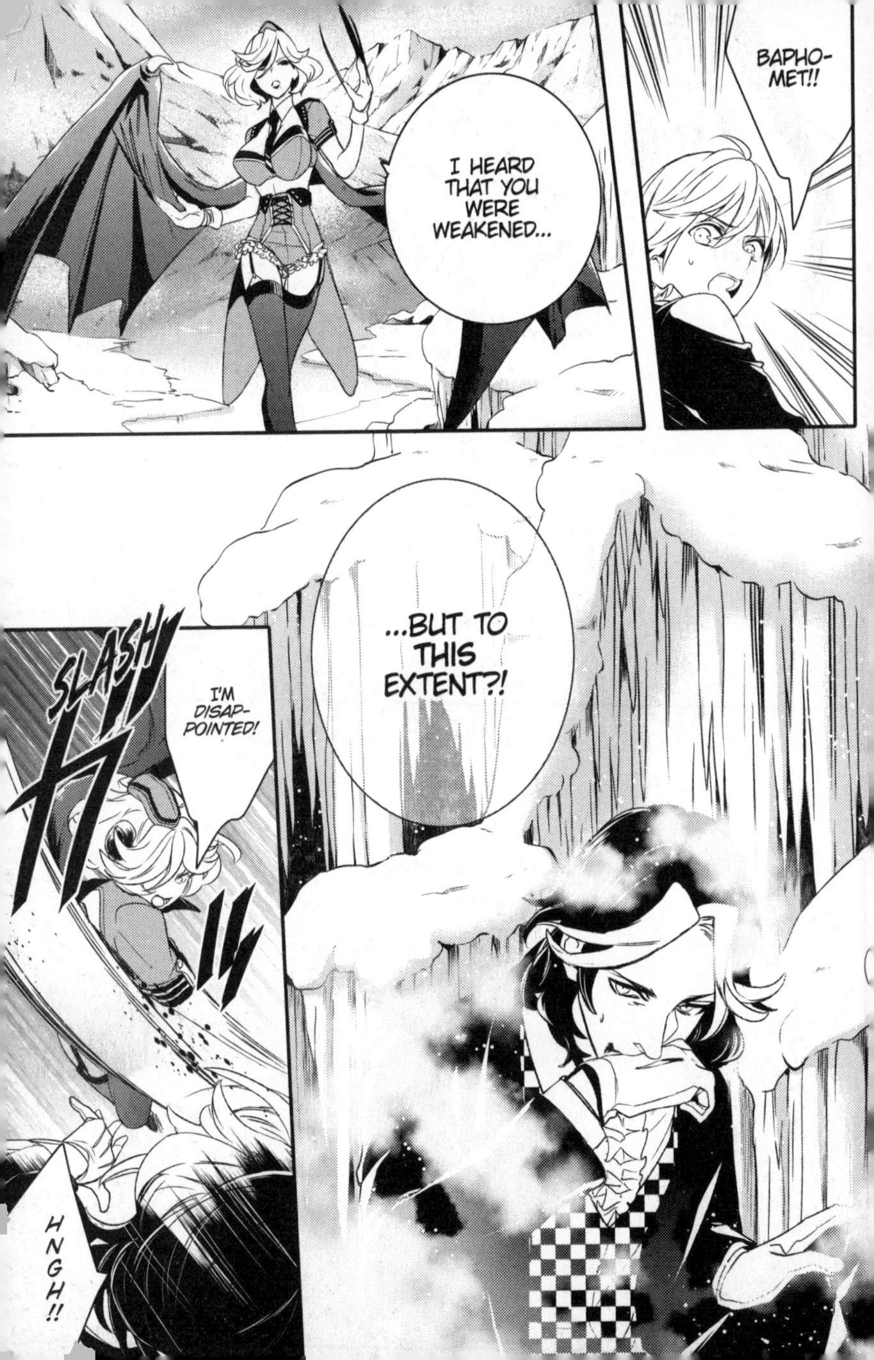
BAPHO-MET!!
I HEARD THAT YOU WERE WEAKENED...
...BUT TO THIS EXTENT?!
SLASH
I'M DISAP-POINTED!
HNGH!!

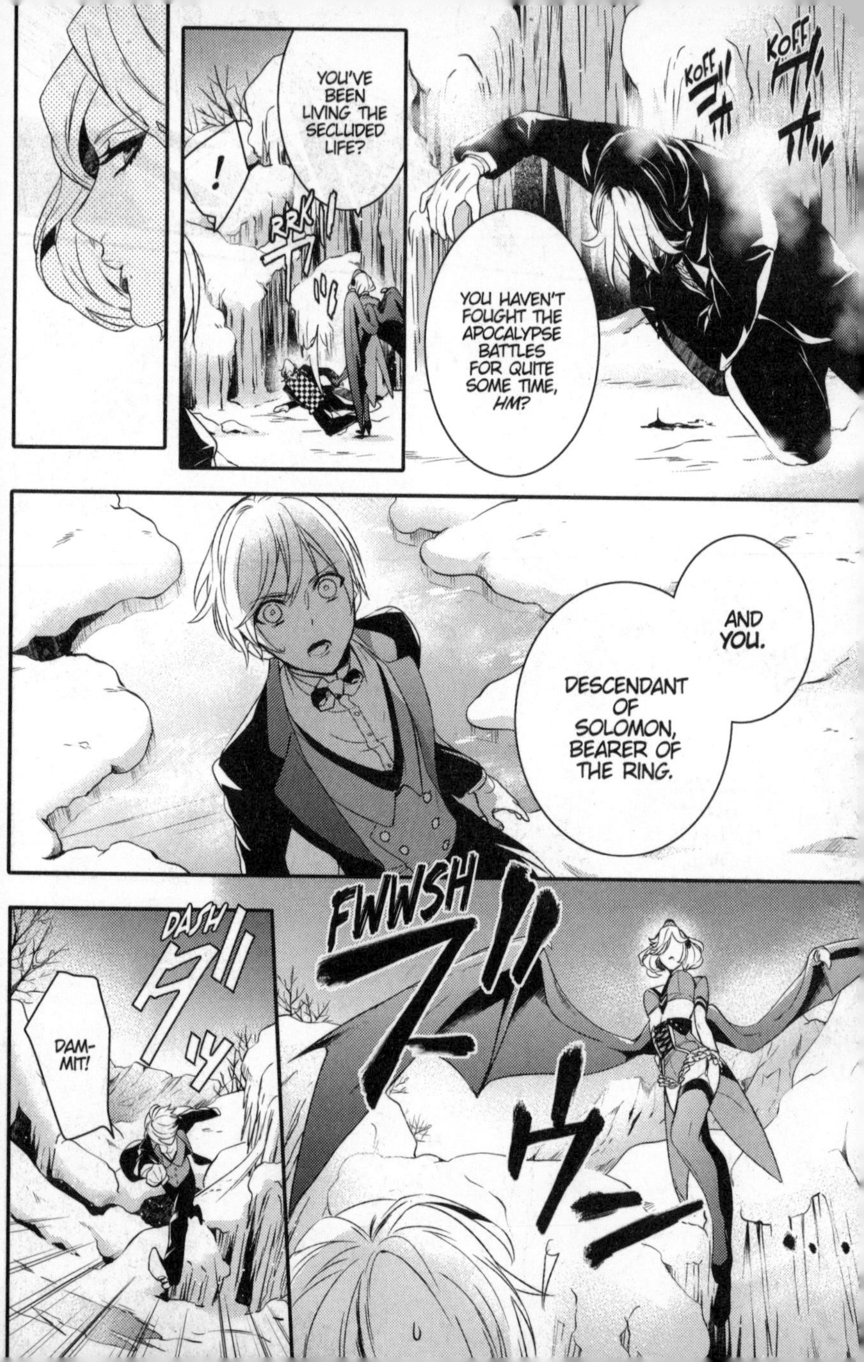
KOFF
KOFF
YOU HAVEN'T FOUGHT THE APOCALYPSE BATTLES FOR QUITE SOME TIME, HM?
YOU'VE BEEN LIVING THE SECLUDED LIFE?
!
RRK
AND YOU.
DESCENDANT OF SOLOMON, BEARER OF THE RING.
FWWSH
DASH
DAM-MIT!

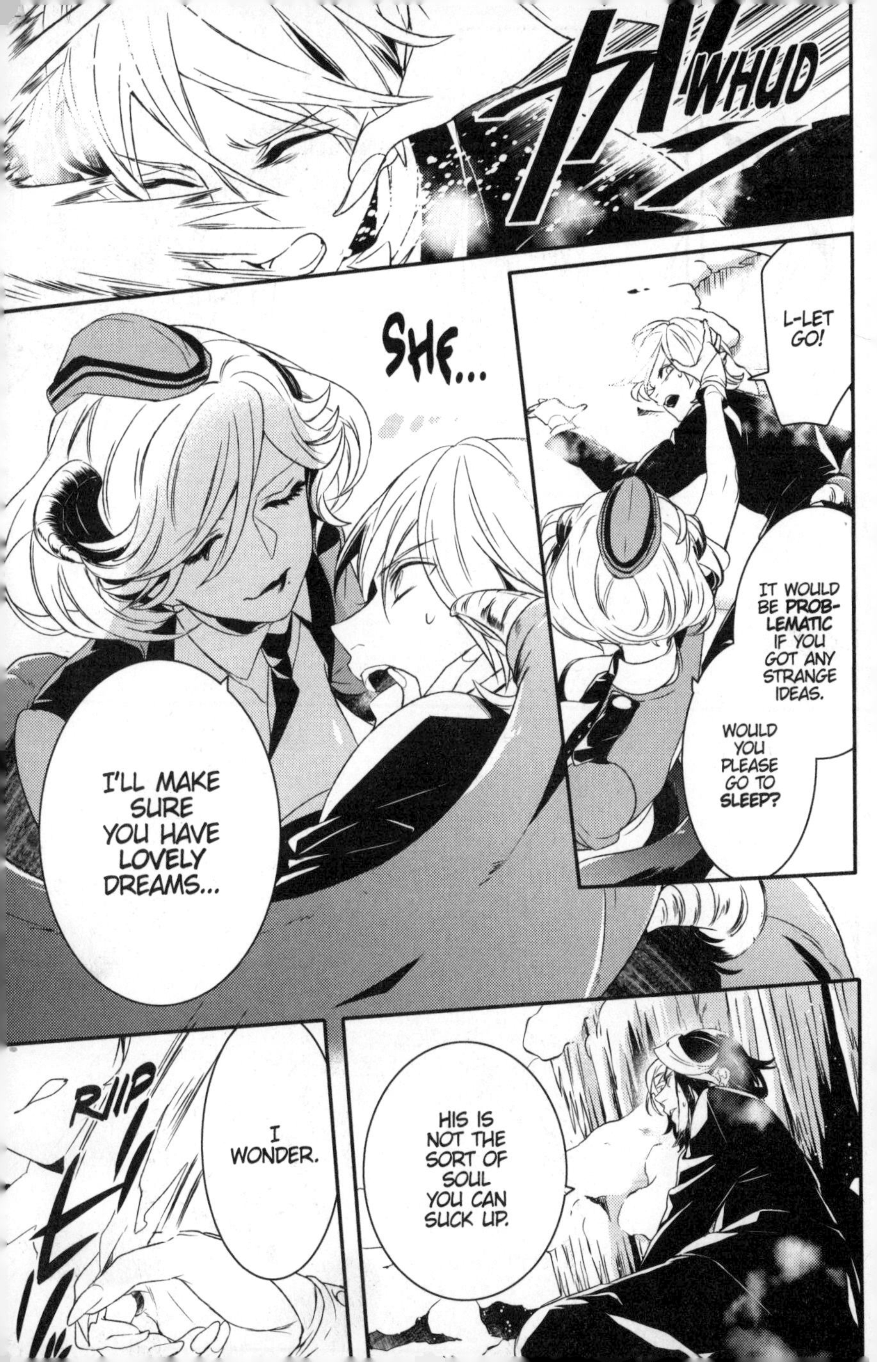
WHUD
L-LET GO!
IT WOULD BE PROBLEMATIC IF YOU GOT ANY STRANGE IDEAS.
WOULD YOU PLEASE GO TO SLEEP?
SHE...
I'LL MAKE SURE YOU HAVE LOVELY DREAMS...
HIS IS NOT THE SORT OF SOUL YOU CAN SUCK UP.
I WONDER.
RIIP

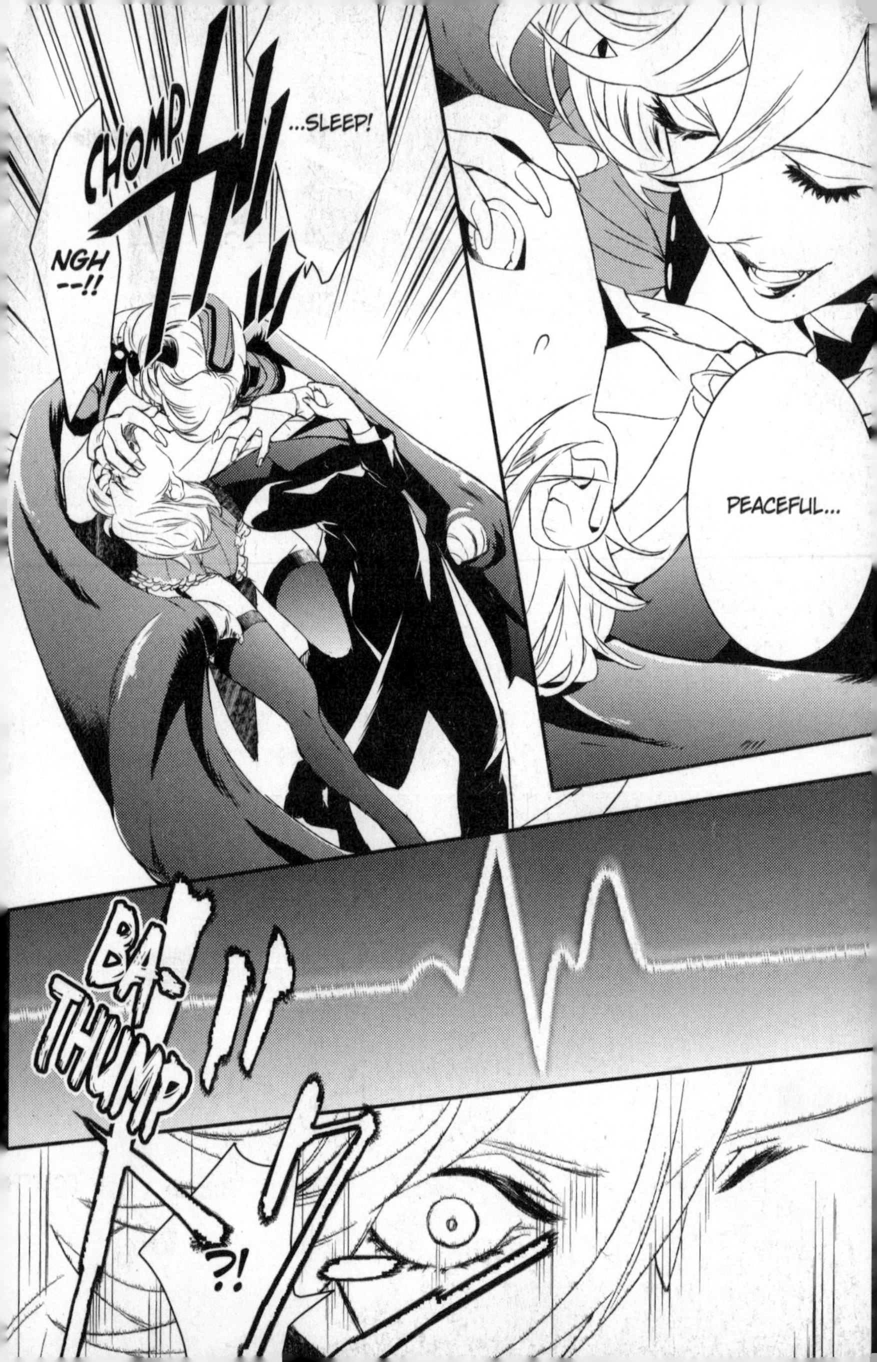
PEACEFUL...
...SLEEP!
CHOMP
NGH --!!
BA-THUMP
?!

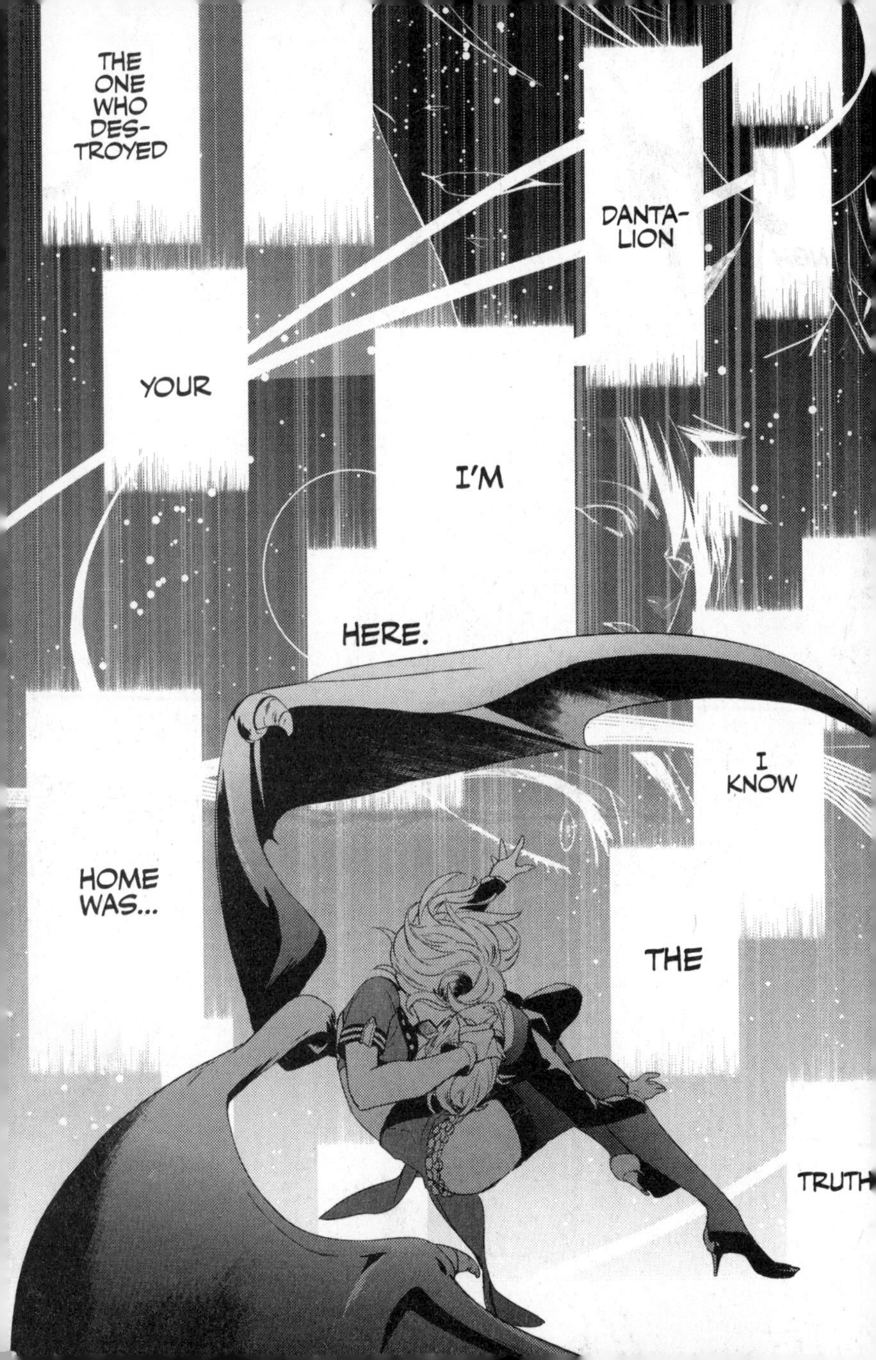
DANTA-
LION
THE
ONE
WHO
DES-
TROYED
YOUR
I'M
HERE.
I
KNOW
HOME
WAS...
THE
TRUTH

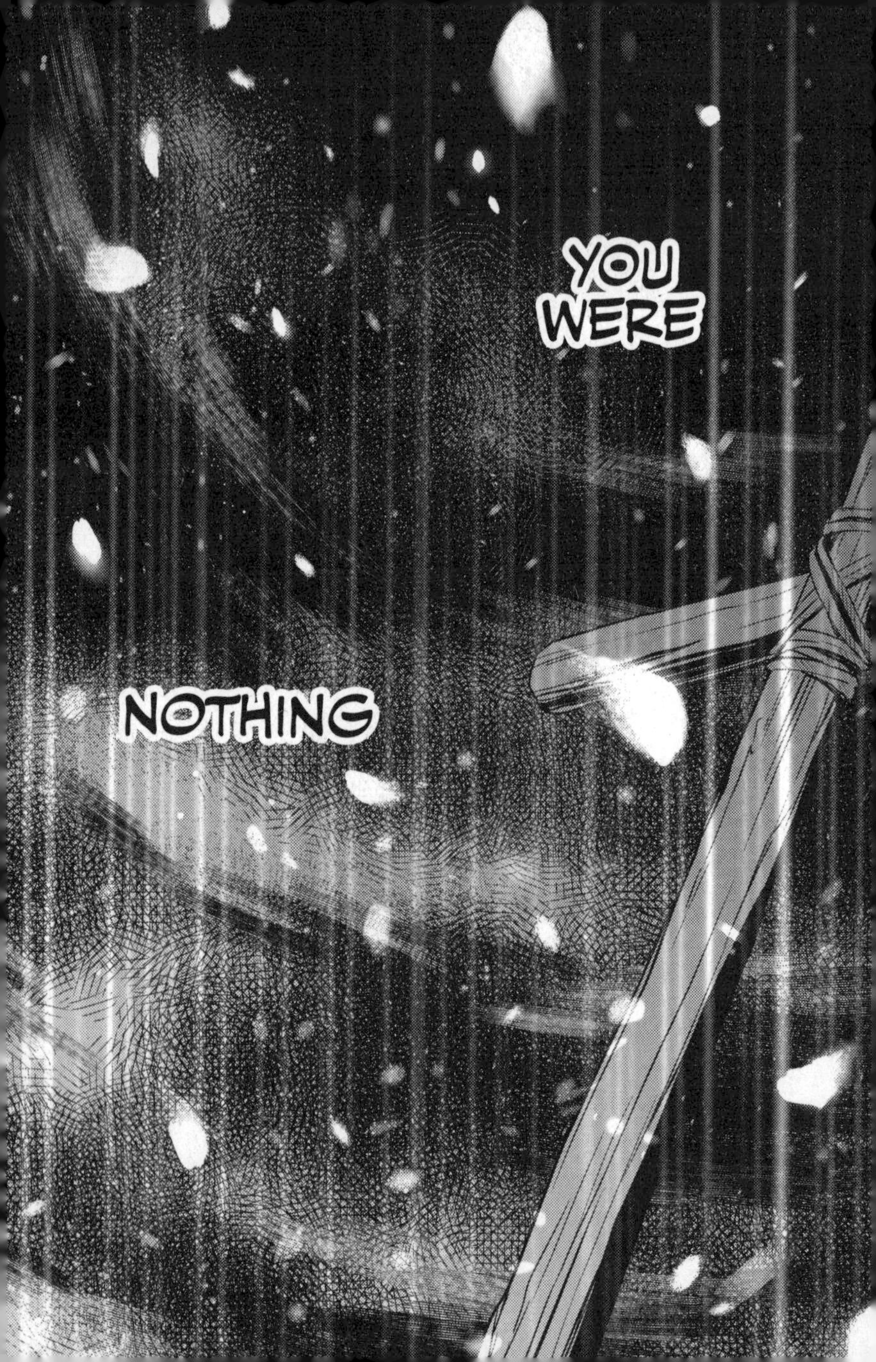
YOU WERE
NOTHING

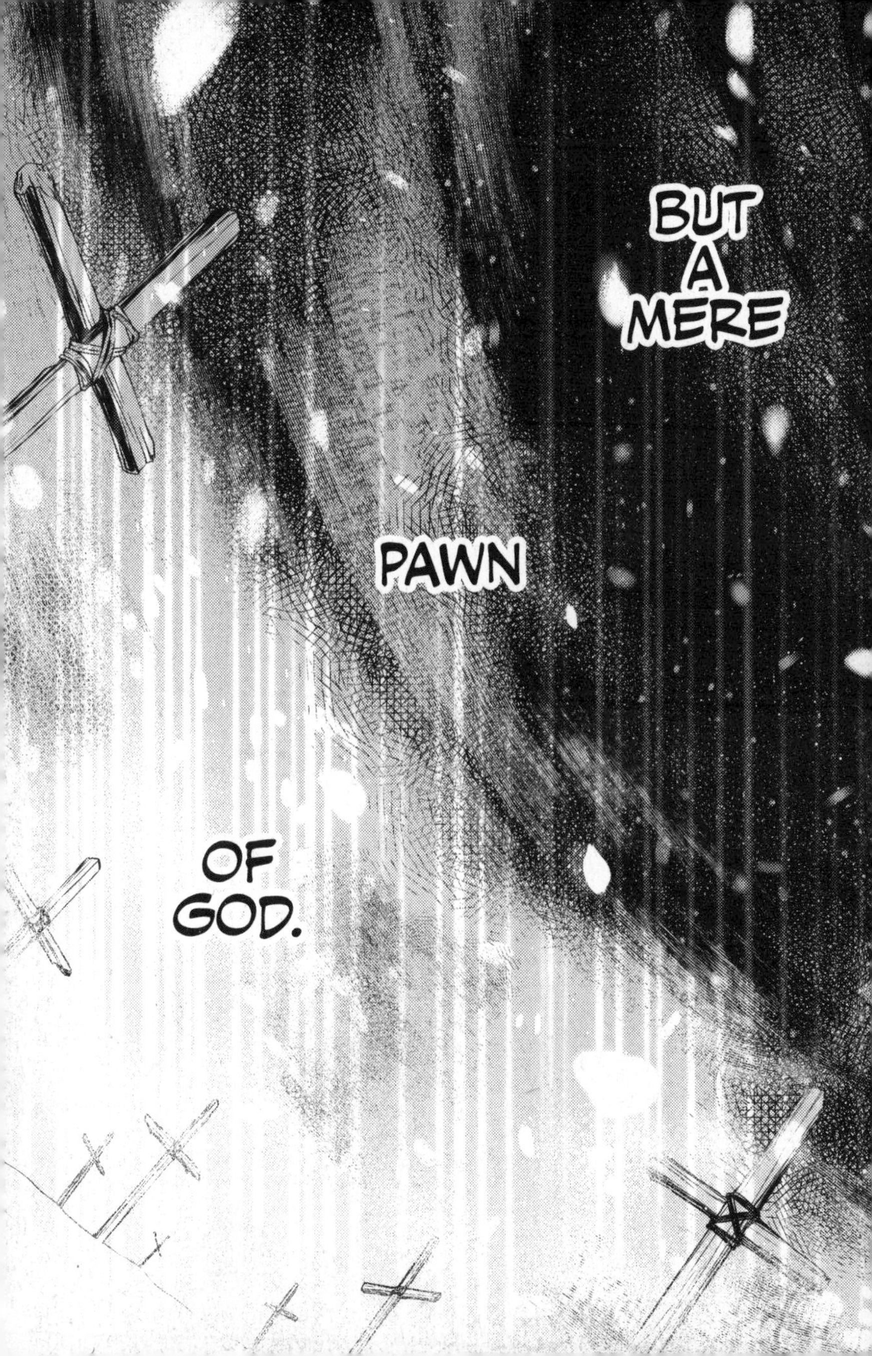
BUT A MERE
PAWN
OF GOD.

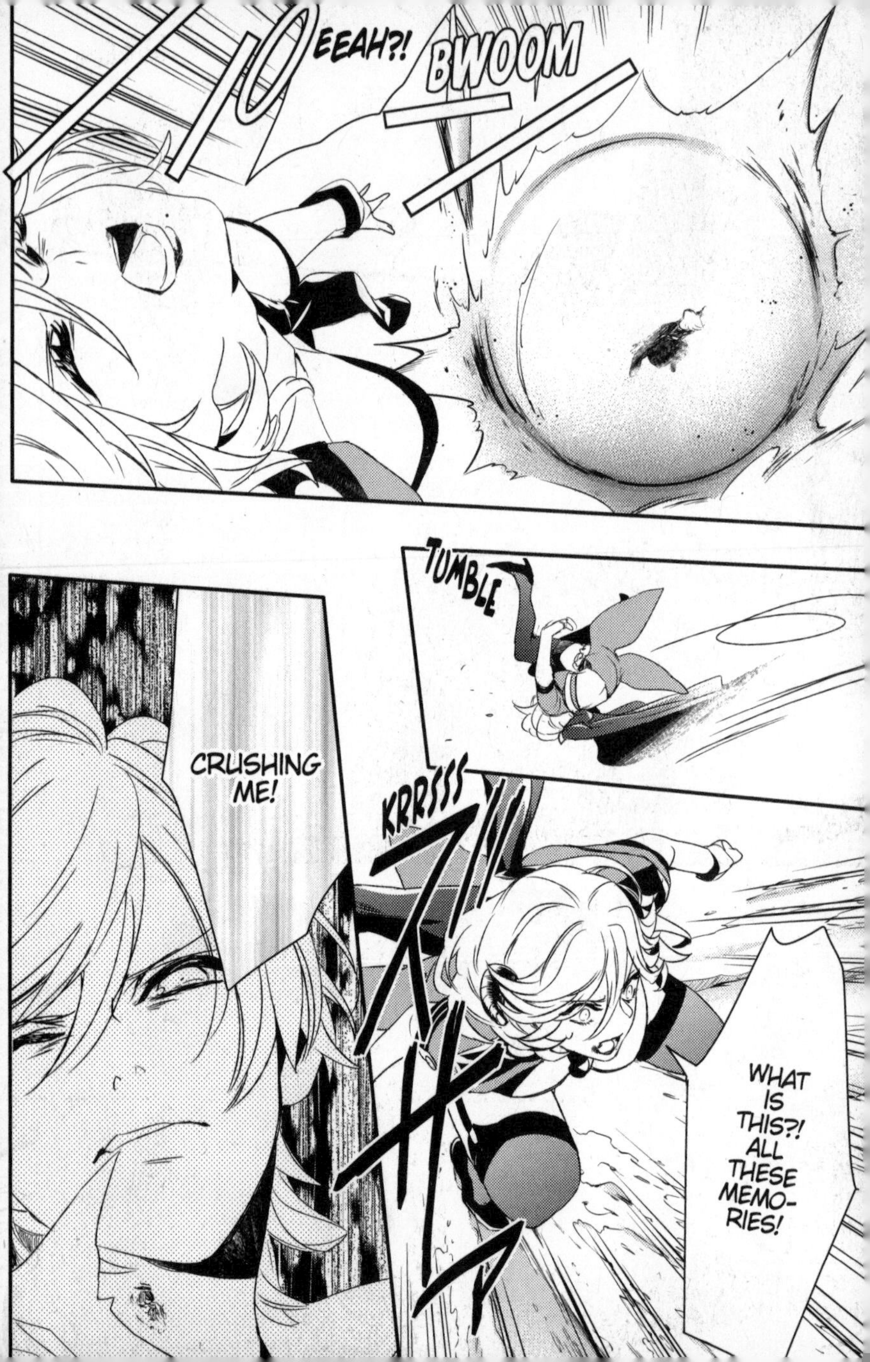
BWOOM
OEEAH?!
TUMBLE
KRRSSS
WHAT IS THIS?! ALL THESE MEMORIES!
CRUSHING ME!

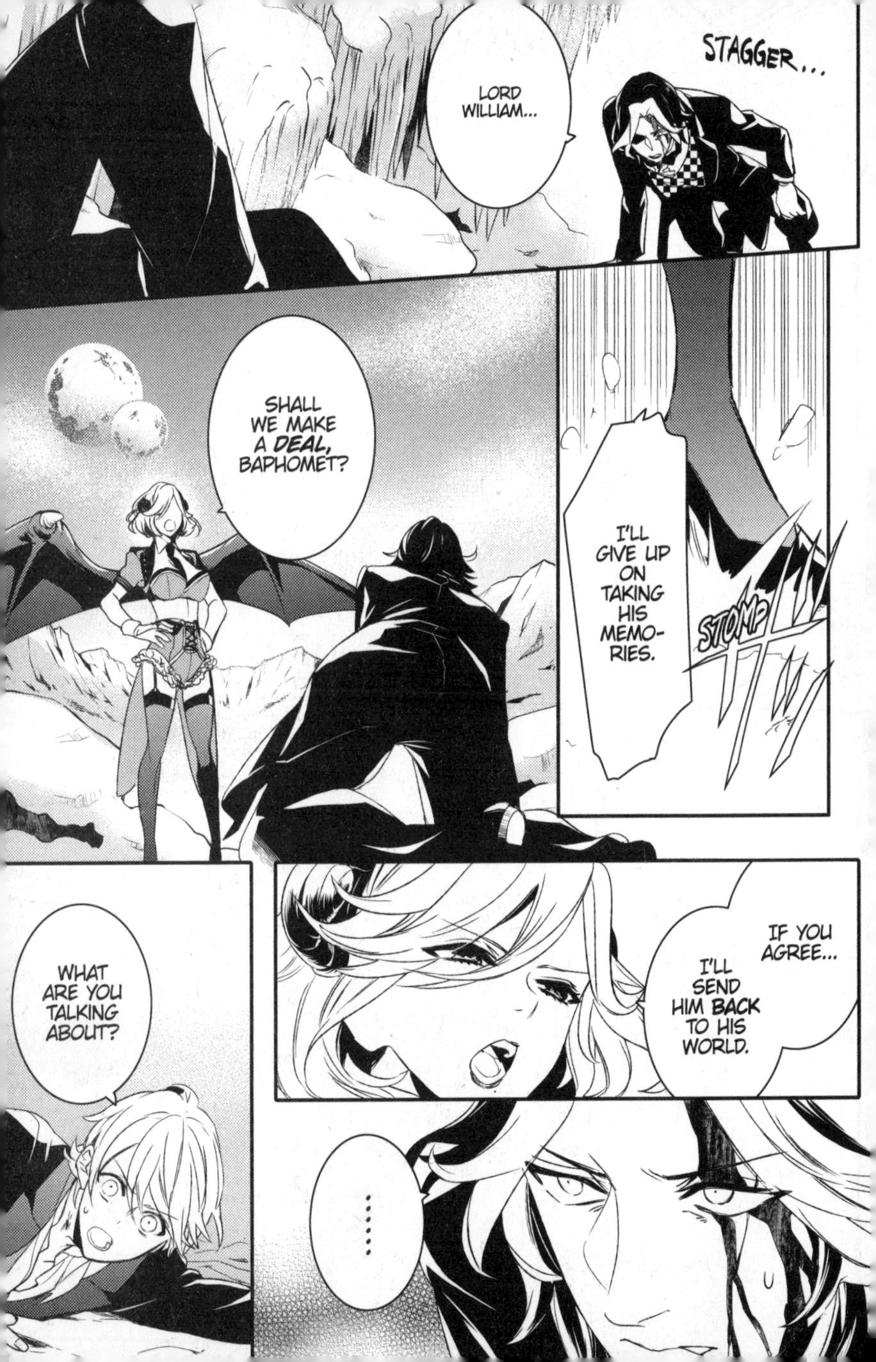
STAGGER...
LORD WILLIAM...
I'LL GIVE UP ON TAKING HIS MEMORIES.
STOMP
SHALL WE MAKE A DEAL, BAPHOMET?
IF YOU AGREE...
I'LL SEND HIM BACK TO HIS WORLD.
......
WHAT ARE YOU TALKING ABOUT?

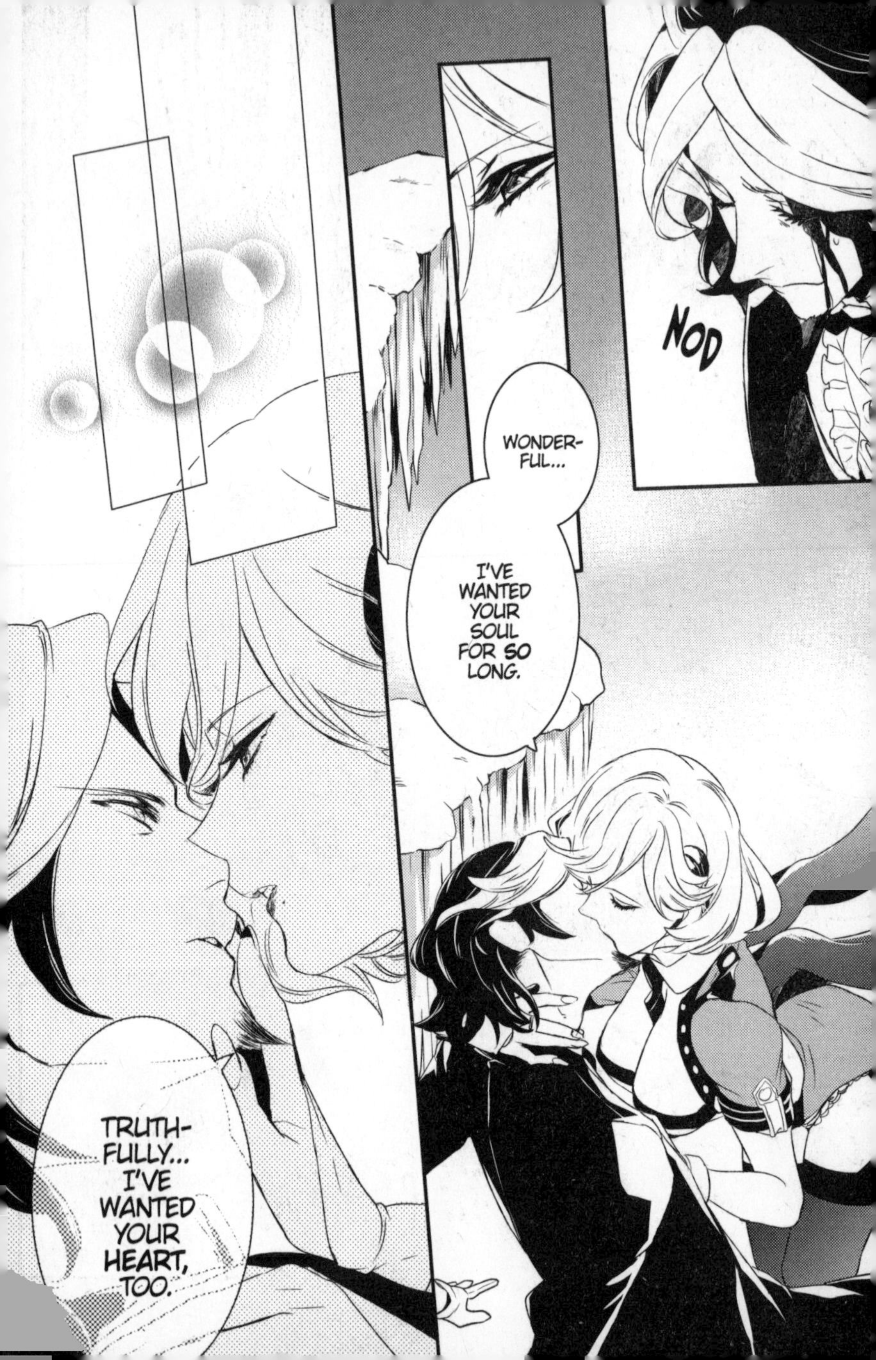
NOD
WONDER-FUL...
I'VE WANTED YOUR SOUL FOR SO LONG.
TRUTH-FULLY... I'VE WANTED YOUR HEART, TOO.

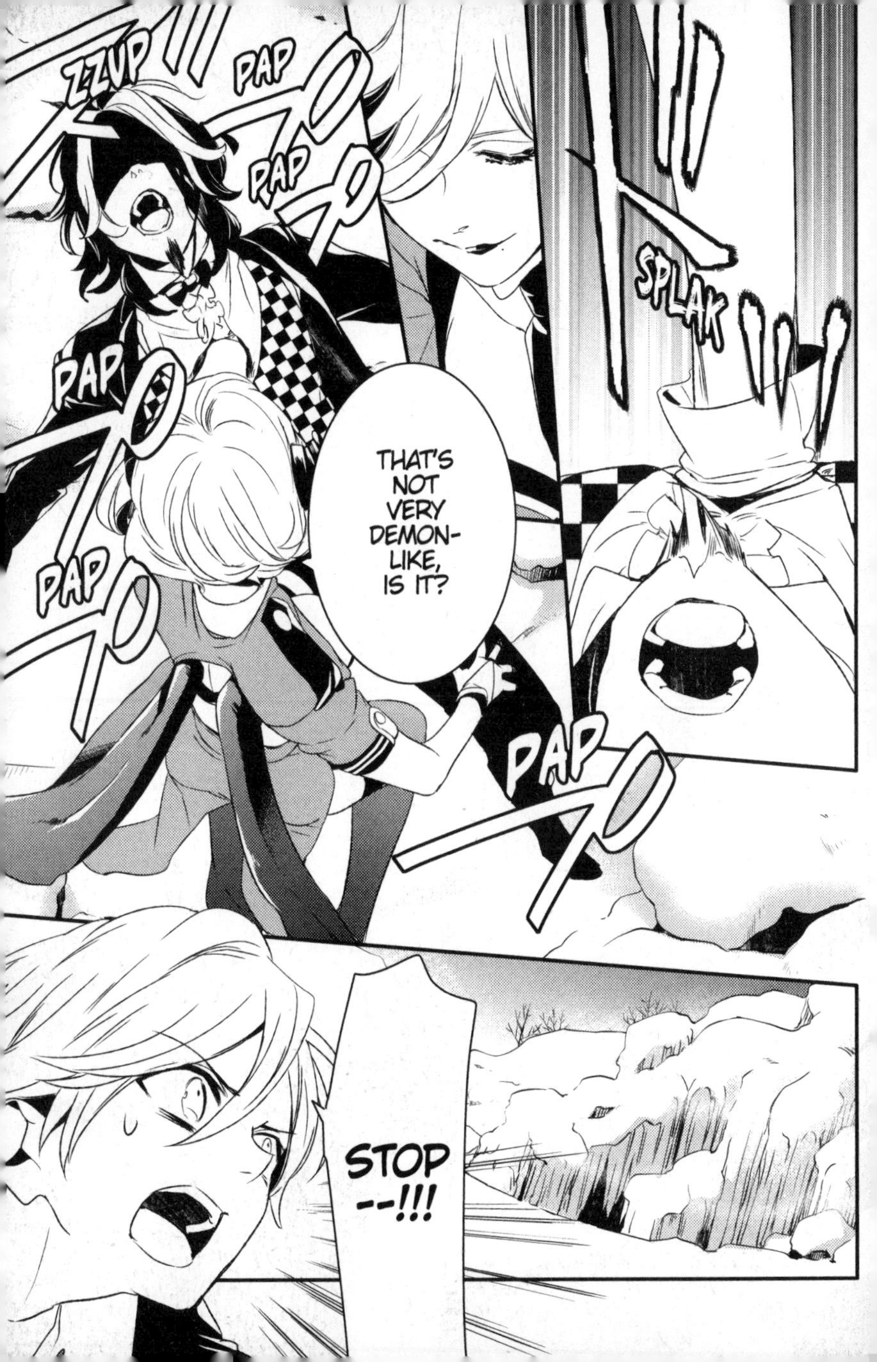
SPLAK
PAP
PAP
ZZUP
THAT'S NOT VERY DEMON-LIKE, IS IT?
PAP
PAP
PAP
STOP --!!!

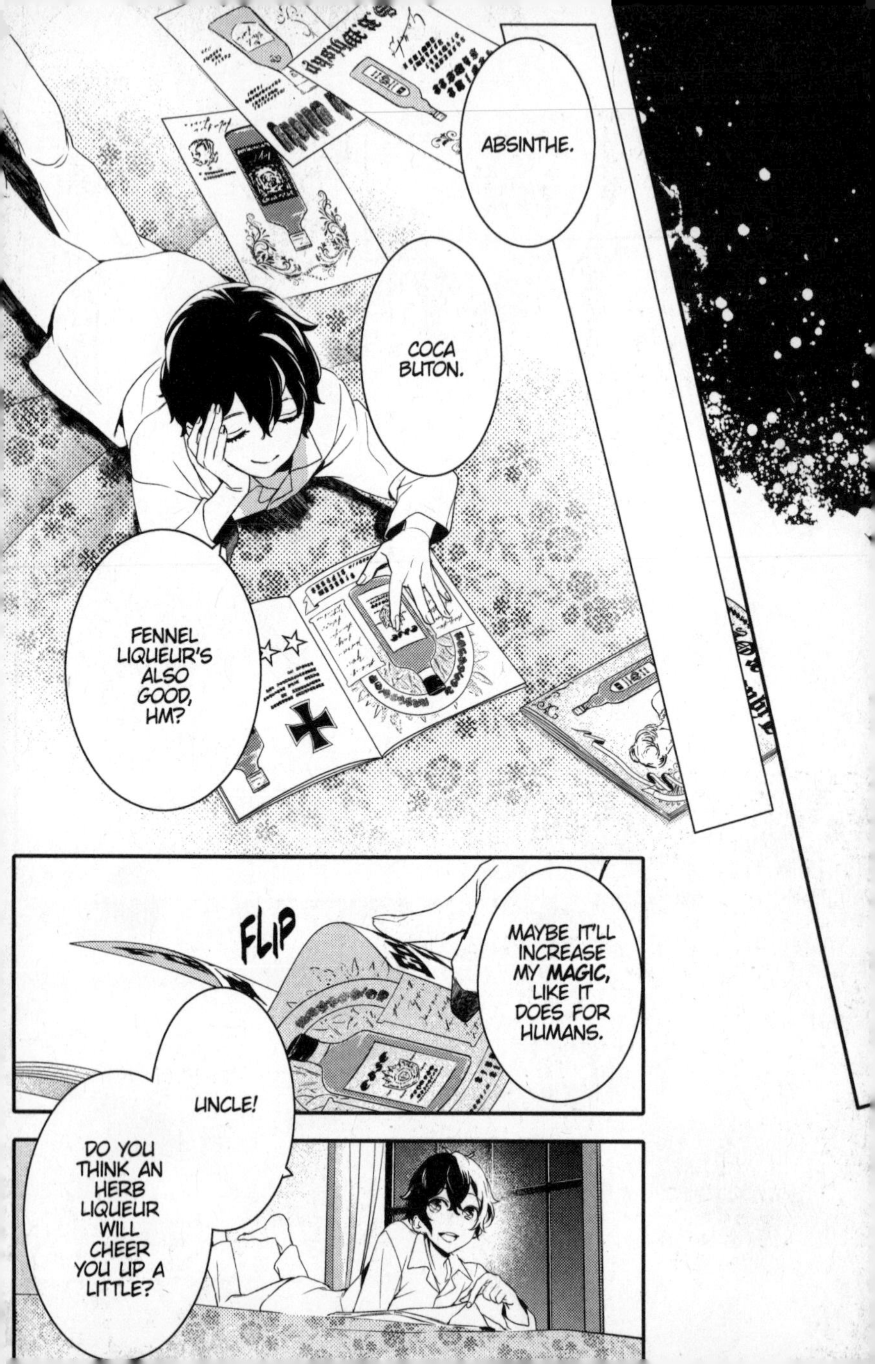
ABSINTHE.
COCA BUTON.
FENNEL LIQUEUR'S ALSO GOOD, HM?
MAYBE IT'LL INCREASE MY **MAGIC**, LIKE IT DOES FOR HUMANS.
FLIP
UNCLE!
DO YOU THINK AN HERB LIQUEUR WILL CHEER YOU UP A LITTLE?

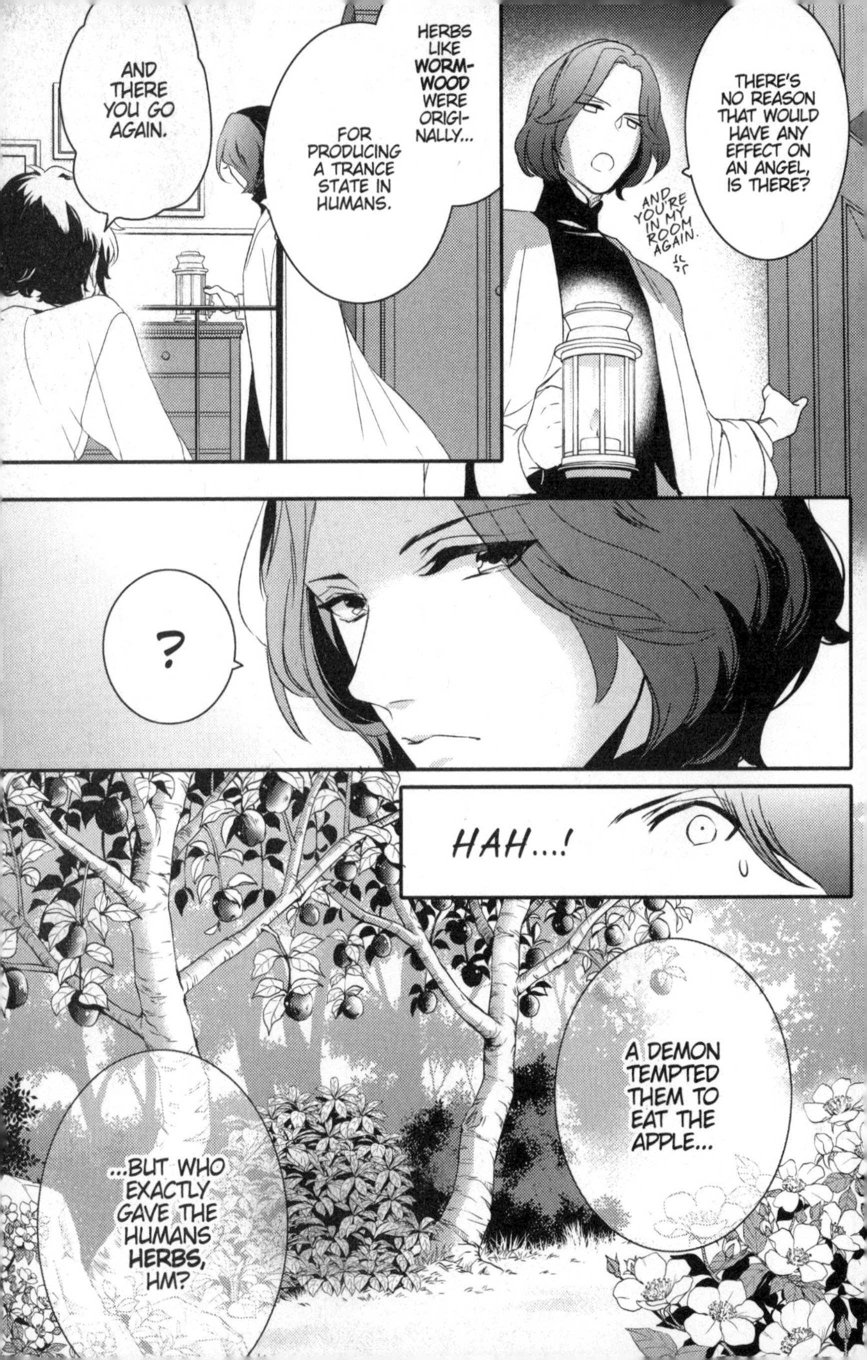
THERE'S NO REASON THAT WOULD HAVE ANY EFFECT ON AN ANGEL, IS THERE?
AND YOU'RE IN MY ROOM AGAIN.
HERBS LIKE WORMWOOD WERE ORIGINALLY...
FOR PRODUCING A TRANCE STATE IN HUMANS.
AND THERE YOU GO AGAIN.
?
HAH...!
A DEMON TEMPTED THEM TO EAT THE APPLE...
...BUT WHO EXACTLY GAVE THE HUMANS HERBS, HM?

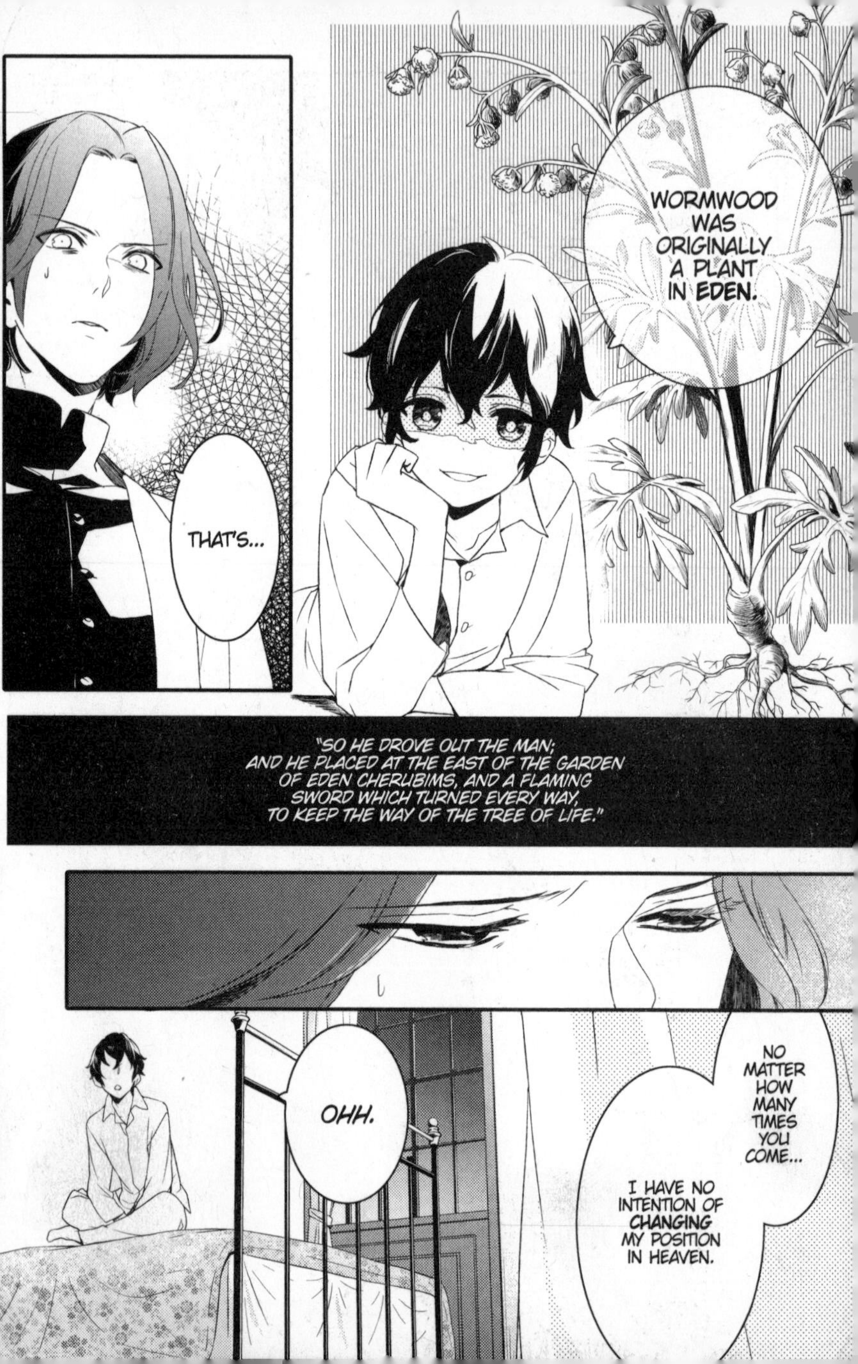
WORMWOOD WAS ORIGINALLY A PLANT IN EDEN.
THAT'S...
"SO HE DROVE OUT THE MAN; AND HE PLACED AT THE EAST OF THE GARDEN OF EDEN CHERUBIMS, AND A FLAMING SWORD WHICH TURNED EVERY WAY, TO KEEP THE WAY OF THE TREE OF LIFE."
NO MATTER HOW MANY TIMES YOU COME...
I HAVE NO INTENTION OF CHANGING MY POSITION IN HEAVEN.
OHH.

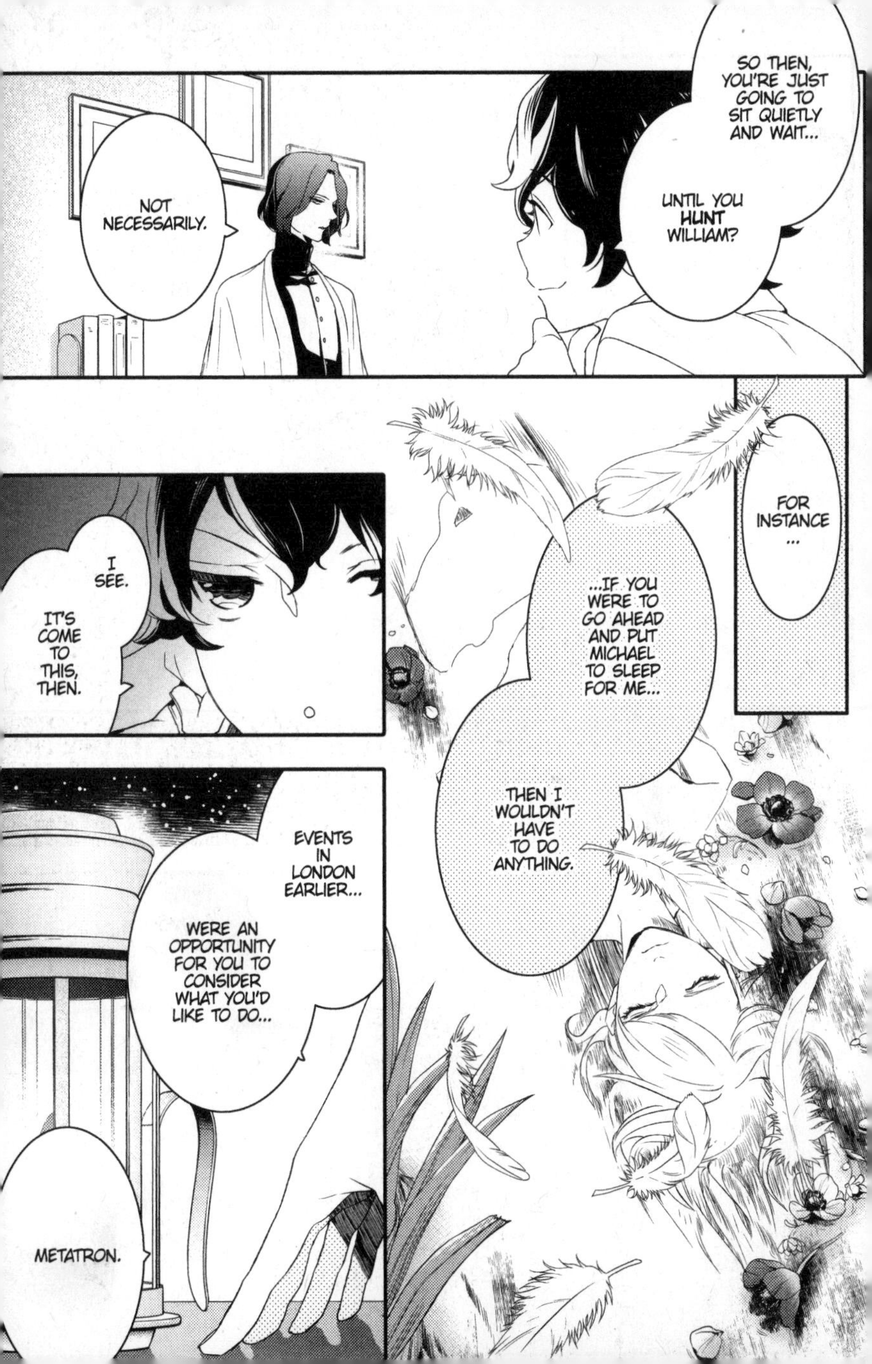
SO THEN, YOU'RE JUST GOING TO SIT QUIETLY AND WAIT...
UNTIL YOU HUNT WILLIAM?
NOT NECESSARILY.
FOR INSTANCE...
...IF YOU WERE TO GO AHEAD AND PUT MICHAEL TO SLEEP FOR ME...
THEN I WOULDN'T HAVE TO DO ANYTHING.
I SEE.
IT'S COME TO THIS, THEN.
EVENTS IN LONDON EARLIER...
WERE AN OPPORTUNITY FOR YOU TO CONSIDER WHAT YOU'D LIKE TO DO...
METATRON.

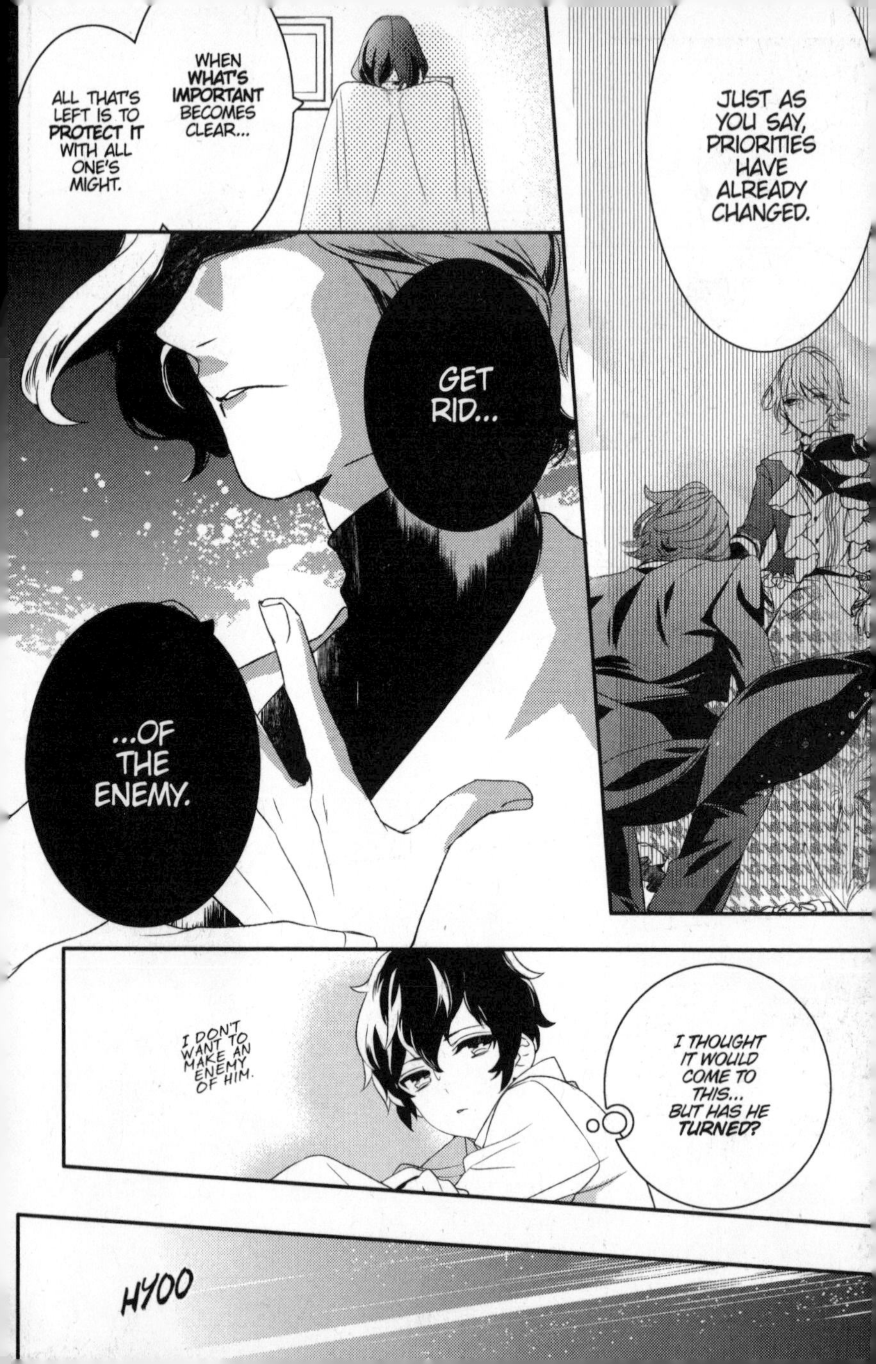
JUST AS YOU SAY, PRIORITIES HAVE ALREADY CHANGED.
WHEN WHAT'S IMPORTANT BECOMES CLEAR...
ALL THAT'S LEFT IS TO PROTECT IT WITH ALL ONE'S MIGHT.
GET RID...
...OF THE ENEMY.
I THOUGHT IT WOULD COME TO THIS... BUT HAS HE TURNED?
I DON'T WANT TO MAKE AN ENEMY OF HIM.
HYOO

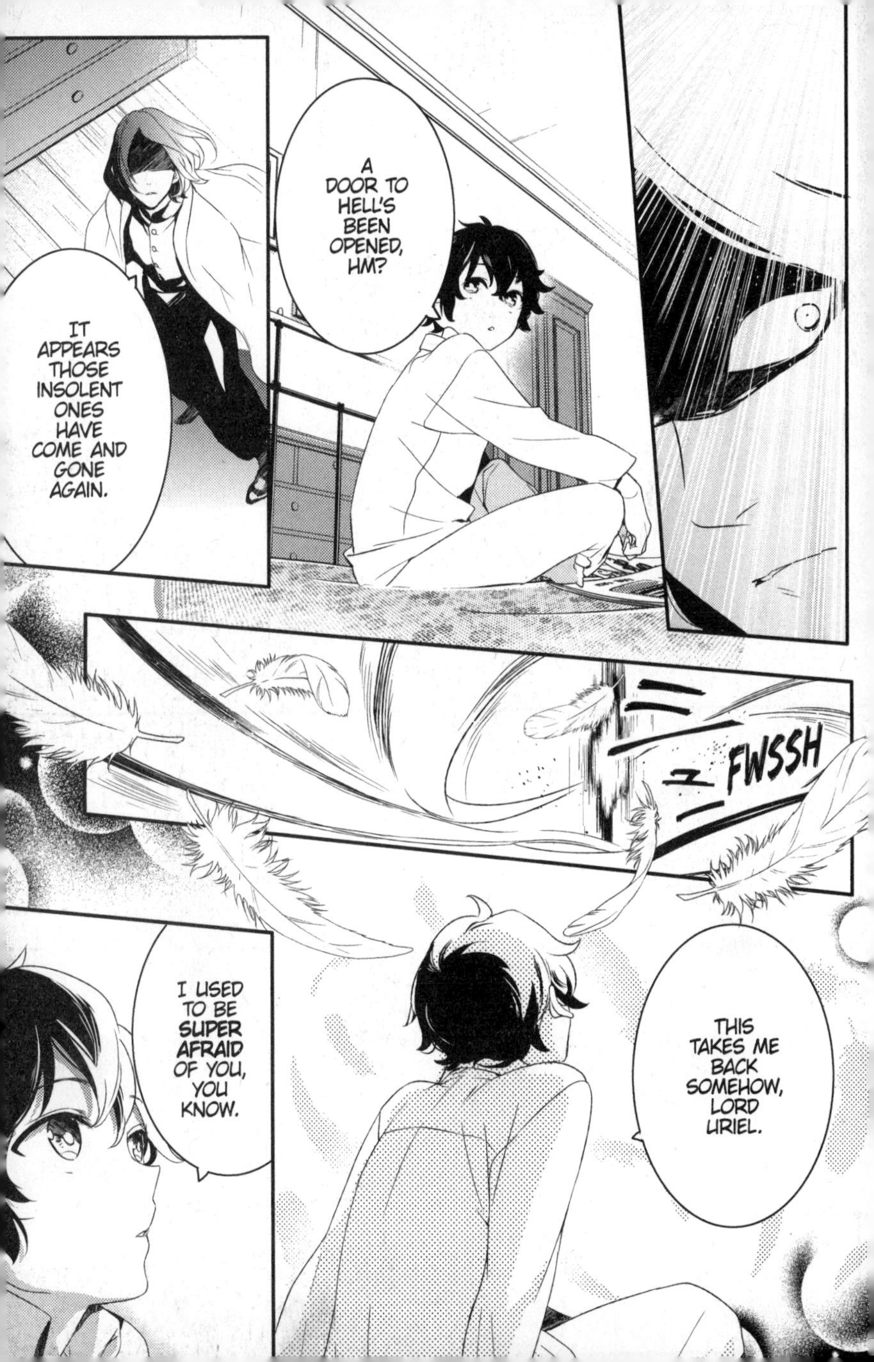
A DOOR TO HELL'S BEEN OPENED, HM?
IT APPEARS THOSE INSOLENT ONES HAVE COME AND GONE AGAIN.
FWSSH
THIS TAKES ME BACK SOMEHOW, LORD URIEL.
I USED TO BE **SUPER AFRAID** OF YOU, YOU KNOW.

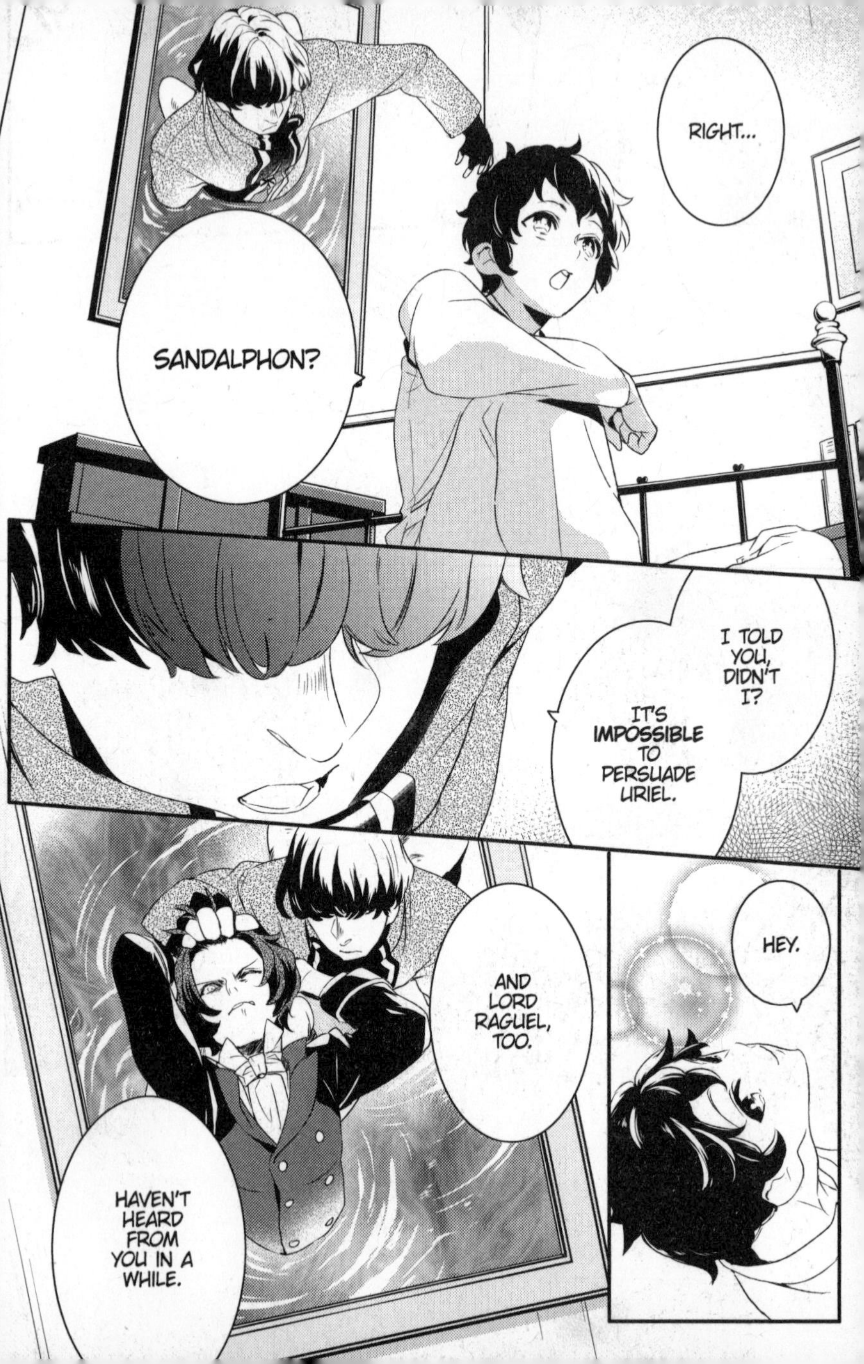
RIGHT...
SANDALPHON?
I TOLD YOU, DIDN'T I?
IT'S IMPOSSIBLE TO PERSUADE URIEL.
HEY.
AND LORD RAGUEL, TOO.
HAVEN'T HEARD FROM YOU IN A WHILE.

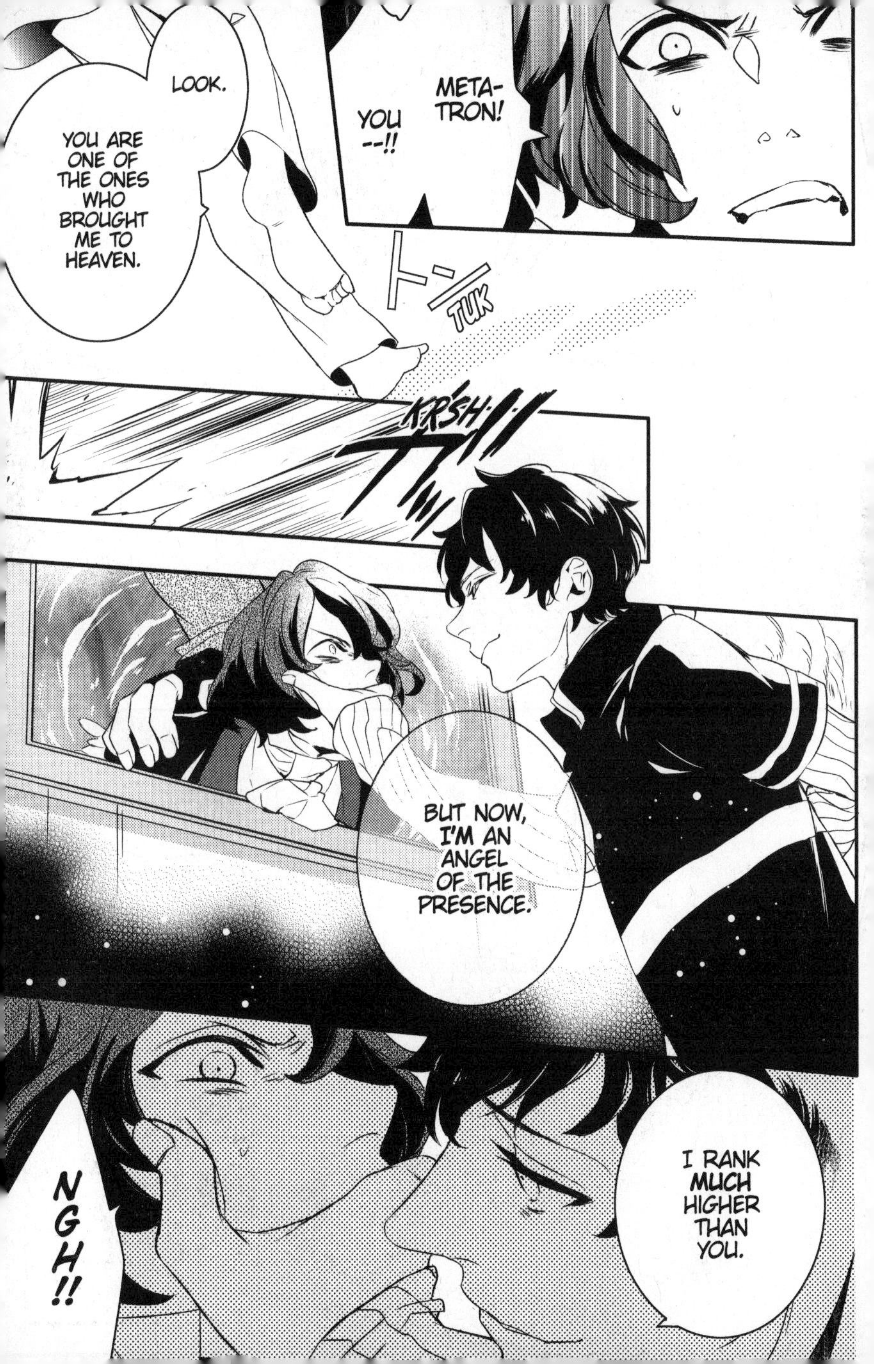
META-TRON!
YOU --!!
LOOK.
YOU ARE ONE OF THE ONES WHO BROUGHT ME TO HEAVEN.
トン
TUK
K-R-S-H
BUT NOW, I'M AN ANGEL OF THE PRESENCE.
I RANK MUCH HIGHER THAN YOU.
NGH!!

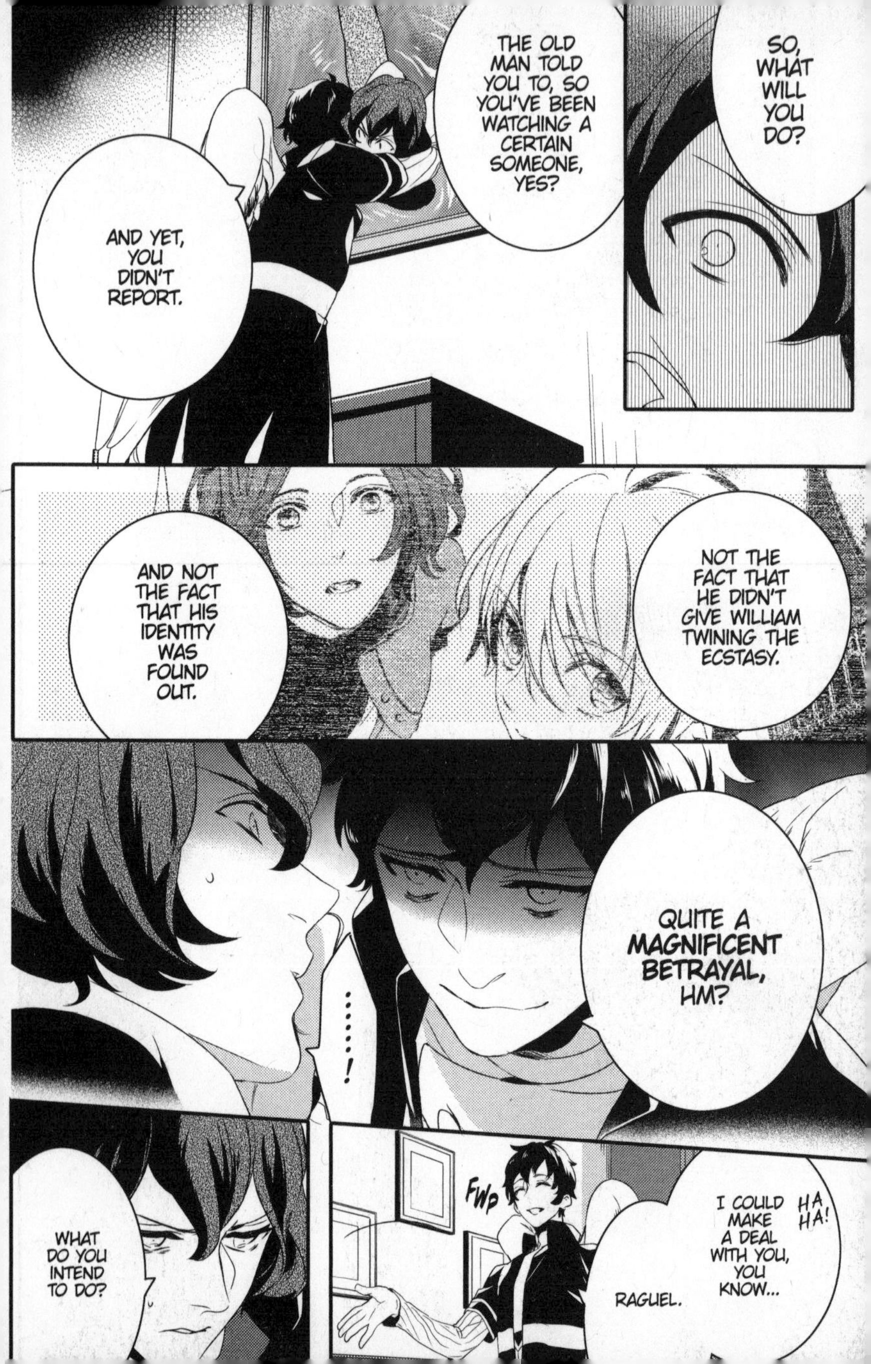
SO, WHAT WILL YOU DO?
THE OLD MAN TOLD YOU TO, SO YOU'VE BEEN WATCHING A CERTAIN SOMEONE, YES?
AND YET, YOU DIDN'T REPORT.
NOT THE FACT THAT HE DIDN'T GIVE WILLIAM TWINING THE ECSTASY.
AND NOT THE FACT THAT HIS IDENTITY WAS FOUND OUT.
QUITE A MAGNIFICENT BETRAYAL, HM?
......!
HA HA!
I COULD MAKE A DEAL WITH YOU, YOU KNOW...
FWP
RAGUEL.
WHAT DO YOU INTEND TO DO?

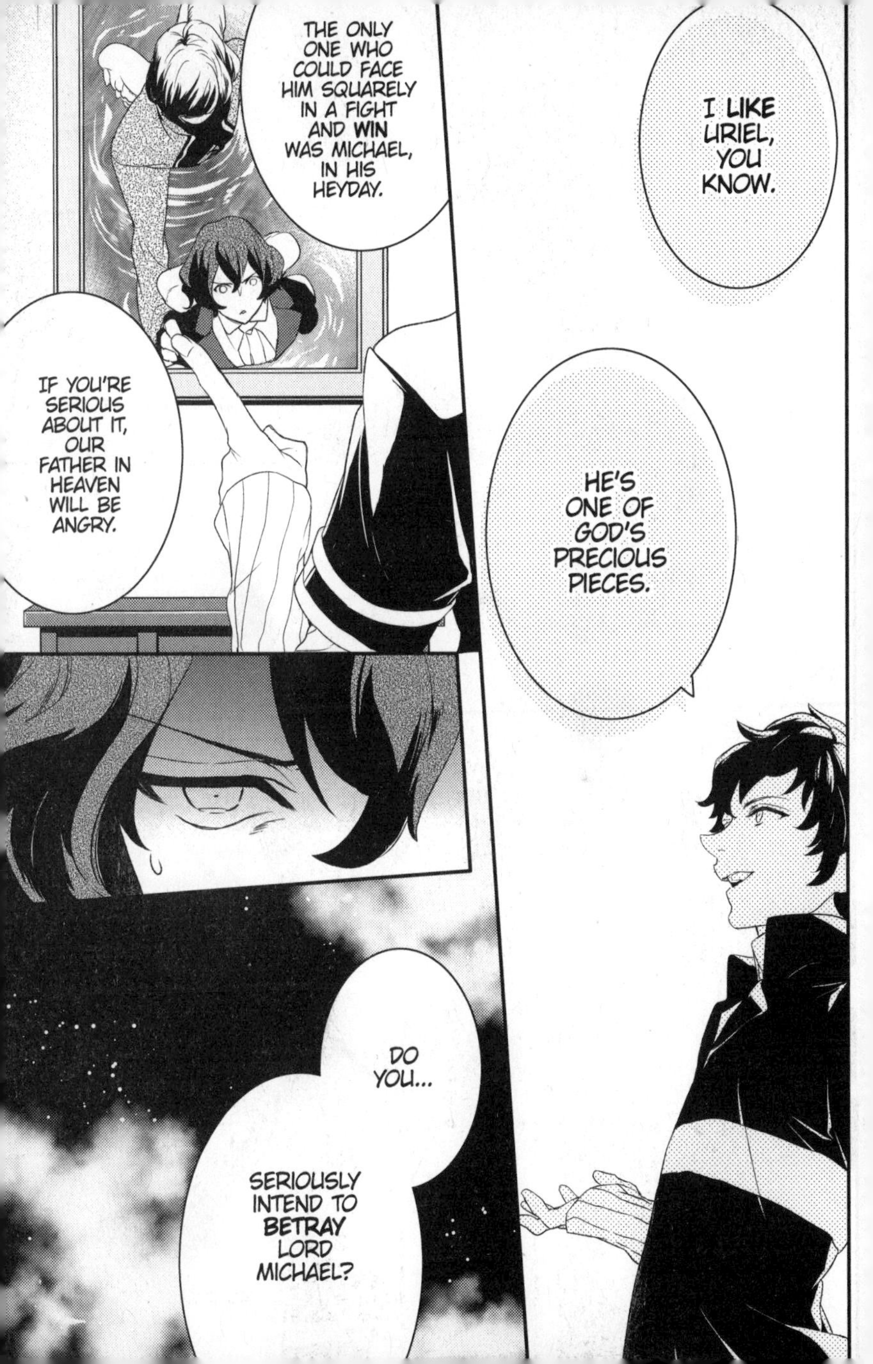
I LIKE URIEL, YOU KNOW.
HE'S ONE OF GOD'S PRECIOUS PIECES.
THE ONLY ONE WHO COULD FACE HIM SQUARELY IN A FIGHT AND WIN WAS MICHAEL, IN HIS HEYDAY.
IF YOU'RE SERIOUS ABOUT IT, OUR FATHER IN HEAVEN WILL BE ANGRY.
DO YOU...
SERIOUSLY INTEND TO BETRAY LORD MICHAEL?

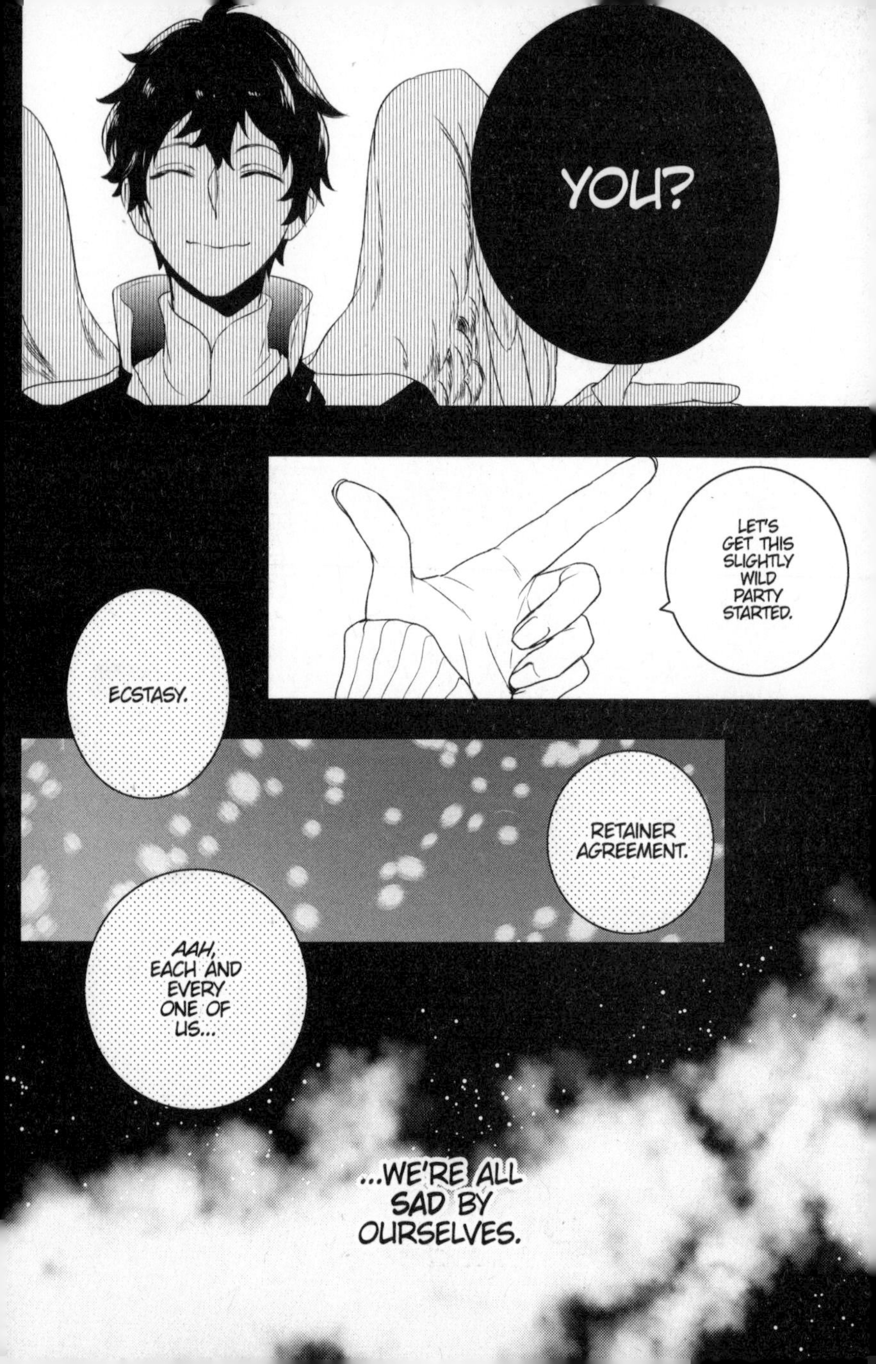
YOU?
LET'S GET THIS SLIGHTLY WILD PARTY STARTED.
ECSTASY.
RETAINER AGREEMENT.
AAH, EACH AND EVERY ONE OF US...
...WE'RE ALL SAD BY OURSELVES.

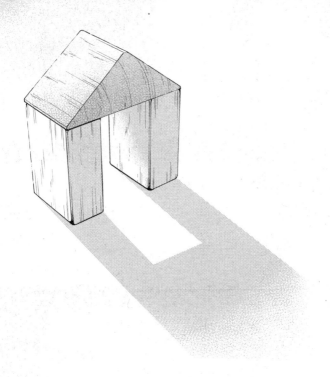

Pillar 57

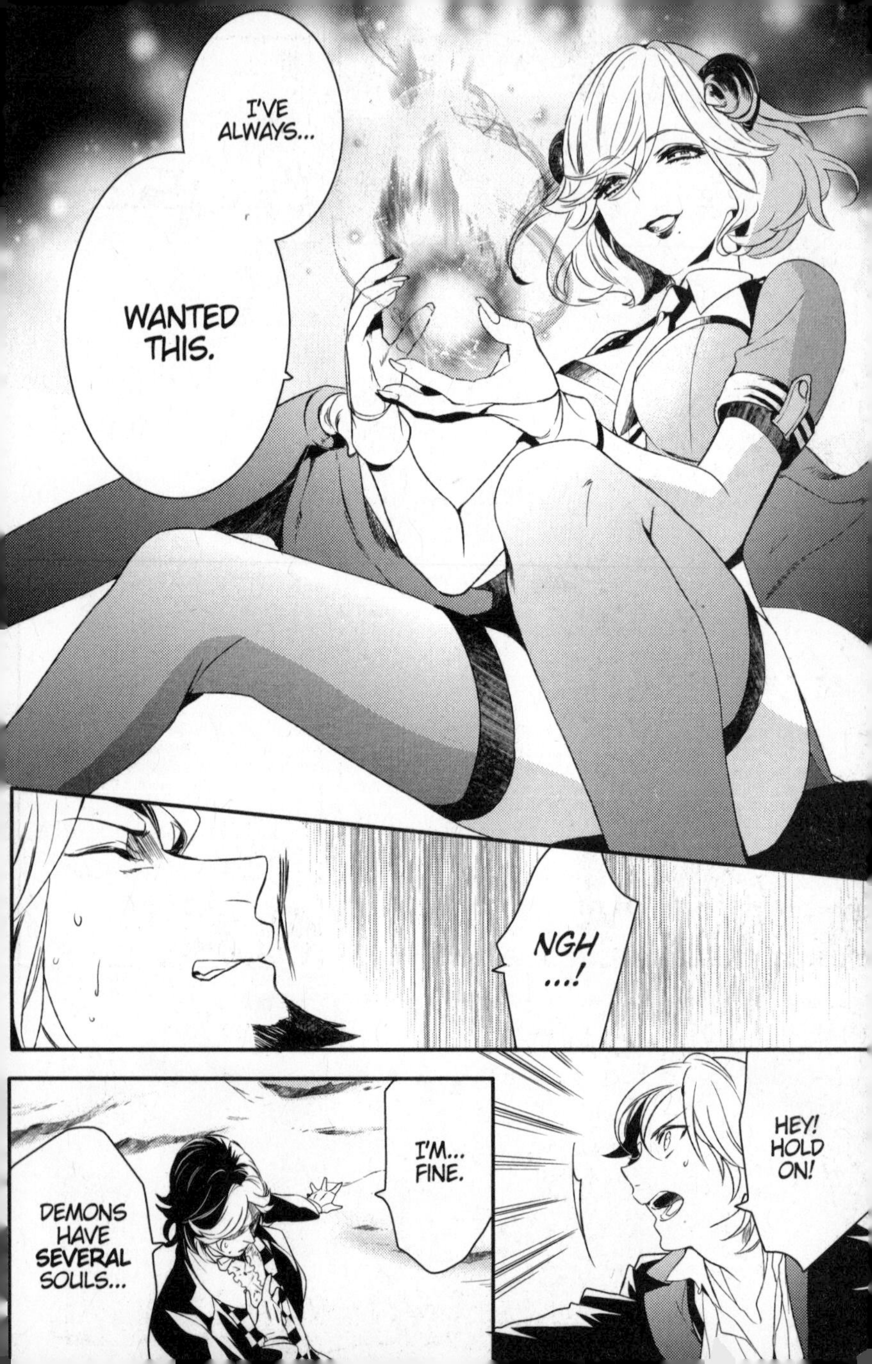
I'VE ALWAYS...
WANTED THIS.
NGH ...!
HEY! HOLD ON!
I'M... FINE.
DEMONS HAVE SEVERAL SOULS...

SAY, BAPHOMET?

WHY DIDN'T YOU GO TO LIMBO?

WHUP

I'M SURE THAT'S WHERE THE UNBAPTIZED GO...

LIMBO?

THE PLACE ON THE BORDER BETWEEN HELL AND THE HUMAN WORLD.

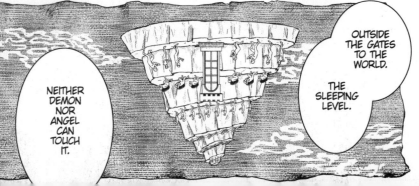

OUTSIDE THE GATES TO THE WORLD.

THE SLEEPING LEVEL.

NEITHER DEMON NOR ANGEL CAN TOUCH IT.

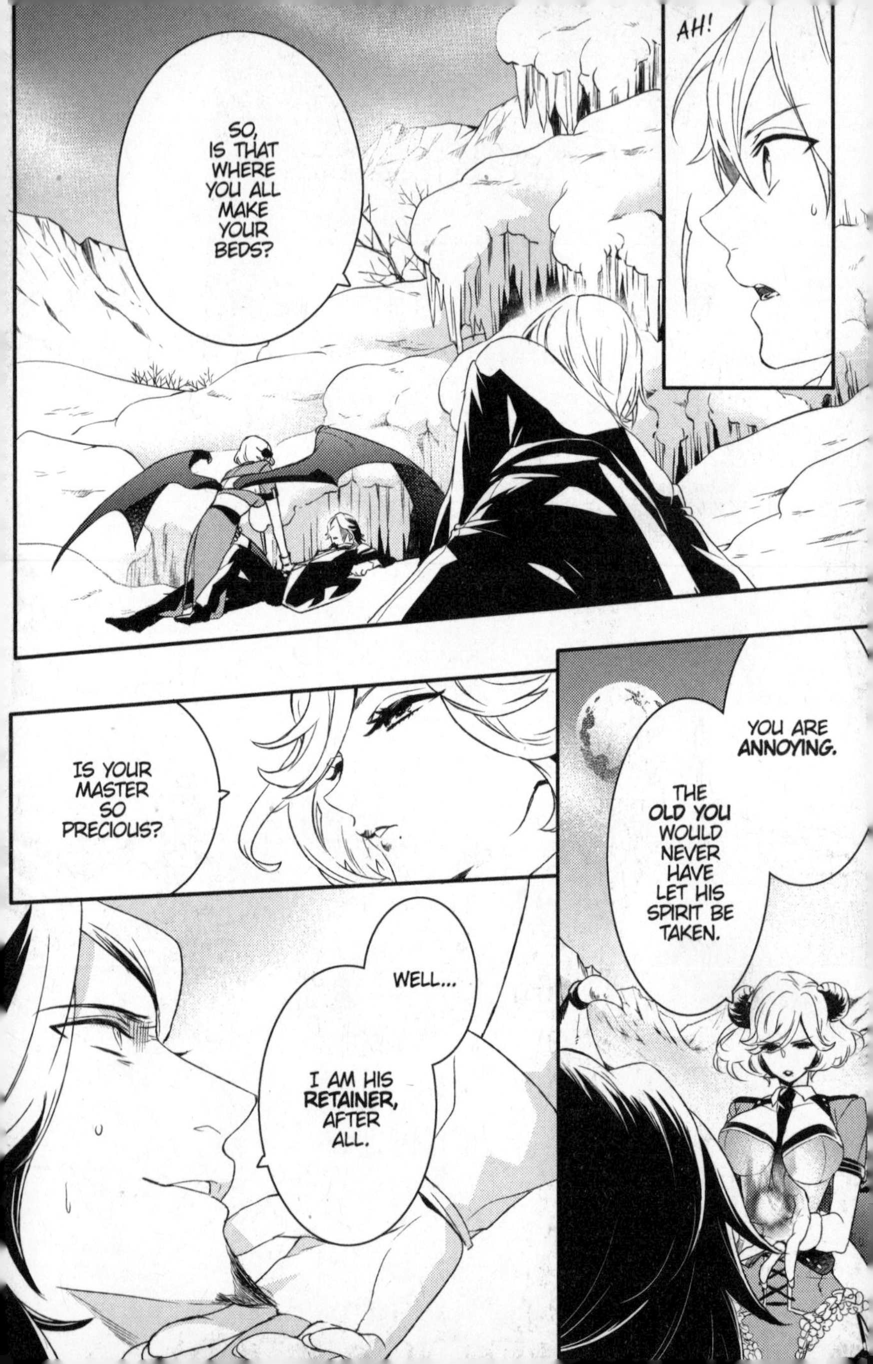
AH!
SO, IS THAT WHERE YOU ALL MAKE YOUR BEDS?
YOU ARE ANNOYING.
THE OLD YOU WOULD NEVER HAVE LET HIS SPIRIT BE TAKEN.
IS YOUR MASTER SO PRECIOUS?
WELL...
I AM HIS RETAINER, AFTER ALL.

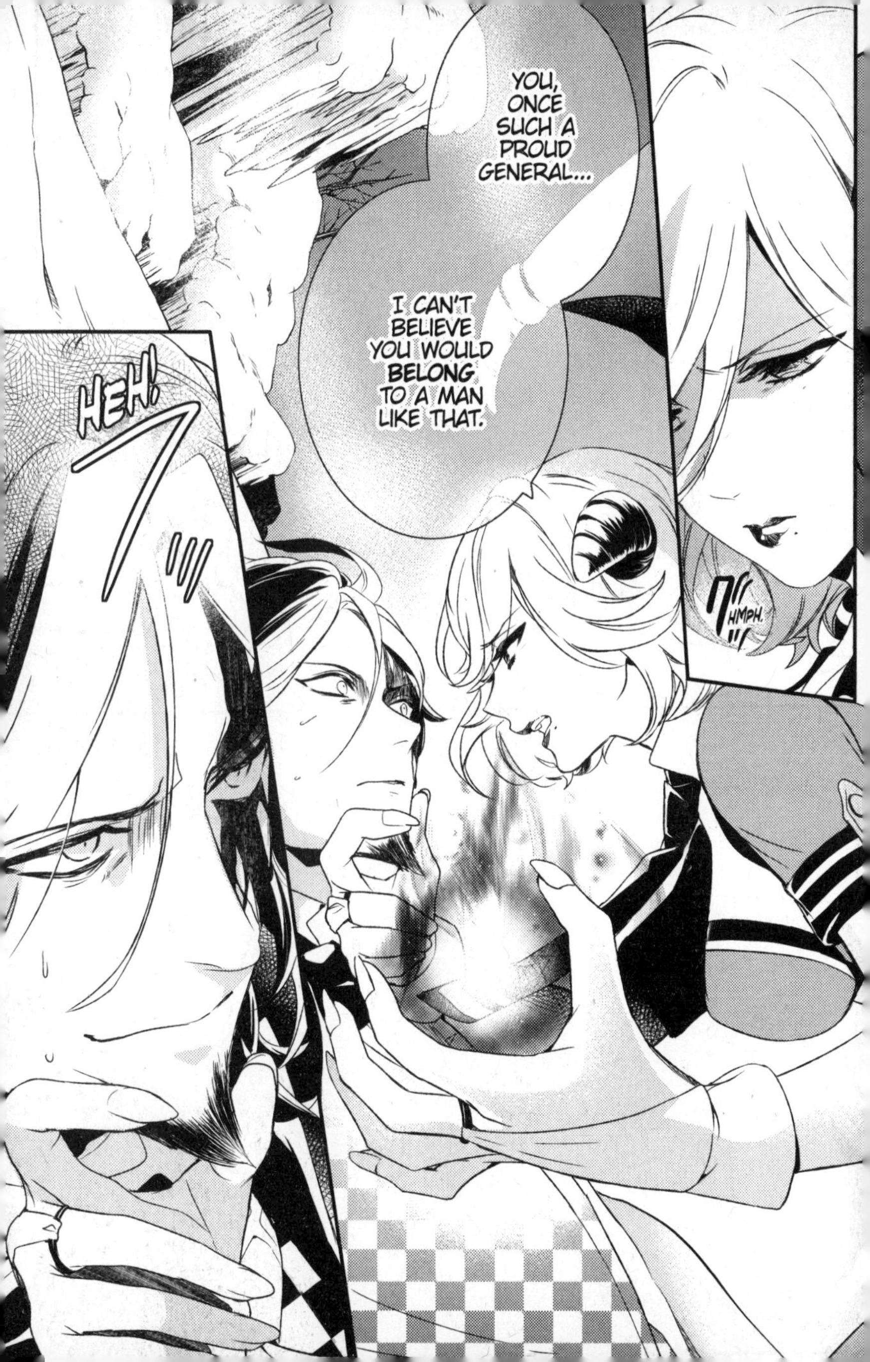
YOU, ONCE SUCH A PROUD GENERAL...
I CAN'T BELIEVE YOU WOULD BELONG TO A MAN LIKE THAT.
HMPH.
HEH!

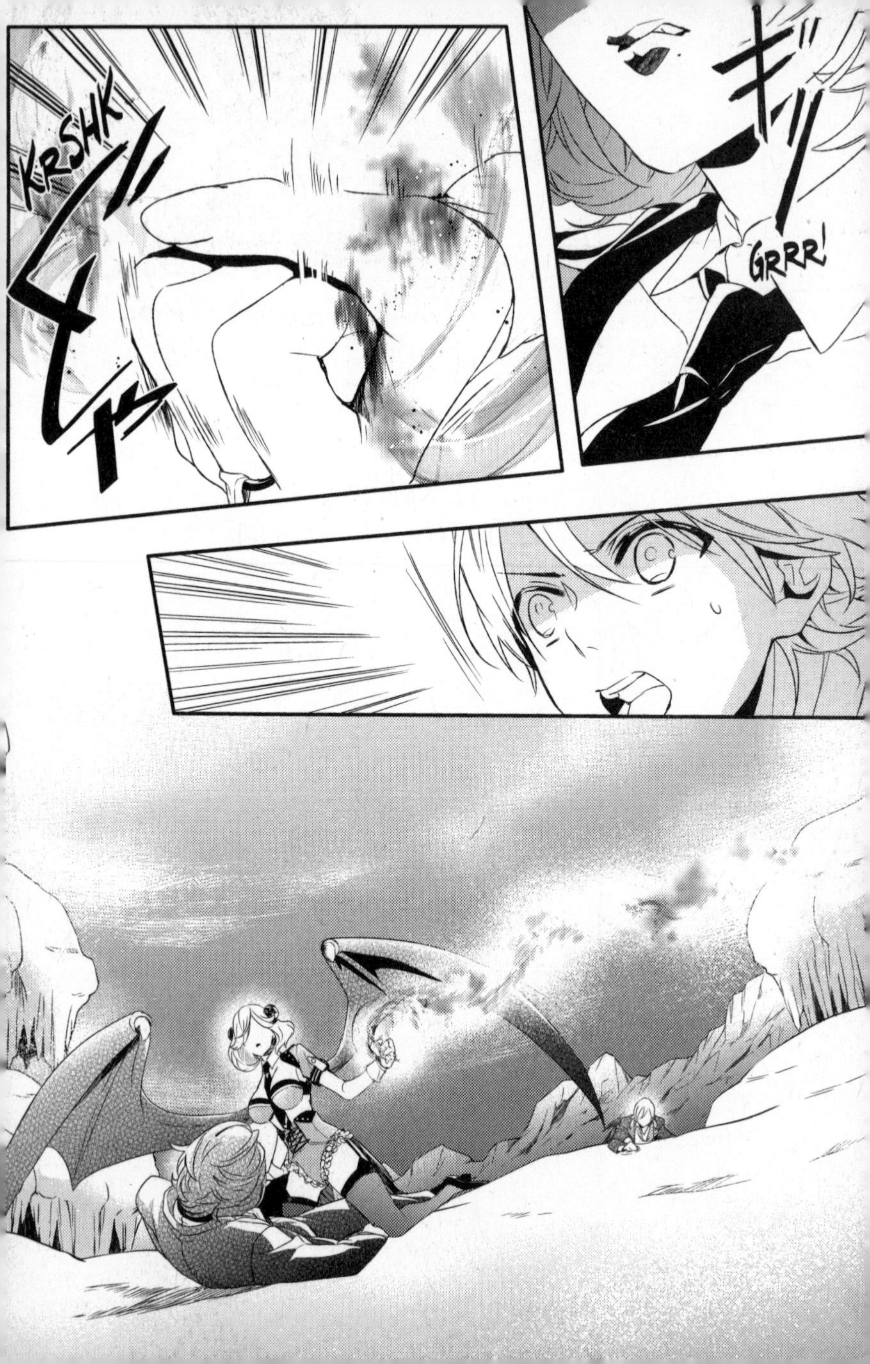
GRRR!
KRSHK

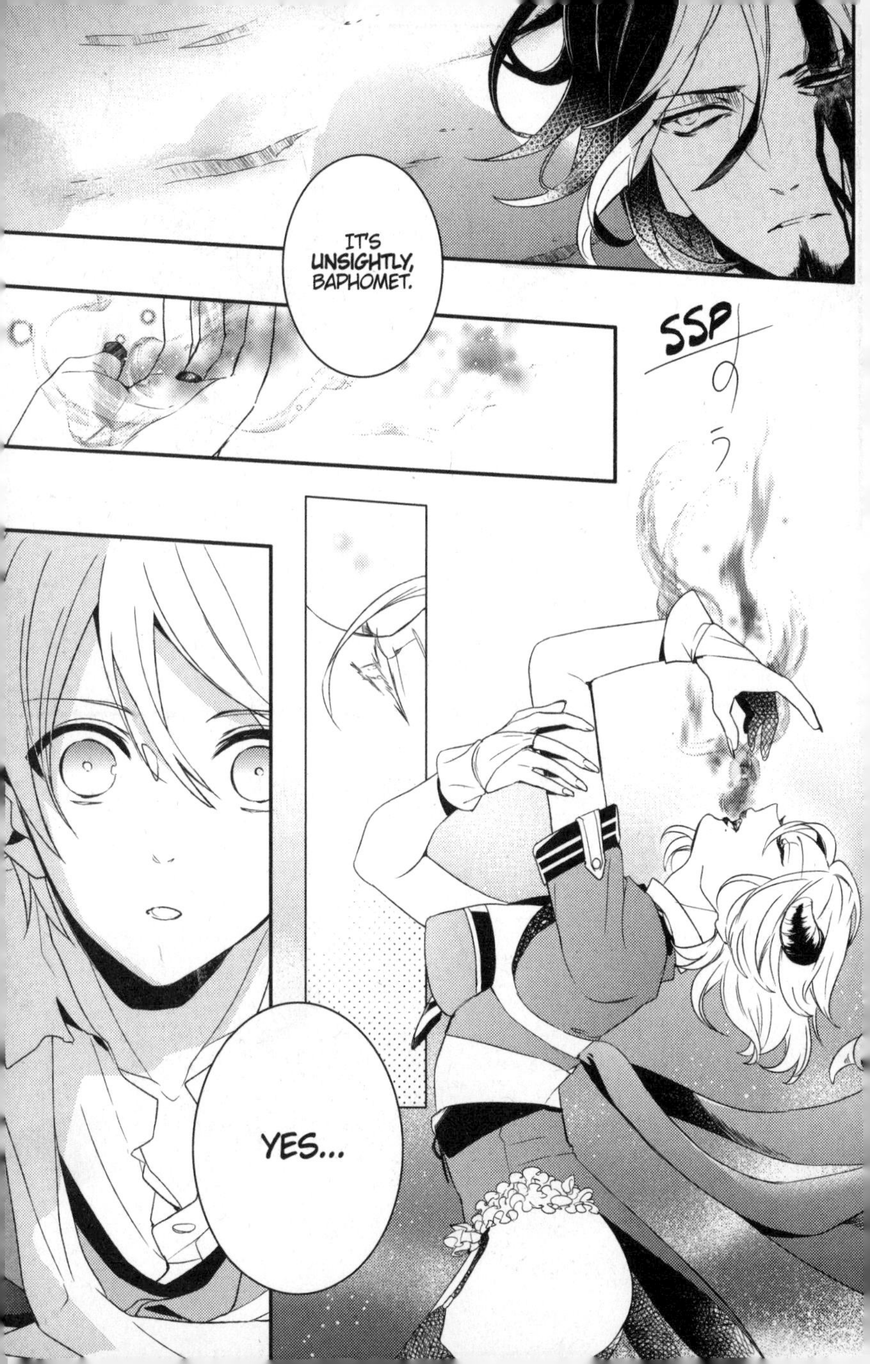
IT'S UNSIGHTLY, BAPHOMET.
SSP
YES...

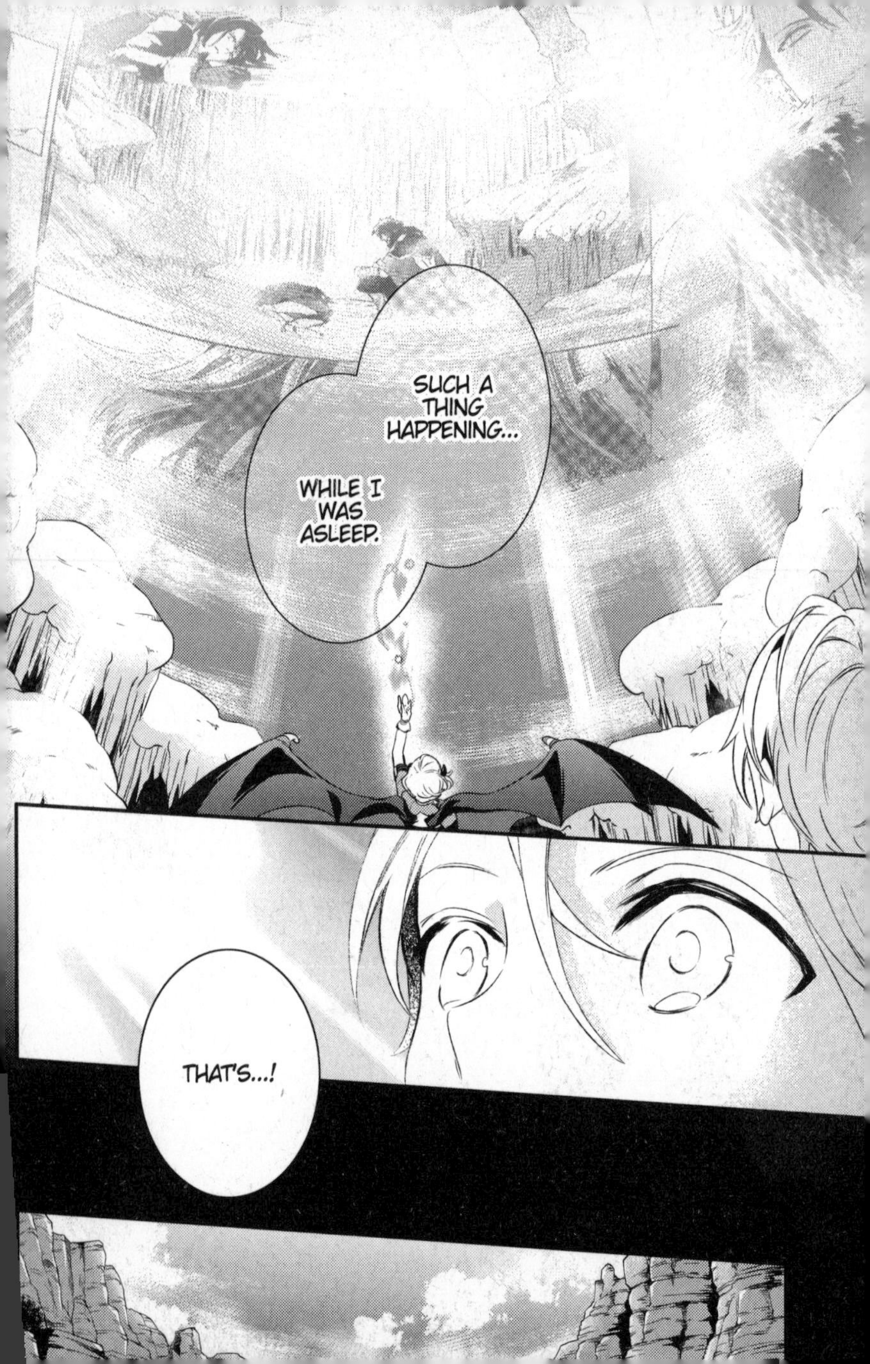
SUCH A THING HAPPENING...
WHILE I WAS ASLEEP.
THAT'S...!

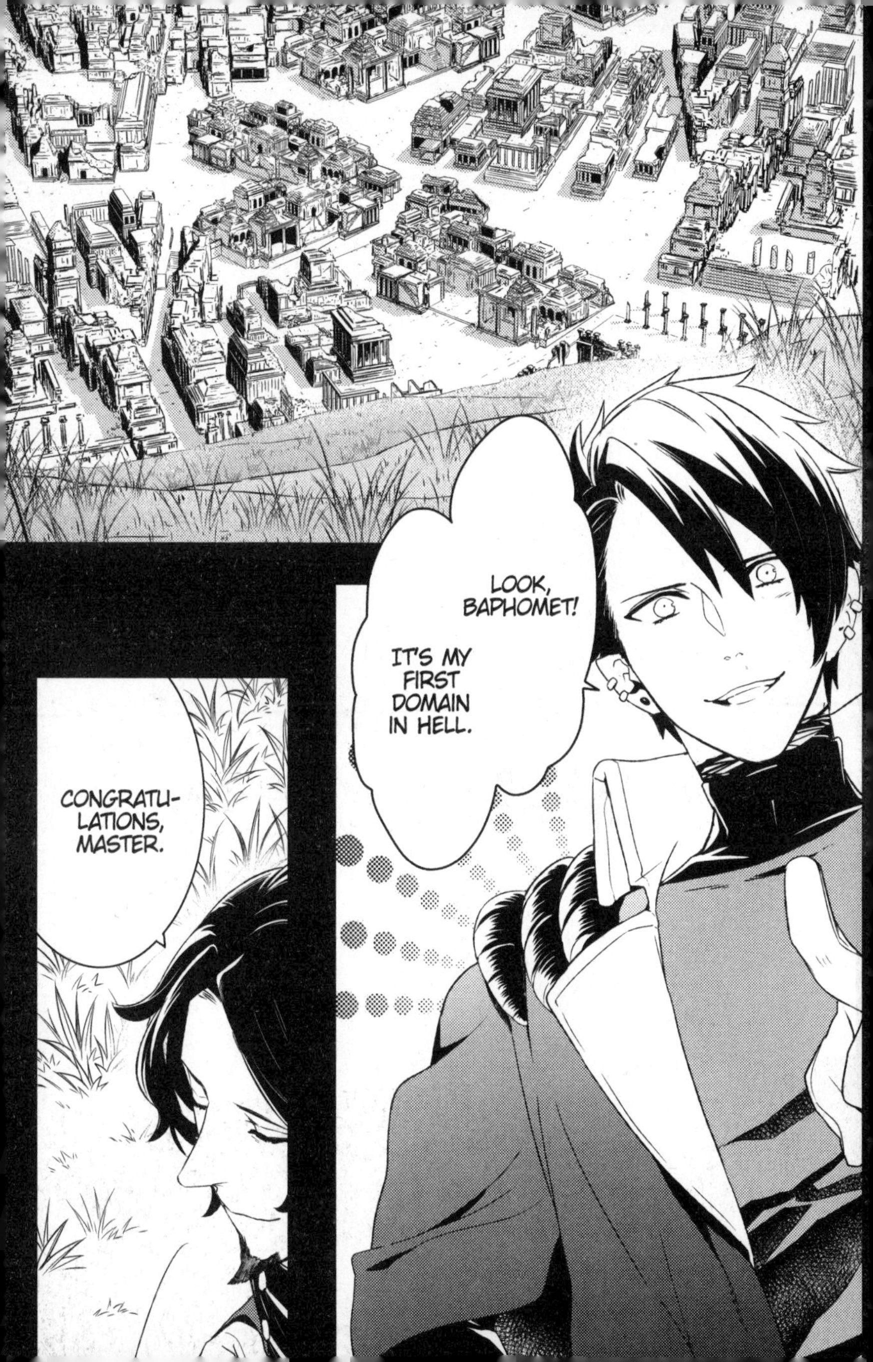
LOOK, BAPHOMET!
IT'S MY FIRST DOMAIN IN HELL.
CONGRATU-LATIONS, MASTER.

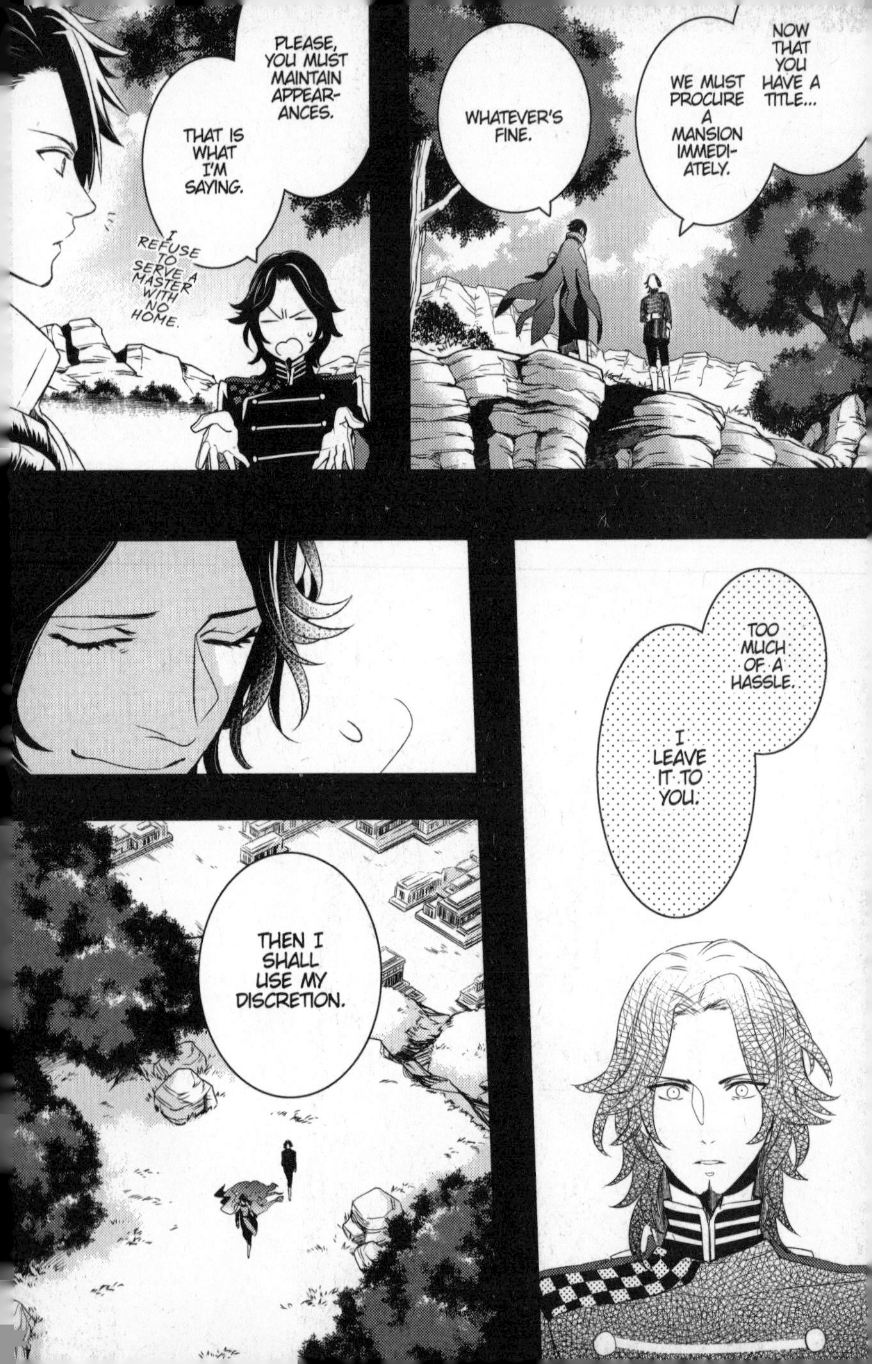
NOW THAT YOU HAVE A TITLE...
WE MUST PROCURE A MANSION IMMEDIATELY.
WHATEVER'S FINE.
PLEASE, YOU MUST MAINTAIN APPEARANCES.
THAT IS WHAT I'M SAYING.
I REFUSE TO SERVE A MASTER WITH NO HOME.
TOO MUCH OF A HASSLE.
I LEAVE IT TO YOU.
THEN I SHALL USE MY DISCRETION.

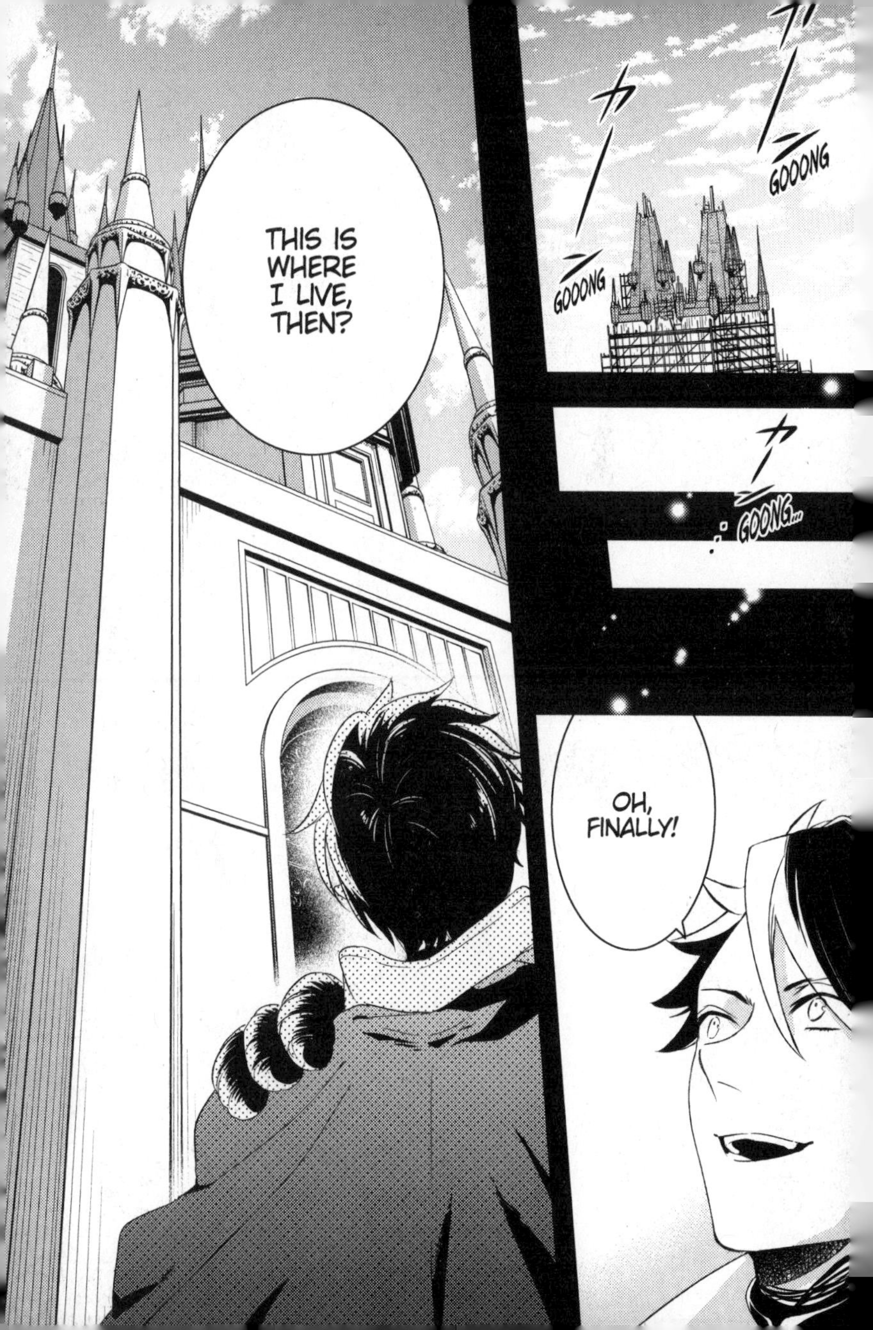
GOOONG
GOOONG
GOONG...
OH, FINALLY!
THIS IS WHERE I LIVE, THEN?

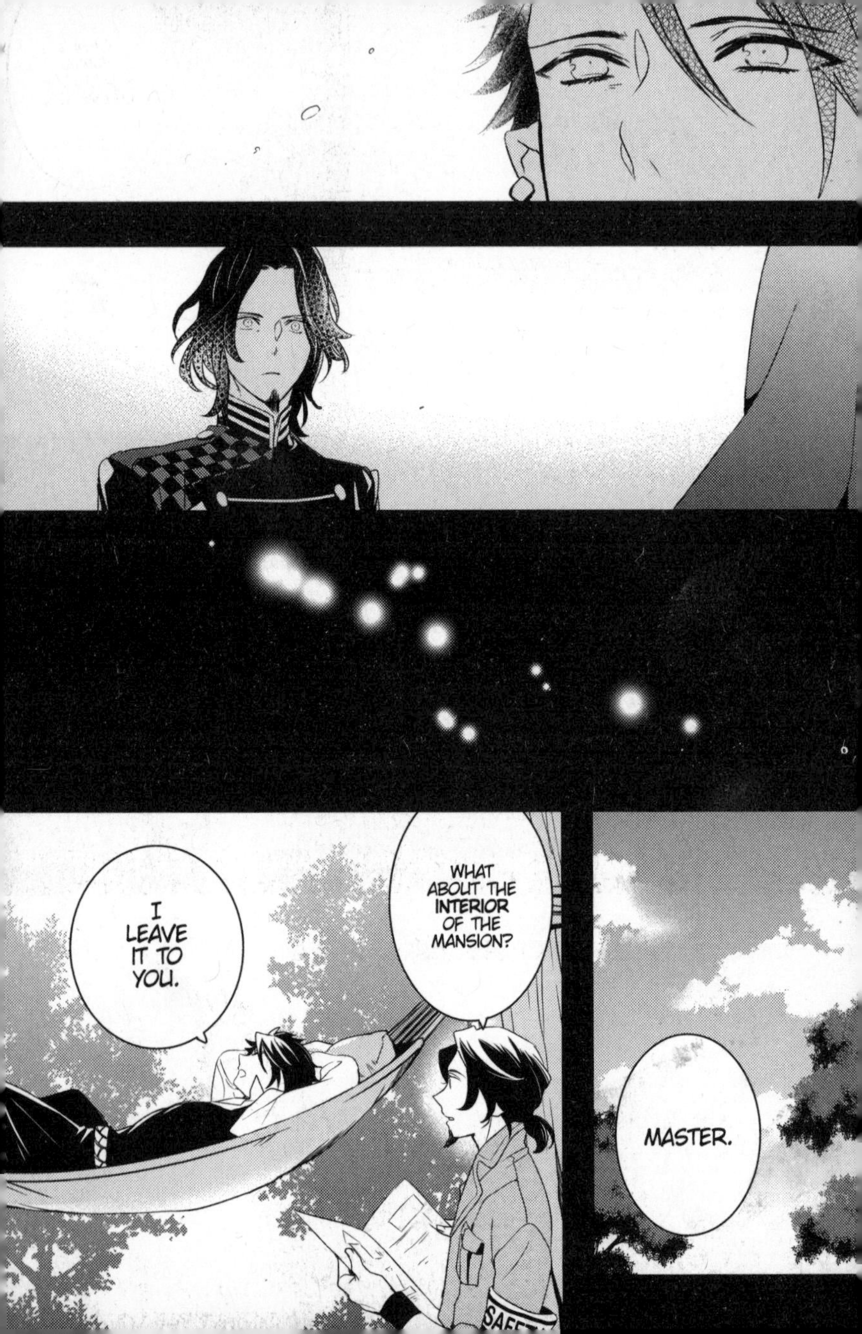
MASTER.
WHAT ABOUT THE INTERIOR OF THE MANSION?
I LEAVE IT TO YOU.

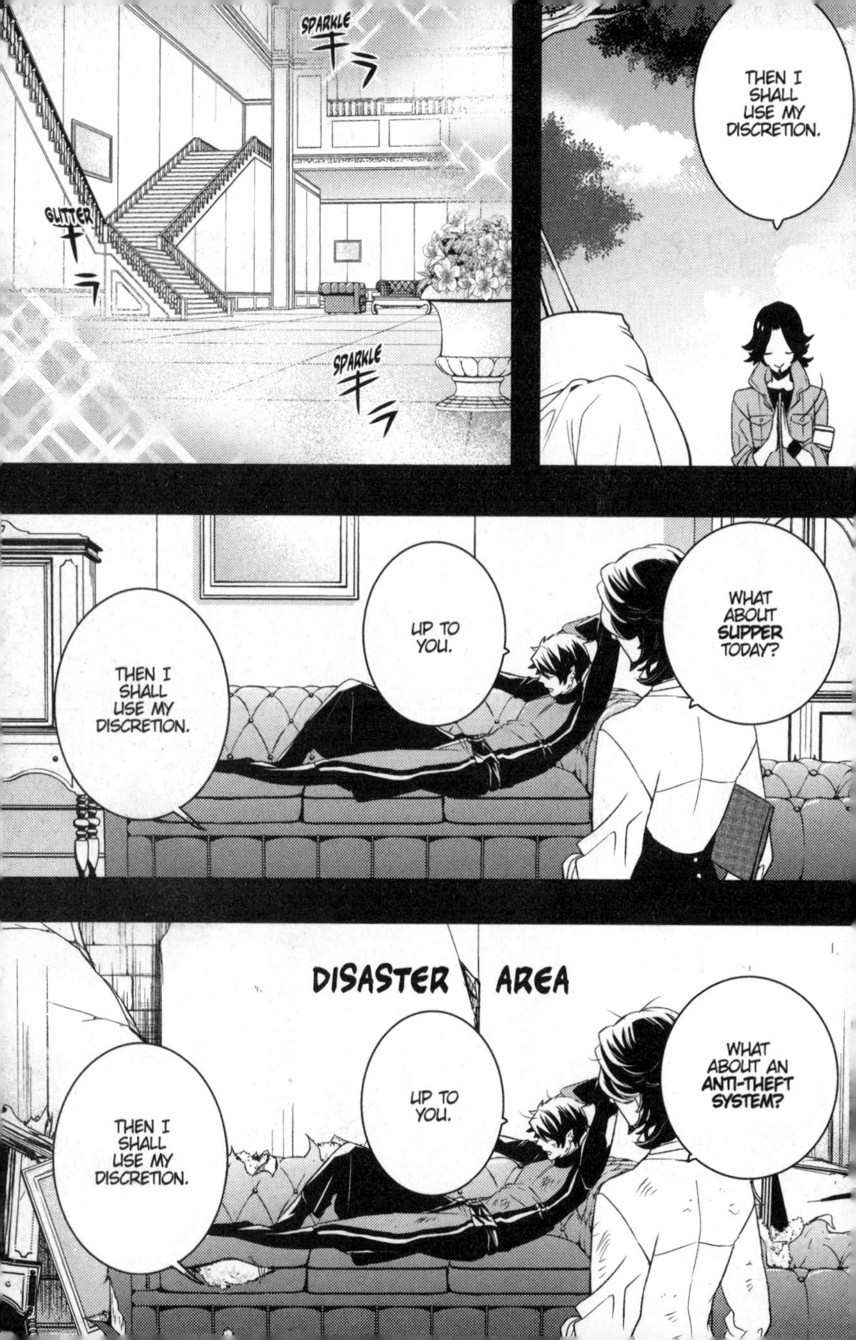
THEN I SHALL USE MY DISCRETION.
SPARKLE キラ
GLITTER キラ
SPARKLE キラ
WHAT ABOUT SUPPER TODAY?
UP TO YOU.
THEN I SHALL USE MY DISCRETION.
DISASTER AREA
WHAT ABOUT AN ANTI-THEFT SYSTEM?
UP TO YOU.
THEN I SHALL USE MY DISCRETION.

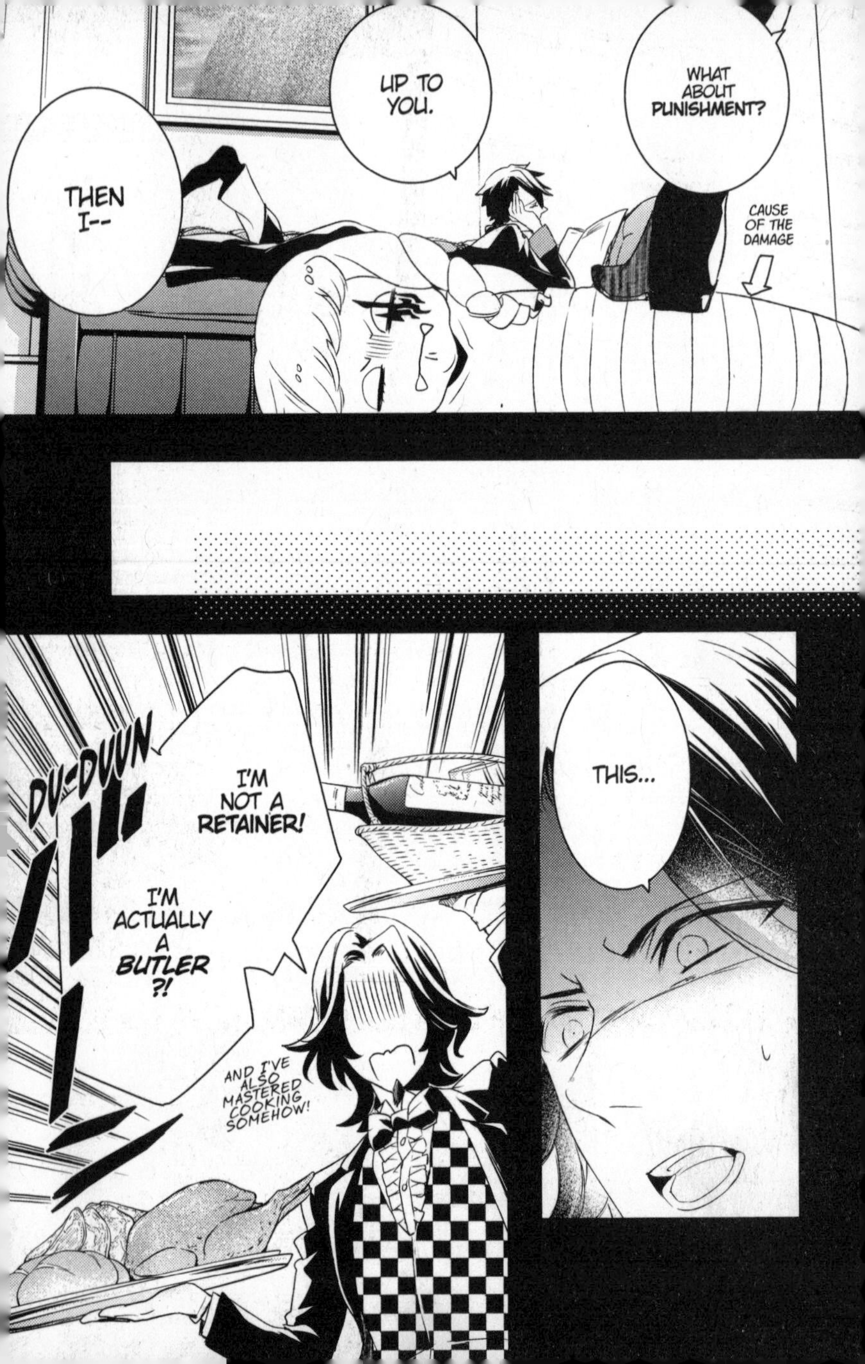
WHAT ABOUT PUNISHMENT?
CAUSE OF THE DAMAGE
UP TO YOU.
THEN I--
THIS...
I'M NOT A RETAINER!
I'M ACTUALLY A BUTLER ?!
DU-DUUN
AND I'VE ALSO MASTERED COOKING SOMEHOW!

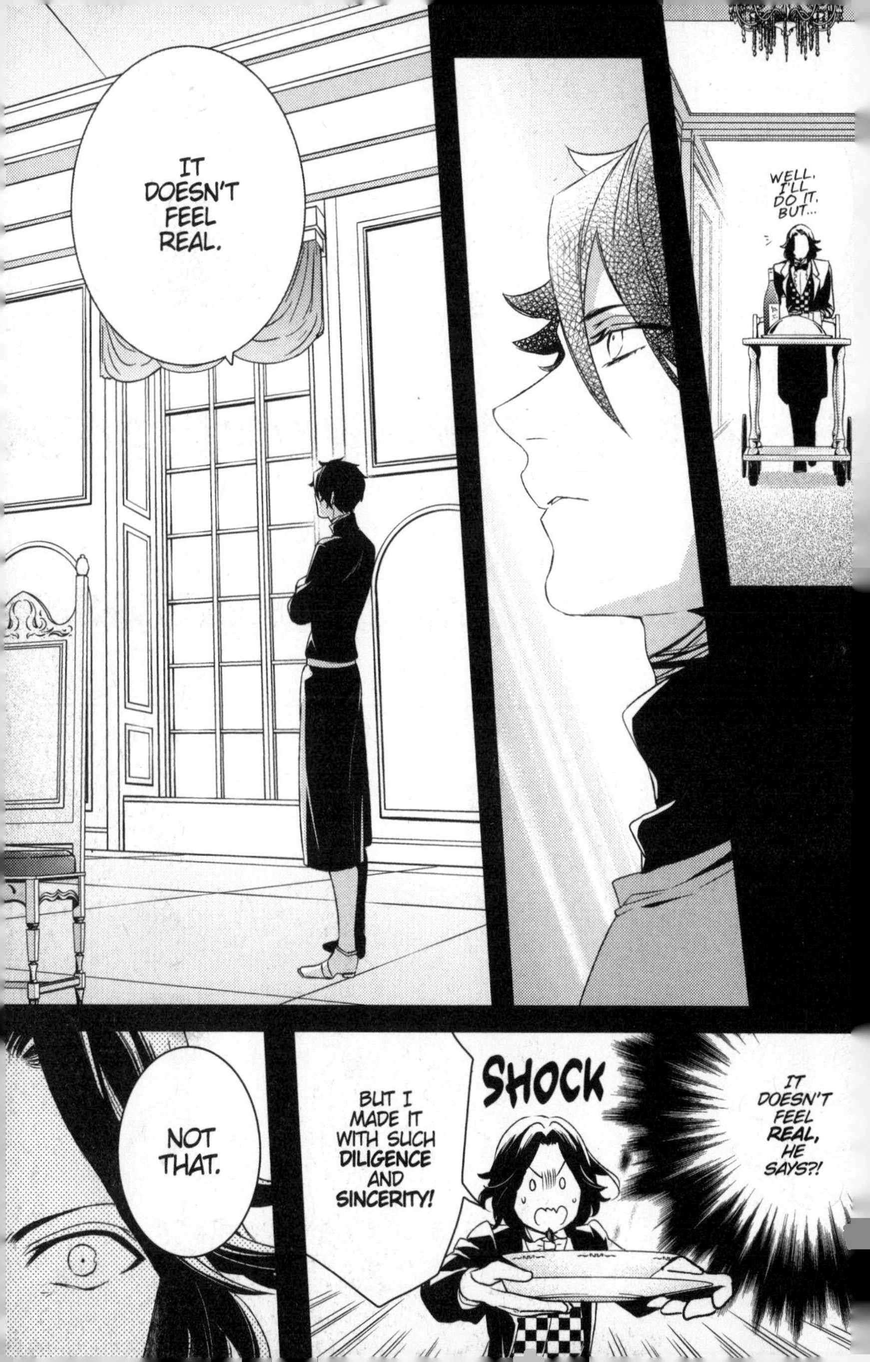
WELL, I'LL DO IT, BUT...
IT DOESN'T FEEL REAL.
IT DOESN'T FEEL REAL, HE SAYS?!
SHOCK
BUT I MADE IT WITH SUCH DILIGENCE AND SINCERITY!
NOT THAT.

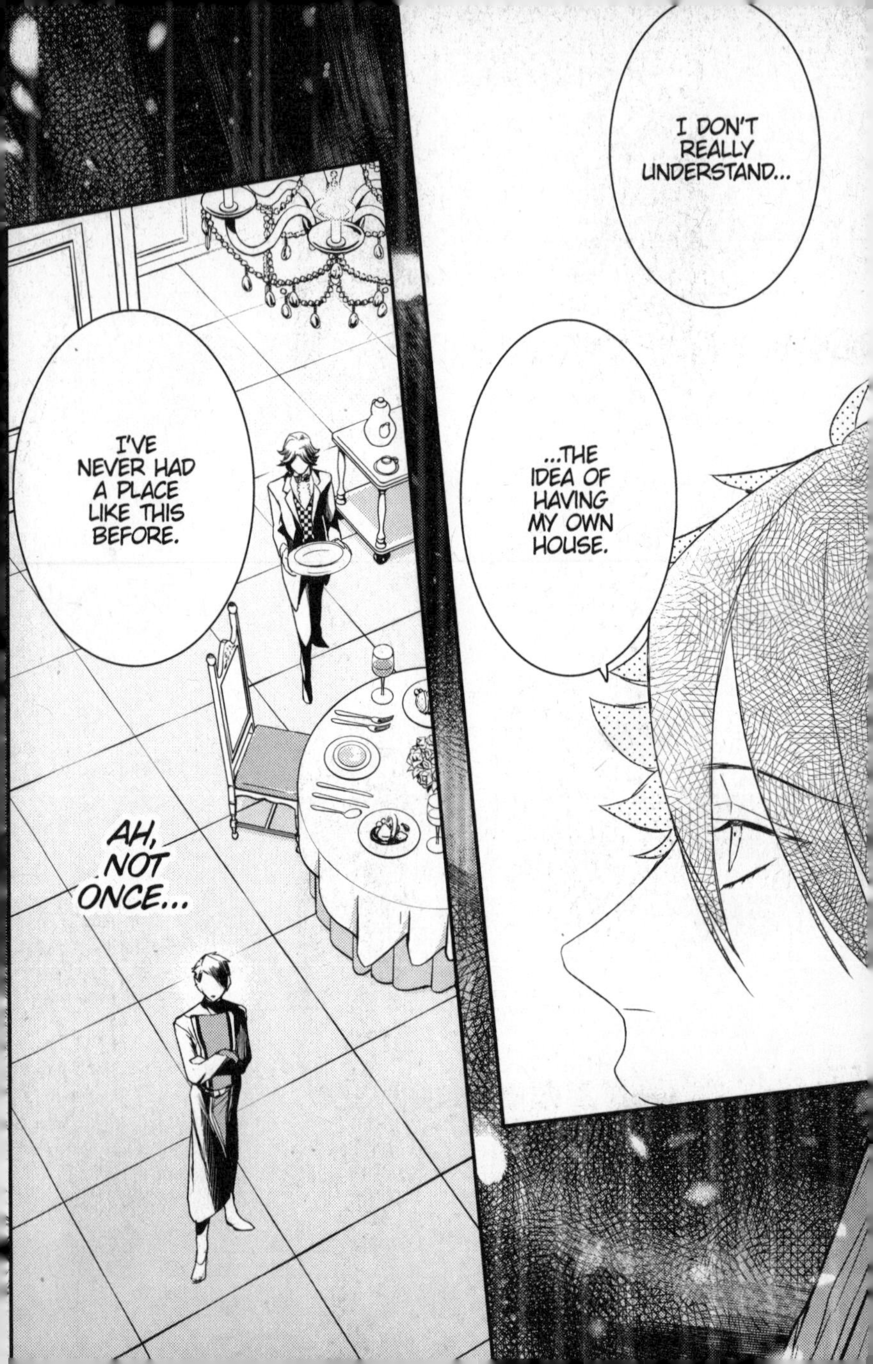
I DON'T REALLY UNDERSTAND...
...THE IDEA OF HAVING MY OWN HOUSE.
I'VE NEVER HAD A PLACE LIKE THIS BEFORE.
AH, NOT ONCE...

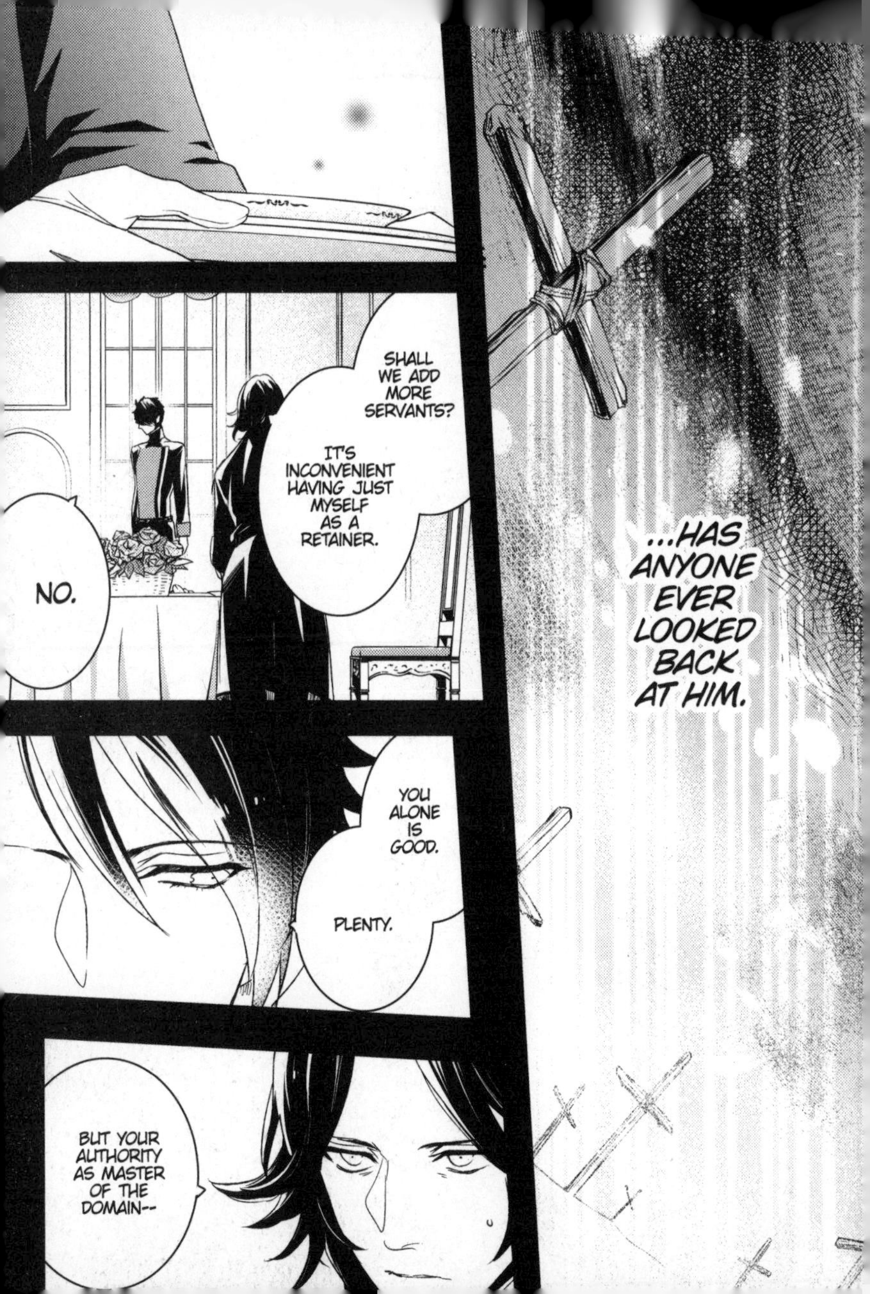
...HAS ANYONE EVER LOOKED BACK AT HIM.
SHALL WE ADD MORE SERVANTS?
IT'S INCONVENIENT HAVING JUST MYSELF AS A RETAINER.
NO.
YOU ALONE IS GOOD.
PLENTY.
BUT YOUR AUTHORITY AS MASTER OF THE DOMAIN--

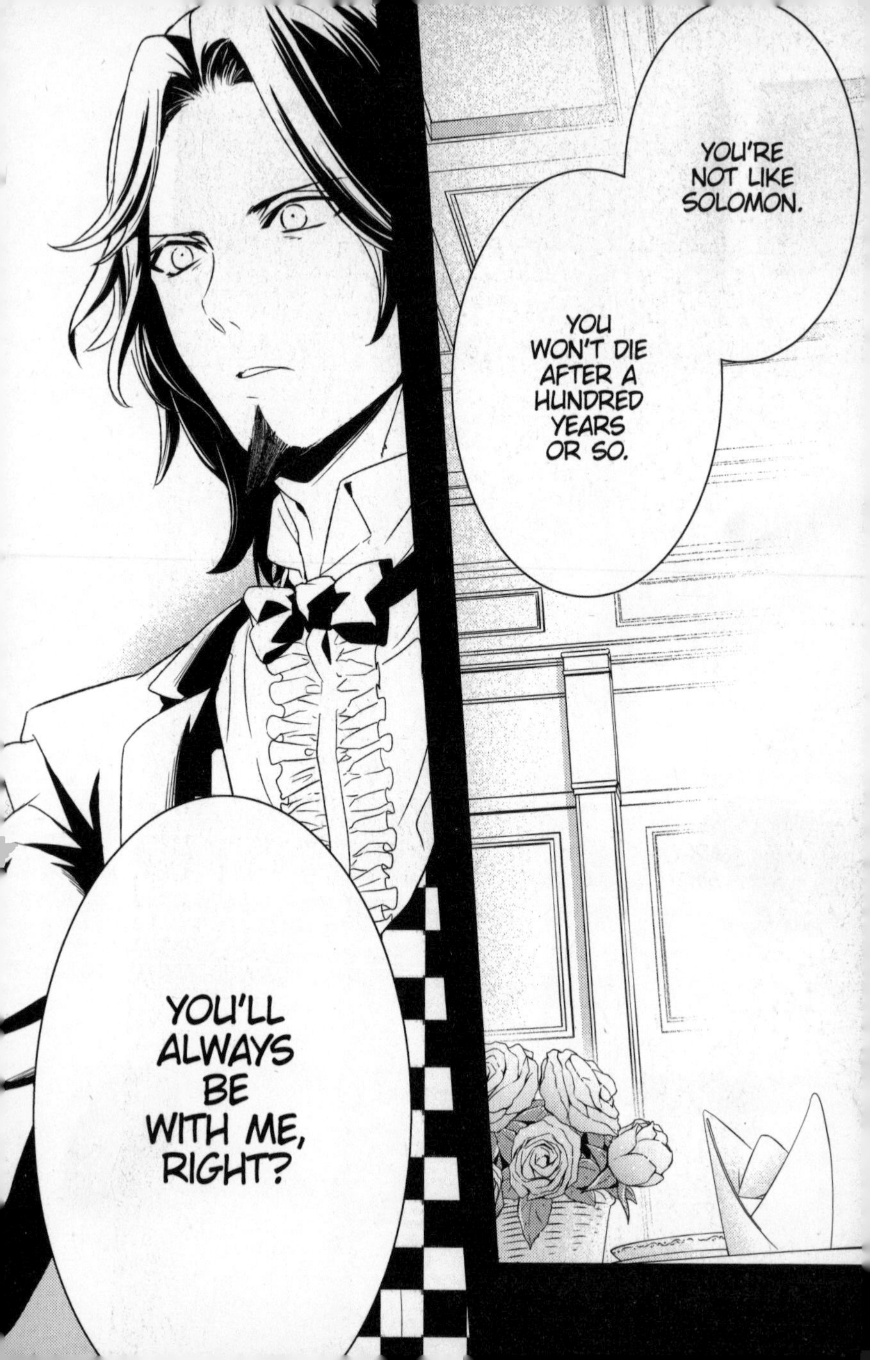
YOU'RE NOT LIKE SOLOMON.
YOU WON'T DIE AFTER A HUNDRED YEARS OR SO.
YOU'LL ALWAYS BE WITH ME, RIGHT?

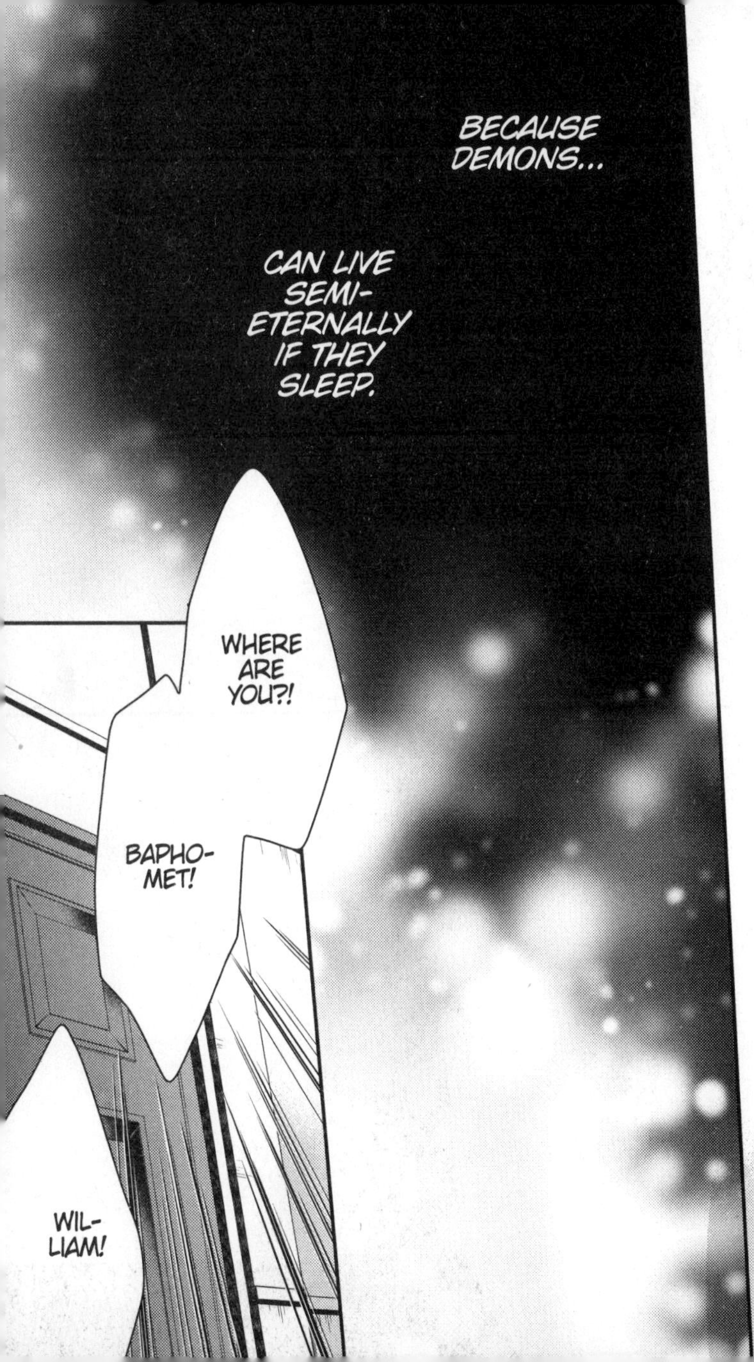
BECAUSE DEMONS...
CAN LIVE SEMI-ETERNALLY IF THEY SLEEP.
WHERE ARE YOU?!
BAPHO-MET!
WIL-LIAM!

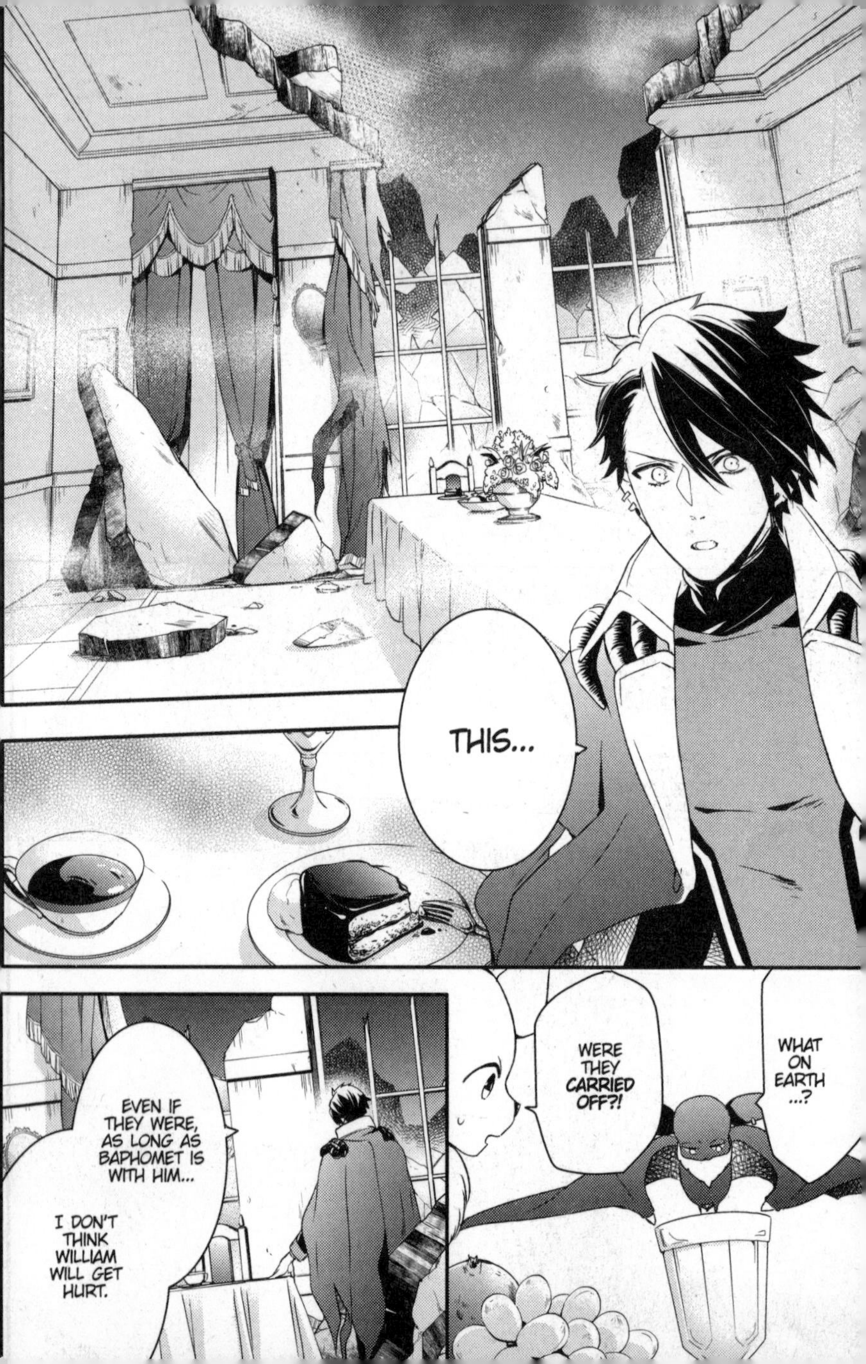
THIS...
WHAT ON EARTH ...?
WERE THEY CARRIED OFF?!
EVEN IF THEY WERE, AS LONG AS BAPHOMET IS WITH HIM...
I DON'T THINK WILLIAM WILL GET HURT.

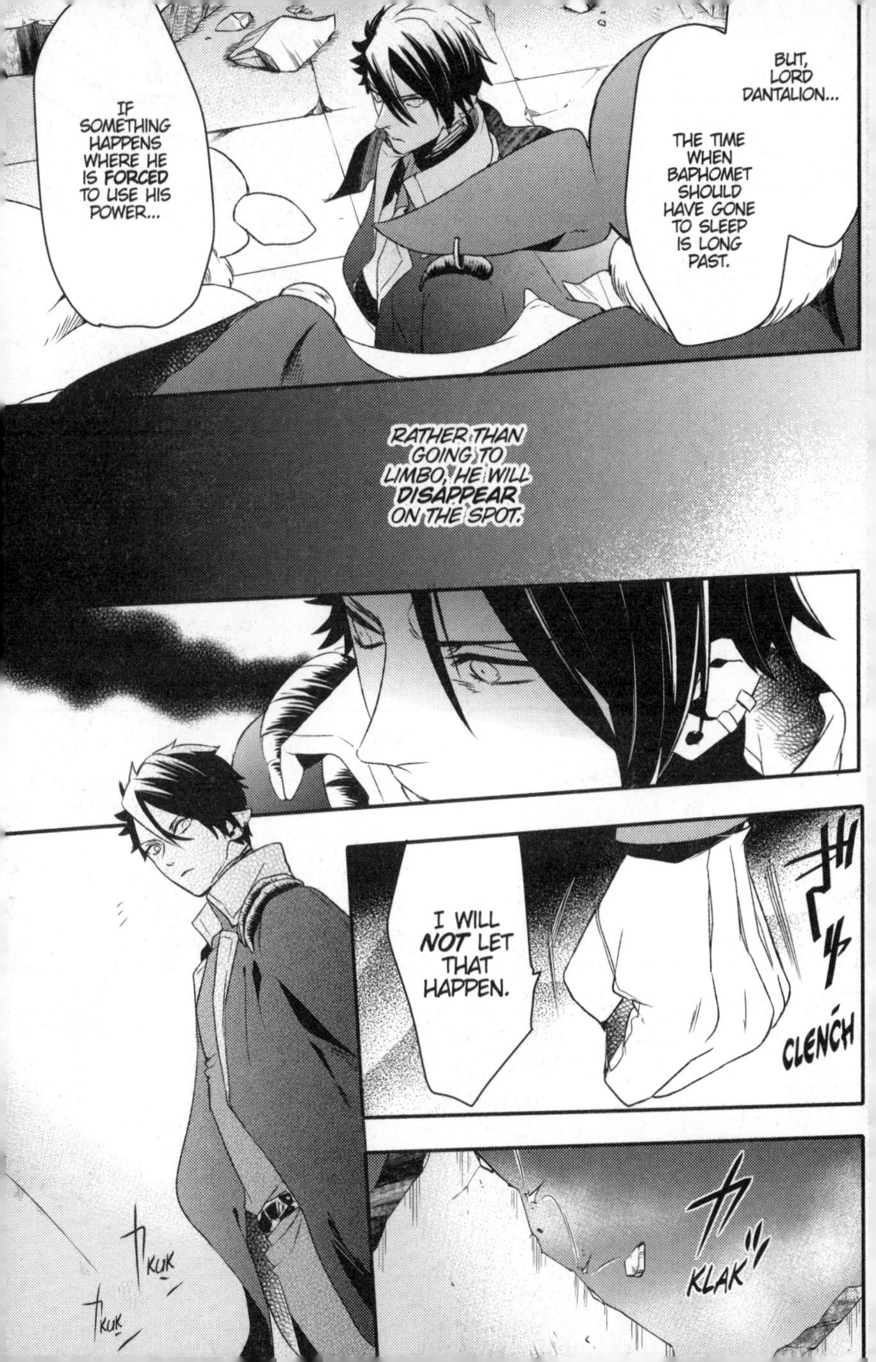
BUT, LORD DANTALION...
THE TIME WHEN BAPHOMET SHOULD HAVE GONE TO SLEEP IS LONG PAST.
IF SOMETHING HAPPENS WHERE HE IS FORCED TO USE HIS POWER...
RATHER THAN GOING TO LIMBO, HE WILL DISAPPEAR ON THE SPOT.
I WILL NOT LET THAT HAPPEN.
CLENCH
KLAK
KUK
KUK

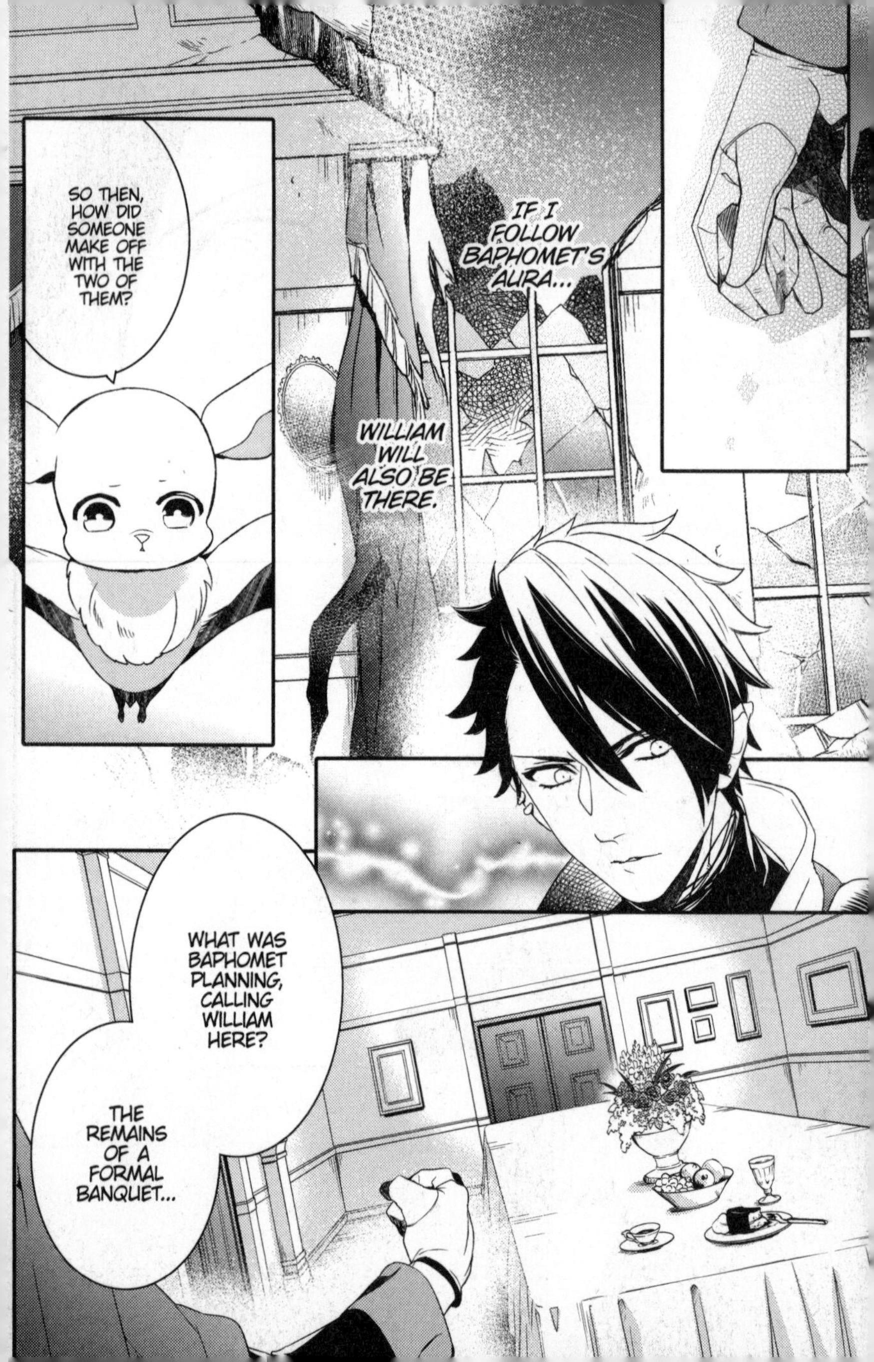
IF I FOLLOW BAPHOMET'S AURA...
WILLIAM WILL ALSO BE THERE.
SO THEN, HOW DID SOMEONE MAKE OFF WITH THE TWO OF THEM?
WHAT WAS BAPHOMET PLANNING, CALLING WILLIAM HERE?
THE REMAINS OF A FORMAL BANQUET...

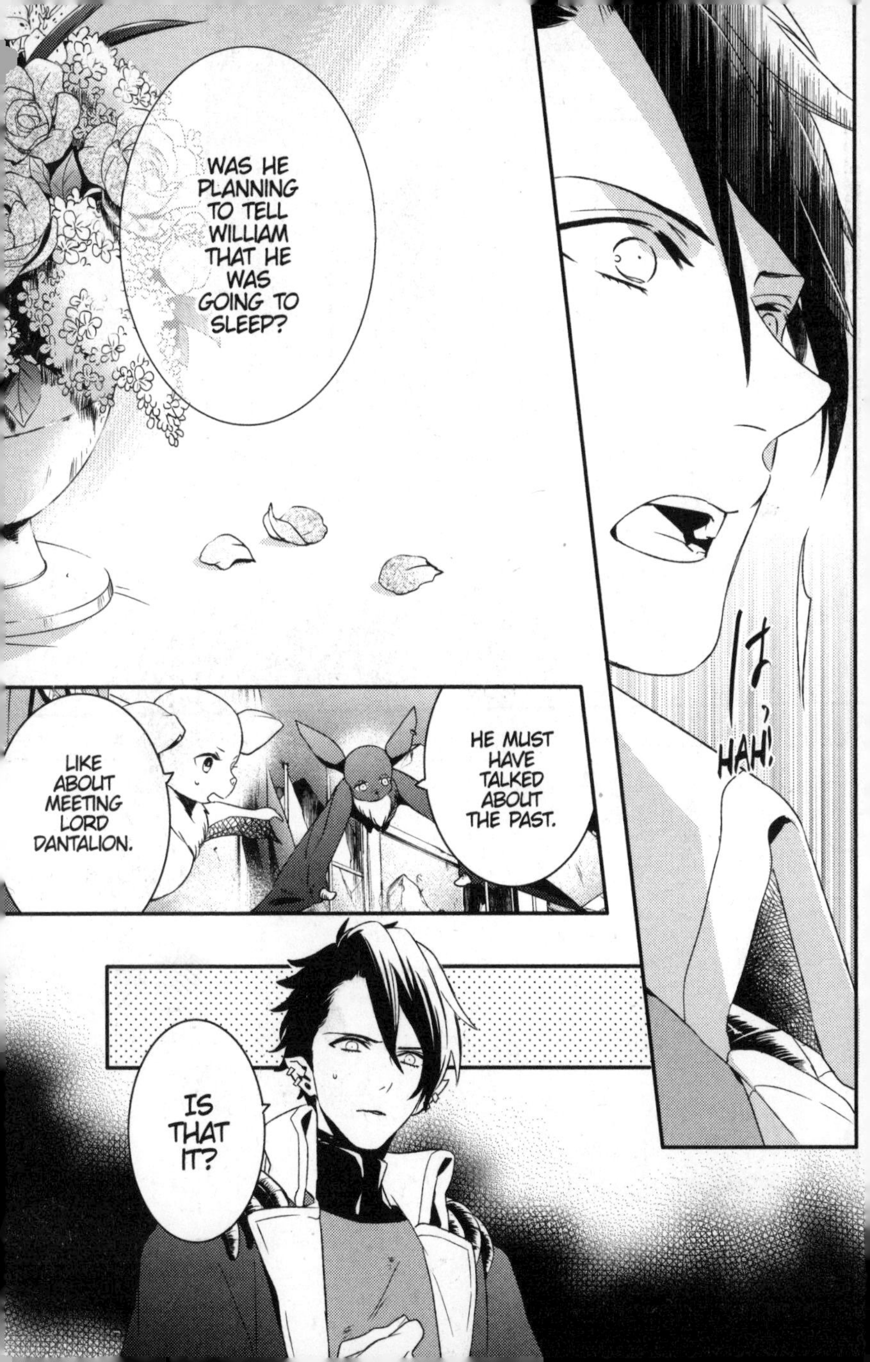
は
HAH!
WAS HE PLANNING TO TELL WILLIAM THAT HE WAS GOING TO SLEEP?
HE MUST HAVE TALKED ABOUT THE PAST.
LIKE ABOUT MEETING LORD DANTALION.
IS THAT IT?

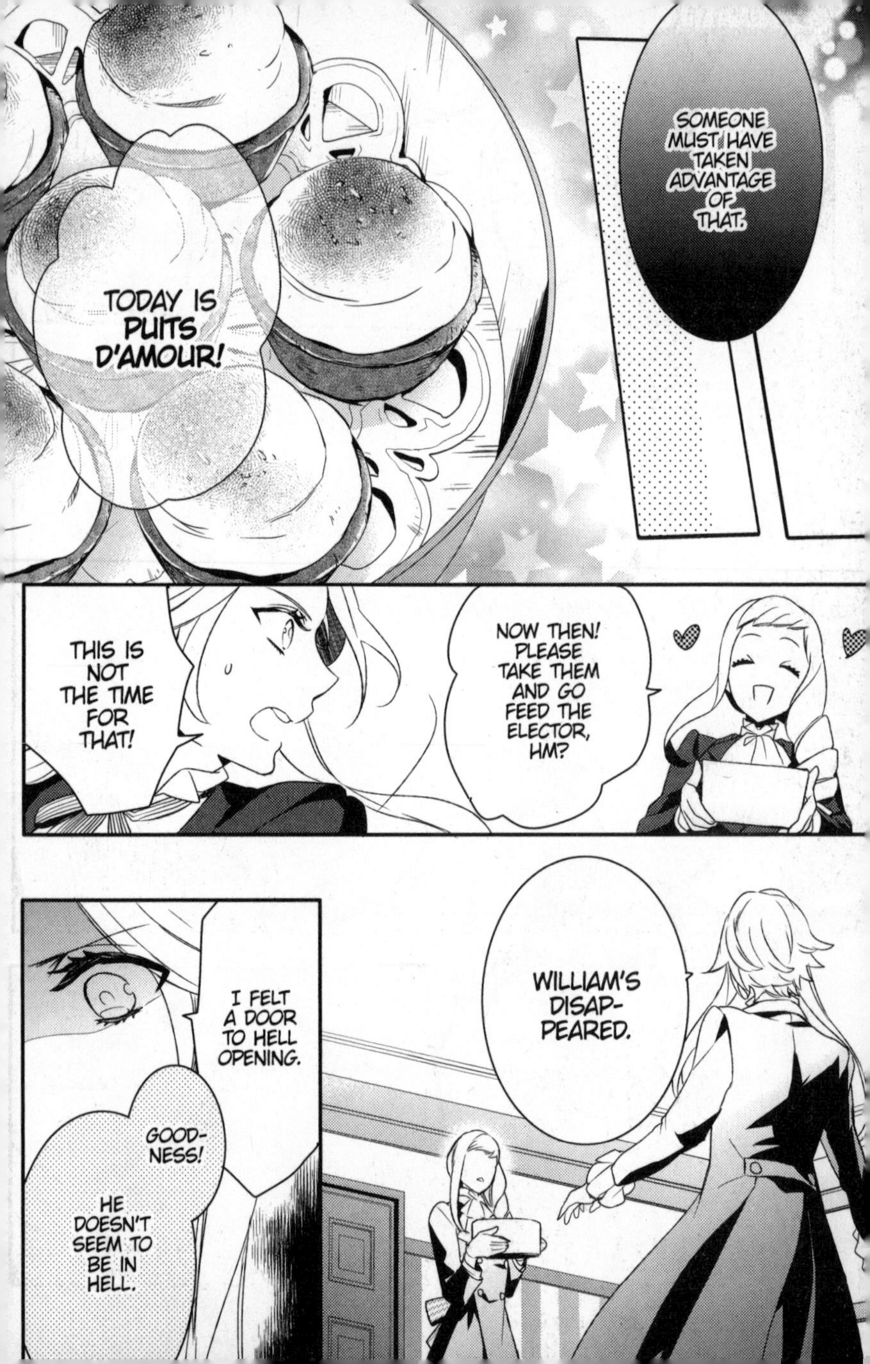
SOMEONE MUST HAVE TAKEN ADVANTAGE OF THAT.
TODAY IS PUITS D'AMOUR!
NOW THEN! PLEASE TAKE THEM AND GO FEED THE ELECTOR, HM?
THIS IS NOT THE TIME FOR THAT!
WILLIAM'S DISAP-PEARED.
I FELT A DOOR TO HELL OPENING.
GOOD-NESS!
HE DOESN'T SEEM TO BE IN HELL.

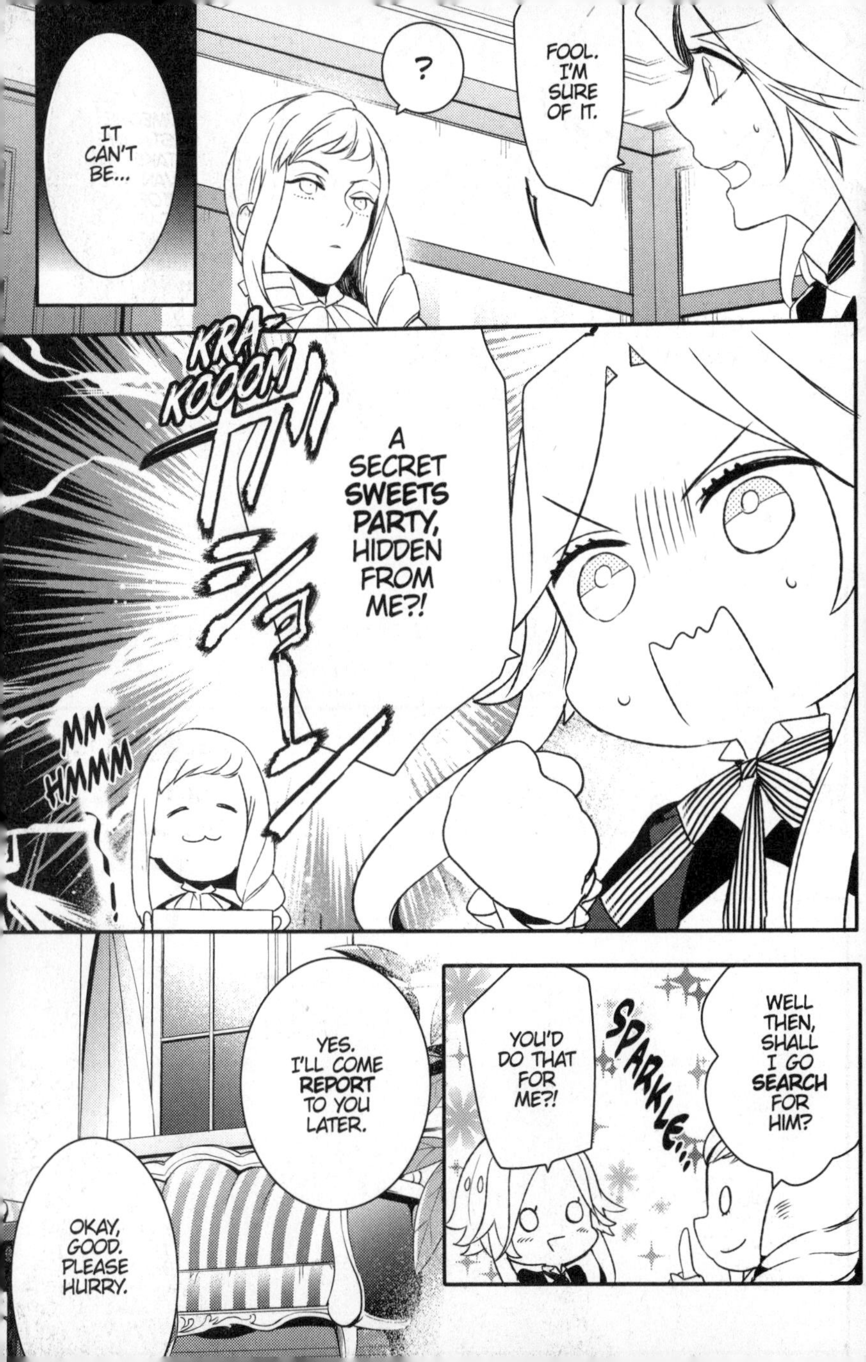
FOOL. I'M SURE OF IT.
?
IT CAN'T BE...
A SECRET SWEETS PARTY, HIDDEN FROM ME?!
KRA-KOOOM
MM HMMM
WELL THEN, SHALL I GO SEARCH FOR HIM?
SPARKLE...
YOU'D DO THAT FOR ME?!
YES. I'LL COME REPORT TO YOU LATER.
OKAY, GOOD. PLEASE HURRY.

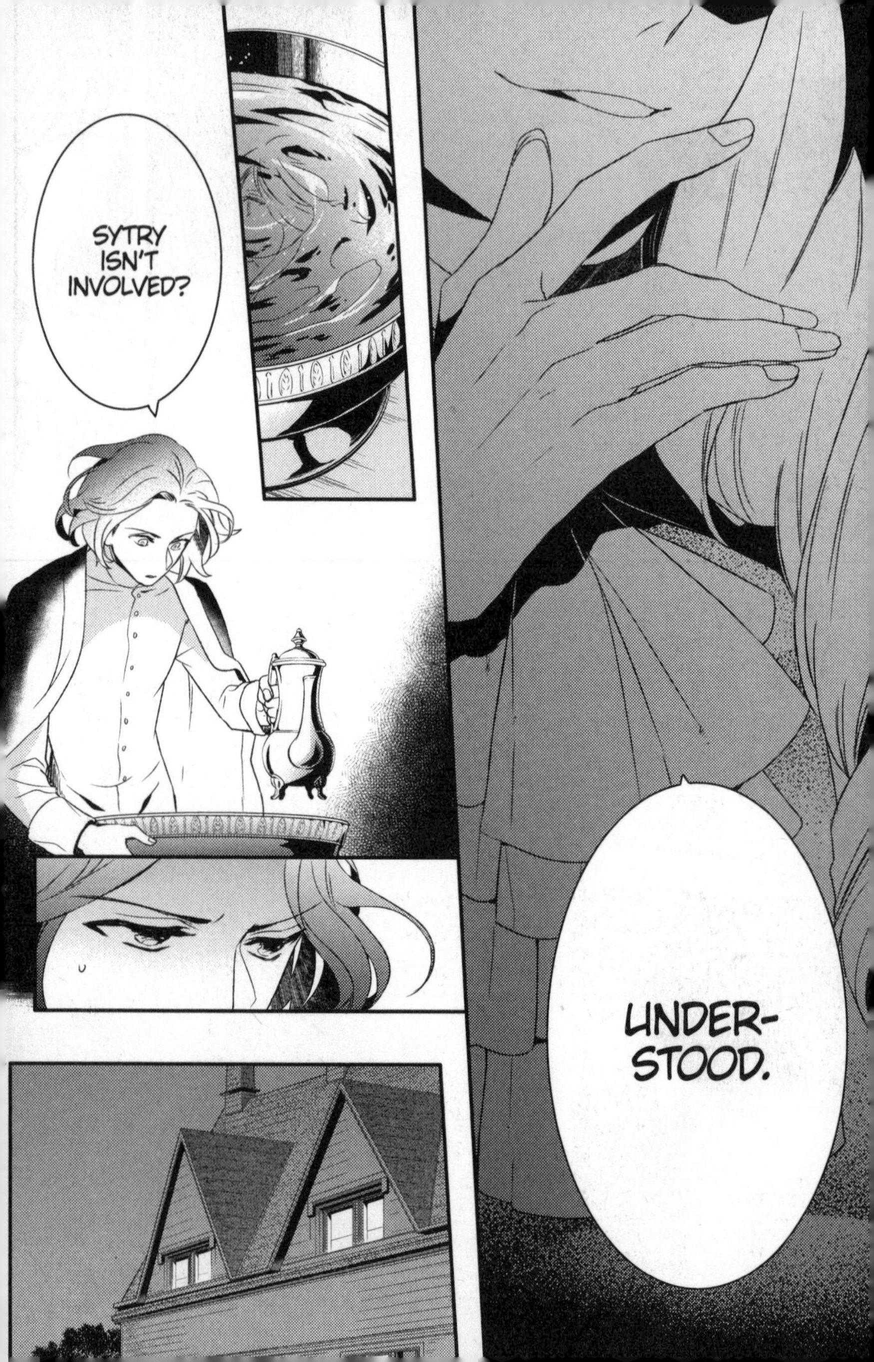
UNDER-STOOD.
SYTRY ISN'T INVOLVED?

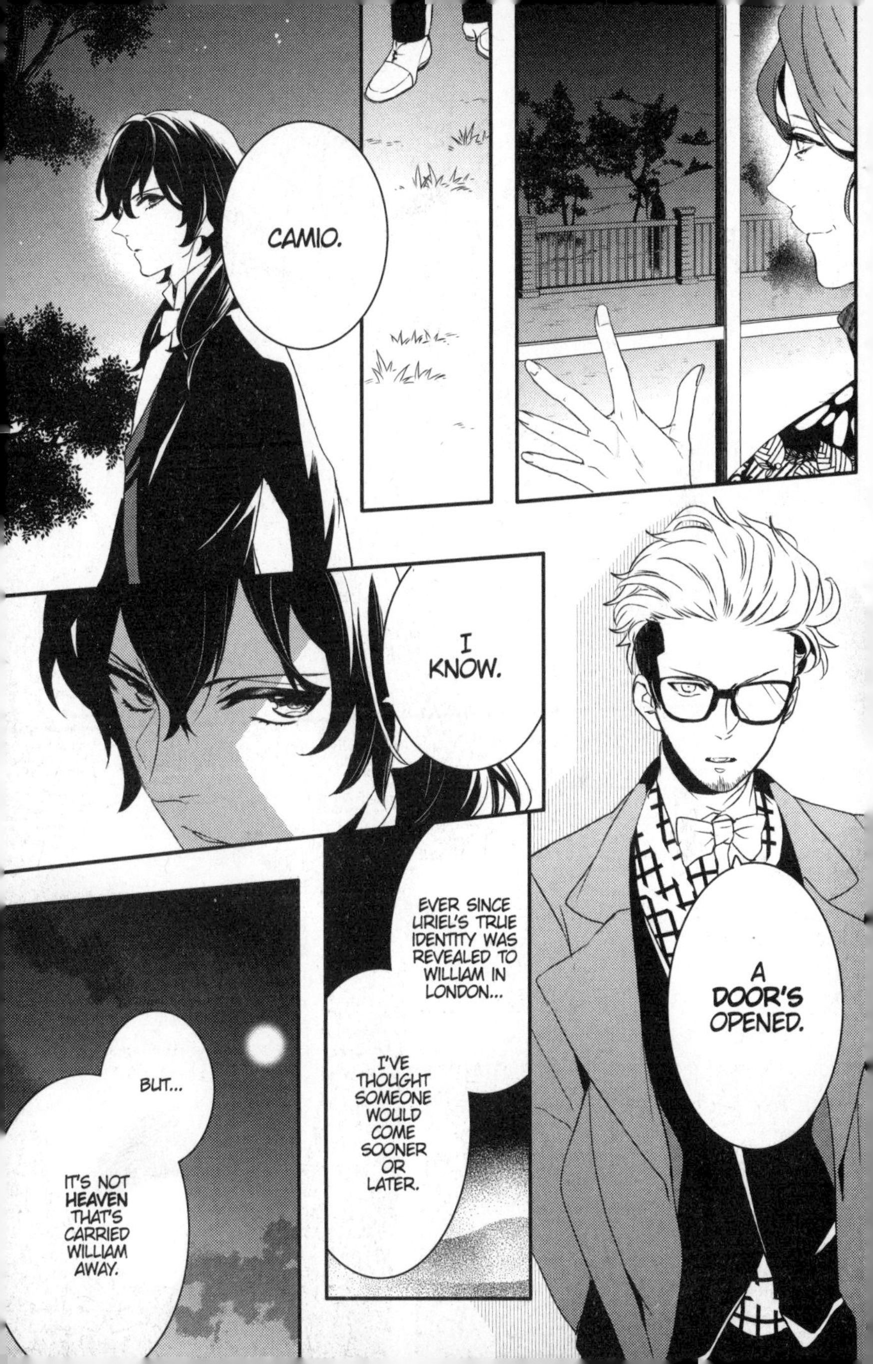
CAMIO.
A DOOR'S OPENED.
I KNOW.
EVER SINCE URIEL'S TRUE IDENTITY WAS REVEALED TO WILLIAM IN LONDON...
I'VE THOUGHT SOMEONE WOULD COME SOONER OR LATER.
BUT...
IT'S NOT HEAVEN THAT'S CARRIED WILLIAM AWAY.

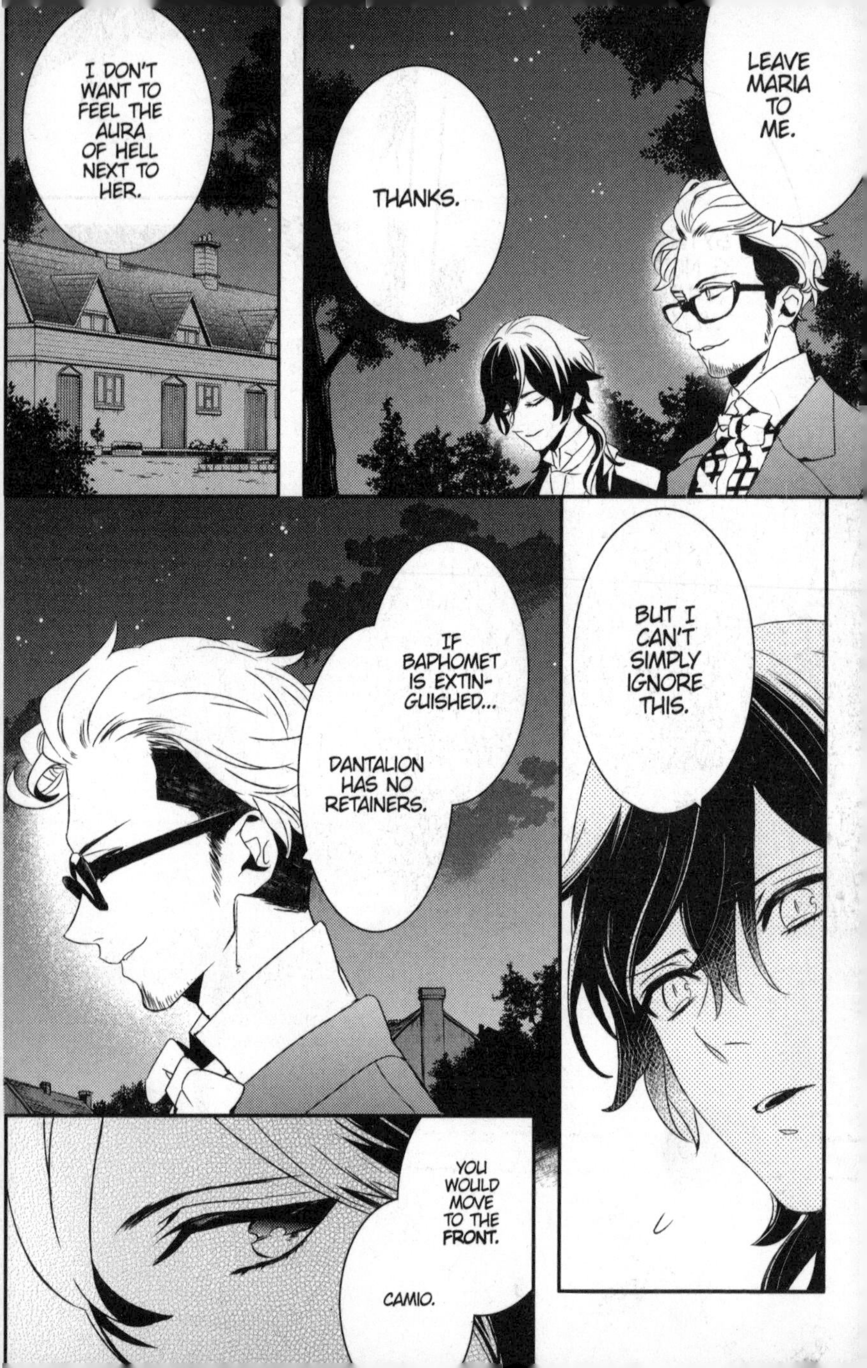
LEAVE MARIA TO ME.
THANKS.
I DON'T WANT TO FEEL THE AURA OF HELL NEXT TO HER.
BUT I CAN'T SIMPLY IGNORE THIS.
IF BAPHOMET IS EXTIN-GUISHED...
DANTALION HAS NO RETAINERS.
YOU WOULD MOVE TO THE FRONT.
CAMIO.

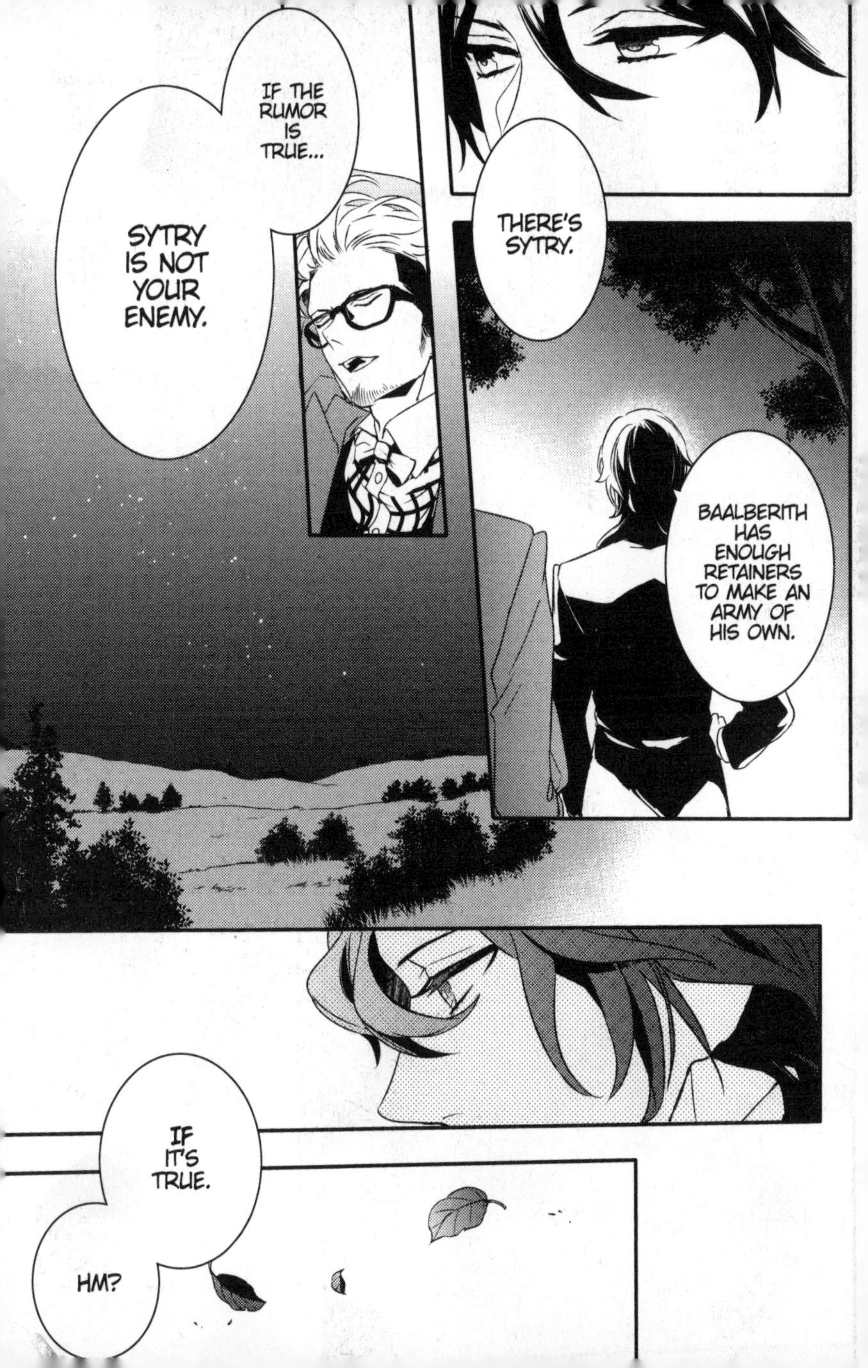
THERE'S SYTRY.
BAALBERITH HAS ENOUGH RETAINERS TO MAKE AN ARMY OF HIS OWN.
IF THE RUMOR IS TRUE...
SYTRY IS NOT YOUR ENEMY.
IF IT'S TRUE.
HM?

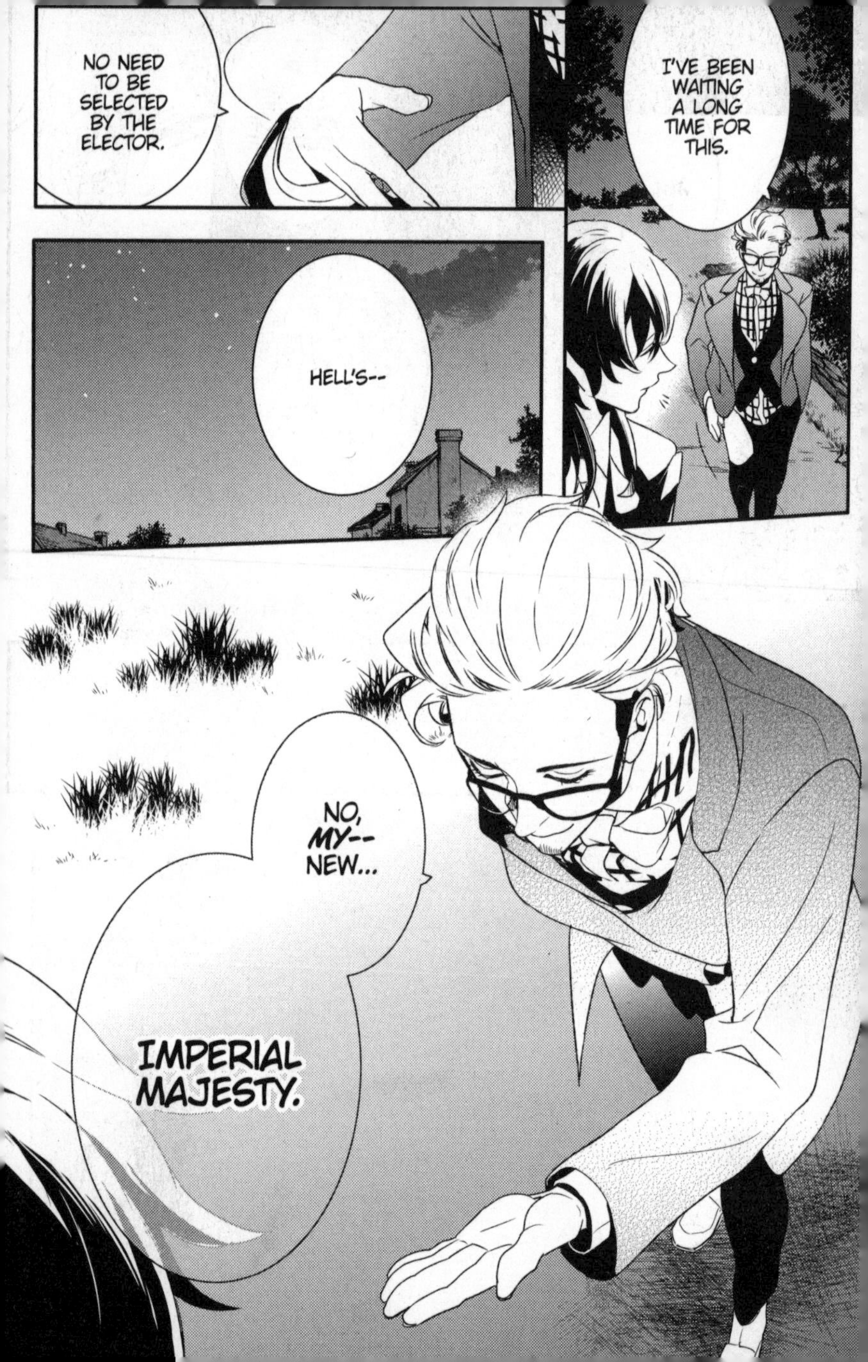
I'VE BEEN WAITING A LONG TIME FOR THIS.
NO NEED TO BE SELECTED BY THE ELECTOR.
HELL'S--
NO, *MY*-- NEW...
IMPERIAL MAJESTY.

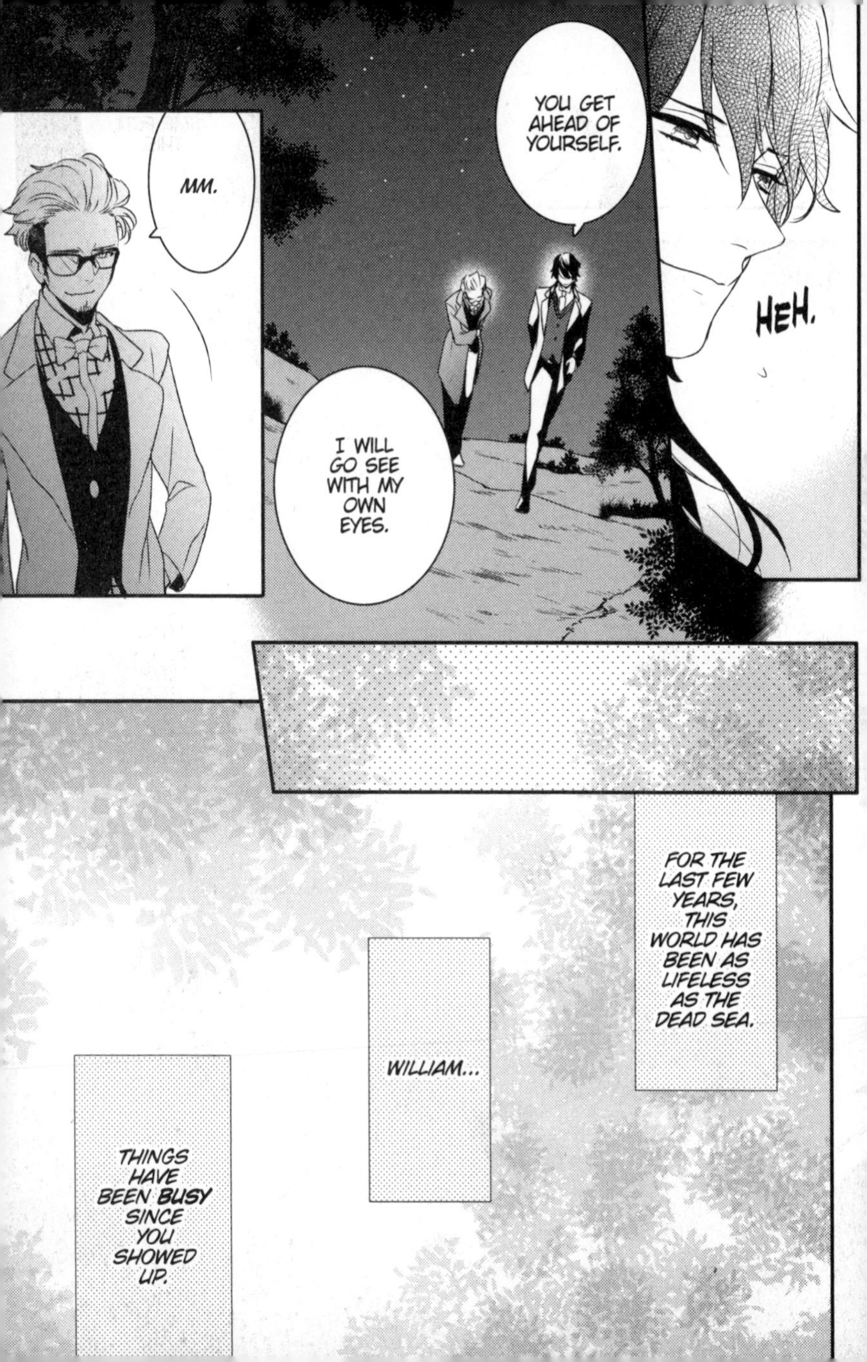
HEH.
YOU GET AHEAD OF YOURSELF.
I WILL GO SEE WITH MY OWN EYES.
MM.
FOR THE LAST FEW YEARS, THIS WORLD HAS BEEN AS LIFELESS AS THE DEAD SEA.
WILLIAM...
THINGS HAVE BEEN **BUSY** SINCE YOU SHOWED UP.

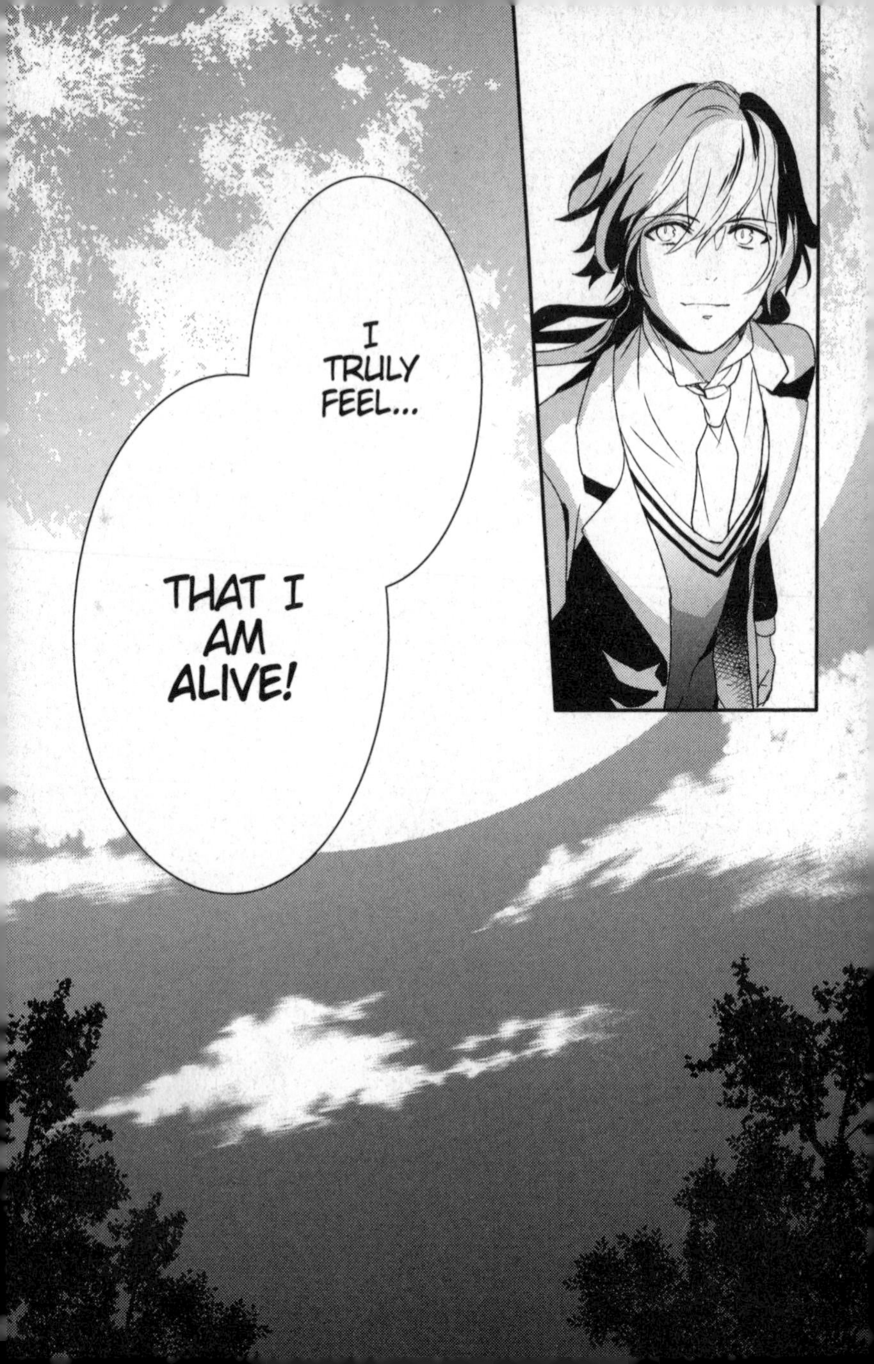
I TRULY FEEL...
THAT I AM ALIVE!

魔界王子

devils and realist

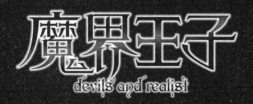

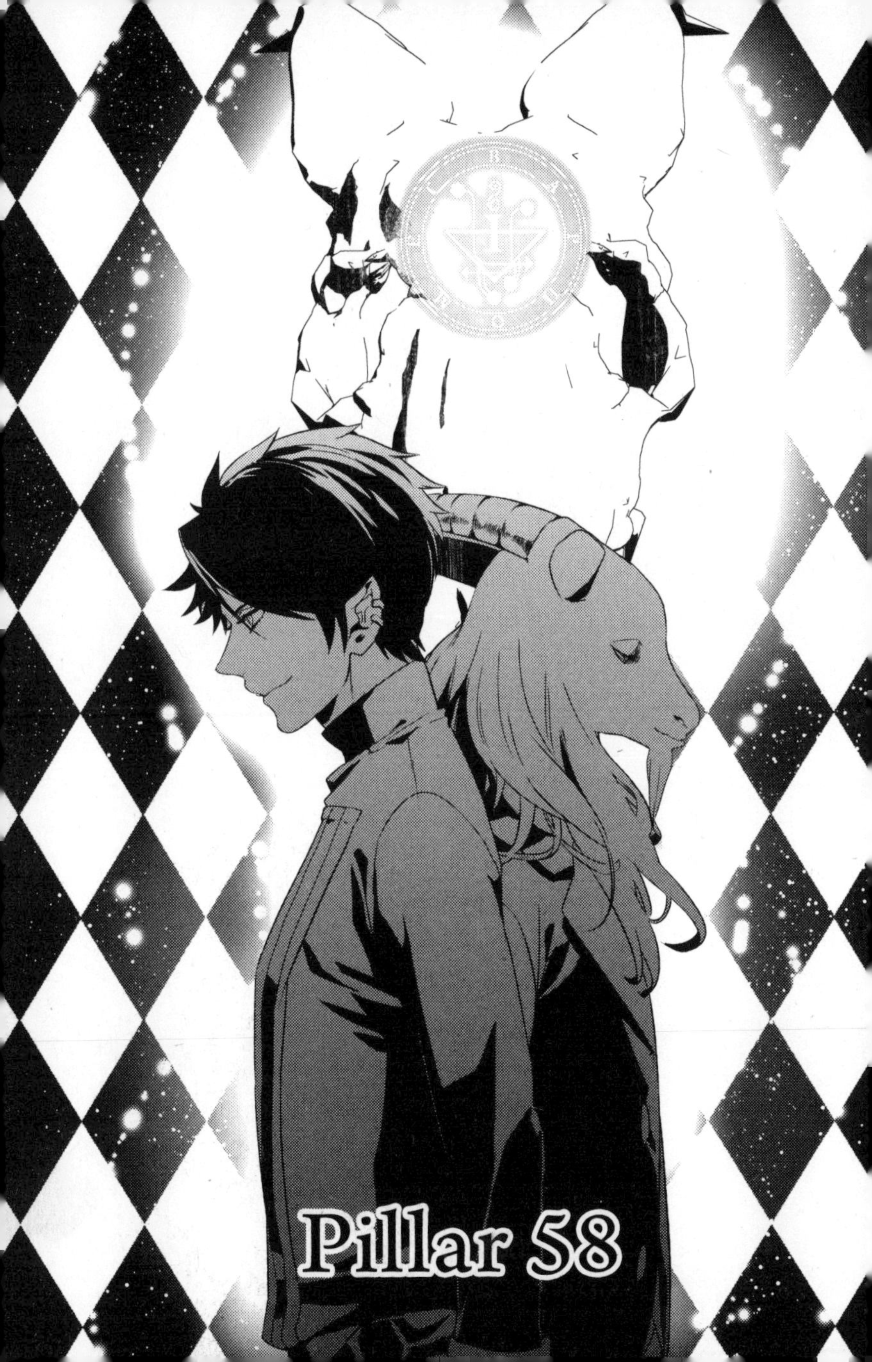
Pillar 58

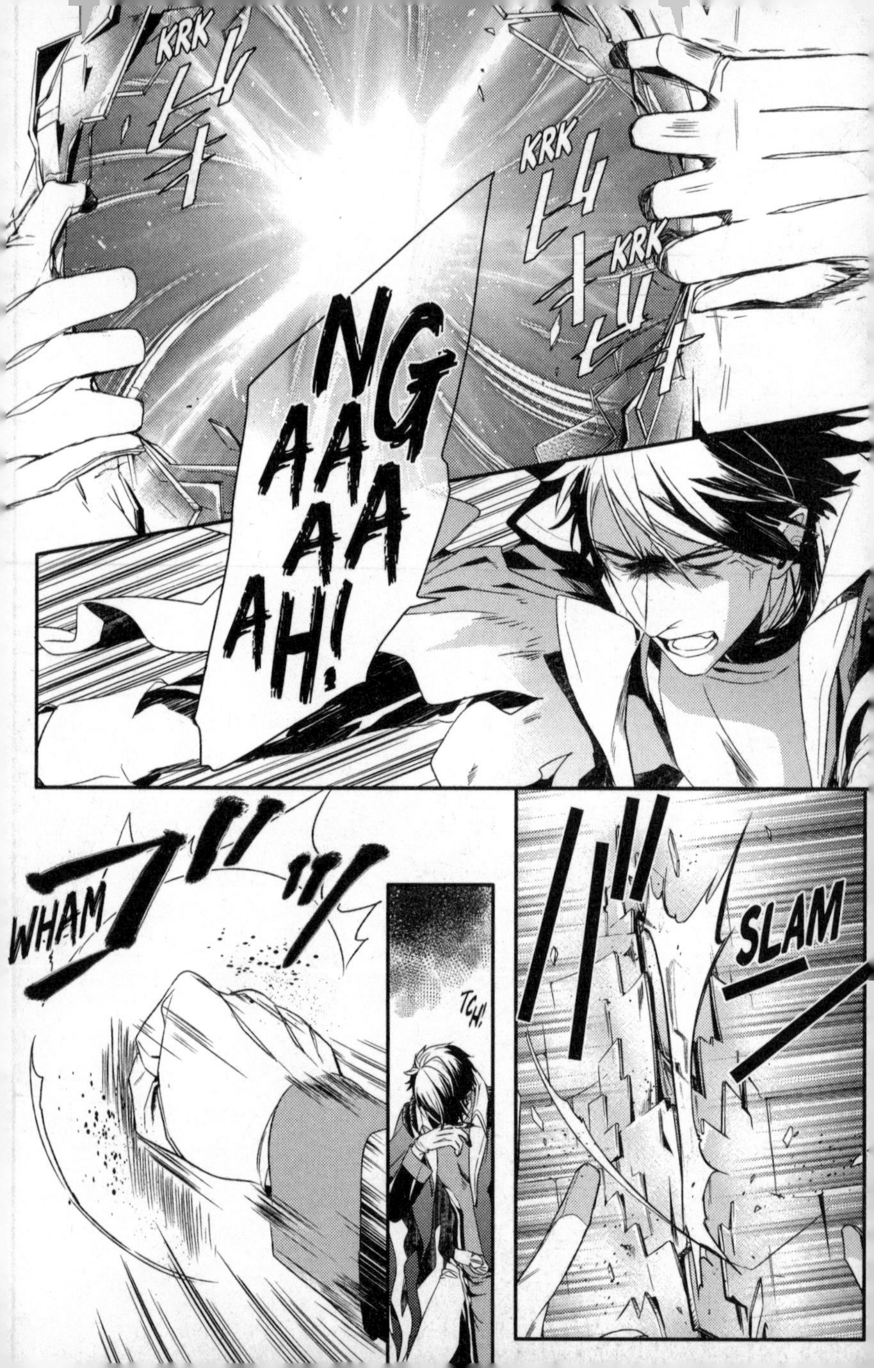
KRK
KRK
KRK
NG AAAAAAH!
SLAM
TCH!
WHAM

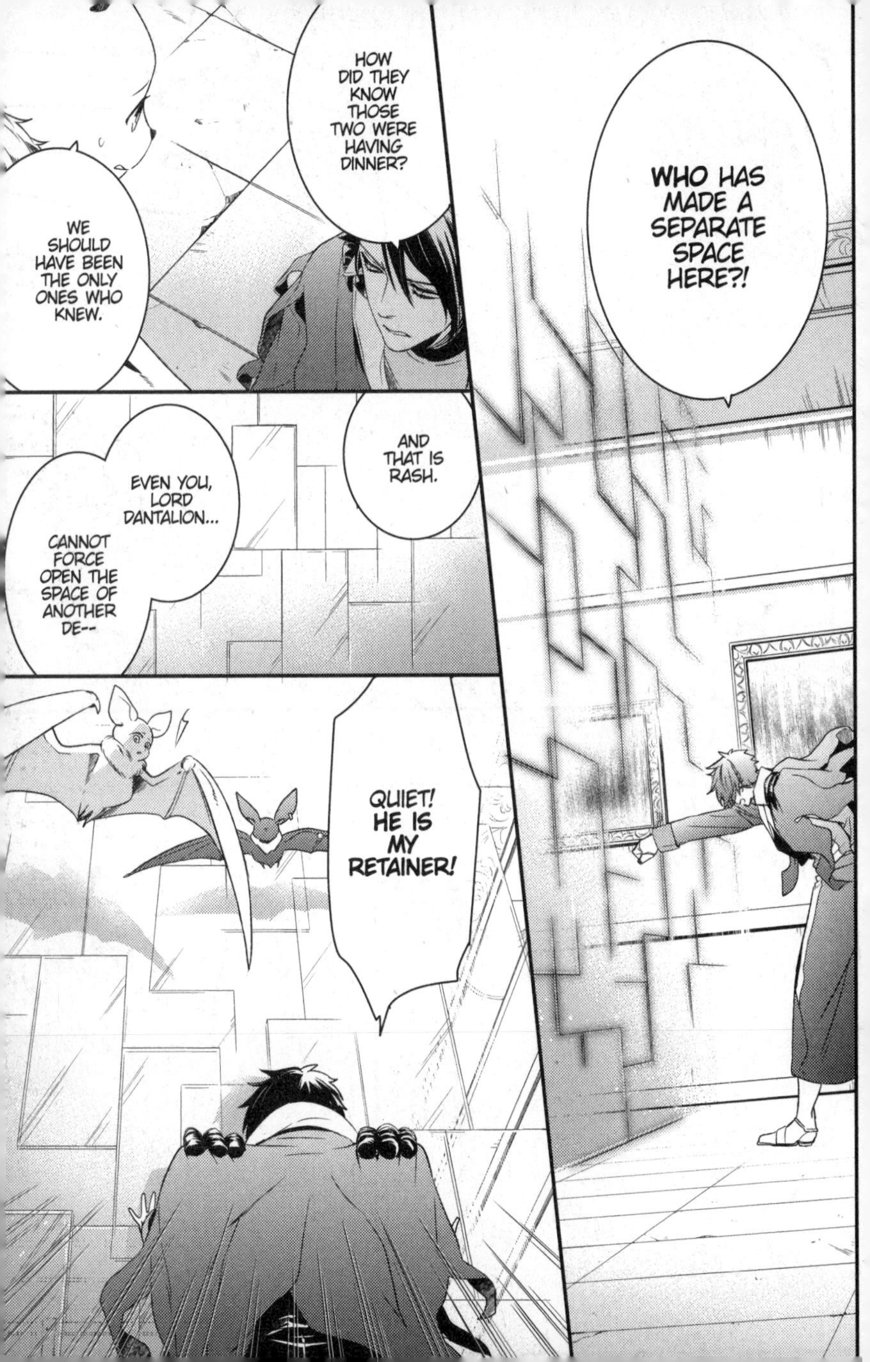
WHO HAS MADE A SEPARATE SPACE HERE?!
HOW DID THEY KNOW THOSE TWO WERE HAVING DINNER?
WE SHOULD HAVE BEEN THE ONLY ONES WHO KNEW.
AND THAT IS RASH.
EVEN YOU, LORD DANTALION...
CANNOT FORCE OPEN THE SPACE OF ANOTHER DE--
QUIET! HE IS MY RETAINER!

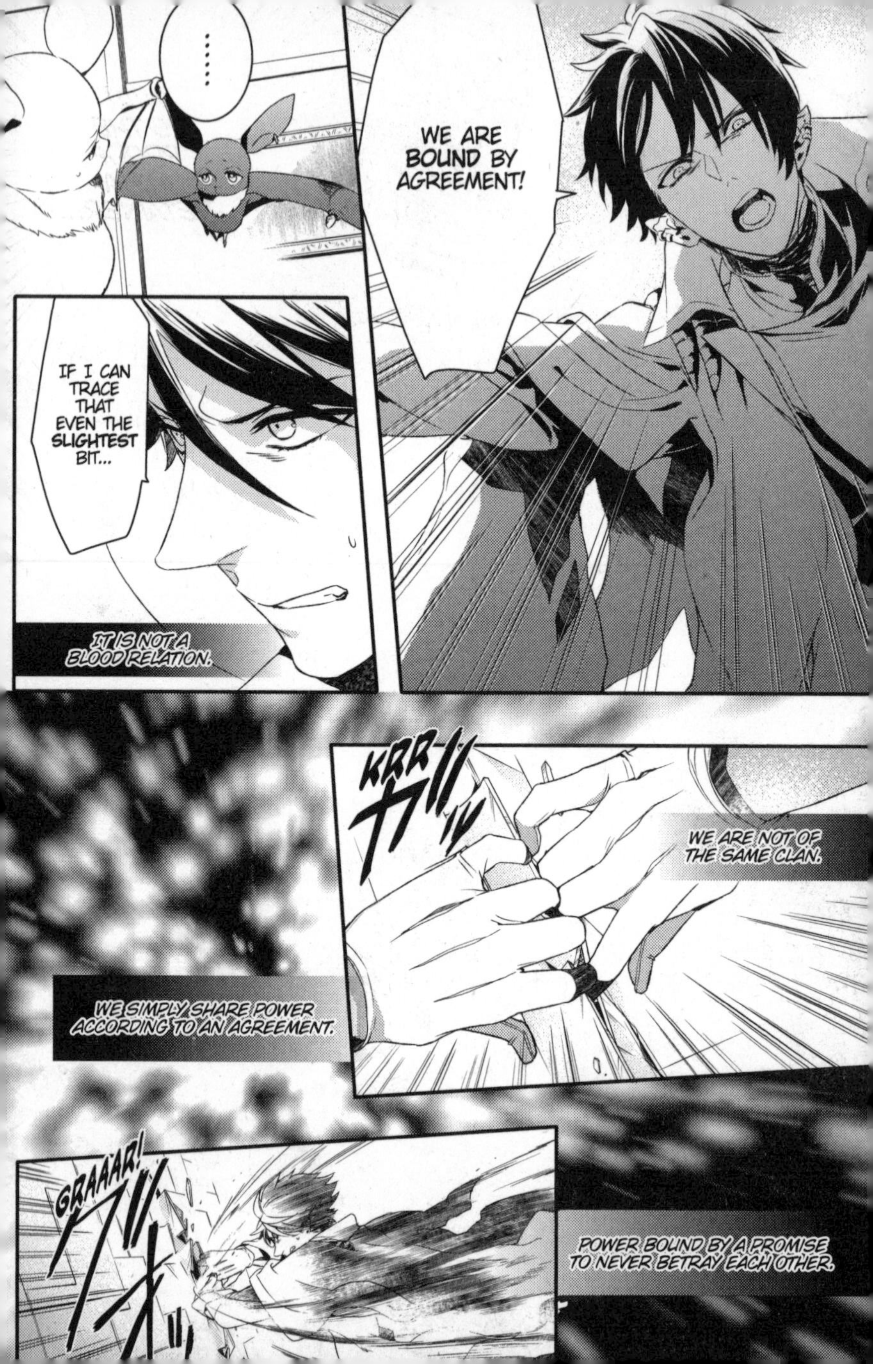
WE ARE BOUND BY AGREEMENT!
......
IF I CAN TRACE THAT EVEN THE SLIGHTEST BIT...
IT IS NOT A BLOOD RELATION.
KRR
WE ARE NOT OF THE SAME CLAN.
WE SIMPLY SHARE POWER ACCORDING TO AN AGREEMENT.
POWER BOUND BY A PROMISE TO NEVER BETRAY EACH OTHER.
GRAAAR!

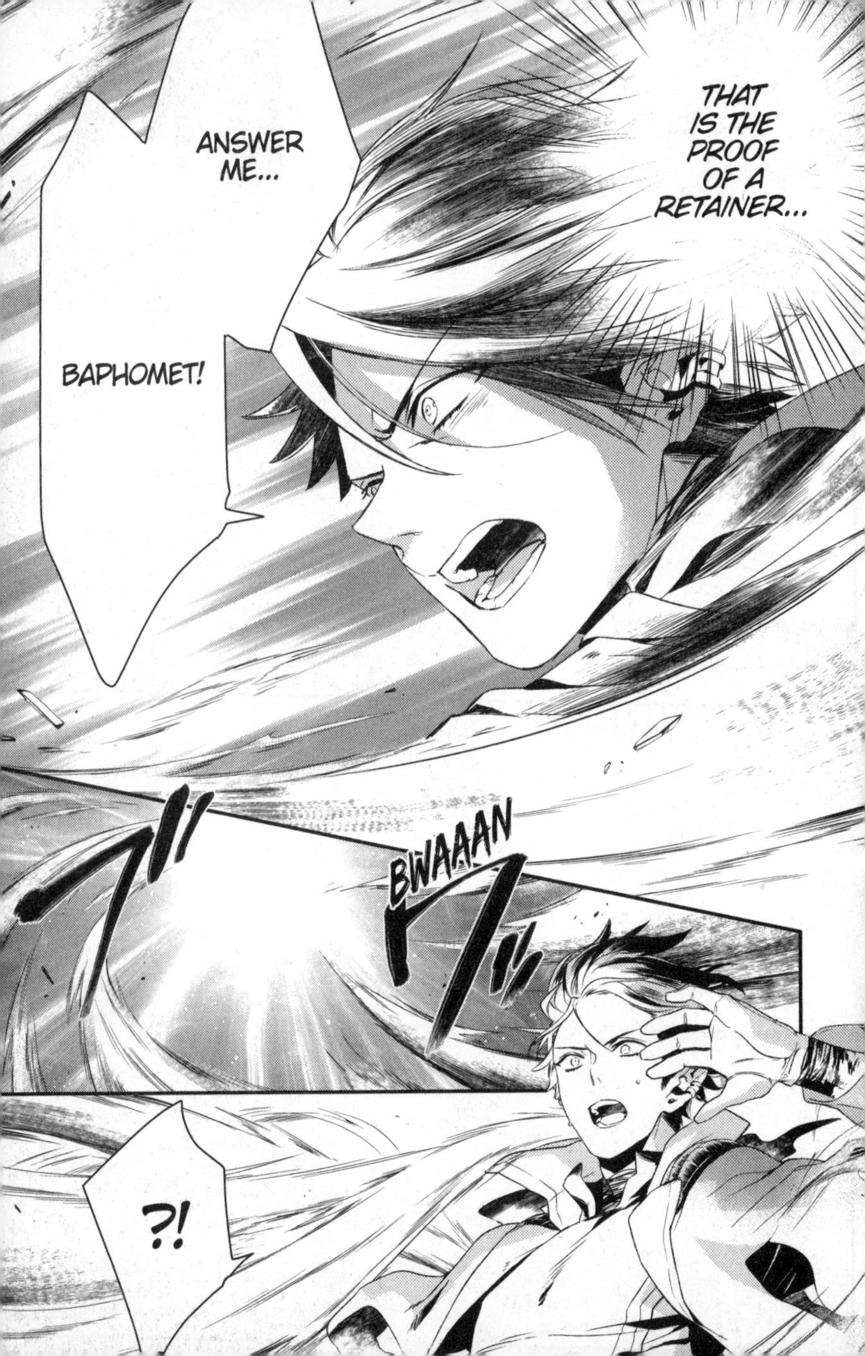
THAT IS THE PROOF OF A RETAINER...
ANSWER ME...
BAPHOMET!
BWAAAN
?!

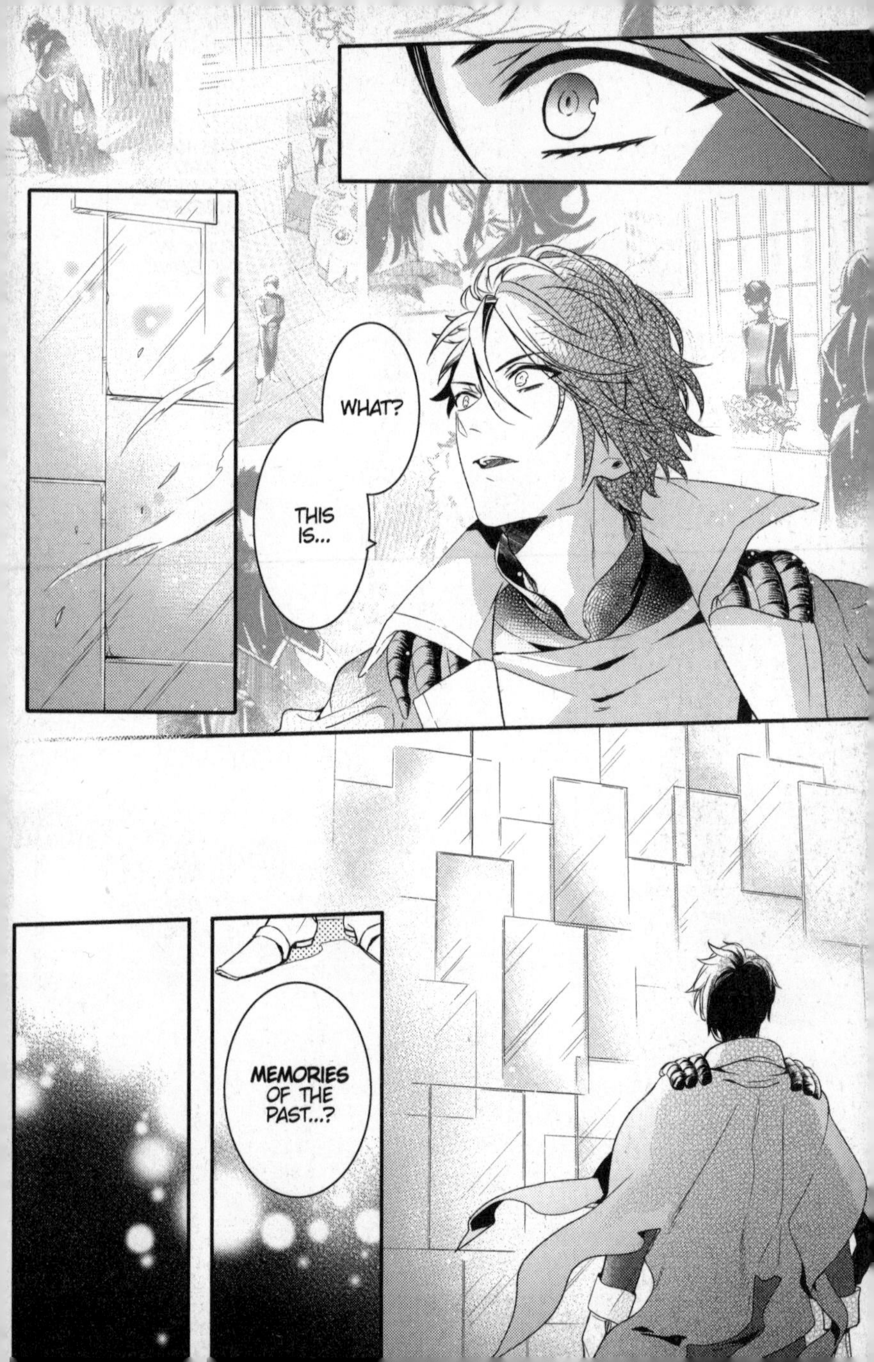
WHAT?
THIS IS...
MEMORIES OF THE PAST...?

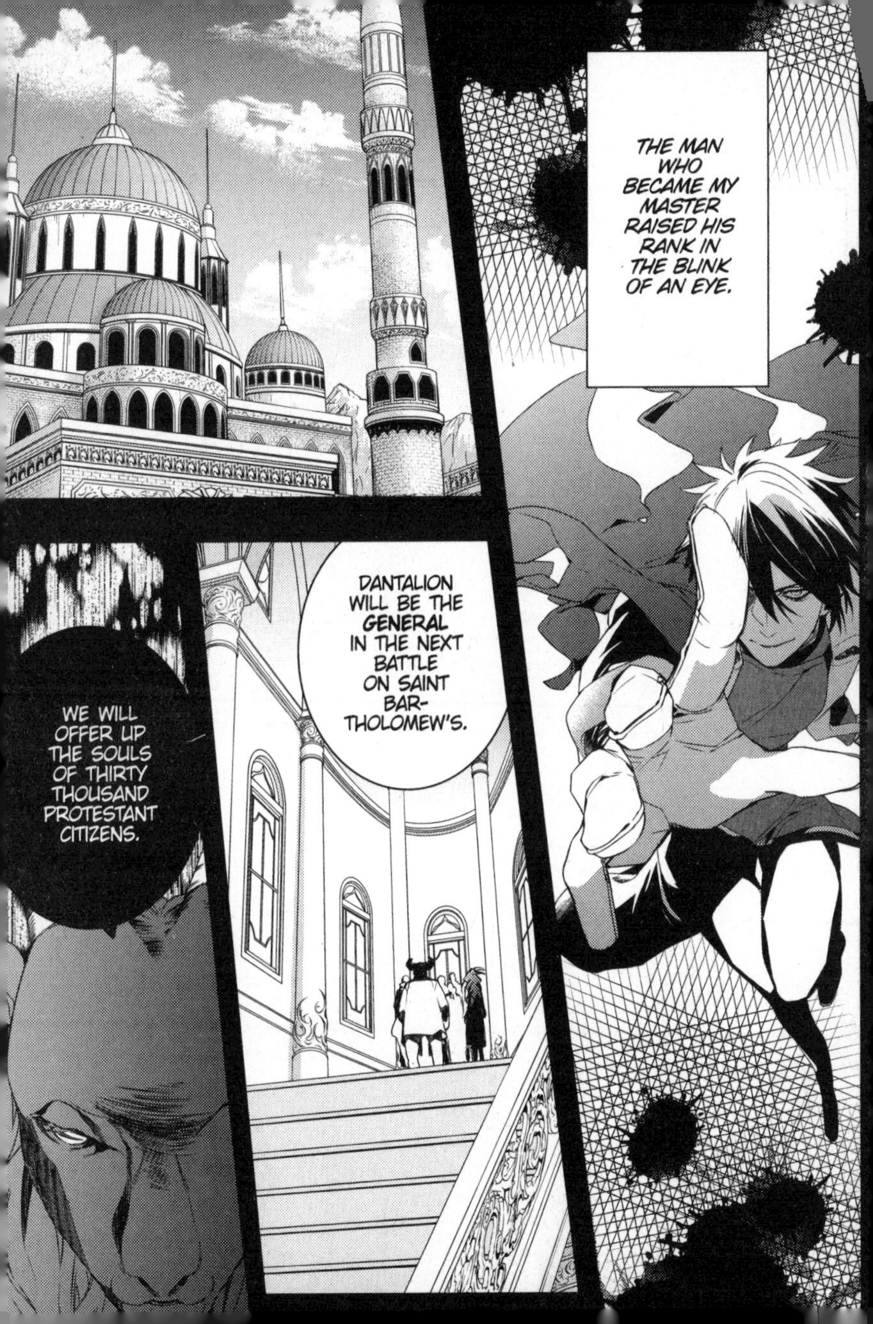
THE MAN WHO BECAME MY MASTER RAISED HIS RANK IN THE BLINK OF AN EYE.
DANTALION WILL BE THE **GENERAL** IN THE NEXT BATTLE ON SAINT BAR-THOLOMEW'S.
WE WILL OFFER UP THE SOULS OF THIRTY THOUSAND PROTESTANT CITIZENS.

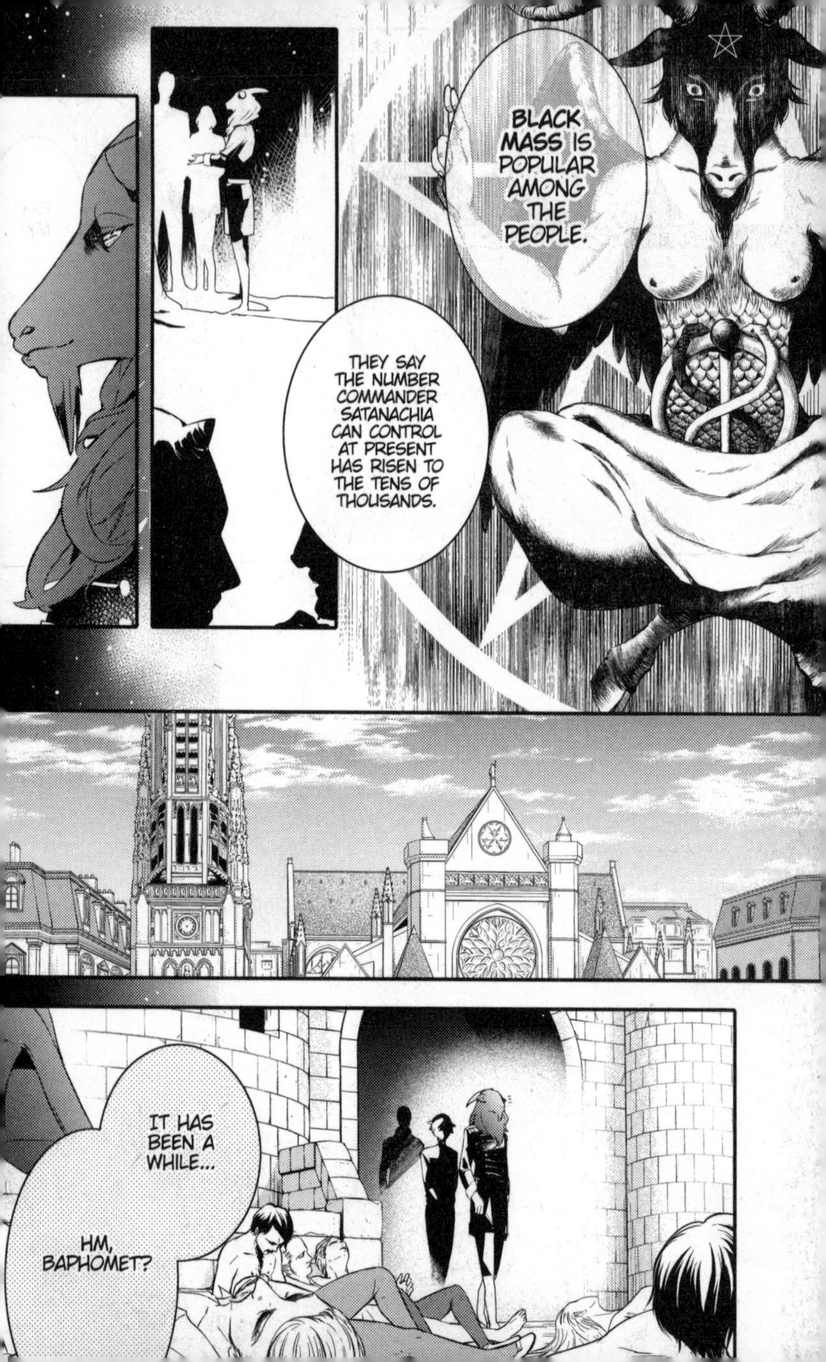
BLACK MASS IS POPULAR AMONG THE PEOPLE.
THEY SAY THE NUMBER COMMANDER SATANACHIA CAN CONTROL AT PRESENT HAS RISEN TO THE TENS OF THOUSANDS.
IT HAS BEEN A WHILE...
HM, BAPHOMET?

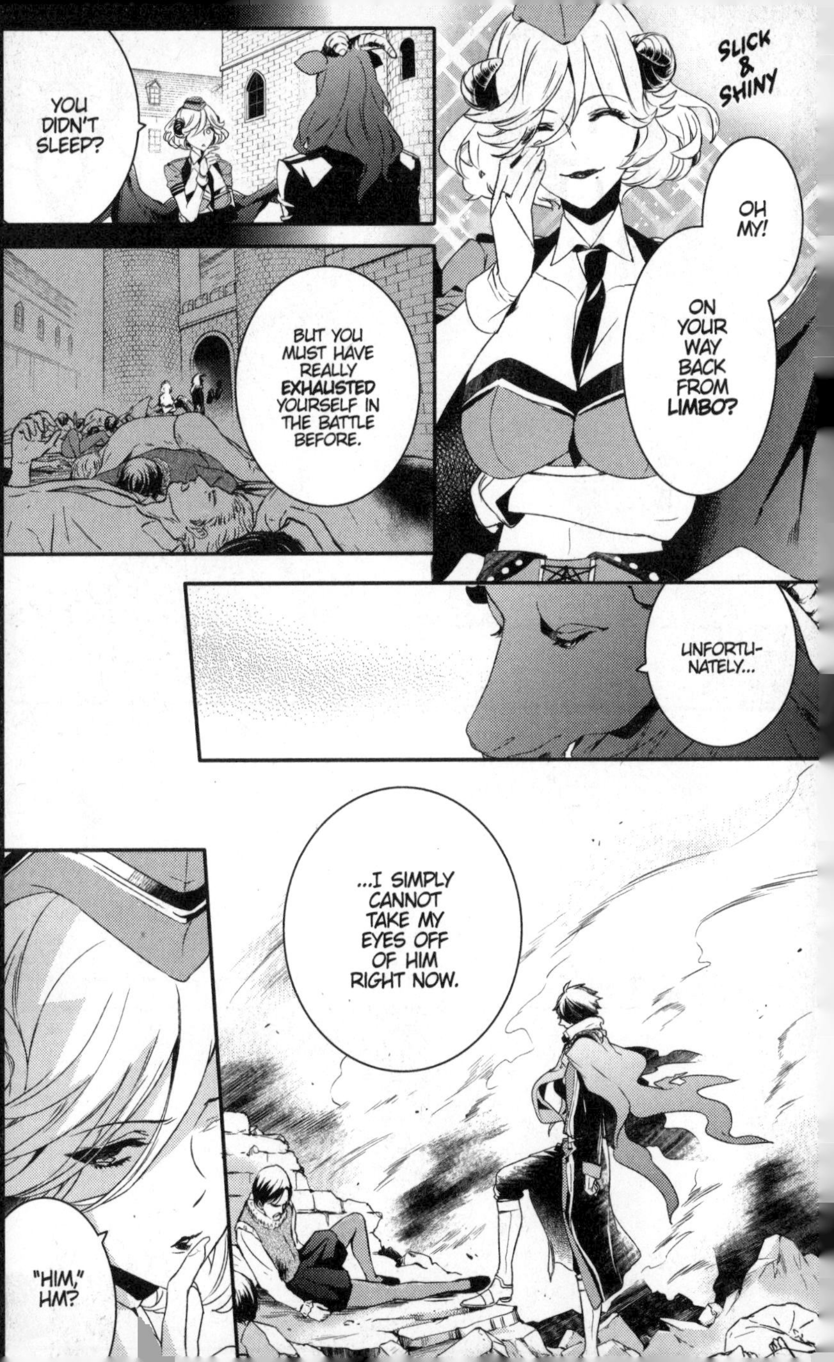
SLICK & SHINY
OH MY!
ON YOUR WAY BACK FROM LIMBO?
YOU DIDN'T SLEEP?
BUT YOU MUST HAVE REALLY **EXHAUSTED** YOURSELF IN THE BATTLE BEFORE.
UNFORTUNATELY...
...I SIMPLY CANNOT TAKE MY EYES OFF OF HIM RIGHT NOW.
"HIM," HM?

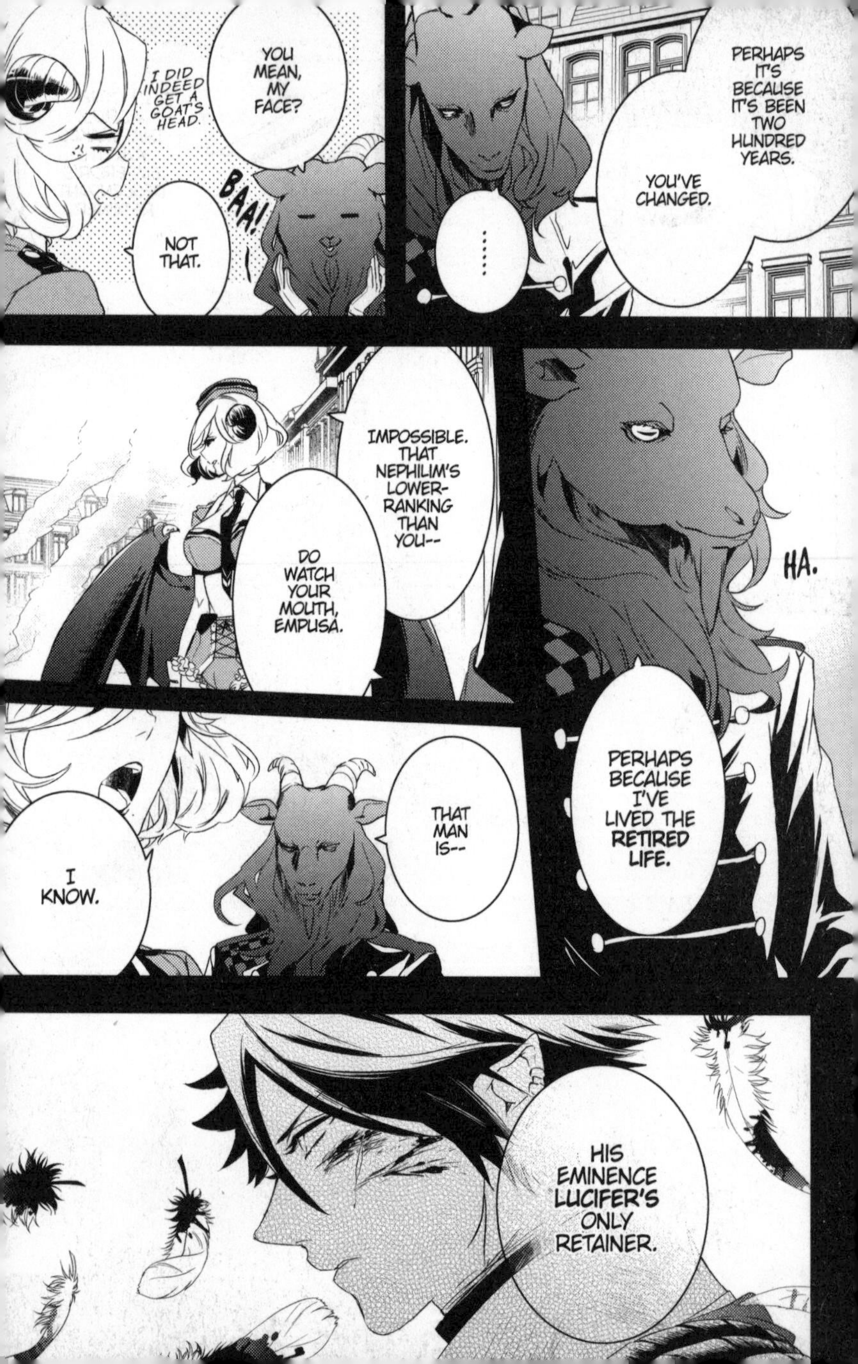
PERHAPS IT'S BECAUSE IT'S BEEN TWO HUNDRED YEARS.
YOU'VE CHANGED.
......
YOU MEAN, MY FACE?
I DID INDEED GET A GOAT'S HEAD.
BAA!
NOT THAT.
HA.
PERHAPS BECAUSE I'VE LIVED THE RETIRED LIFE.
IMPOSSIBLE. THAT NEPHILIM'S LOWER-RANKING THAN YOU--
DO WATCH YOUR MOUTH, EMPUSA.
THAT MAN IS--
I KNOW.
HIS EMINENCE LUCIFER'S ONLY RETAINER.

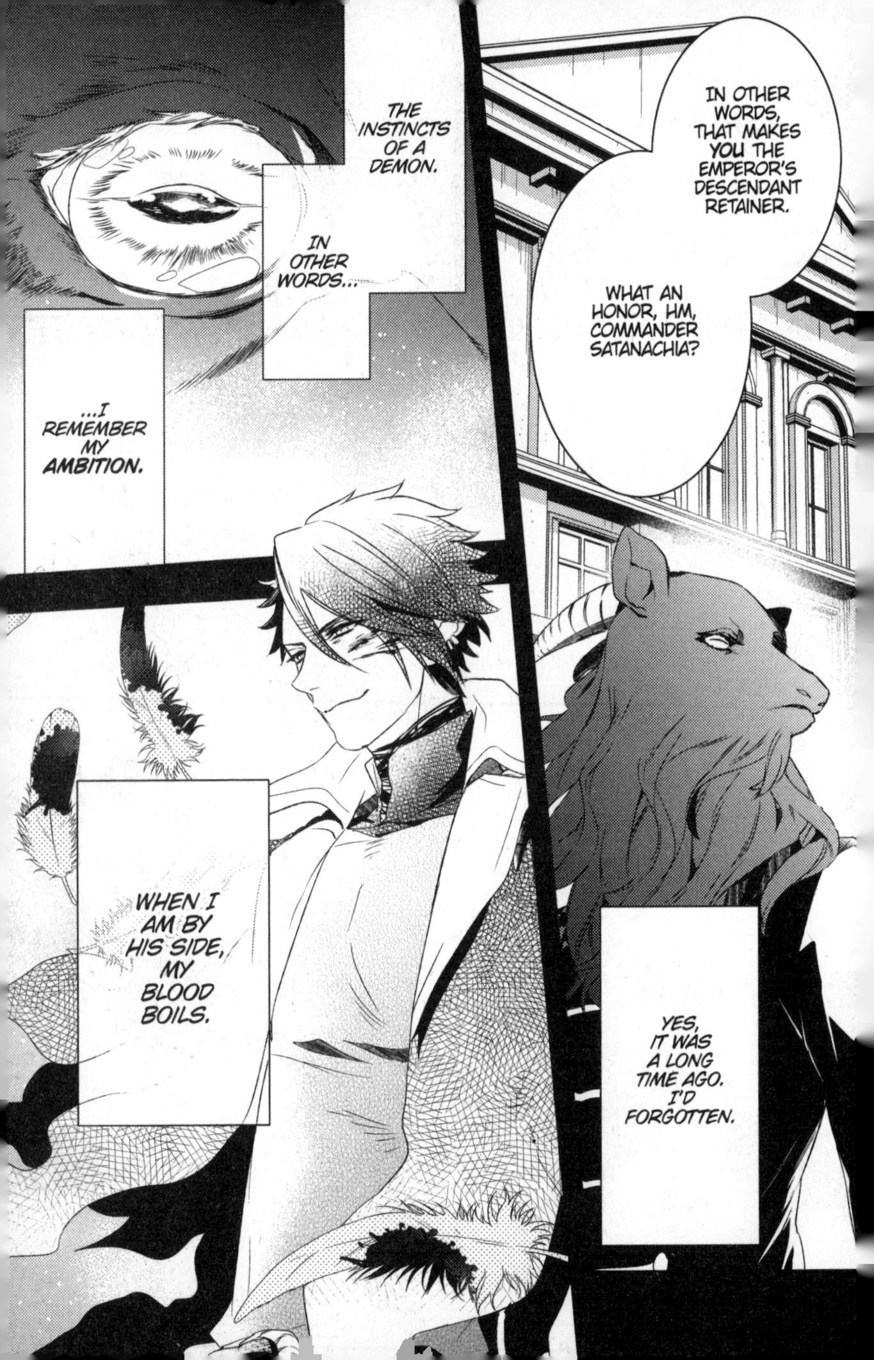
IN OTHER WORDS, THAT MAKES YOU THE EMPEROR'S DESCENDANT RETAINER.
WHAT AN HONOR, HM, COMMANDER SATANACHIA?
YES, IT WAS A LONG TIME AGO. I'D FORGOTTEN.
THE INSTINCTS OF A DEMON.
IN OTHER WORDS...
...I REMEMBER MY AMBITION.
WHEN I AM BY HIS SIDE, MY BLOOD BOILS.

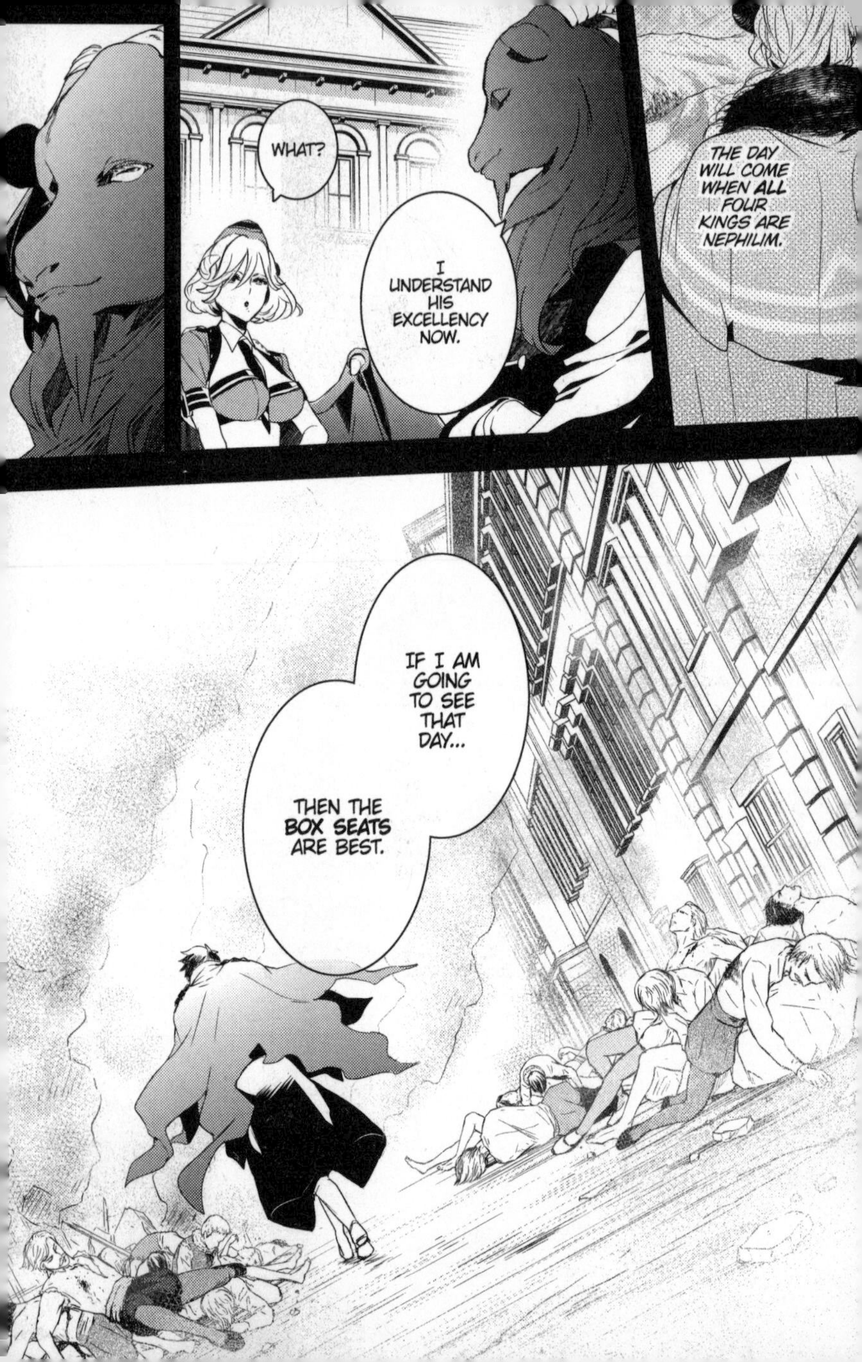
THE DAY WILL COME WHEN ALL FOUR KINGS ARE NEPHILIM.
WHAT?
I UNDERSTAND HIS EXCELLENCY NOW.
IF I AM GOING TO SEE THAT DAY...
THEN THE BOX SEATS ARE BEST.

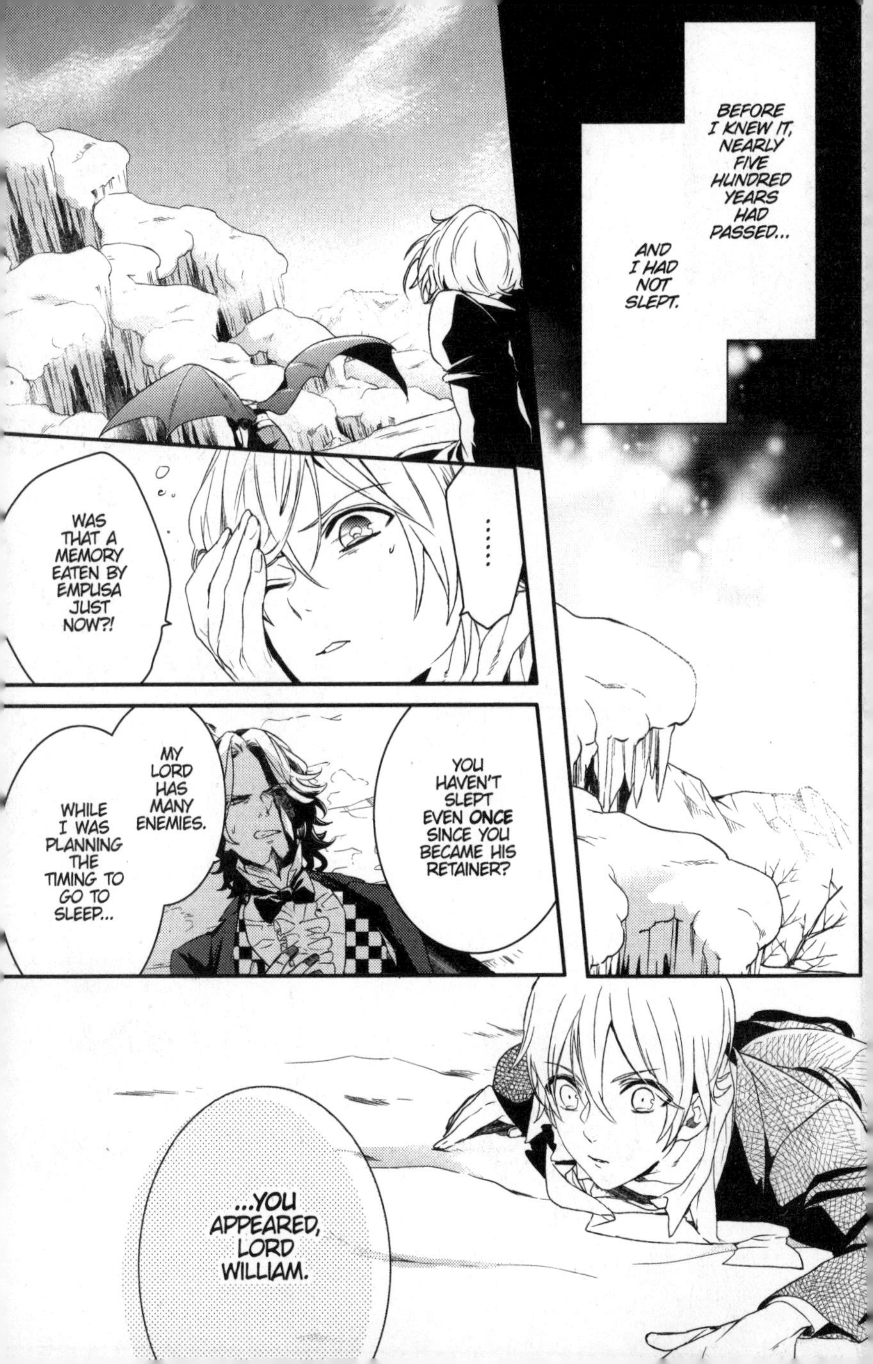
BEFORE I KNEW IT, NEARLY FIVE HUNDRED YEARS HAD PASSED...
AND I HAD NOT SLEPT.
......
WAS THAT A MEMORY EATEN BY EMPUSA JUST NOW?!
YOU HAVEN'T SLEPT EVEN ONCE SINCE YOU BECAME HIS RETAINER?
MY LORD HAS MANY ENEMIES.
WHILE I WAS PLANNING THE TIMING TO GO TO SLEEP...
...YOU APPEARED, LORD WILLIAM.

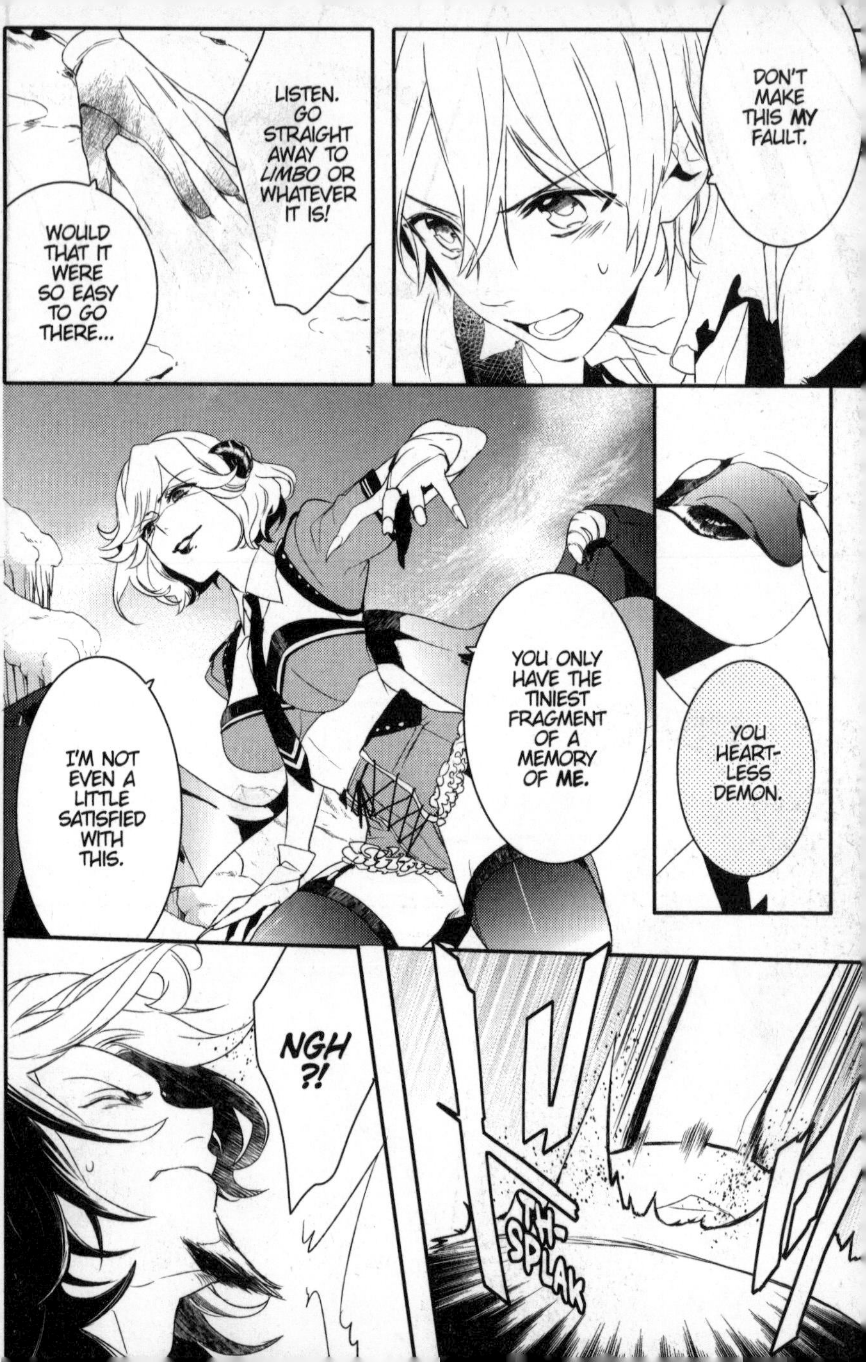
DON'T MAKE THIS MY FAULT.
LISTEN. GO STRAIGHT AWAY TO *LIMBO* OR WHATEVER IT IS!
WOULD THAT IT WERE SO EASY TO GO THERE...
YOU HEARTLESS DEMON.
YOU ONLY HAVE THE TINIEST FRAGMENT OF A MEMORY OF ME.
I'M NOT EVEN A LITTLE SATISFIED WITH THIS.
TH-SPLAK
NGH?!

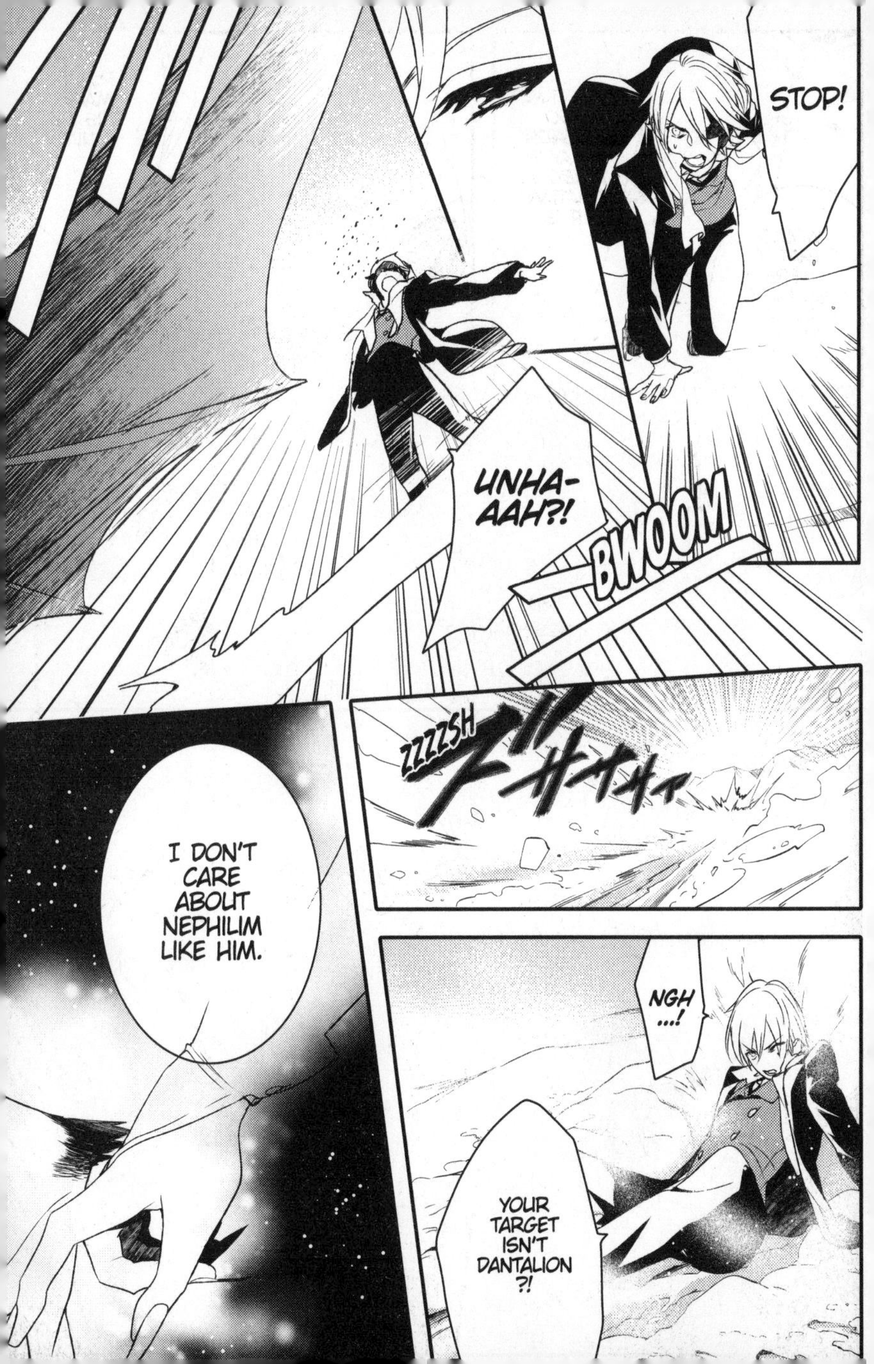
STOP!
UNHA-AAH?!
BWOOM
ZZZZSH
NGH ...!
YOUR TARGET ISN'T DANTALION ?!
I DON'T CARE ABOUT NEPHILIM LIKE HIM.

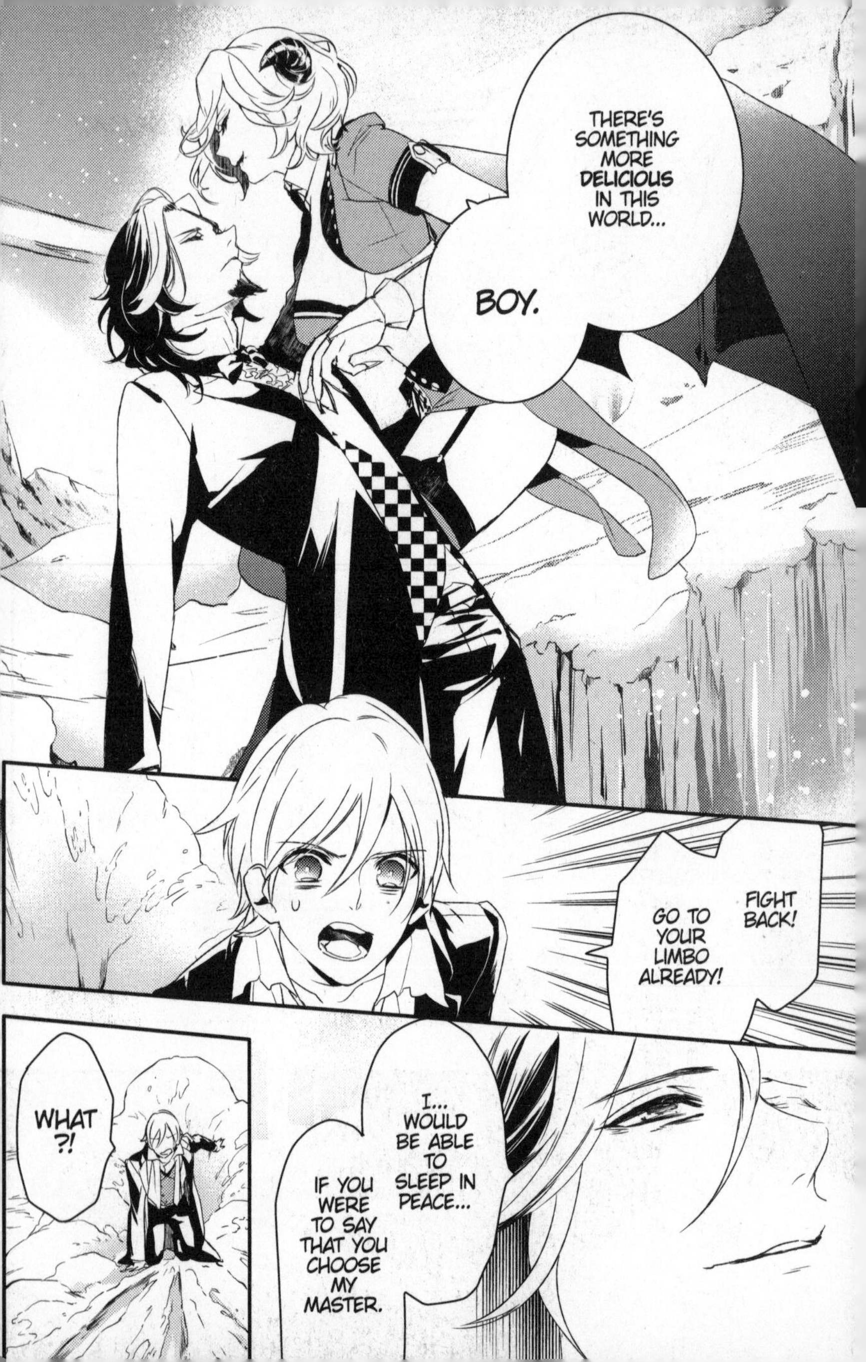
THERE'S SOMETHING MORE DELICIOUS IN THIS WORLD...
BOY.
FIGHT BACK!
GO TO YOUR LIMBO ALREADY!
I... WOULD BE ABLE TO SLEEP IN PEACE...
IF YOU WERE TO SAY THAT YOU CHOOSE MY MASTER.
WHAT ?!

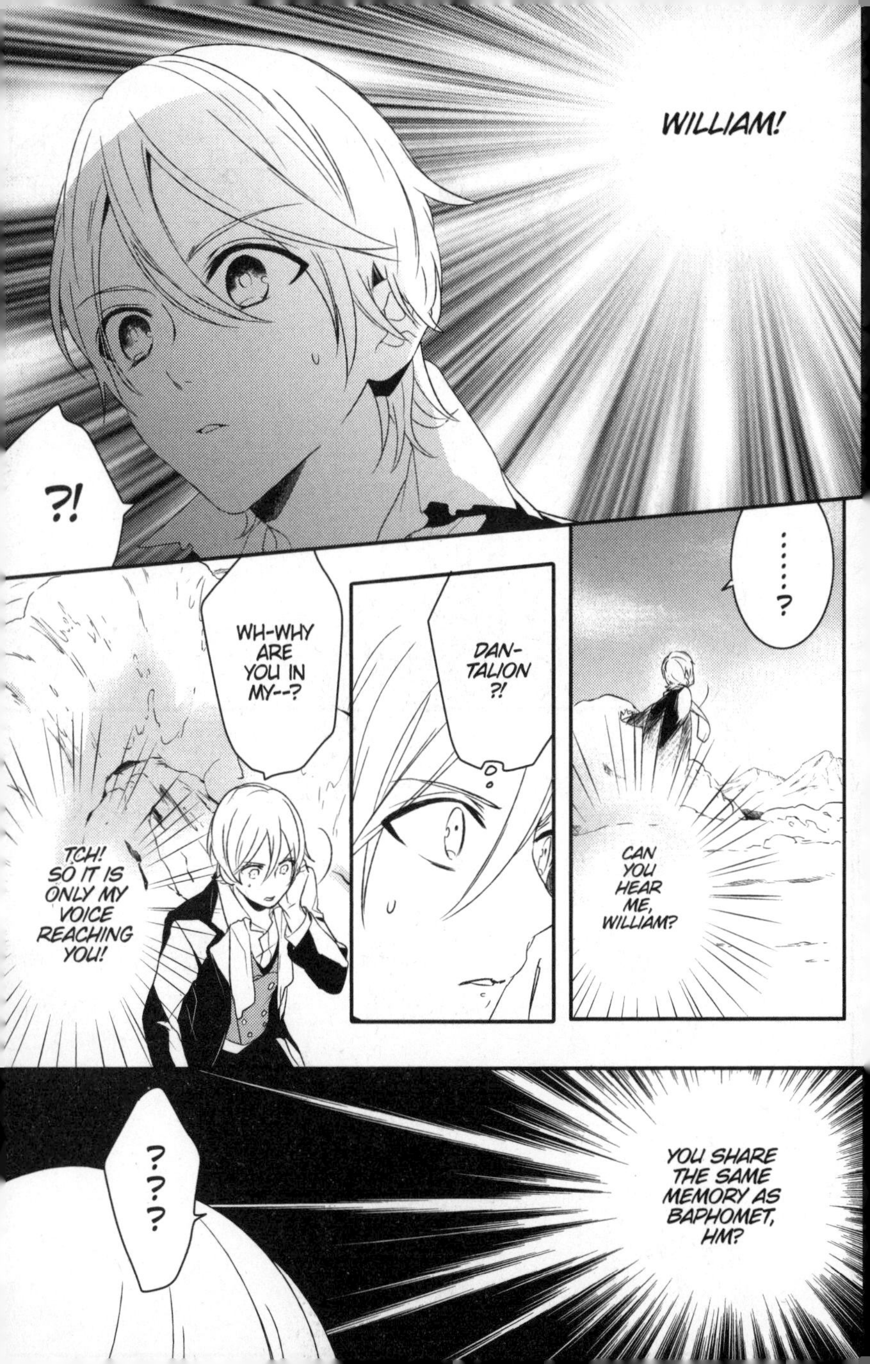
WILLIAM!
?!
......?
CAN YOU HEAR ME, WILLIAM?
DAN-TALION ?!
WH-WHY ARE YOU IN MY--?
TCH! SO IT IS ONLY MY VOICE REACHING YOU!
YOU SHARE THE SAME MEMORY AS BAPHOMET, HM?
???

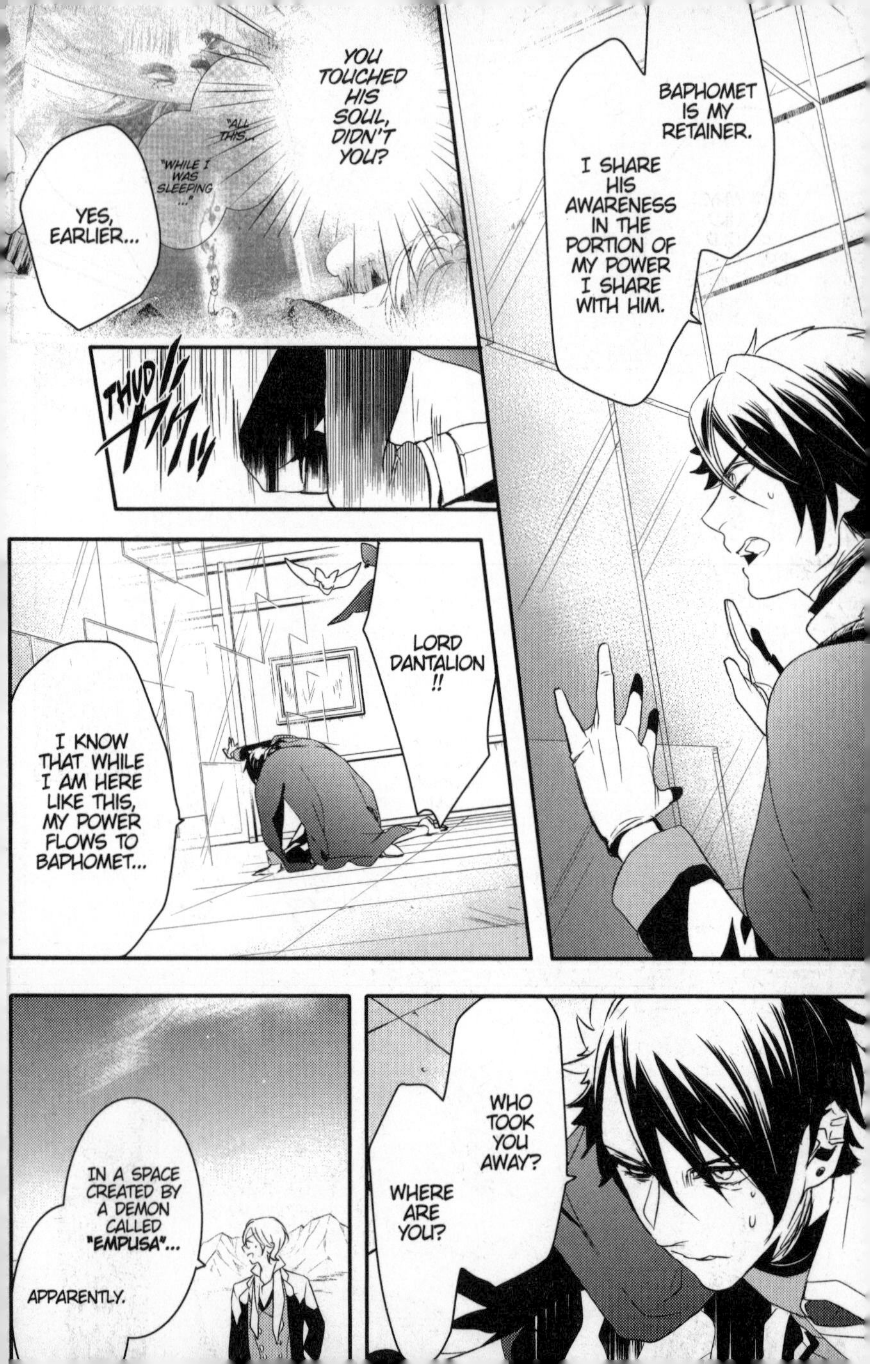
BAPHOMET IS MY RETAINER.
I SHARE HIS AWARENESS IN THE PORTION OF MY POWER I SHARE WITH HIM.
YOU TOUCHED HIS SOUL, DIDN'T YOU?
"ALL THIS..."
"WHILE I WAS SLEEPING..."
YES, EARLIER...
THUD!!
LORD DANTALION!!
I KNOW THAT WHILE I AM HERE LIKE THIS, MY POWER FLOWS TO BAPHOMET...
WHO TOOK YOU AWAY?
WHERE ARE YOU?
IN A SPACE CREATED BY A DEMON CALLED "EMPUSA"...
APPARENTLY.

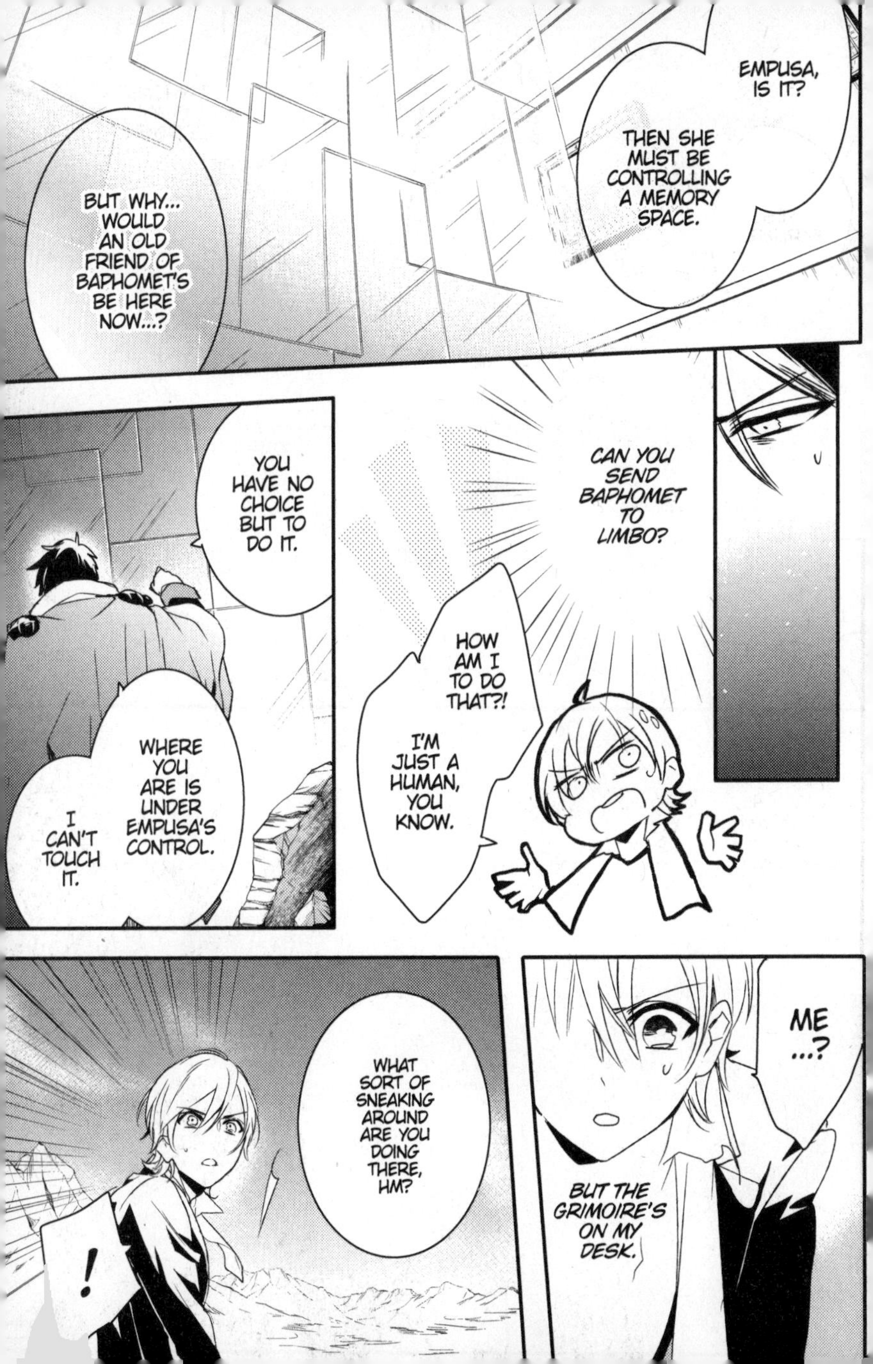
EMPUSA, IS IT?
THEN SHE MUST BE CONTROLLING A MEMORY SPACE.
BUT WHY... WOULD AN OLD FRIEND OF BAPHOMET'S BE HERE NOW...?
CAN YOU SEND BAPHOMET TO LIMBO?
HOW AM I TO DO THAT?!
I'M JUST A HUMAN, YOU KNOW.
YOU HAVE NO CHOICE BUT TO DO IT.
WHERE YOU ARE IS UNDER EMPUSA'S CONTROL.
I CAN'T TOUCH IT.
ME ...?
BUT THE GRIMOIRE'S ON MY DESK.
WHAT SORT OF SNEAKING AROUND ARE YOU DOING THERE, HM?
!

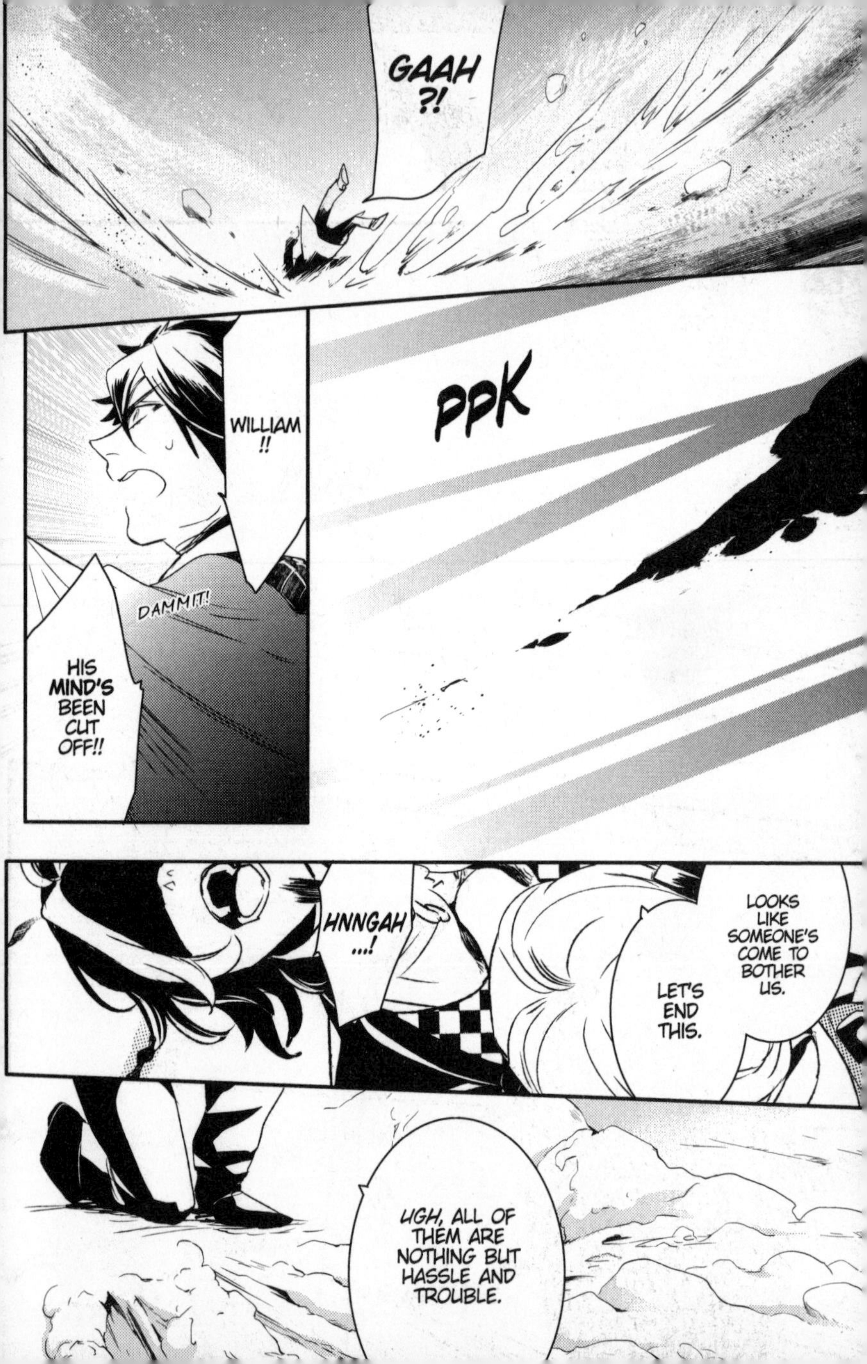
GAAH ?!
PPK
WILLIAM !!
DAMMIT!
HIS MIND'S BEEN CUT OFF!!
LOOKS LIKE SOMEONE'S COME TO BOTHER US.
LET'S END THIS.
HNNGAH ...!
UGH, ALL OF THEM ARE NOTHING BUT HASSLE AND TROUBLE.

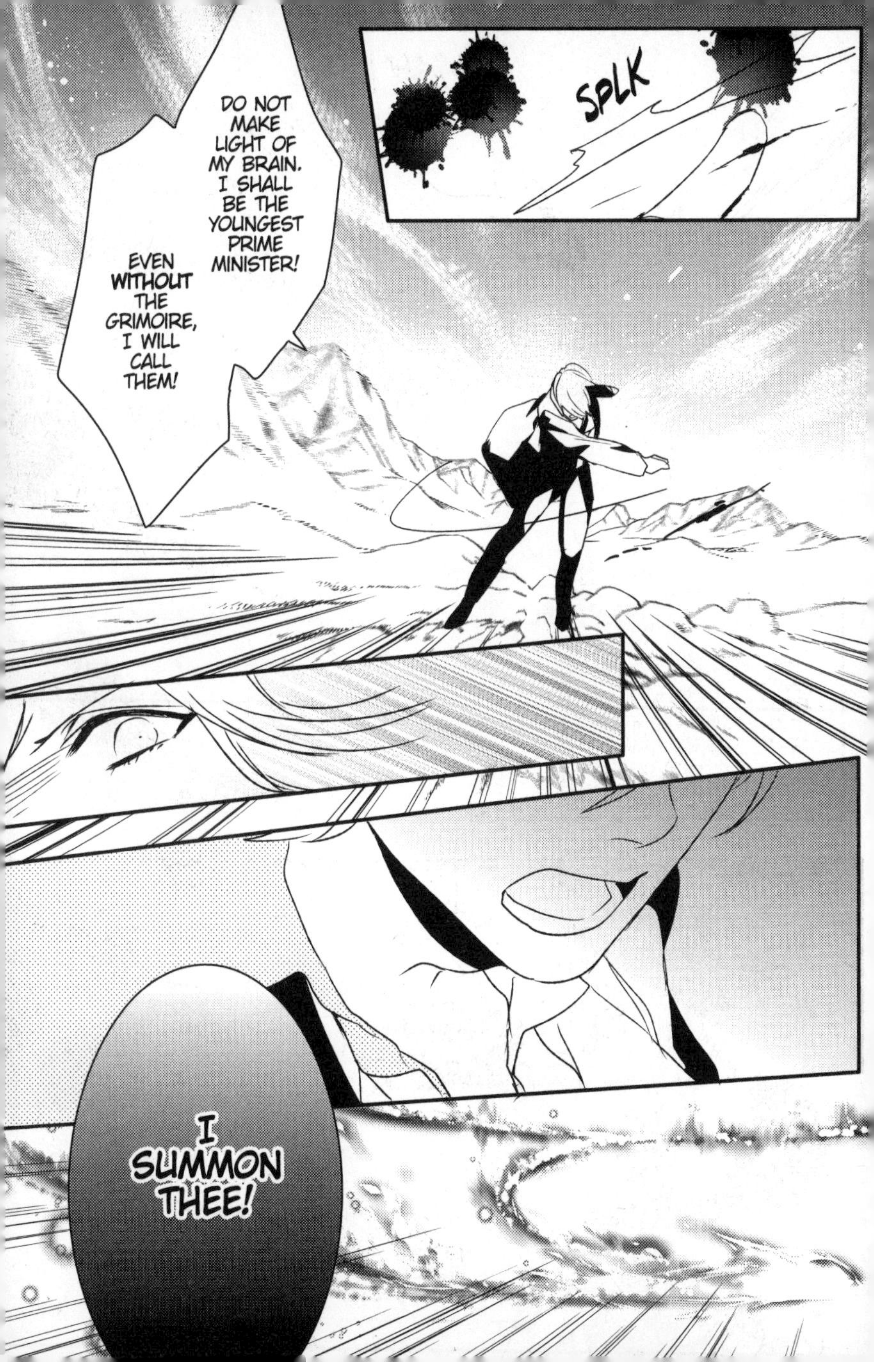
SPLK
DO NOT MAKE LIGHT OF MY BRAIN. I SHALL BE THE YOUNGEST PRIME MINISTER!
EVEN WITHOUT THE GRIMOIRE, I WILL CALL THEM!
I SUMMON THEE!

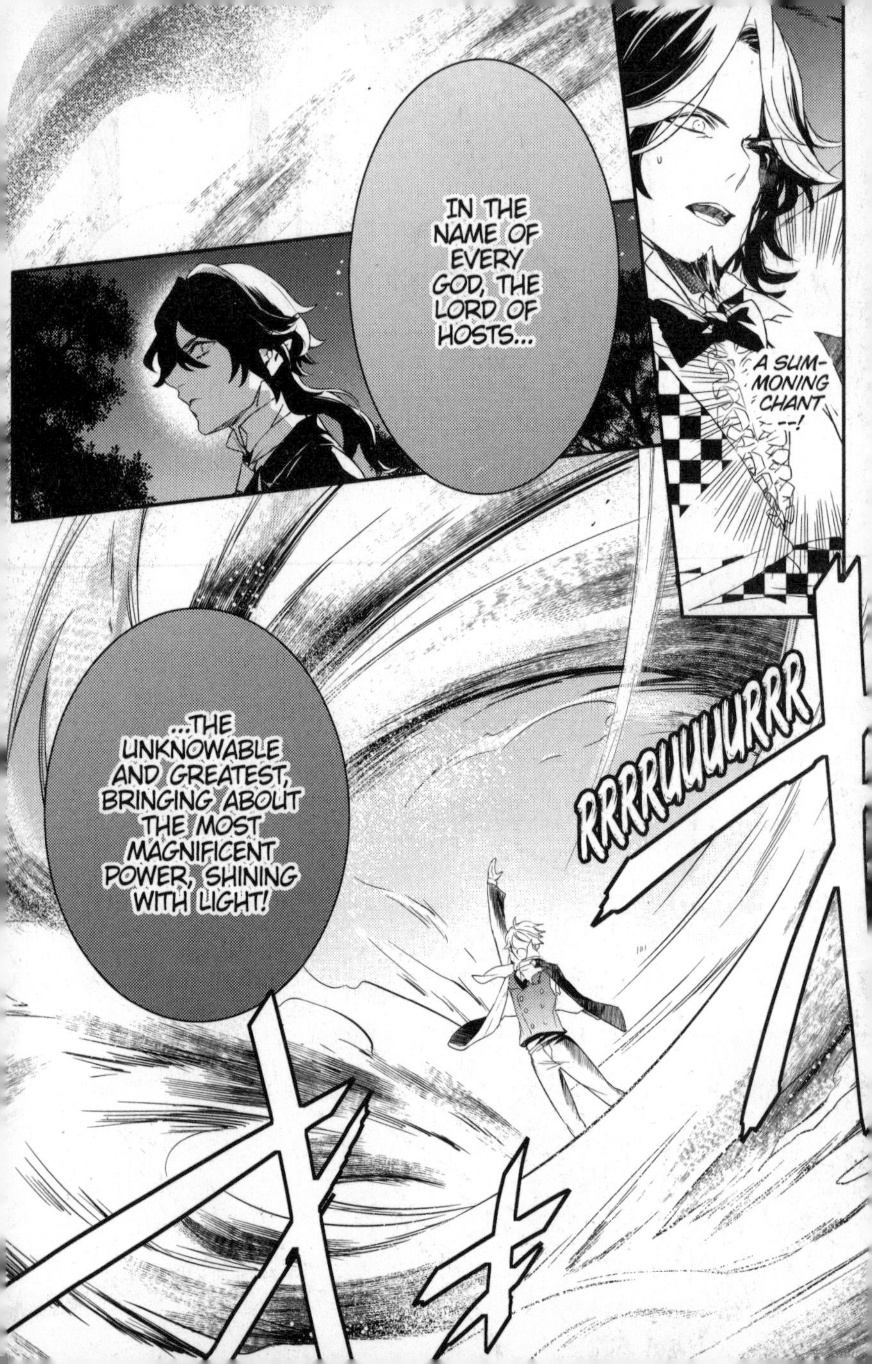
IN THE NAME OF EVERY GOD, THE LORD OF HOSTS...
A SUM-MONING CHANT --!
RRRRUUUURRR
...THE UNKNOWABLE AND GREATEST, BRINGING ABOUT THE MOST MAGNIFICENT POWER, SHINING WITH LIGHT!

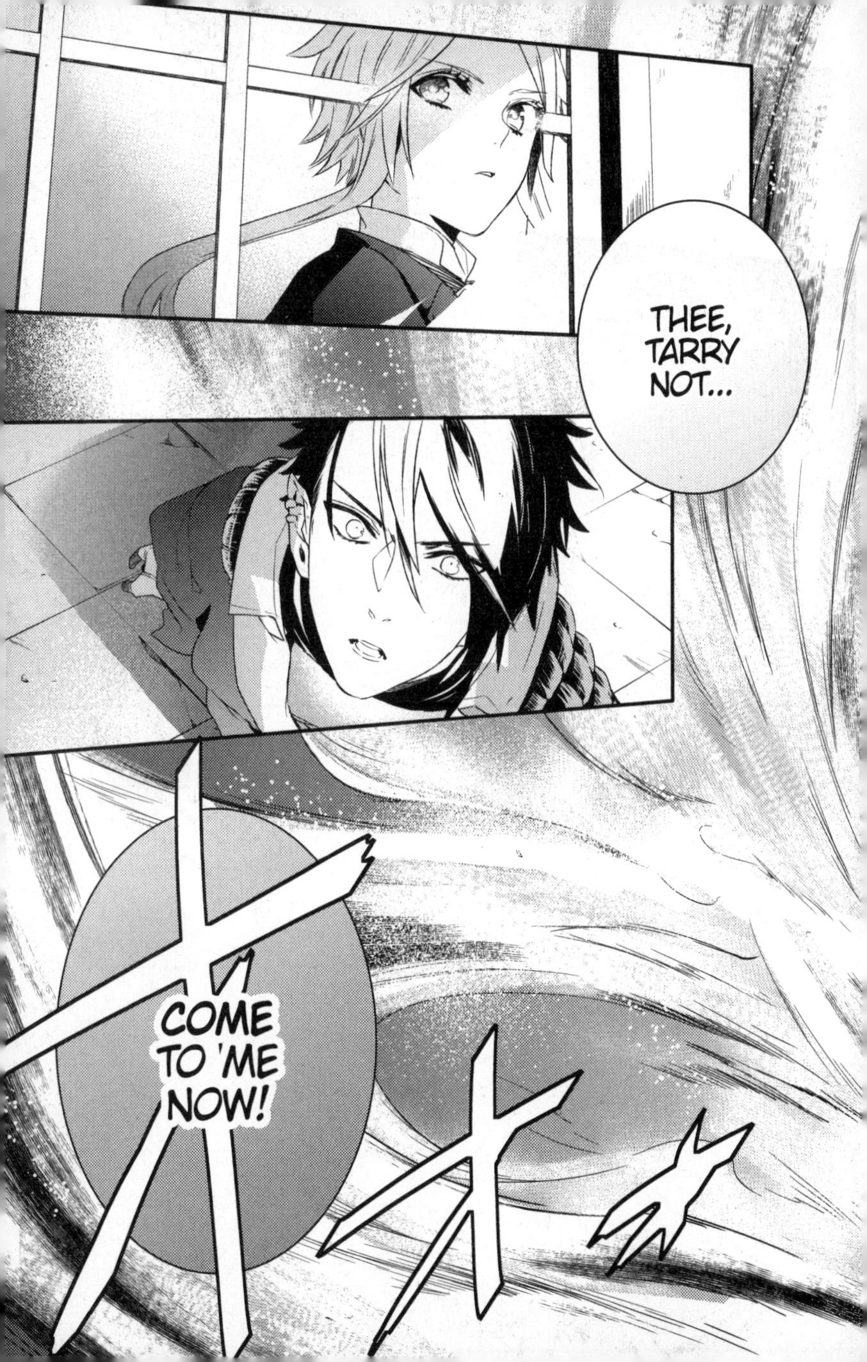
THEE, TARRY NOT...
COME TO 'ME NOW!

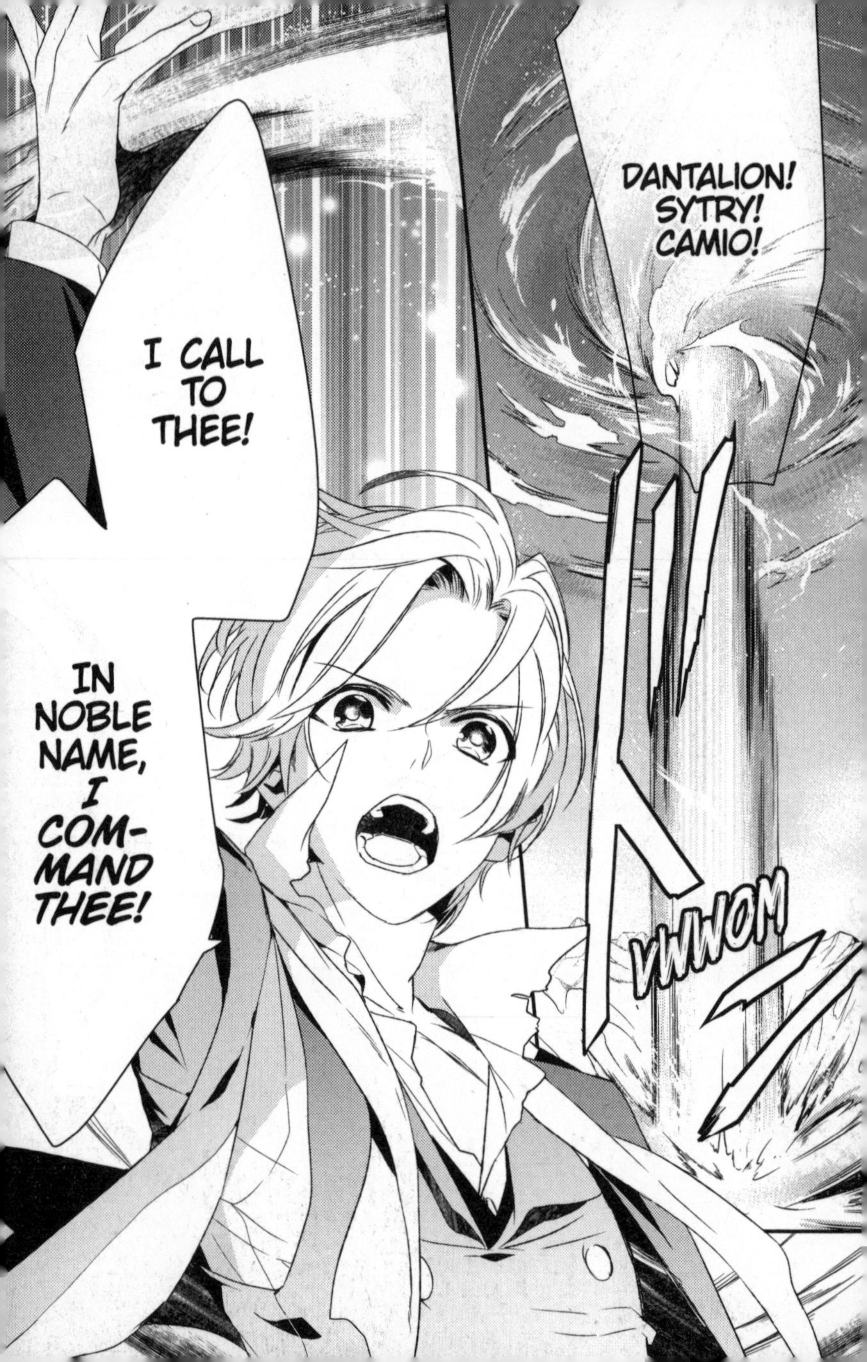
DANTALION! SYTRY! CAMIO!
I CALL TO THEE!
IN NOBLE NAME, I COMMAND THEE!
VWWOM

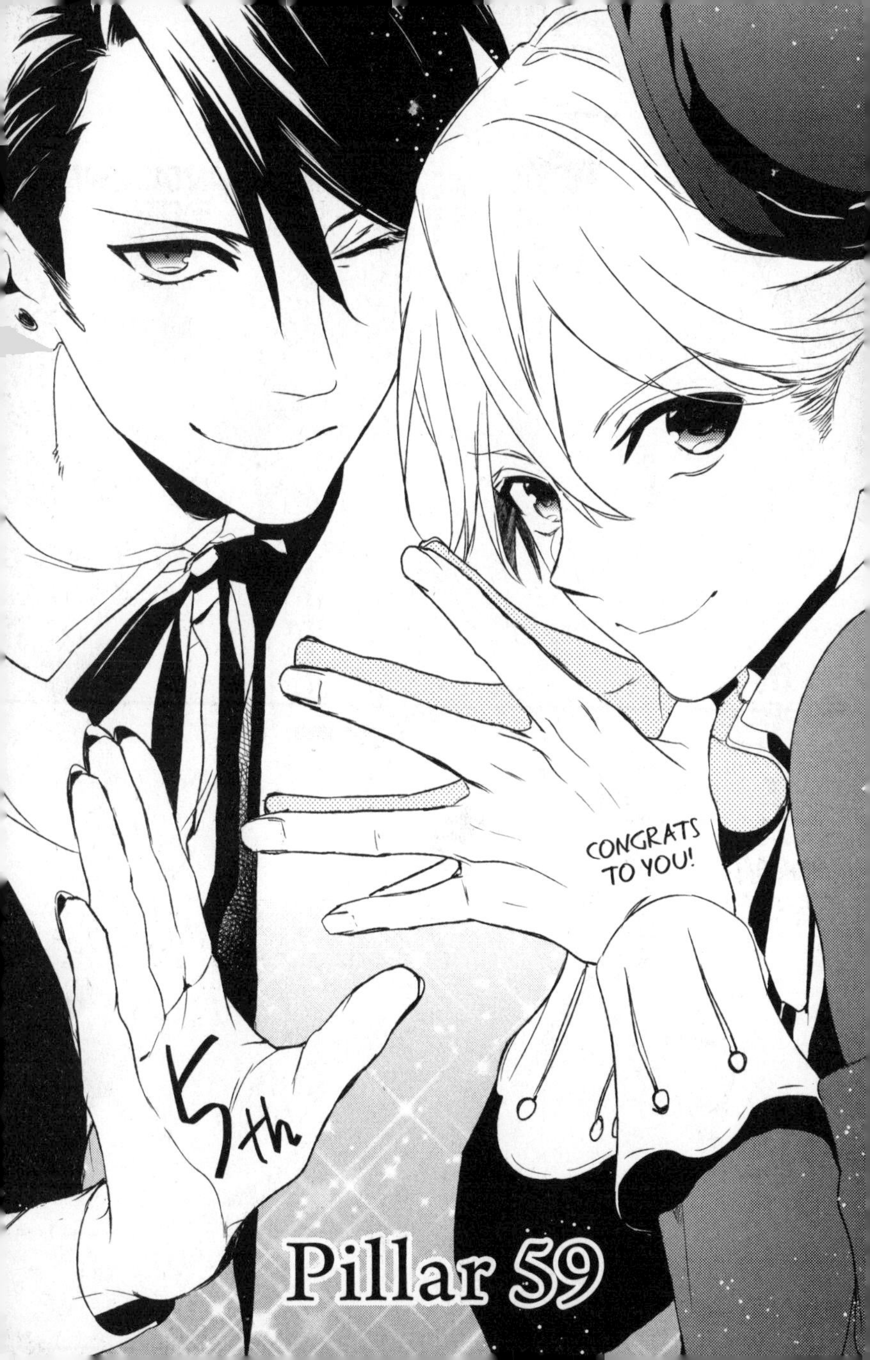
5th
CONGRATS TO YOU!

Pillar 59

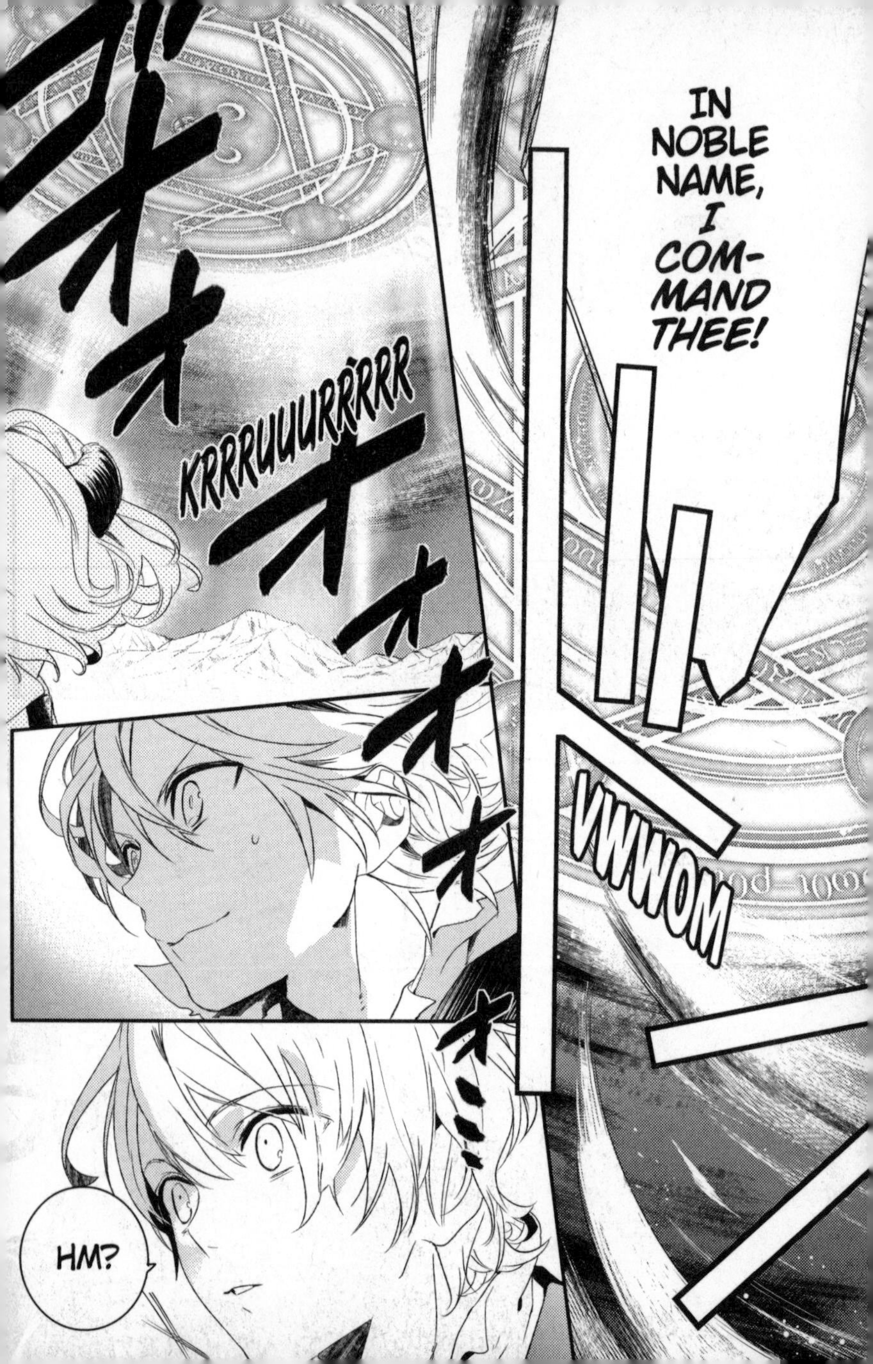
IN NOBLE NAME, I COMMAND THEE!
VWWOM
KRRRUUURRRR
HM?

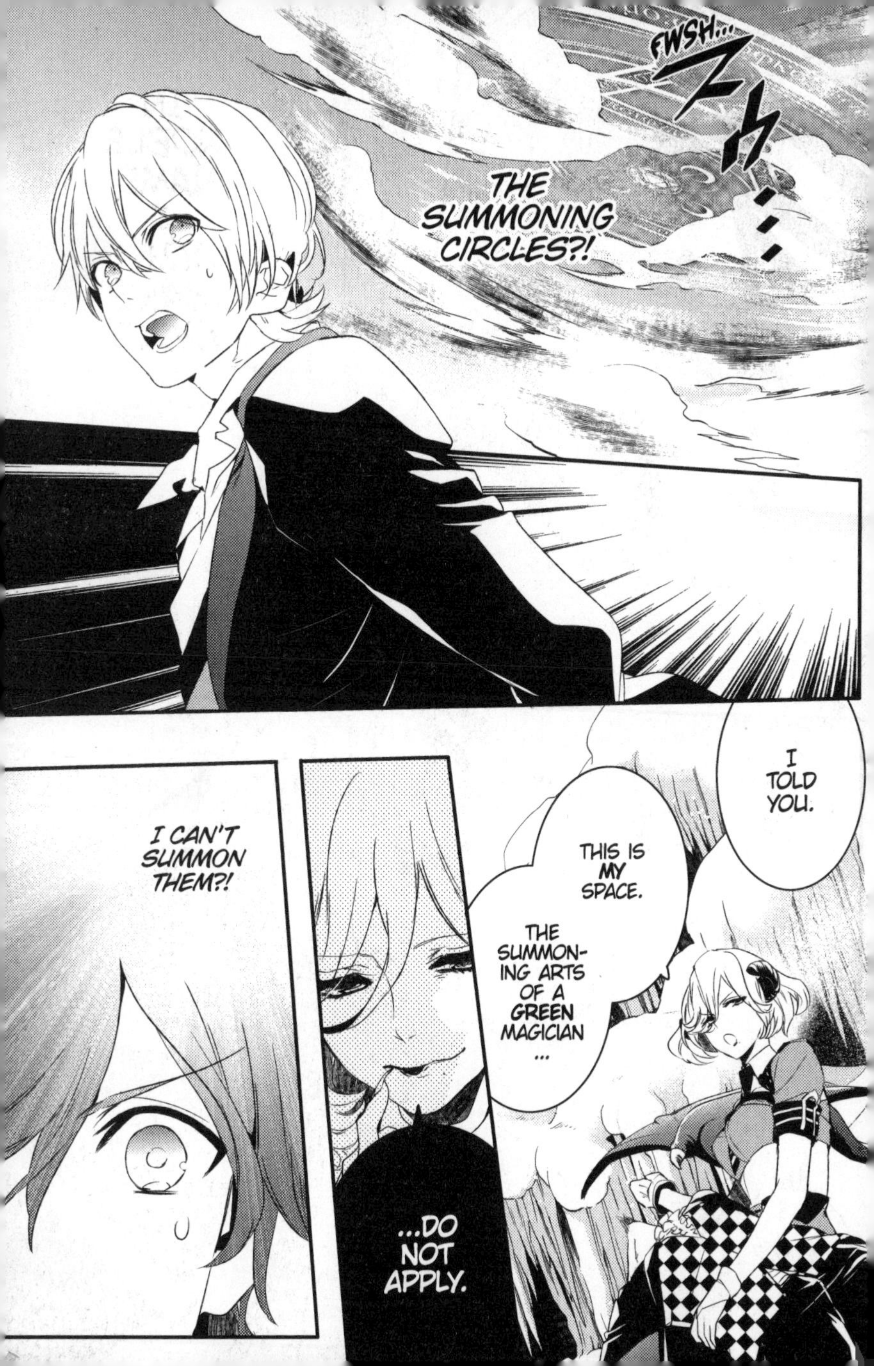
FWSH...
THE SUMMONING CIRCLES?!
I TOLD YOU.
THIS IS MY SPACE.
THE SUMMONING ARTS OF A GREEN MAGICIAN ...
...DO NOT APPLY.
I CAN'T SUMMON THEM?!

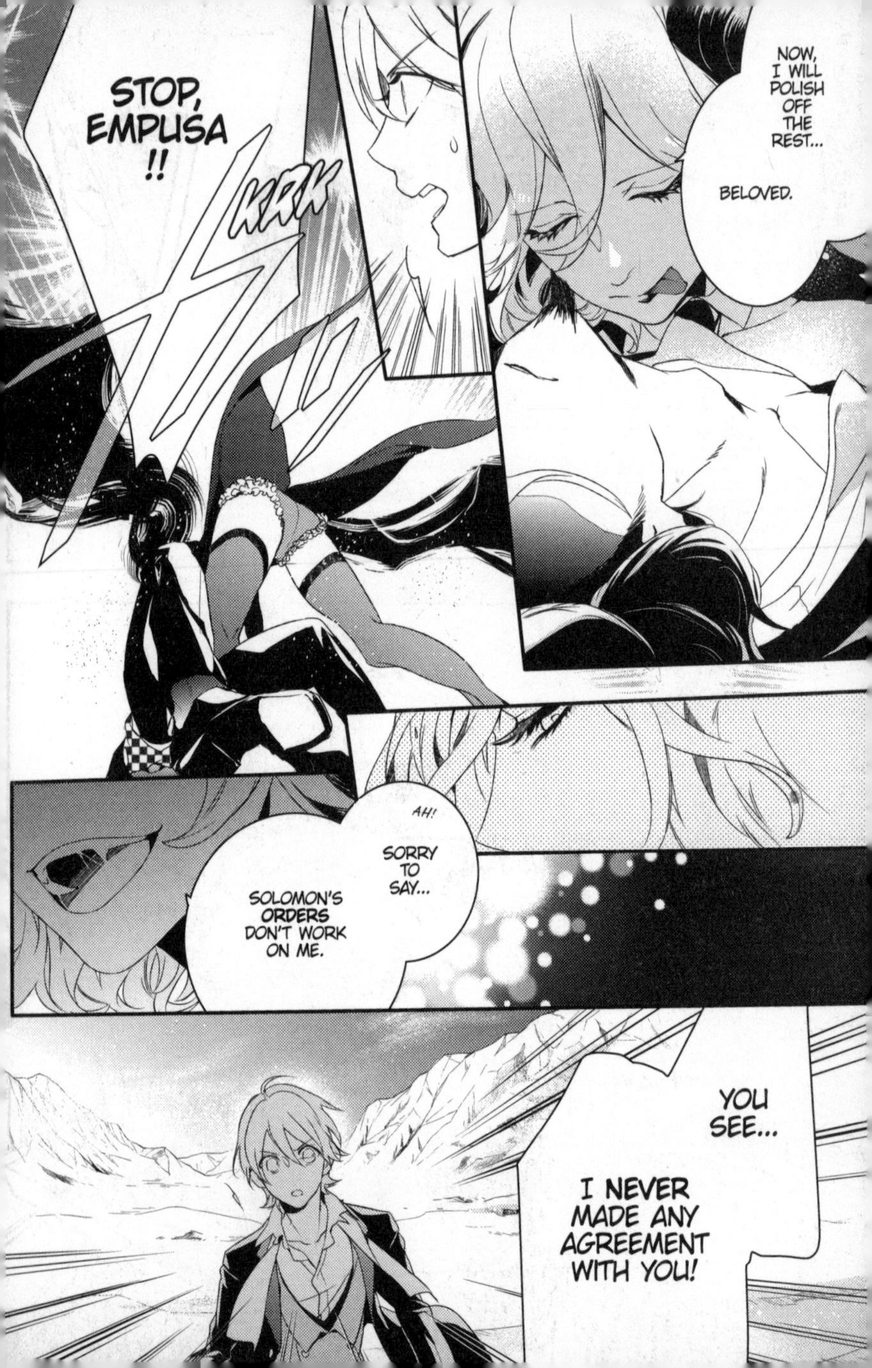
NOW, I WILL POLISH OFF THE REST...
BELOVED.
KRRK
STOP, EMPUSA !!
AH!
SORRY TO SAY...
SOLOMON'S ORDERS DON'T WORK ON ME.
YOU SEE...
I NEVER MADE ANY AGREEMENT WITH YOU!

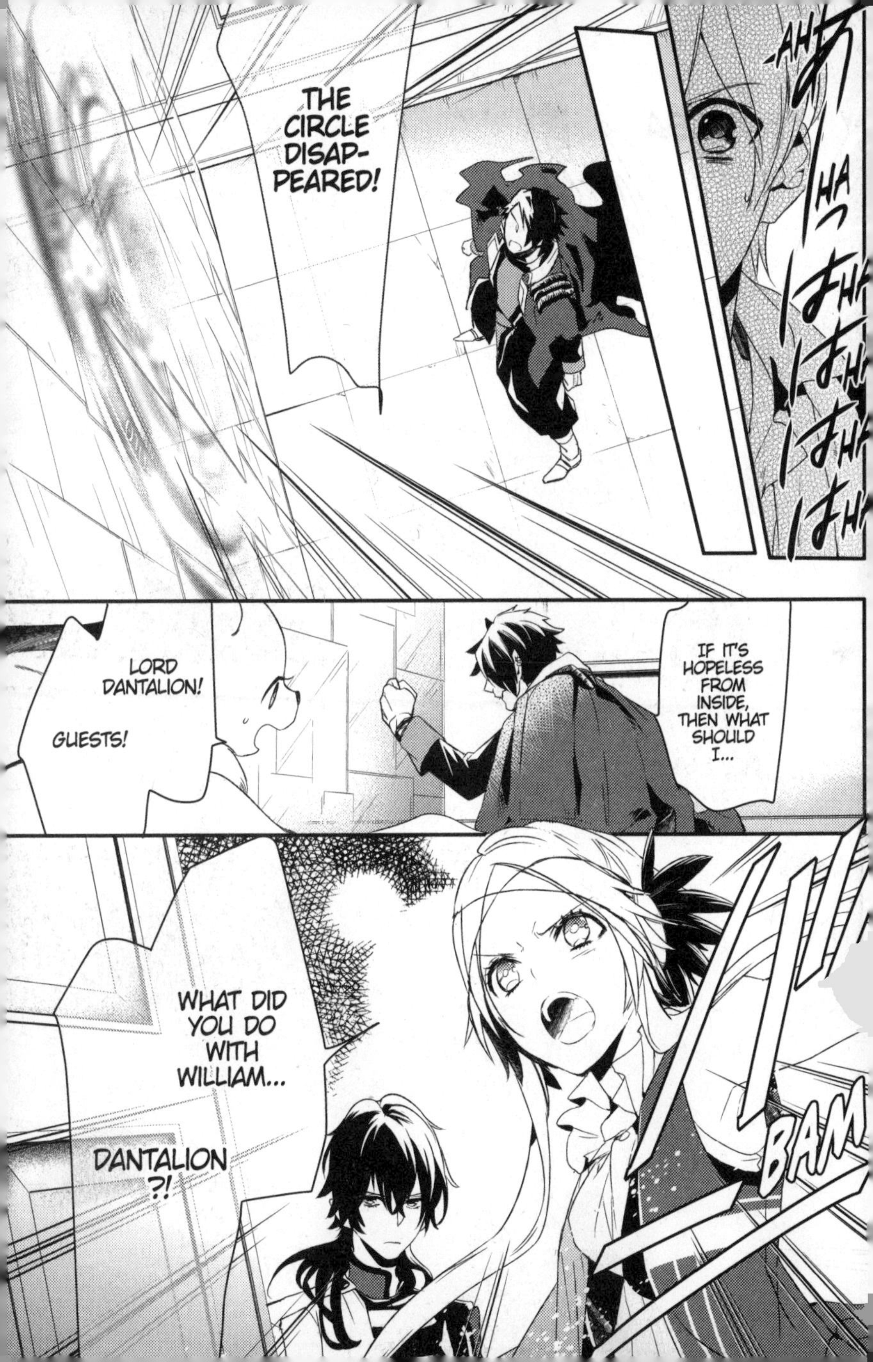

-AH HA HA HA HA
THE CIRCLE DISAP-PEARED!
IF IT'S HOPELESS FROM INSIDE, THEN WHAT SHOULD I...
LORD DANTALION!
GUESTS!
BAM
WHAT DID YOU DO WITH WILLIAM...
DANTALION ?!

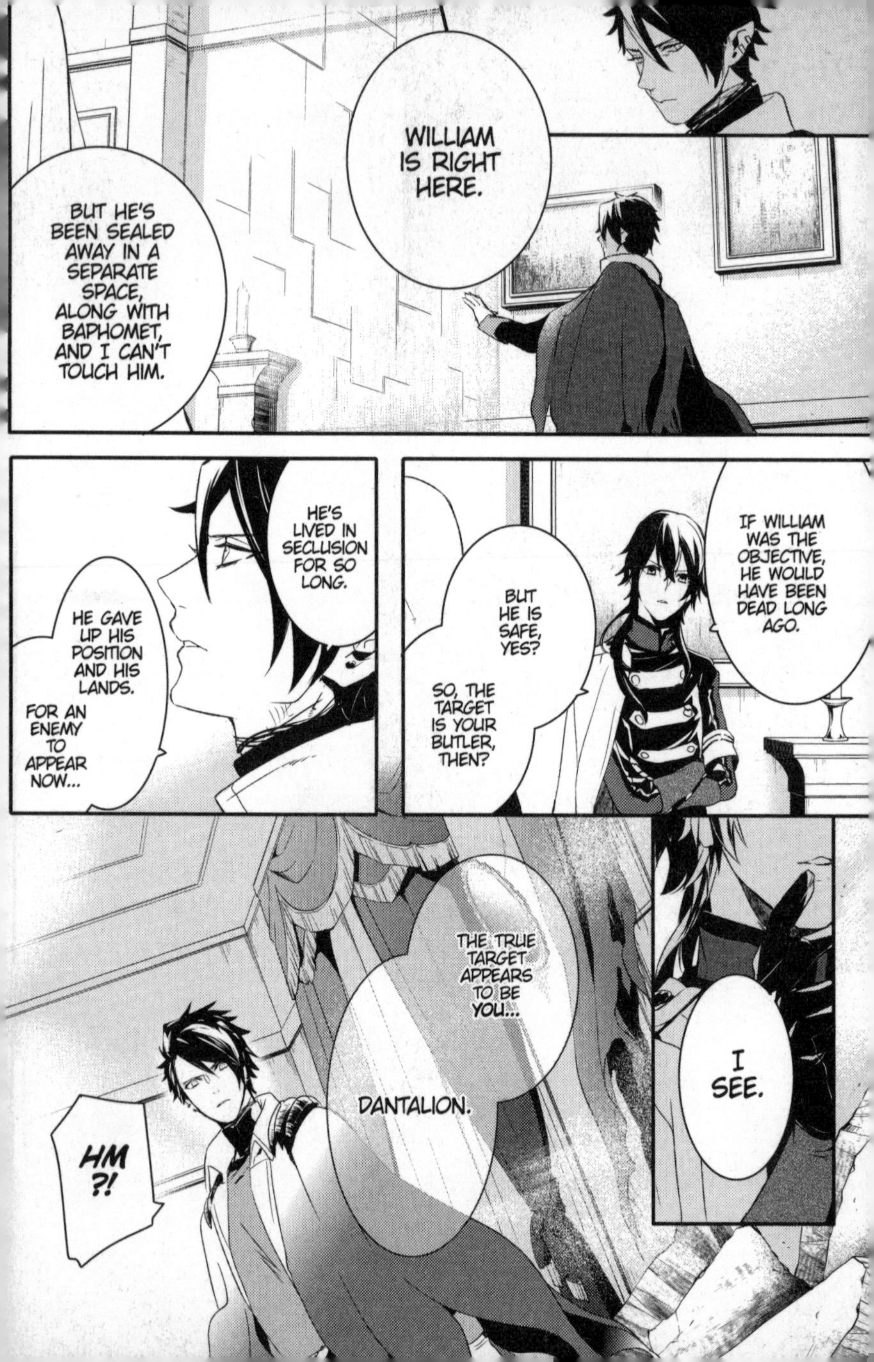
WILLIAM IS RIGHT HERE.
BUT HE'S BEEN SEALED AWAY IN A SEPARATE SPACE, ALONG WITH BAPHOMET, AND I CAN'T TOUCH HIM.
IF WILLIAM WAS THE OBJECTIVE, HE WOULD HAVE BEEN DEAD LONG AGO.
BUT HE IS SAFE, YES?
SO, THE TARGET IS YOUR BUTLER, THEN?
HE'S LIVED IN SECLUSION FOR SO LONG.
HE GAVE UP HIS POSITION AND HIS LANDS.
FOR AN ENEMY TO APPEAR NOW...
I SEE.
THE TRUE TARGET APPEARS TO BE YOU...
DANTALION.
HM ?!

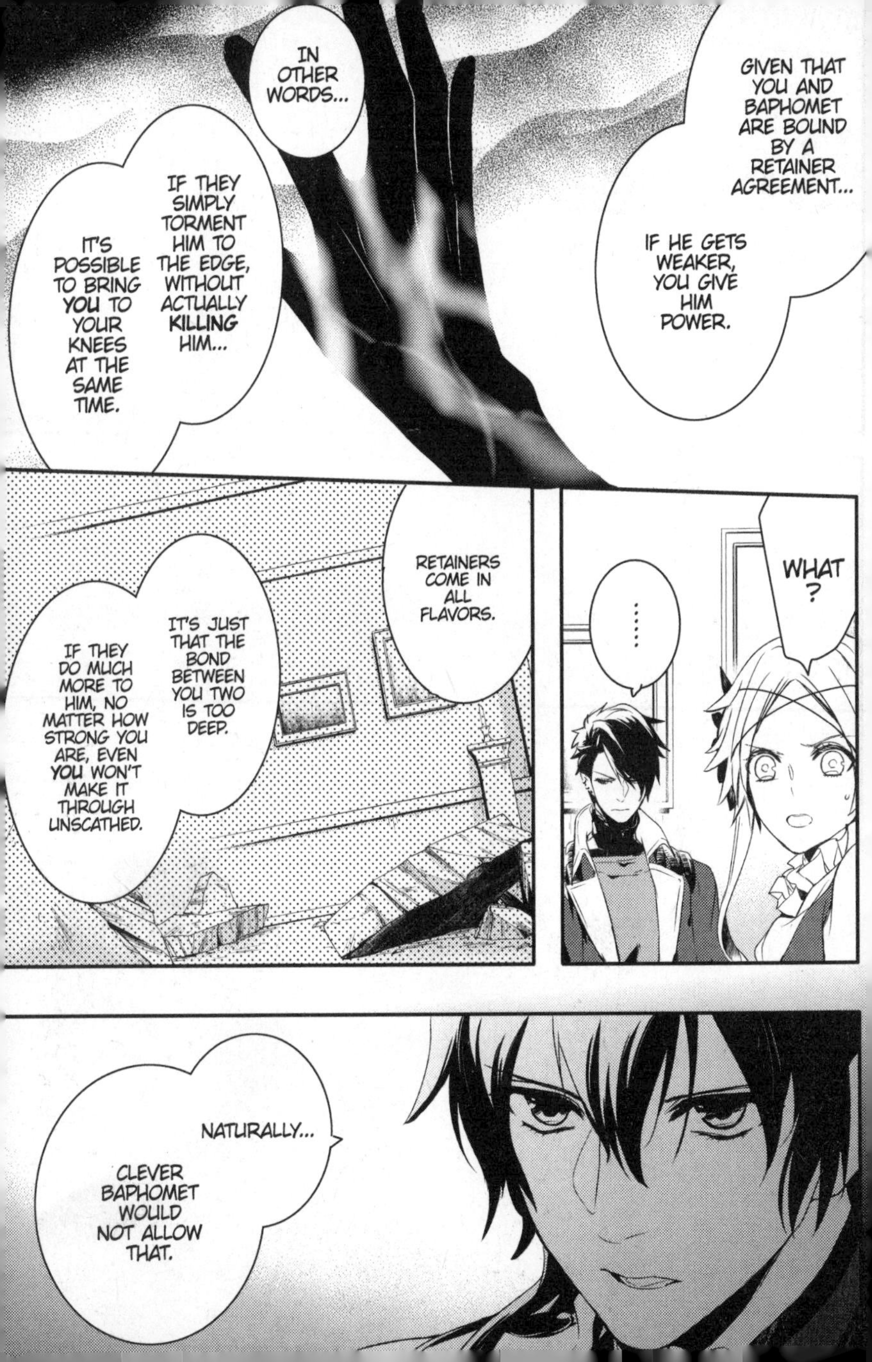
GIVEN THAT YOU AND BAPHOMET ARE BOUND BY A RETAINER AGREEMENT...
IF HE GETS WEAKER, YOU GIVE HIM POWER.
IN OTHER WORDS...
IF THEY SIMPLY TORMENT HIM TO THE EDGE, WITHOUT ACTUALLY **KILLING** HIM...
IT'S POSSIBLE TO BRING **YOU** TO YOUR KNEES AT THE SAME TIME.
WHAT?
......
RETAINERS COME IN ALL FLAVORS.
IT'S JUST THAT THE BOND BETWEEN YOU TWO IS TOO DEEP.
IF THEY DO MUCH MORE TO HIM, NO MATTER HOW STRONG YOU ARE, EVEN **YOU** WON'T MAKE IT THROUGH UNSCATHED.
NATURALLY...
CLEVER BAPHOMET WOULD NOT ALLOW THAT.

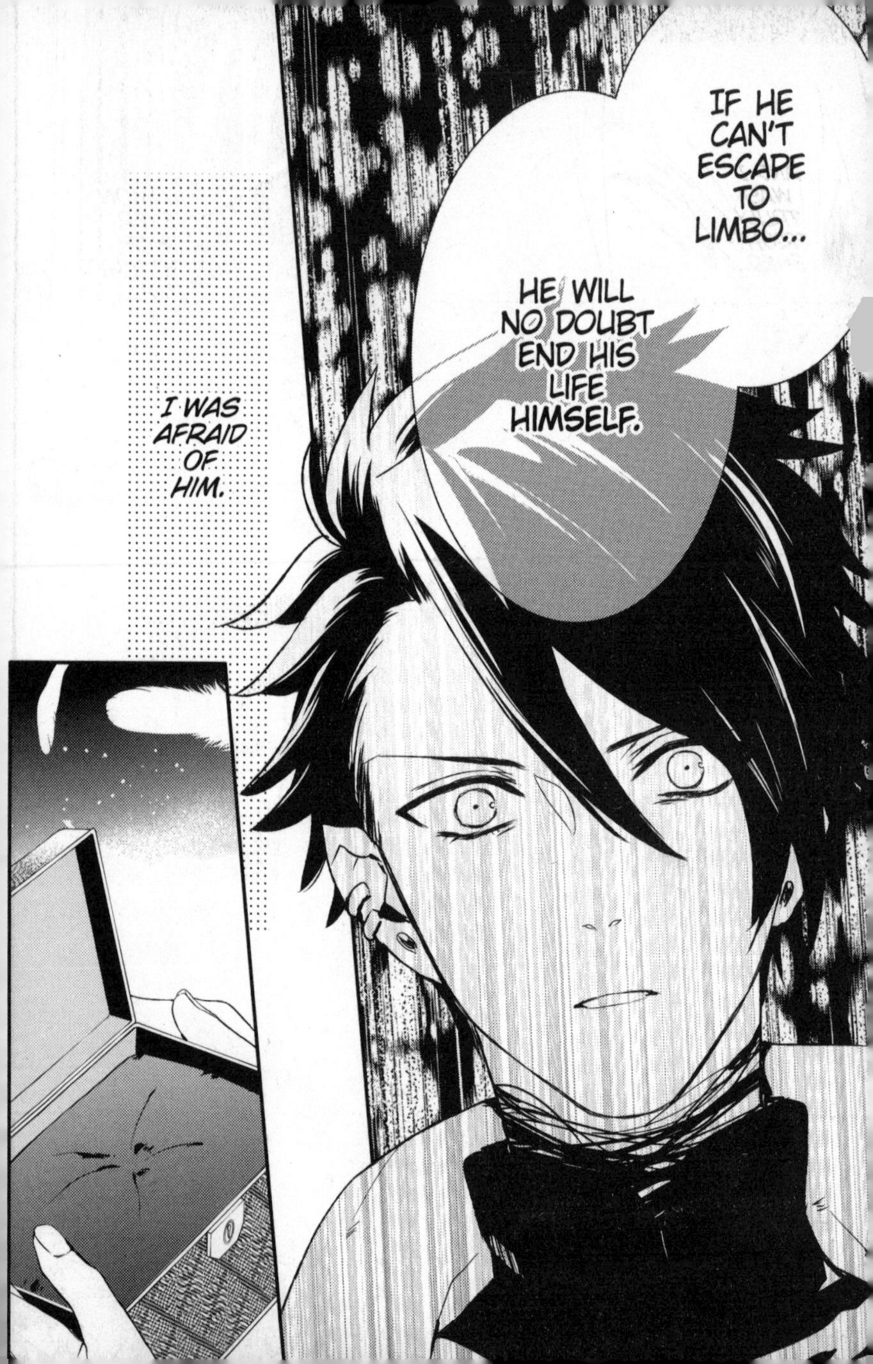
IF HE CAN'T ESCAPE TO LIMBO...
HE WILL NO DOUBT END HIS LIFE HIMSELF.
I WAS AFRAID OF HIM.

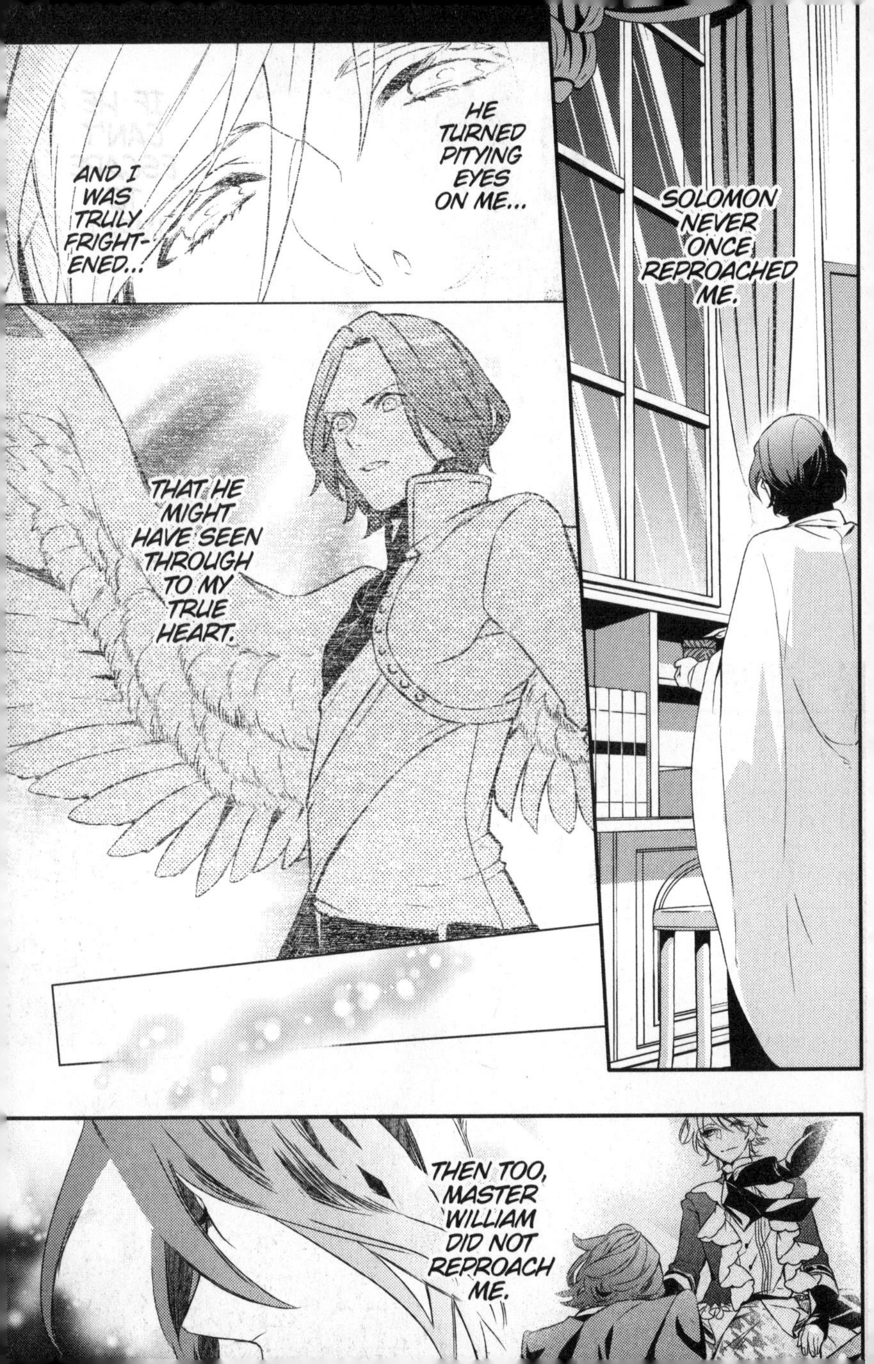
SOLOMON NEVER ONCE REPROACHED ME.
HE TURNED PITYING EYES ON ME...
AND I WAS TRULY FRIGHT-ENED...
THAT HE MIGHT HAVE SEEN THROUGH TO MY TRUE HEART.
THEN TOO, MASTER WILLIAM DID NOT REPROACH ME.

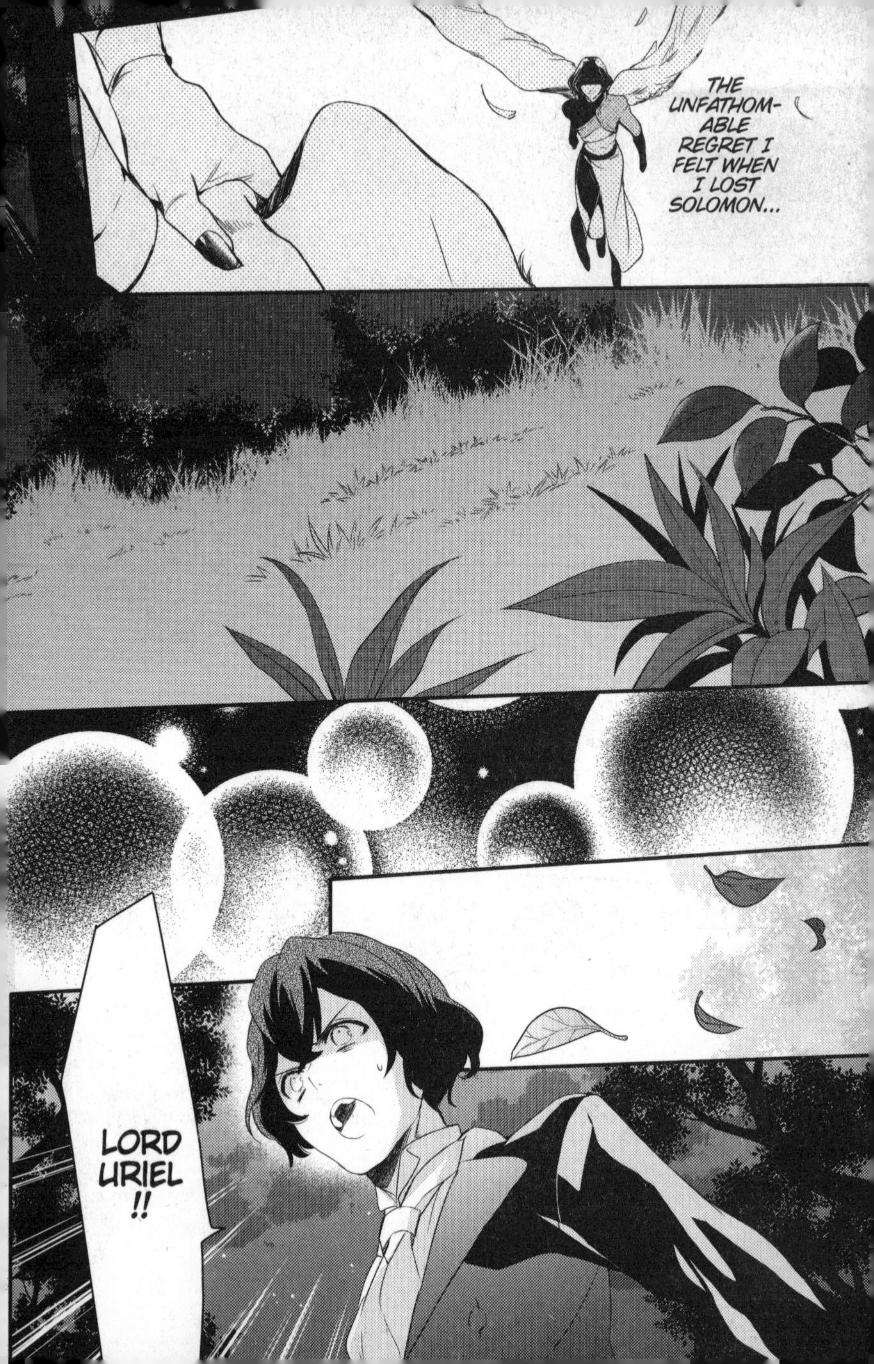
THE UNFATHOMABLE REGRET I FELT WHEN I LOST SOLOMON...
LORD URIEL !!

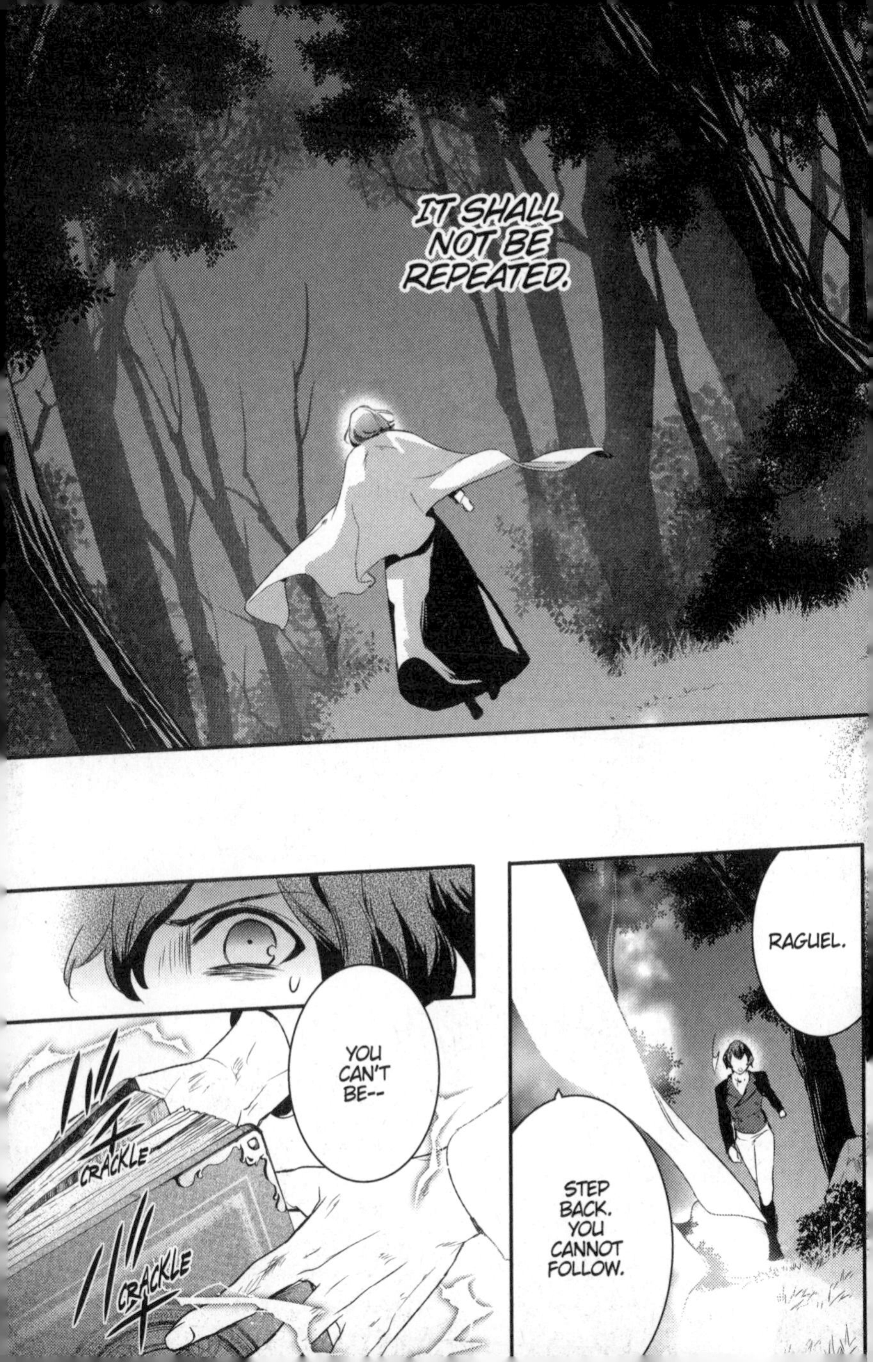
IT SHALL NOT BE REPEATED.
RAGUEL.
STEP BACK. YOU CANNOT FOLLOW.
YOU CAN'T BE--
CRACKLE
CRACKLE

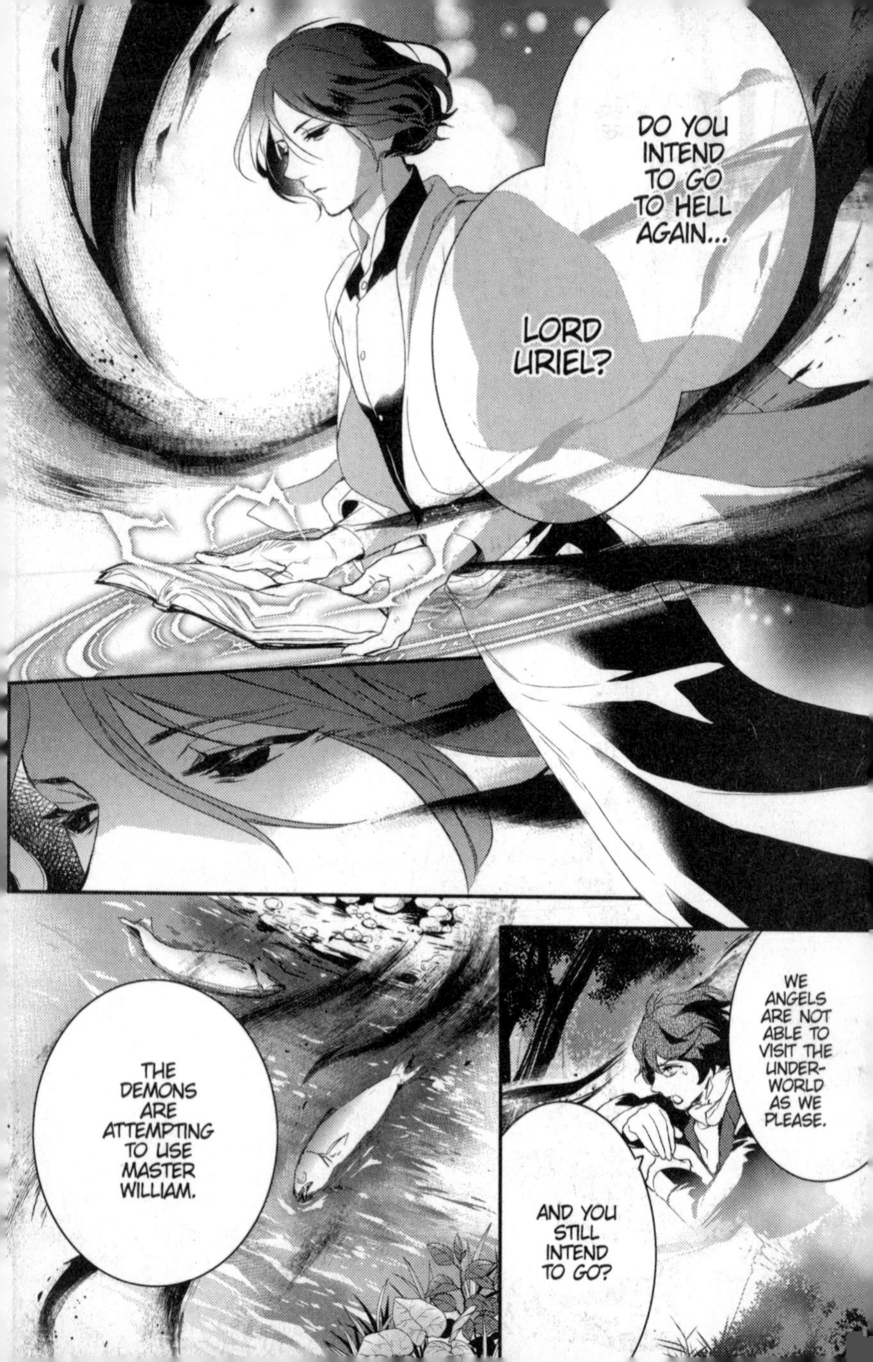
DO YOU INTEND TO GO TO HELL AGAIN...
LORD URIEL?
WE ANGELS ARE NOT ABLE TO VISIT THE UNDER-WORLD AS WE PLEASE.
AND YOU STILL INTEND TO GO?
THE DEMONS ARE ATTEMPTING TO USE MASTER WILLIAM.

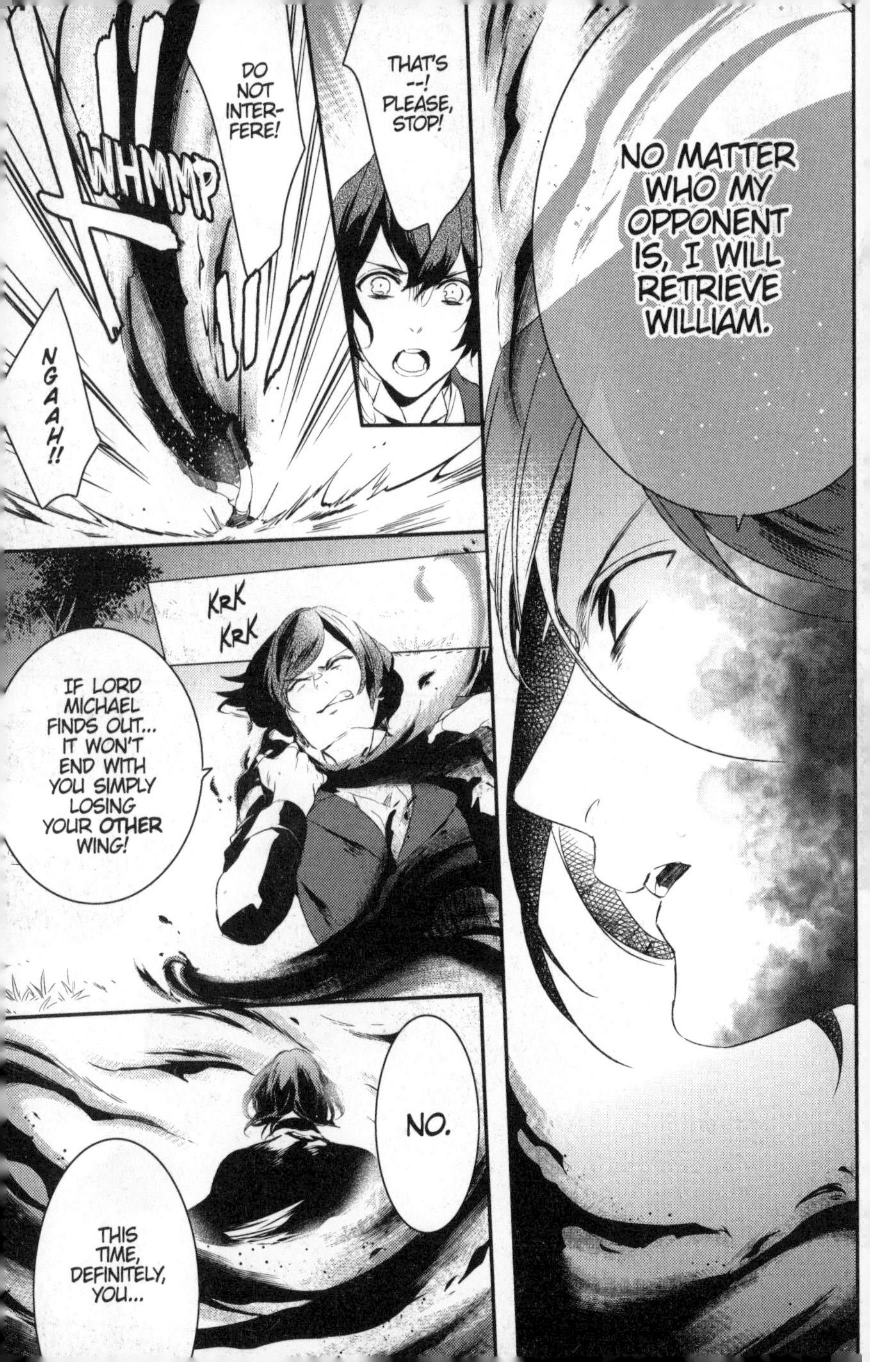
NO MATTER WHO MY OPPONENT IS, I WILL RETRIEVE WILLIAM.
THAT'S --! PLEASE, STOP!
DO NOT INTERFERE!
WHMMP
NGAAH!!
KRK KRK
IF LORD MICHAEL FINDS OUT... IT WON'T END WITH YOU SIMPLY LOSING YOUR OTHER WING!
NO.
THIS TIME, DEFINITELY, YOU...

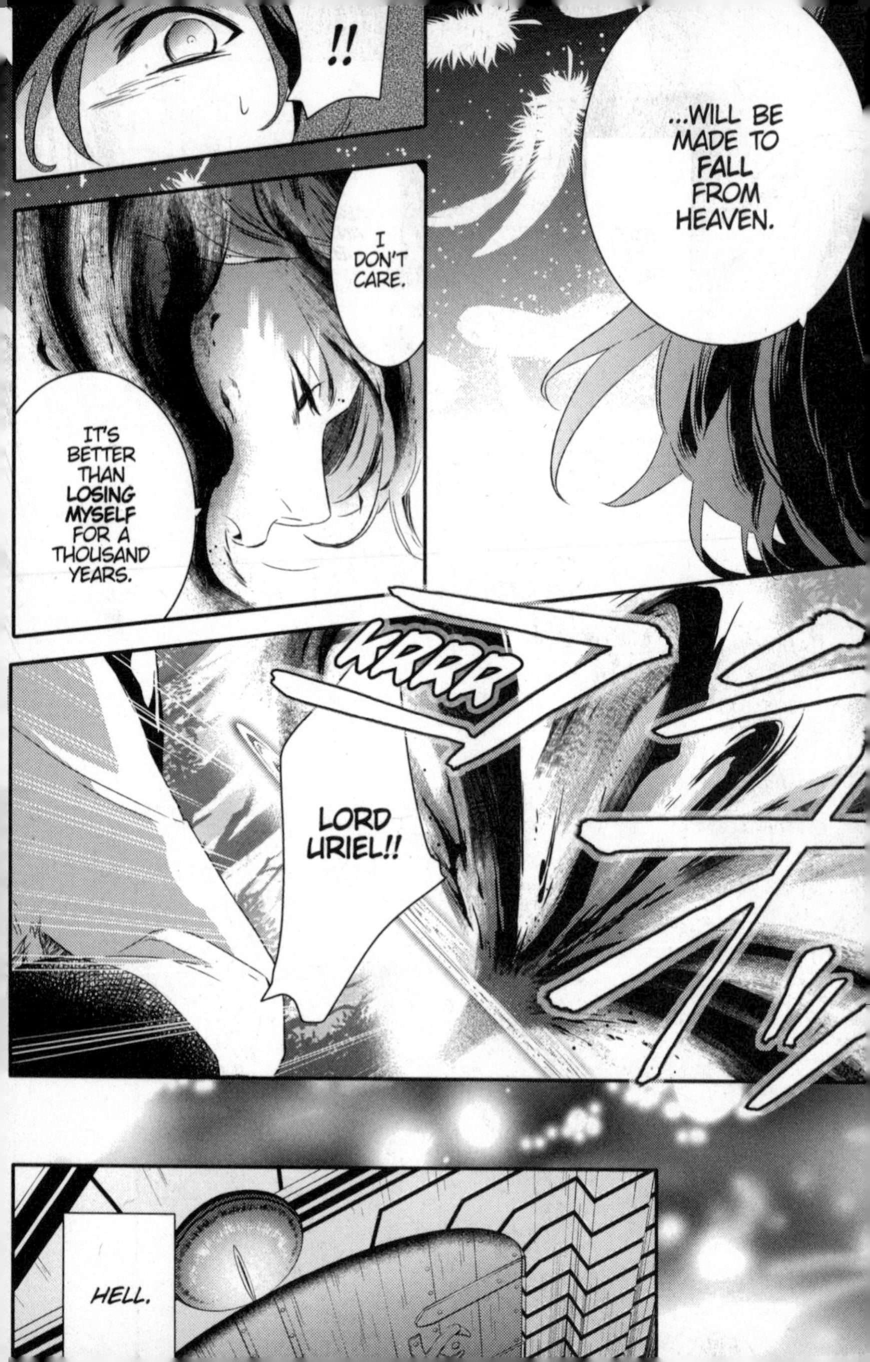
...WILL BE MADE TO FALL FROM HEAVEN.
!!
I DON'T CARE.
IT'S BETTER THAN LOSING MYSELF FOR A THOUSAND YEARS.
KRRR
LORD URIEL!!
HELL.

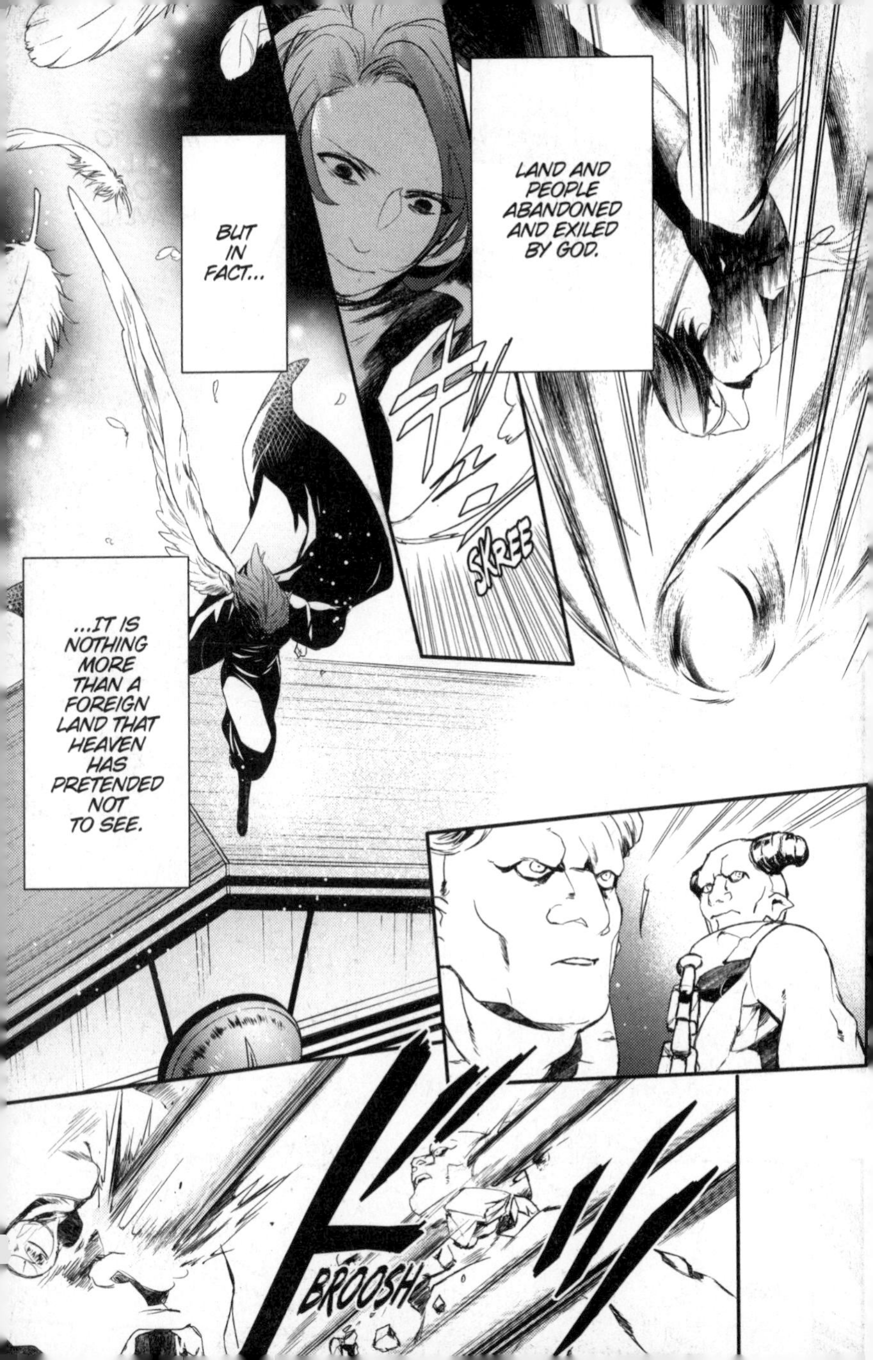
LAND AND PEOPLE ABANDONED AND EXILED BY GOD.
BUT IN FACT...
SKREE
...IT IS NOTHING MORE THAN A FOREIGN LAND THAT HEAVEN HAS PRETENDED NOT TO SEE.
BROOSH

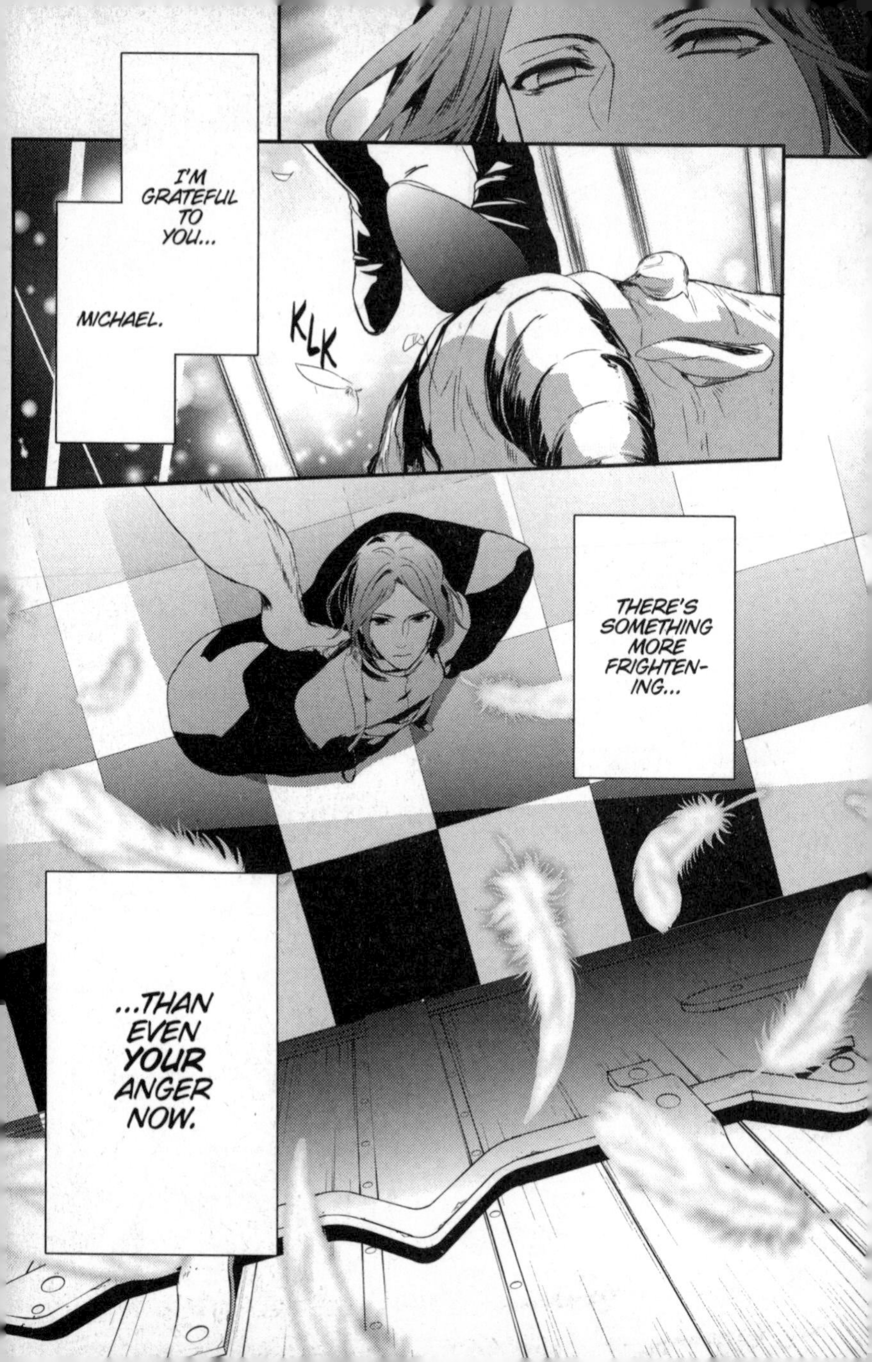
I'M GRATEFUL TO YOU...
MICHAEL.
KLK
THERE'S SOMETHING MORE FRIGHTEN-ING...
...THAN EVEN YOUR ANGER NOW.

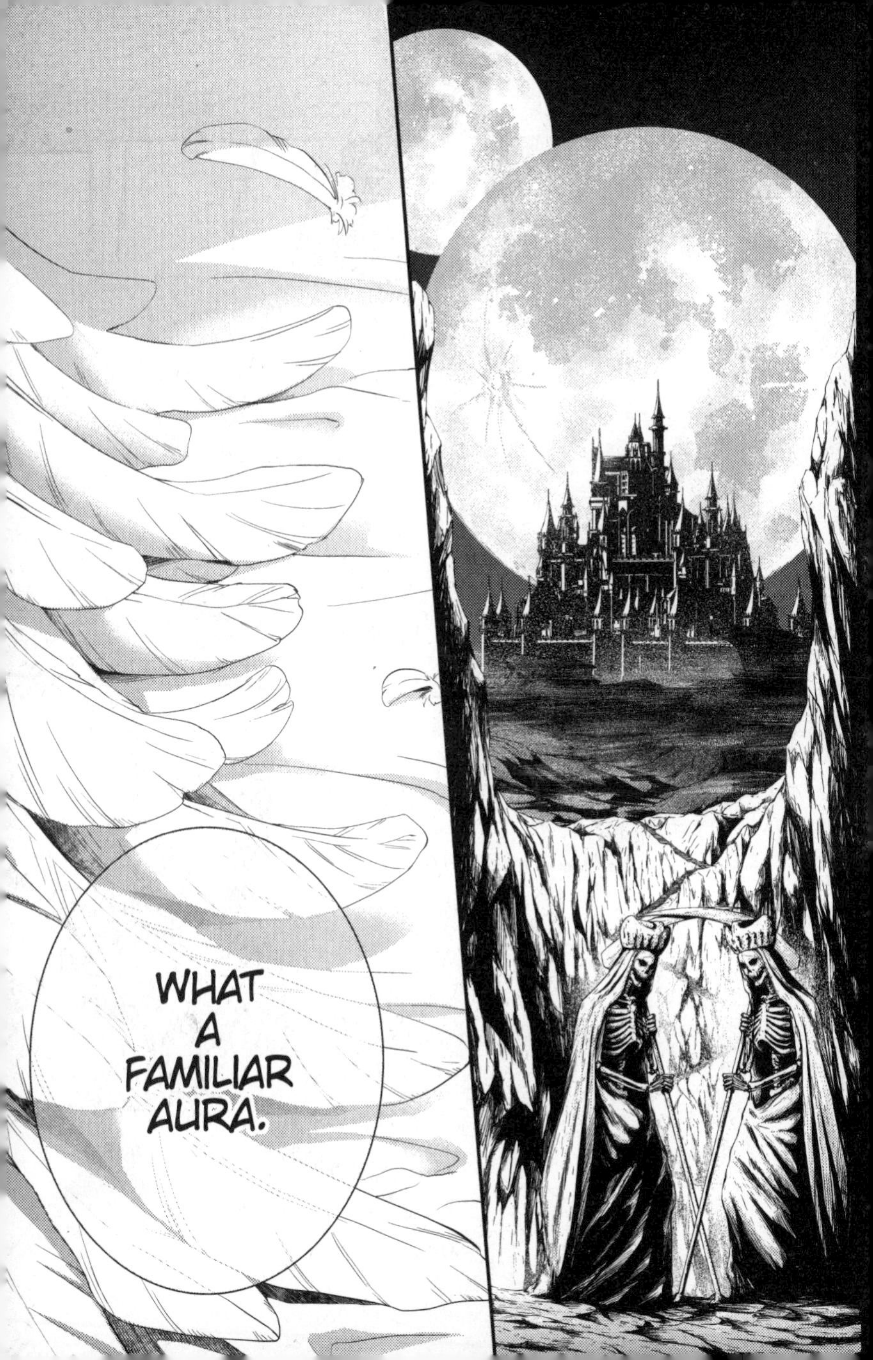
WHAT A FAMILIAR AURA.

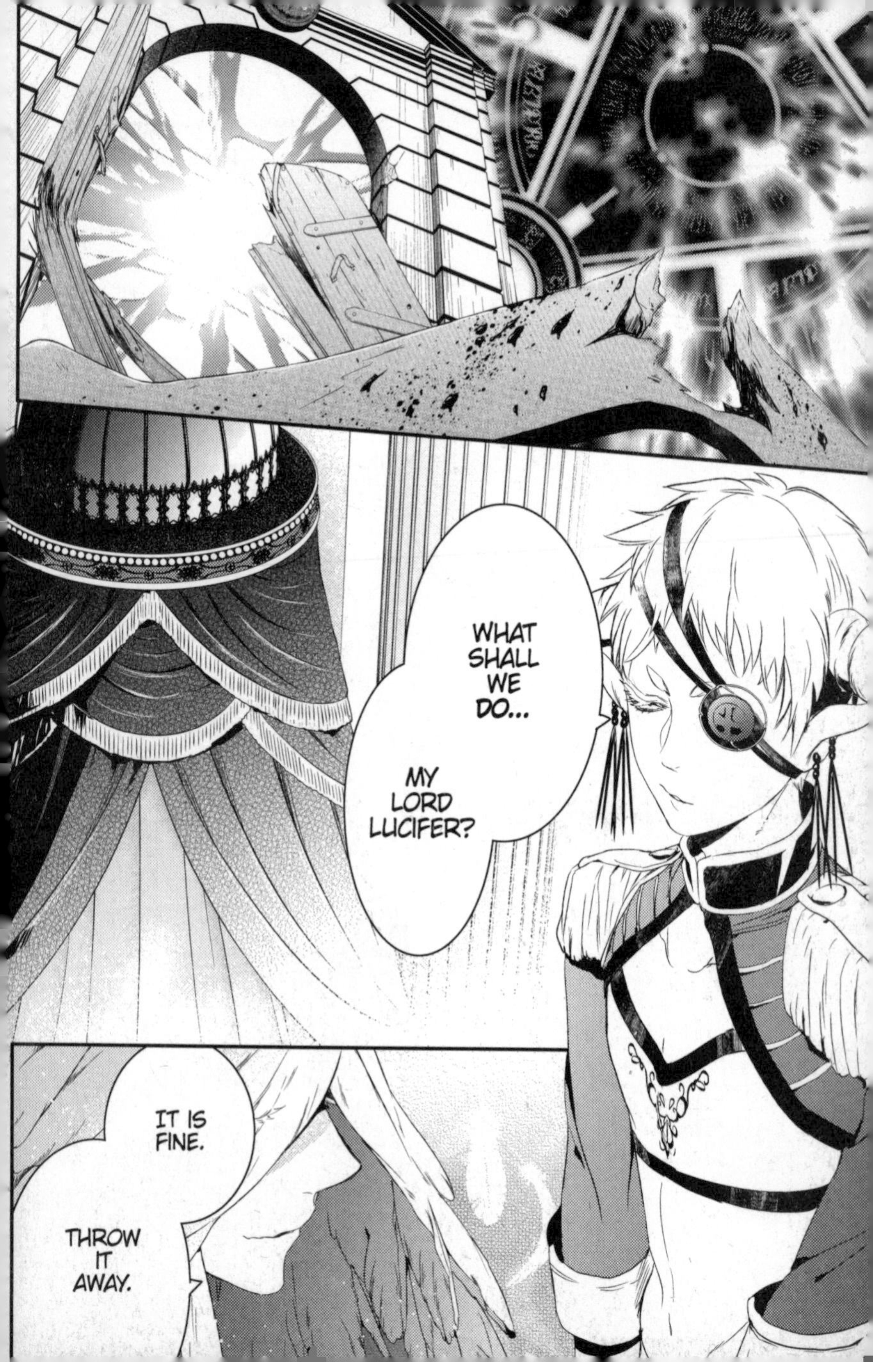

WHAT SHALL WE DO...
MY LORD LUCIFER?
IT IS FINE.
THROW IT AWAY.

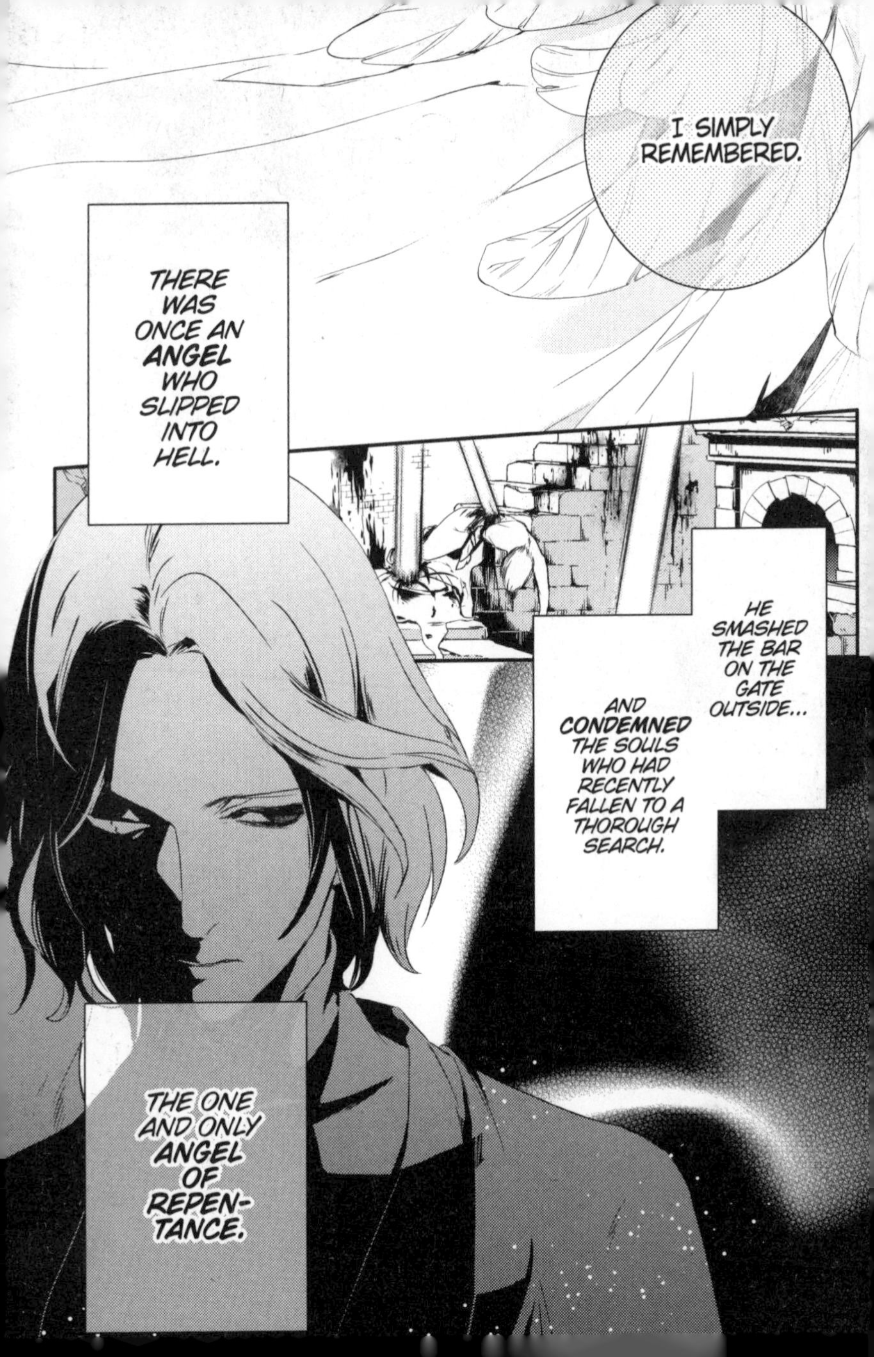
I SIMPLY REMEMBERED.
THERE WAS ONCE AN ANGEL WHO SLIPPED INTO HELL.
HE SMASHED THE BAR ON THE GATE OUTSIDE...
AND CONDEMNED THE SOULS WHO HAD RECENTLY FALLEN TO A THOROUGH SEARCH.
THE ONE AND ONLY ANGEL OF REPENTANCE.

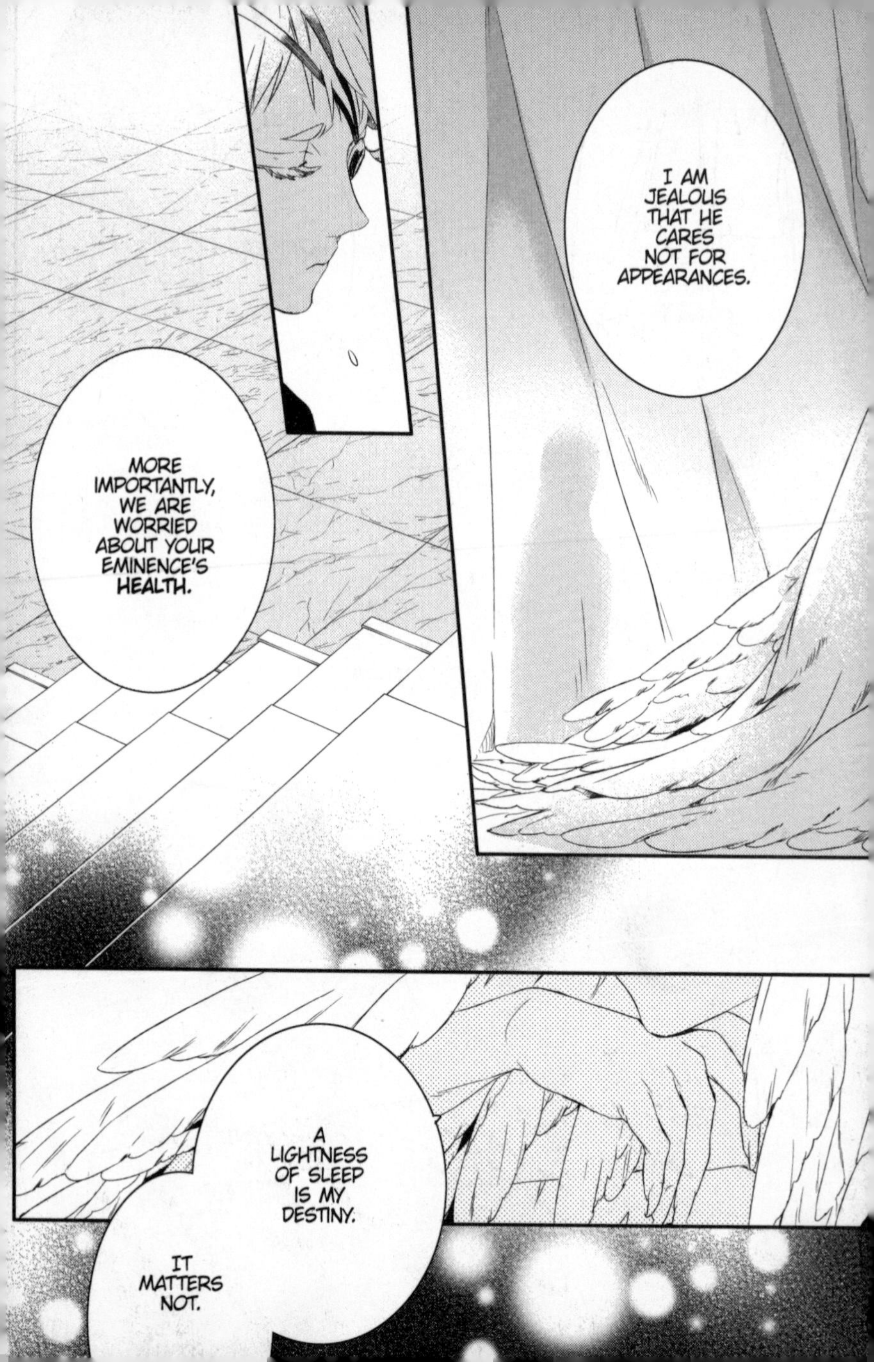
I AM JEALOUS THAT HE CARES NOT FOR APPEARANCES.
MORE IMPORTANTLY, WE ARE WORRIED ABOUT YOUR EMINENCE'S HEALTH.
A LIGHTNESS OF SLEEP IS MY DESTINY.
IT MATTERS NOT.

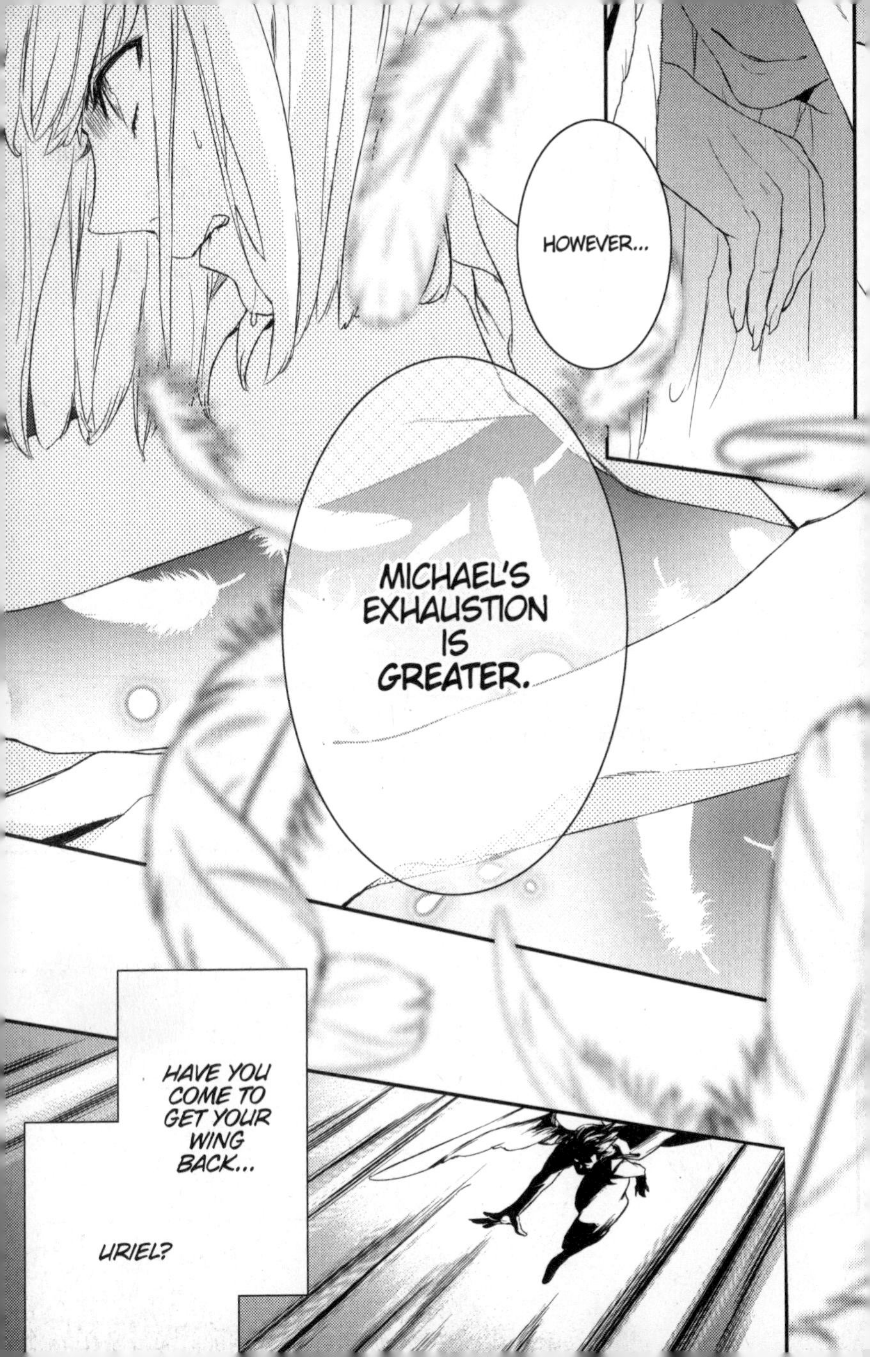
HOWEVER...
MICHAEL'S EXHAUSTION IS GREATER.
HAVE YOU COME TO GET YOUR WING BACK...
URIEL?

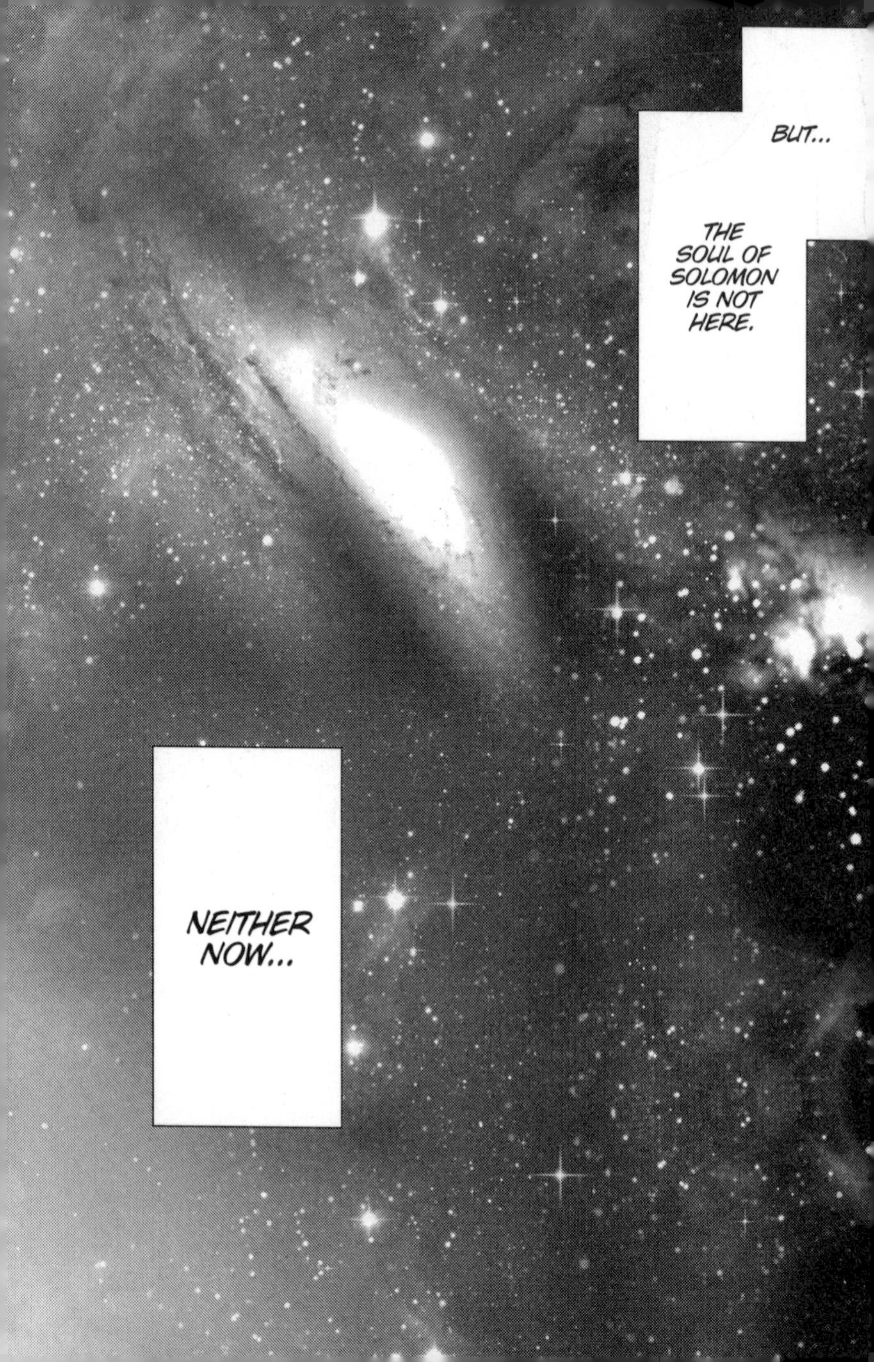
BUT...
THE SOUL OF SOLOMON IS NOT HERE.
NEITHER NOW...

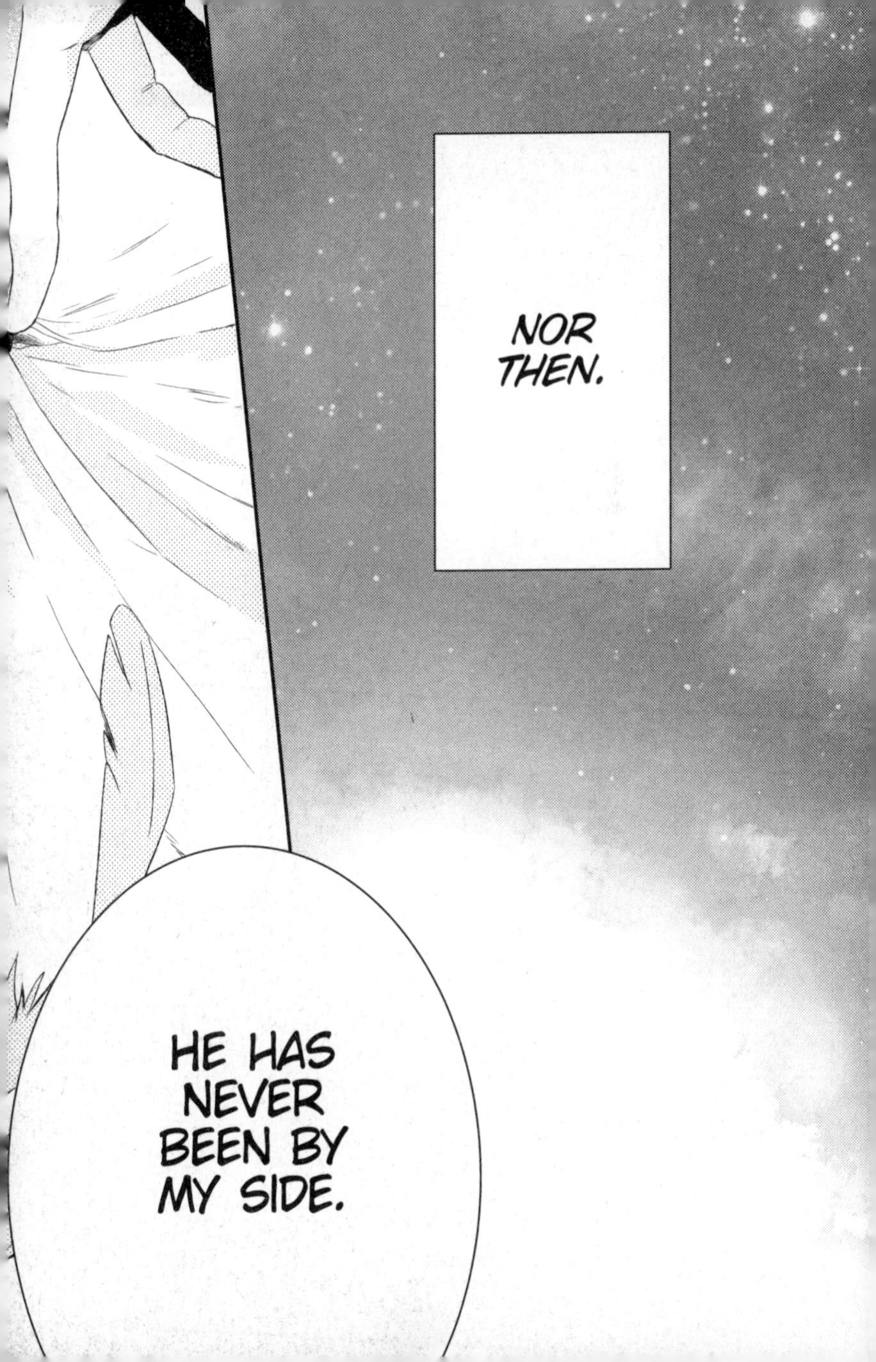
NOR THEN.
HE HAS NEVER BEEN BY MY SIDE.

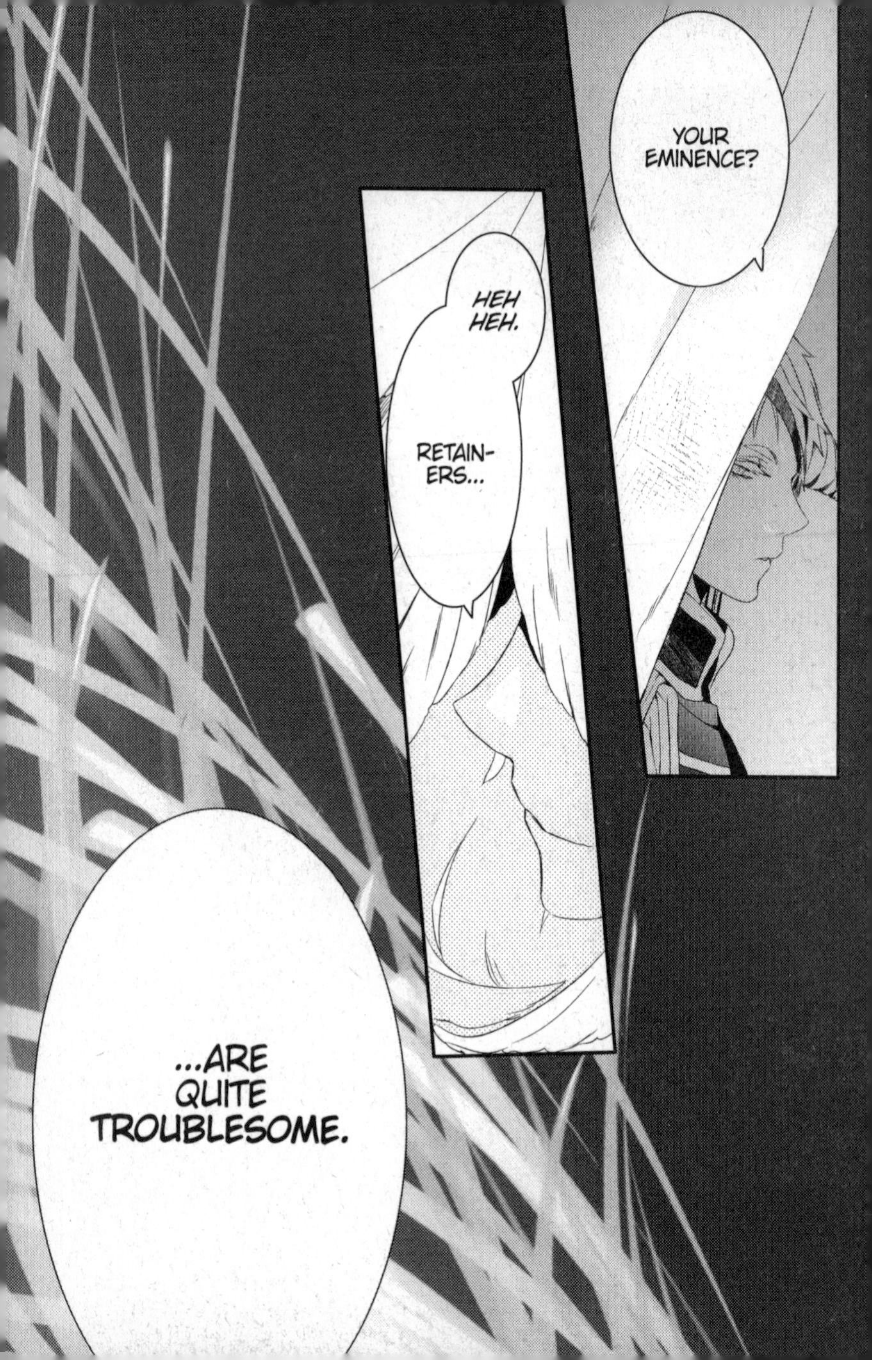
YOUR EMINENCE?
HEH HEH.
RETAIN-ERS...
...ARE QUITE TROUBLESOME.

魔界王子

devils and realist

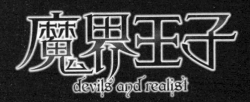

SHOCK

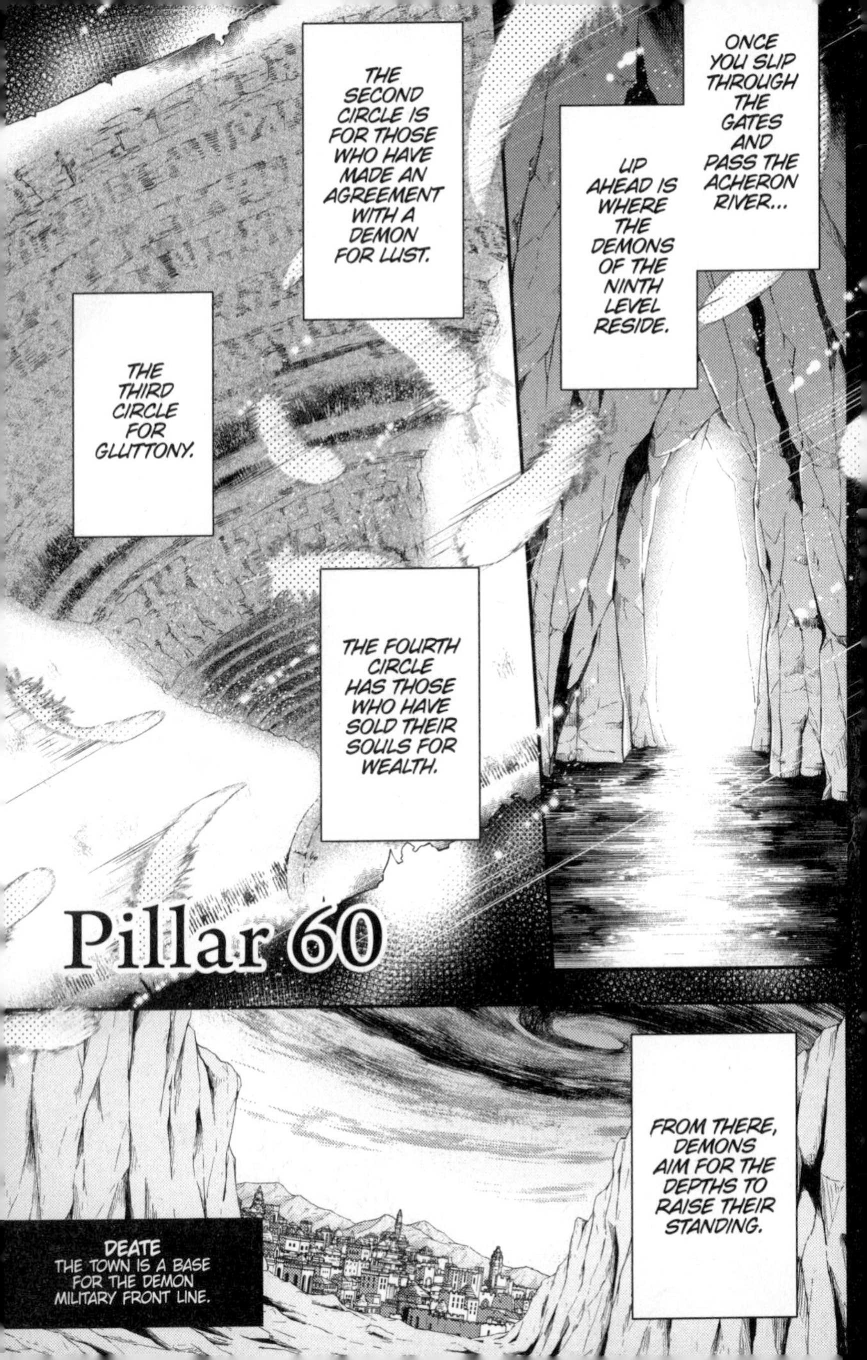
ONCE YOU SLIP THROUGH THE GATES AND PASS THE ACHERON RIVER...
UP AHEAD IS WHERE THE DEMONS OF THE NINTH LEVEL RESIDE.
THE SECOND CIRCLE IS FOR THOSE WHO HAVE MADE AN AGREEMENT WITH A DEMON FOR LUST.
THE THIRD CIRCLE FOR GLUTTONY.
THE FOURTH CIRCLE HAS THOSE WHO HAVE SOLD THEIR SOULS FOR WEALTH.
Pillar 60
FROM THERE, DEMONS AIM FOR THE DEPTHS TO RAISE THEIR STANDING.
DEATE
THE TOWN IS A BASE FOR THE DEMON MILITARY FRONT LINE.

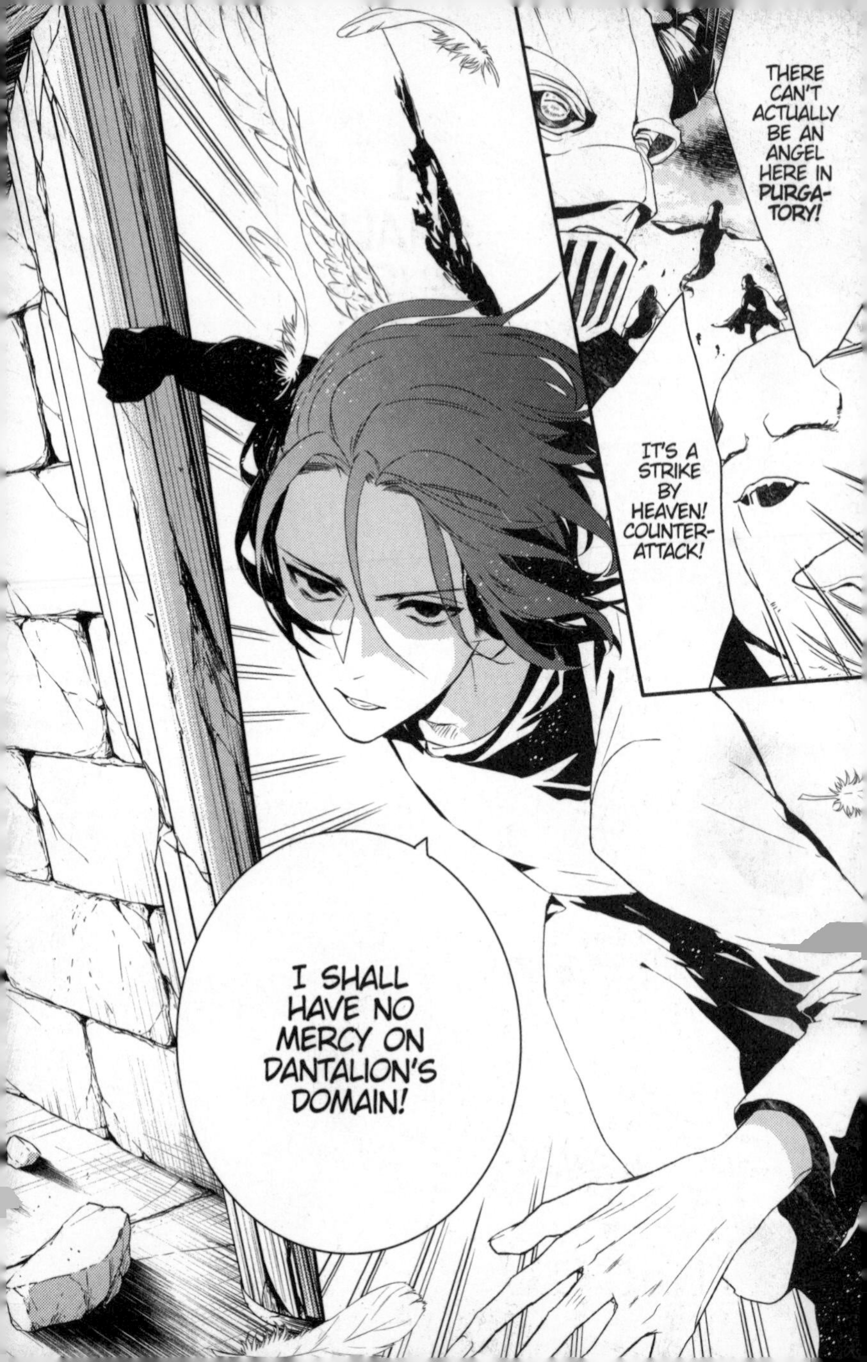
THERE CAN'T ACTUALLY BE AN ANGEL HERE IN PURGA-TORY!
IT'S A STRIKE BY HEAVEN! COUNTER-ATTACK!
I SHALL HAVE NO MERCY ON DANTALION'S DOMAIN!

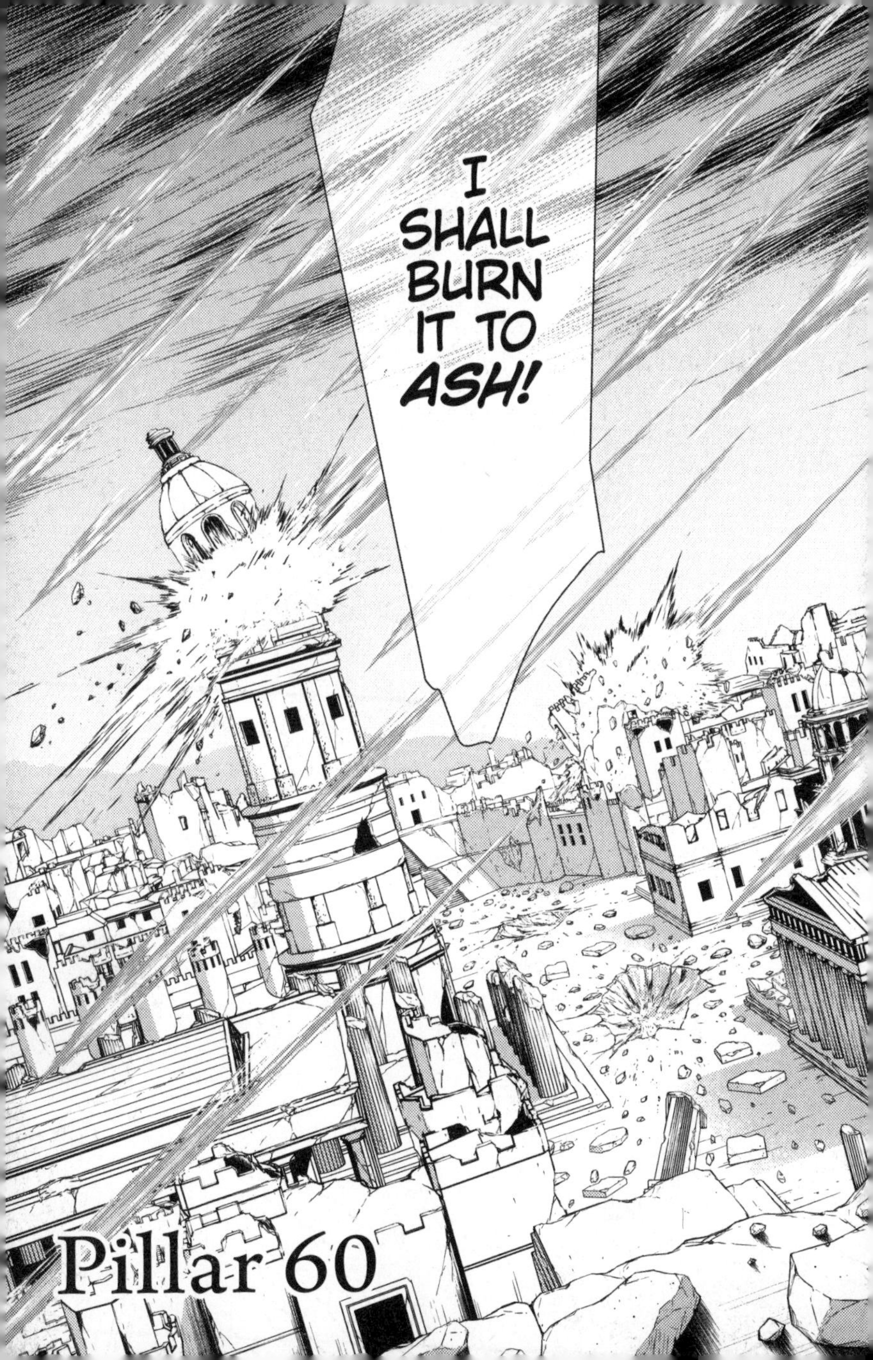
I SHALL BURN IT TO ASH!
Pillar 60

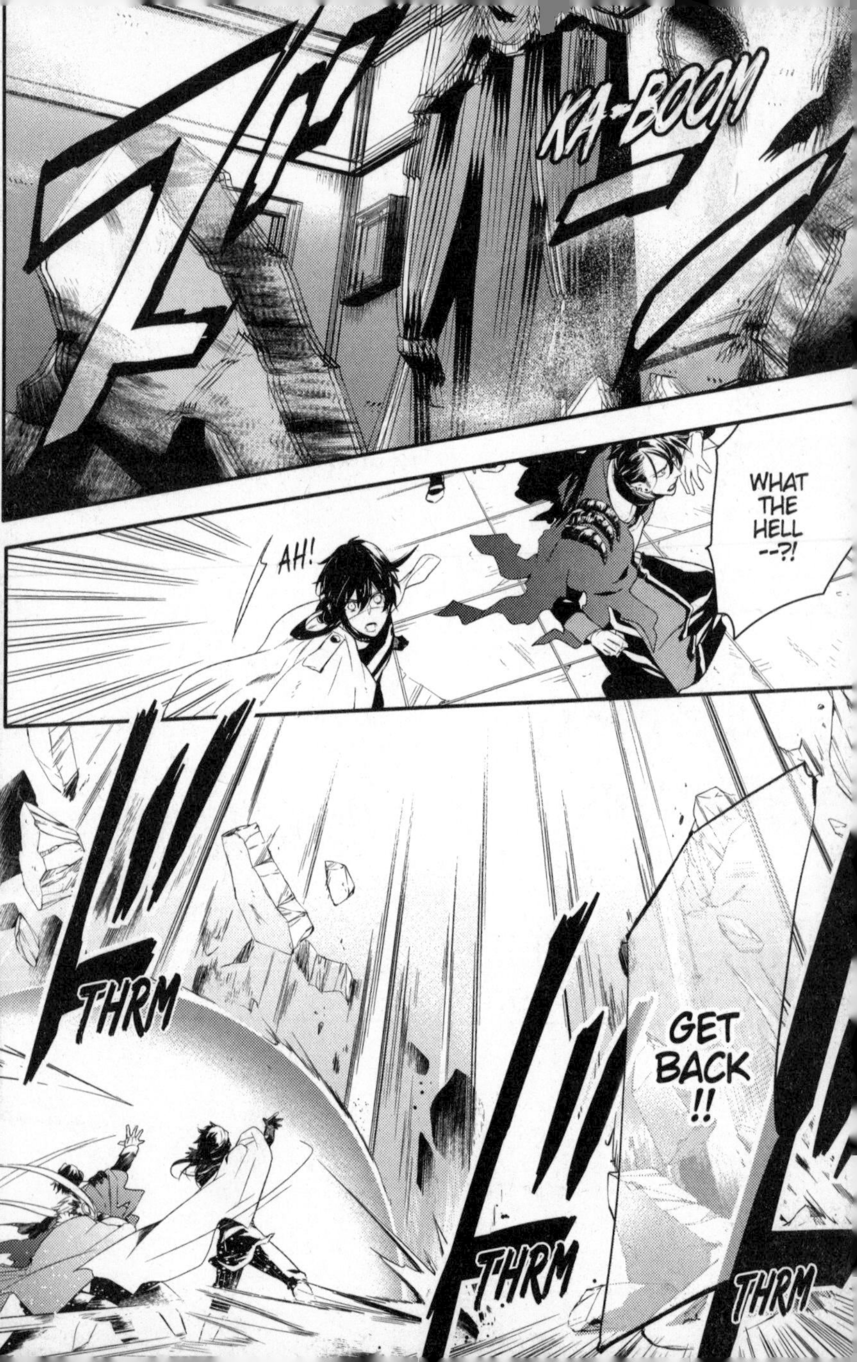
KA-BOOM
WHAT THE HELL --?!
AH!
GET BACK !!
THRM
THRM
THRM

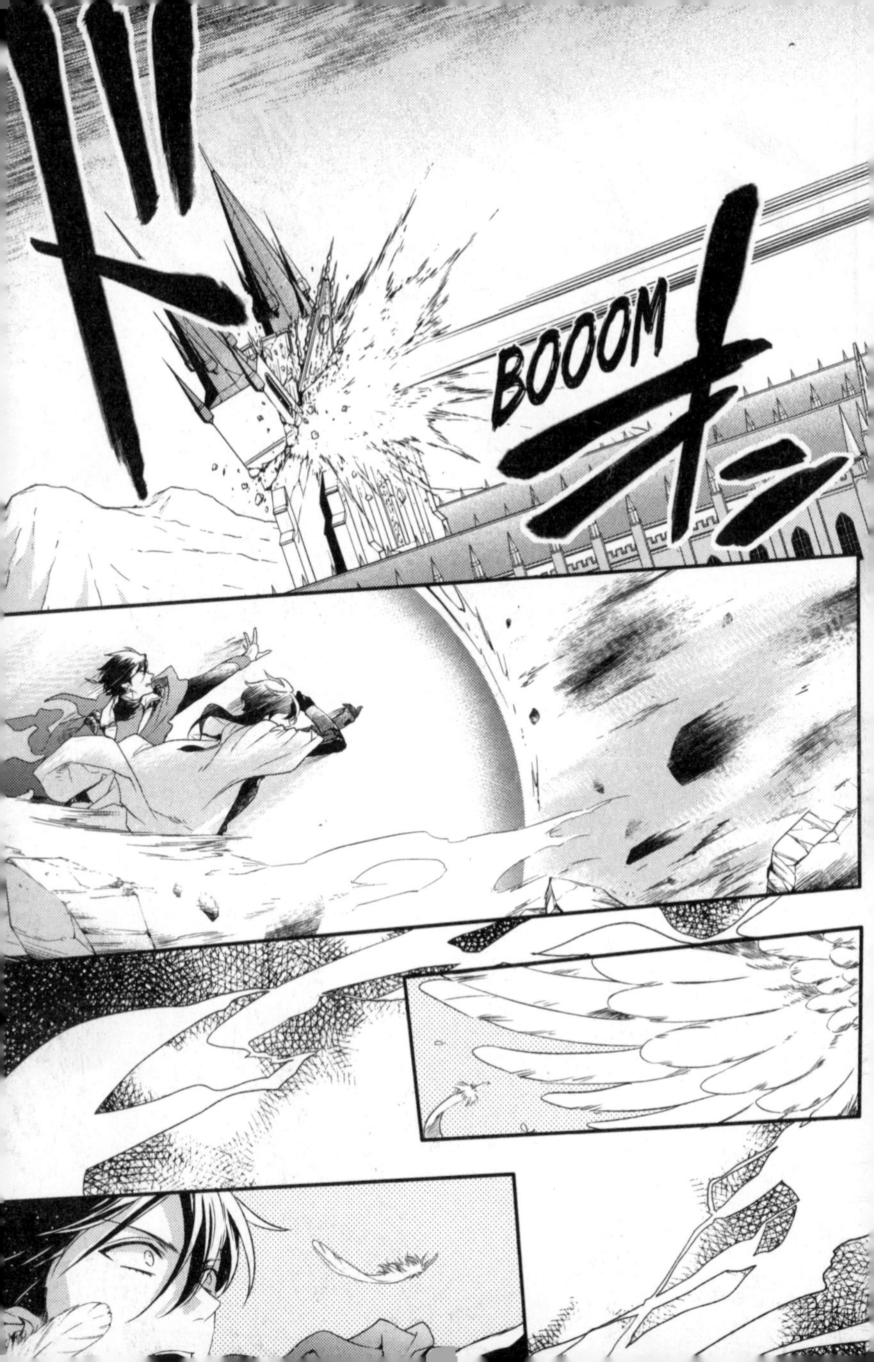
BOOOM

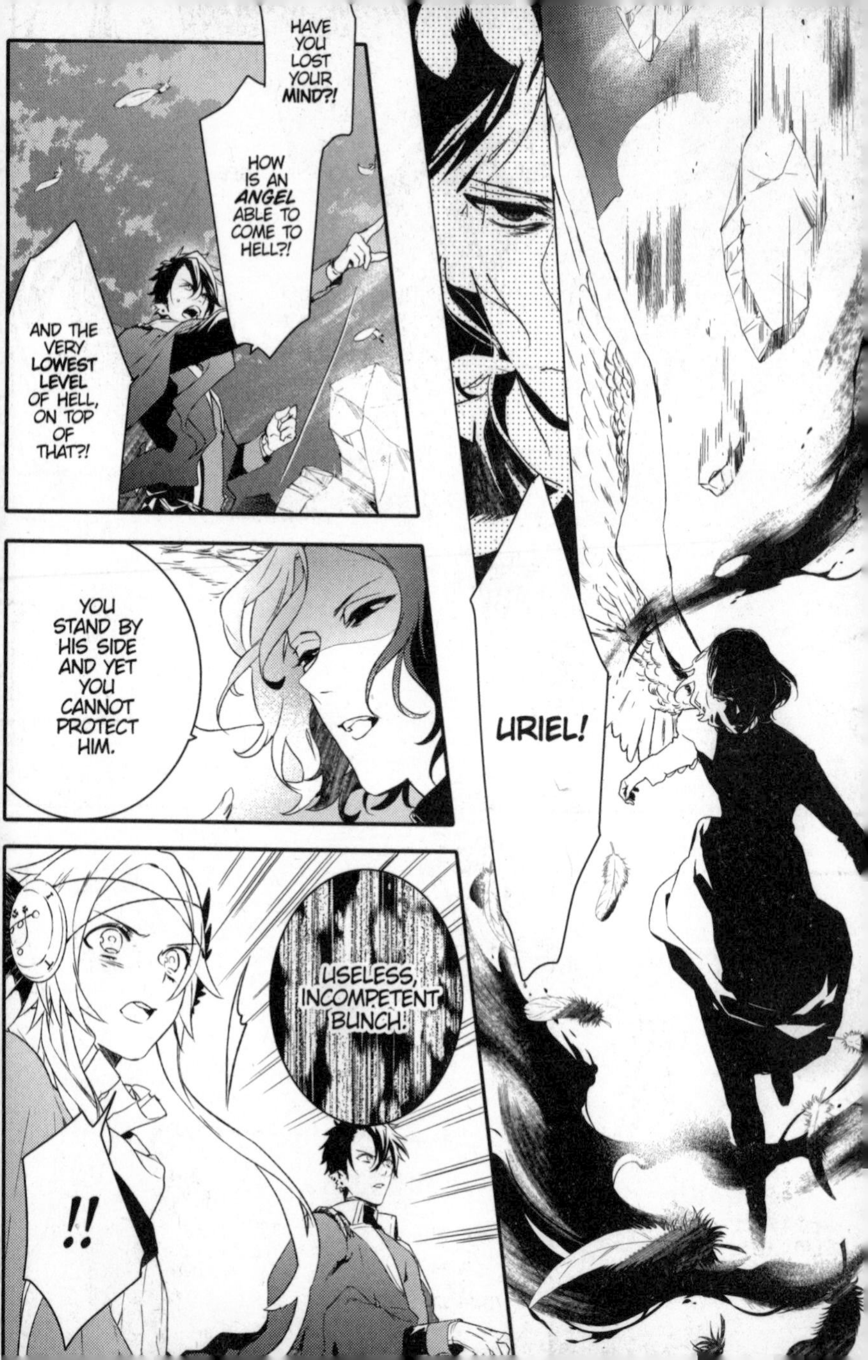
URIEL!
HAVE YOU LOST YOUR MIND?!
HOW IS AN ANGEL ABLE TO COME TO HELL?!
AND THE VERY LOWEST LEVEL OF HELL, ON TOP OF THAT?!
YOU STAND BY HIS SIDE AND YET YOU CANNOT PROTECT HIM.
USELESS, INCOMPETENT BUNCH.
!!

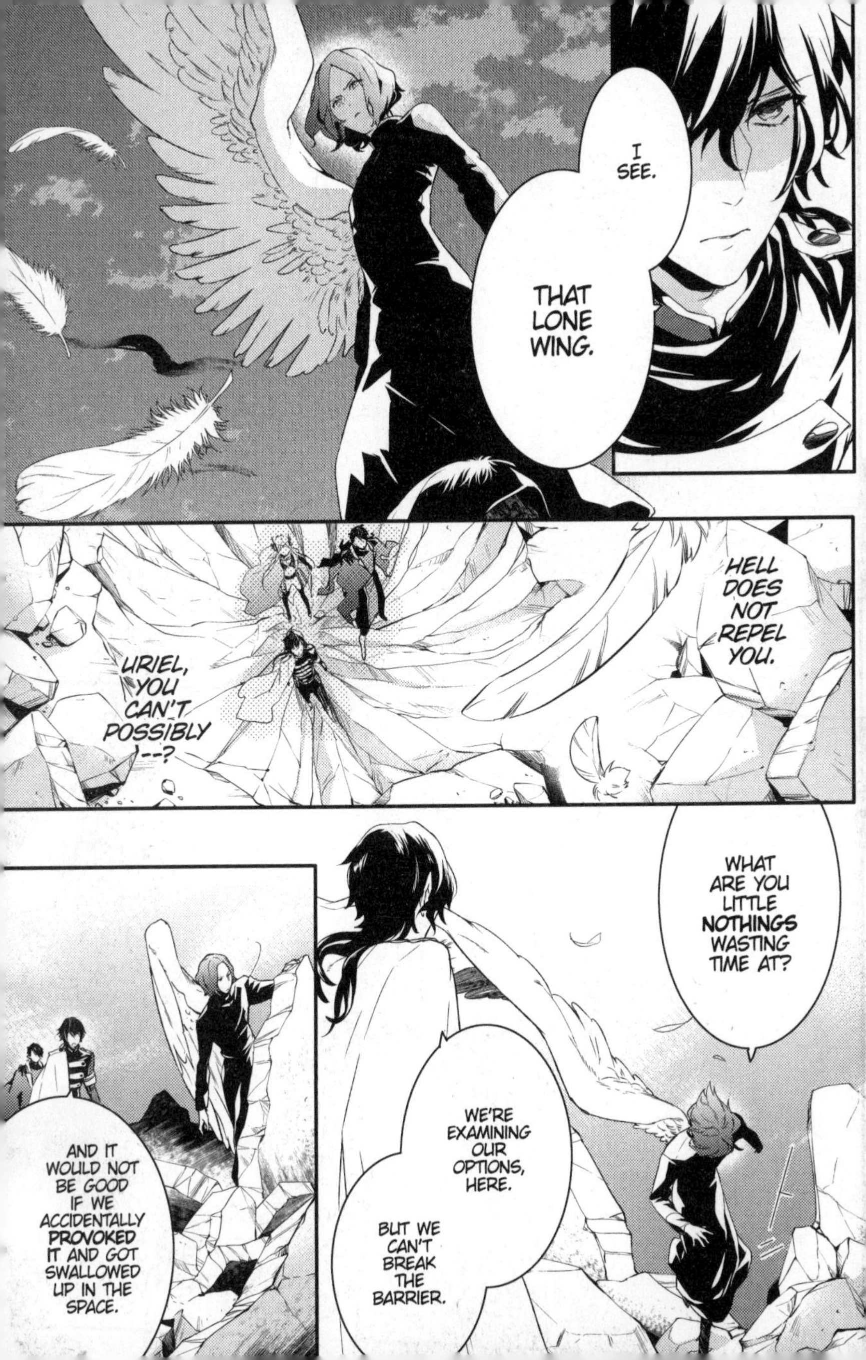
I SEE.
THAT LONE WING.
HELL DOES NOT REPEL YOU.
URIEL, YOU CAN'T POSSIBLY --?
WHAT ARE YOU LITTLE **NOTHINGS** WASTING TIME AT?
WE'RE EXAMINING OUR OPTIONS, HERE.
BUT WE CAN'T BREAK THE BARRIER.
AND IT WOULD NOT BE GOOD IF WE ACCIDENTALLY **PROVOKED** IT AND GOT SWALLOWED UP IN THE SPACE.

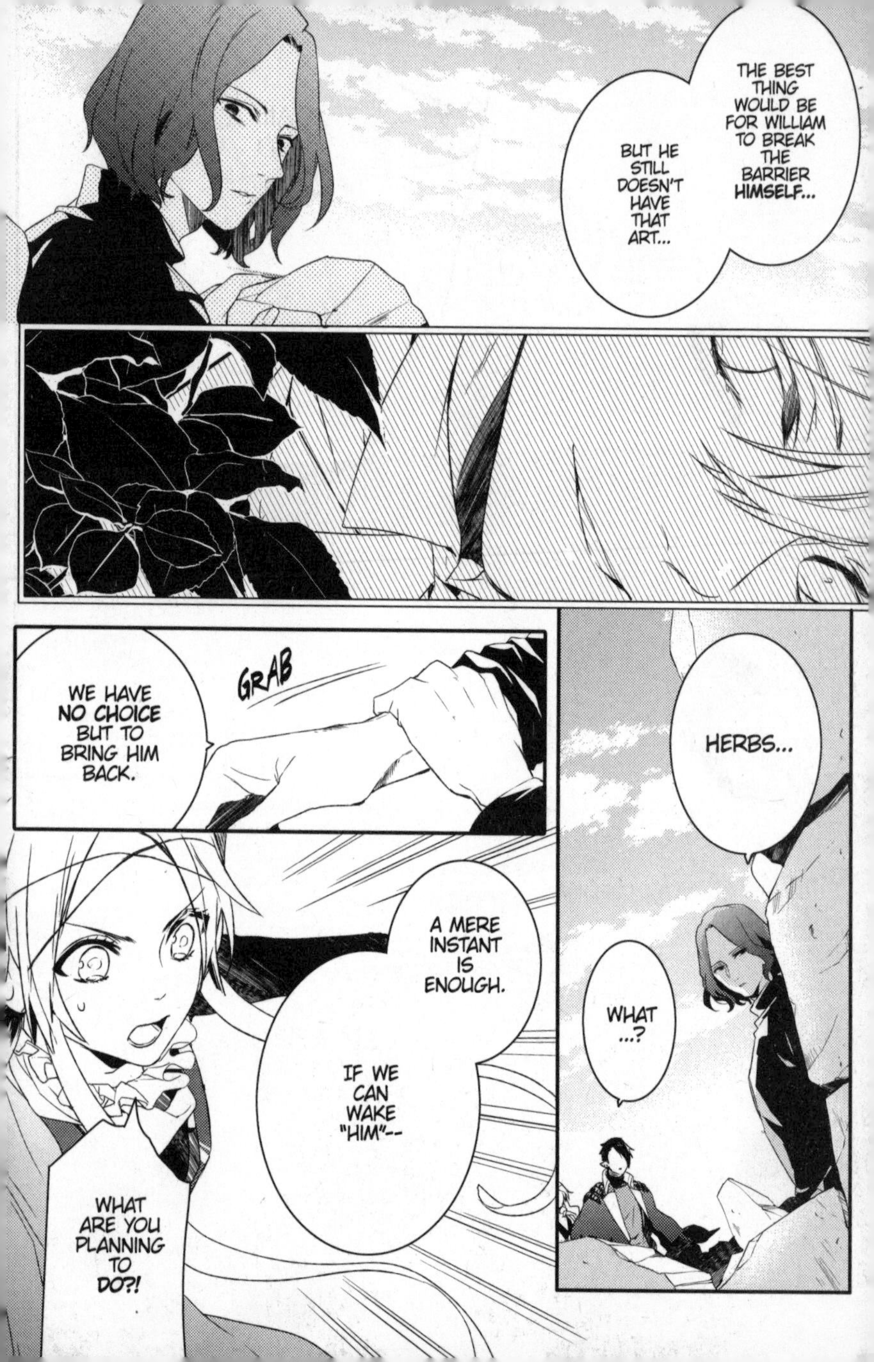
THE BEST THING WOULD BE FOR WILLIAM TO BREAK THE BARRIER HIMSELF...
BUT HE STILL DOESN'T HAVE THAT ART...
HERBS...
WHAT ...?
GRAB
WE HAVE NO CHOICE BUT TO BRING HIM BACK.
A MERE INSTANT IS ENOUGH.
IF WE CAN WAKE "HIM"--
WHAT ARE YOU PLANNING TO DO?!

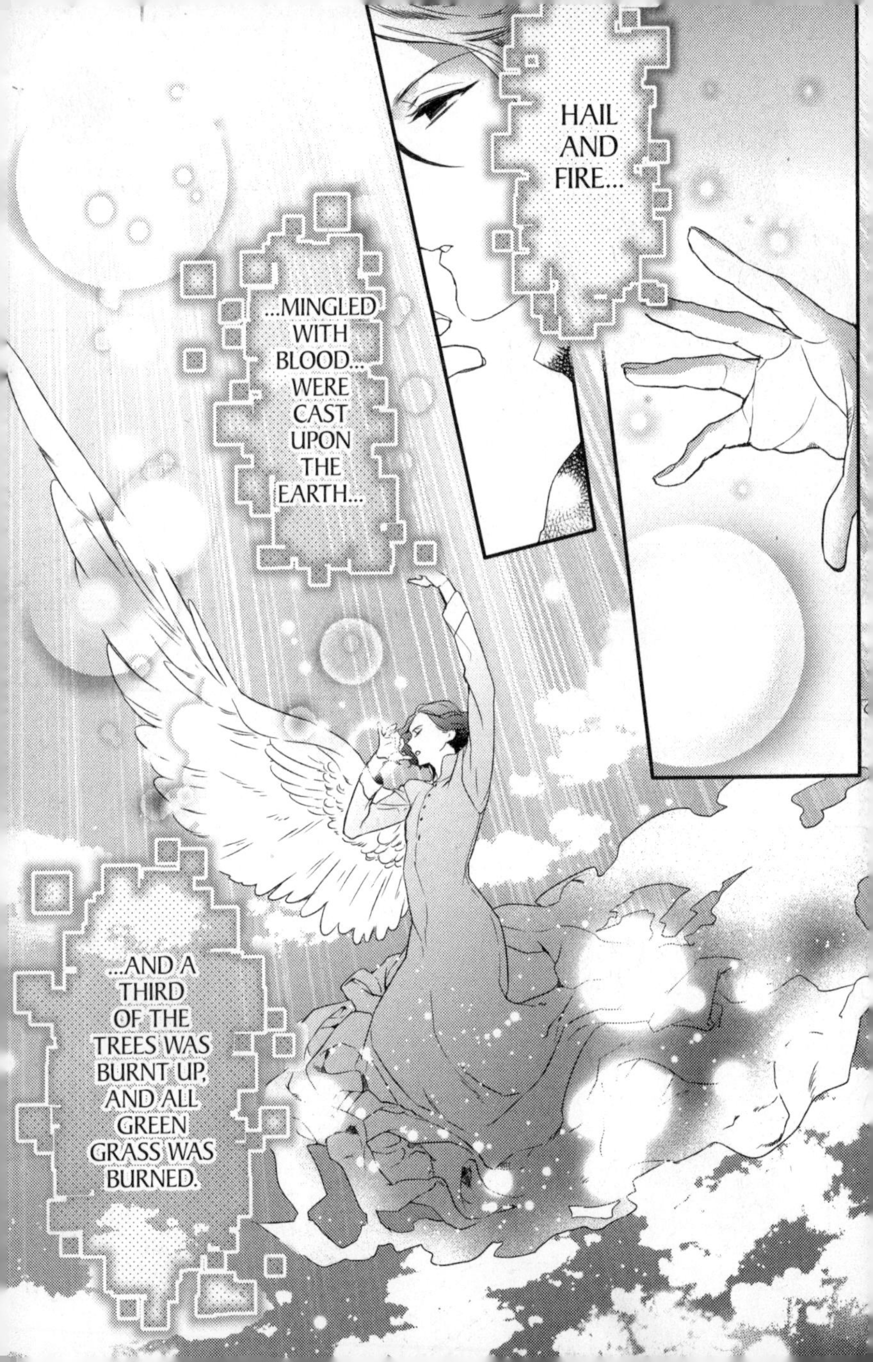
HAIL AND FIRE...
...MINGLED WITH BLOOD... WERE CAST UPON THE EARTH...
...AND A THIRD OF THE TREES WAS BURNT UP, AND ALL GREEN GRASS WAS BURNED.

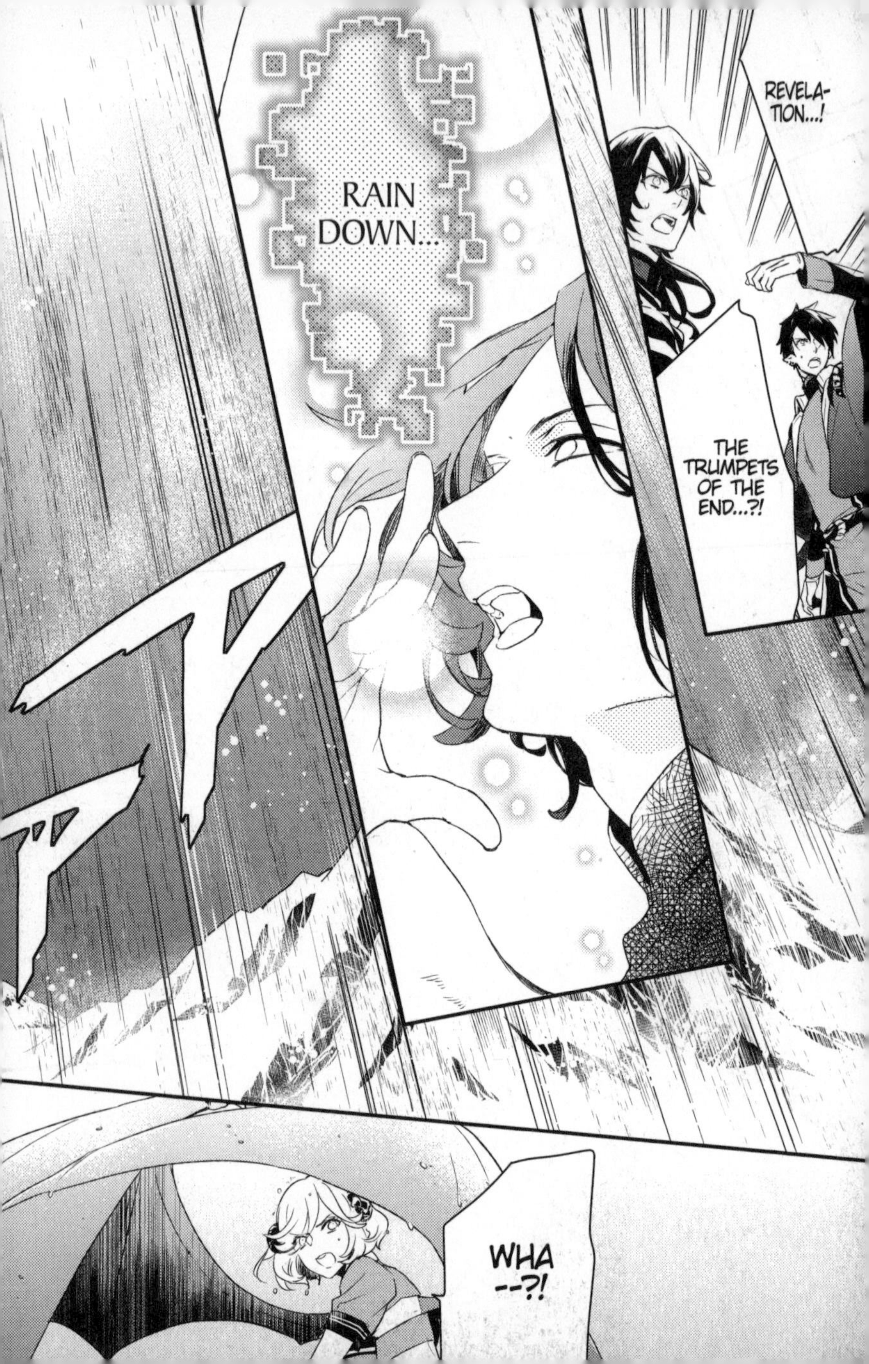
REVELA-
TION...!
THE TRUMPETS OF THE END...?!
RAIN DOWN...
WHA--?!

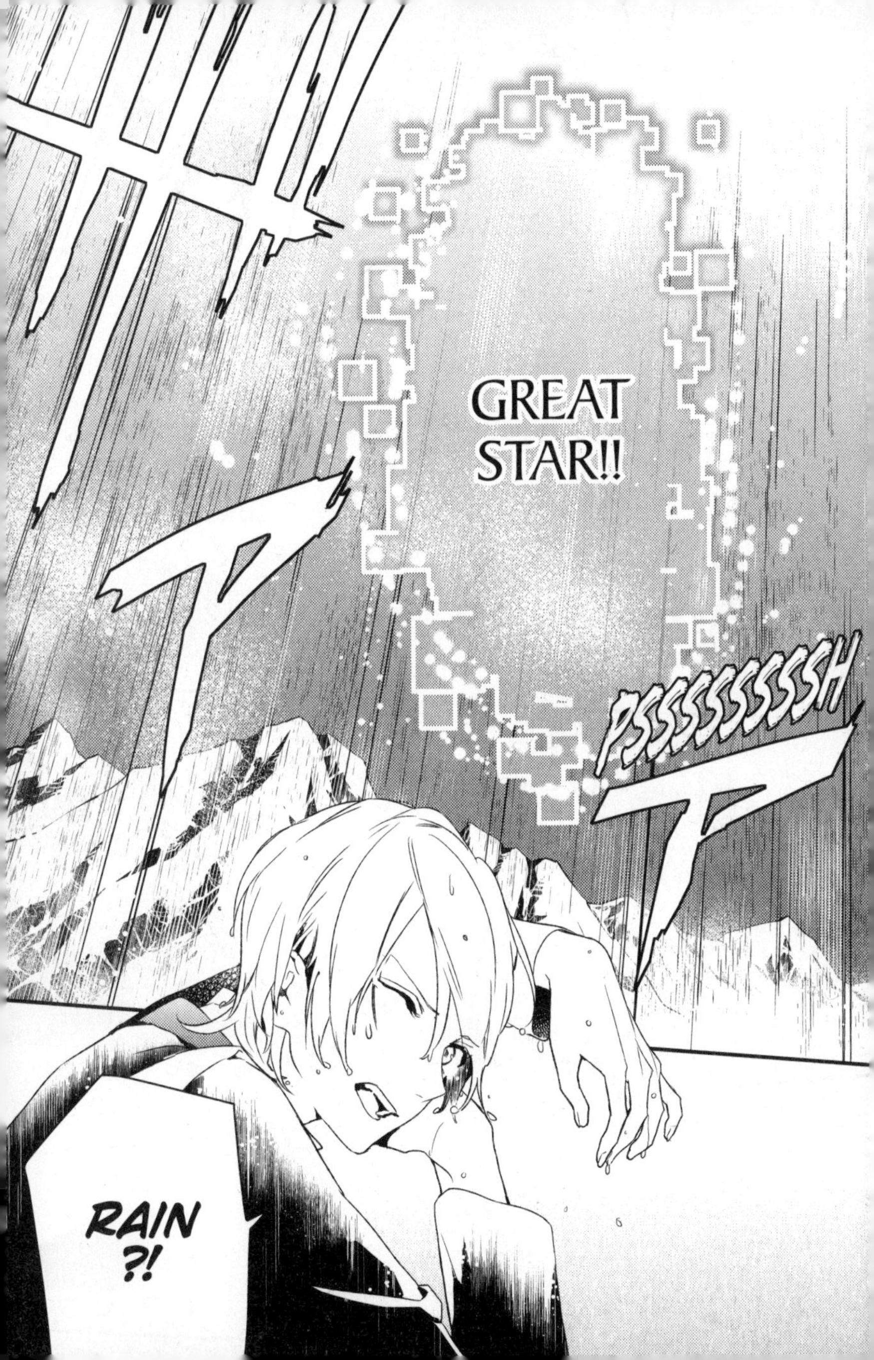
GREAT STAR!!
PSSSSSSSSSH
RAIN ?!

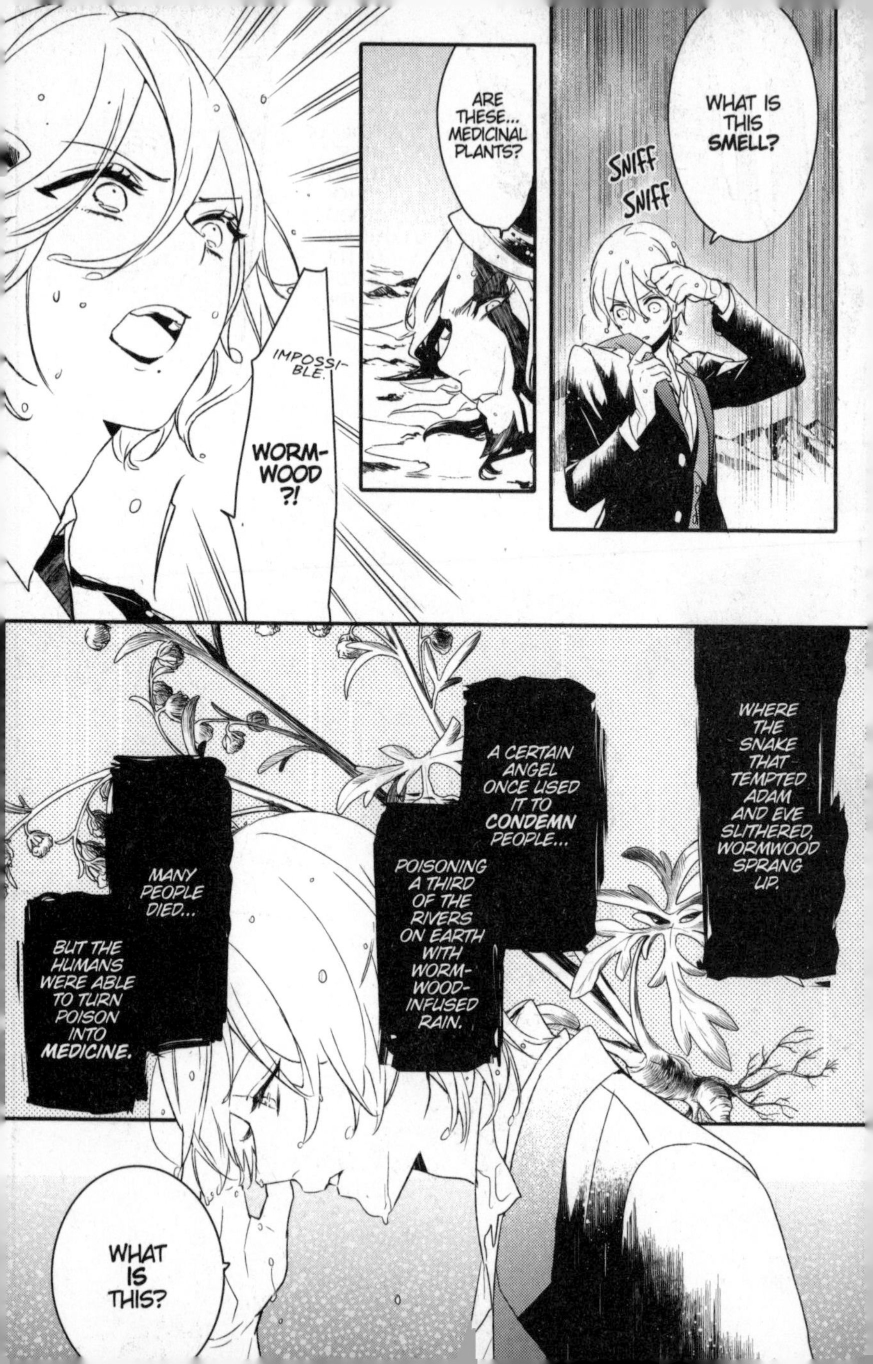
WHAT IS THIS SMELL?
SNIFF SNIFF
ARE THESE... MEDICINAL PLANTS?
IMPOSSIBLE.
WORMWOOD?!
WHERE THE SNAKE THAT TEMPTED ADAM AND EVE SLITHERED, WORMWOOD SPRANG UP.
A CERTAIN ANGEL ONCE USED IT TO **CONDEMN** PEOPLE...
POISONING A THIRD OF THE RIVERS ON EARTH WITH WORMWOOD-INFUSED RAIN.
MANY PEOPLE DIED...
BUT THE HUMANS WERE ABLE TO TURN POISON INTO **MEDICINE**.
WHAT IS THIS?

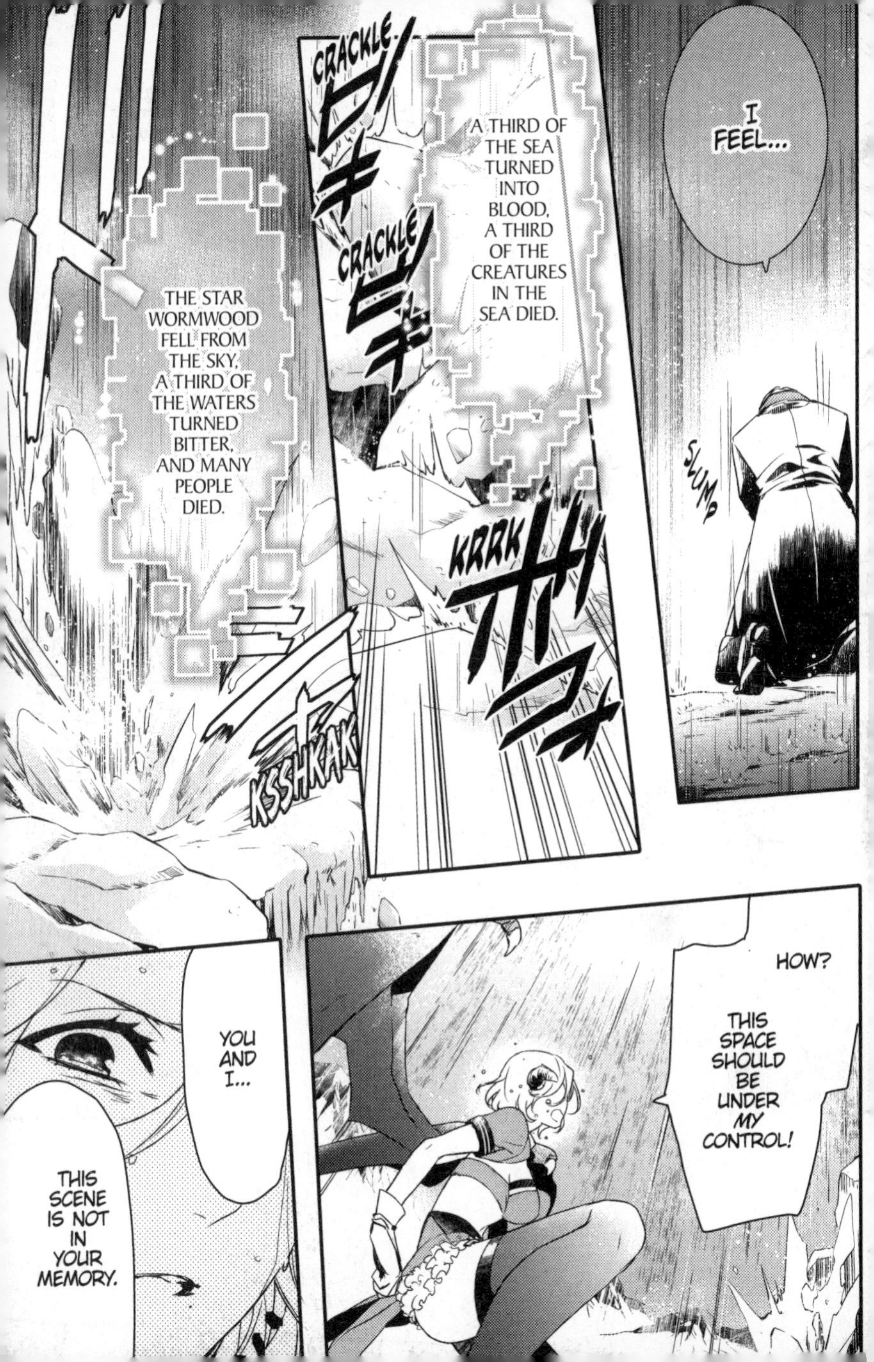
I FEEL...
SLUMP
CRACKLE
CRACKLE
A THIRD OF THE SEA TURNED INTO BLOOD, A THIRD OF THE CREATURES IN THE SEA DIED.
KRRK
THE STAR WORMWOOD FELL FROM THE SKY, A THIRD OF THE WATERS TURNED BITTER, AND MANY PEOPLE DIED.
KSSHKAK
HOW?
THIS SPACE SHOULD BE UNDER MY CONTROL!
YOU AND I...
THIS SCENE IS NOT IN YOUR MEMORY.

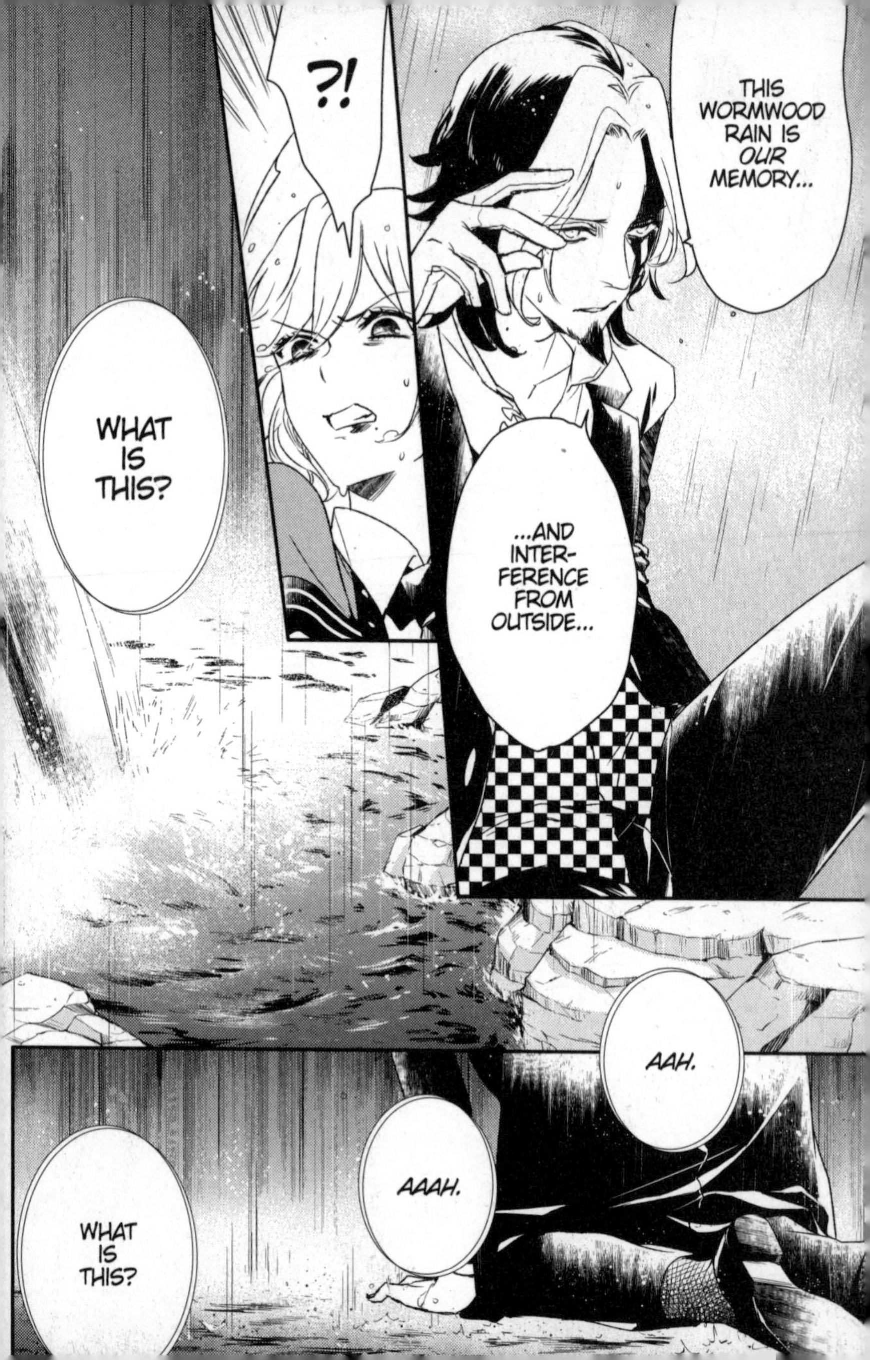
THIS WORMWOOD RAIN IS *OUR* MEMORY...
?!
...AND INTER-FERENCE FROM OUTSIDE...
WHAT IS THIS?
AAH.
AAAH.
WHAT IS THIS?

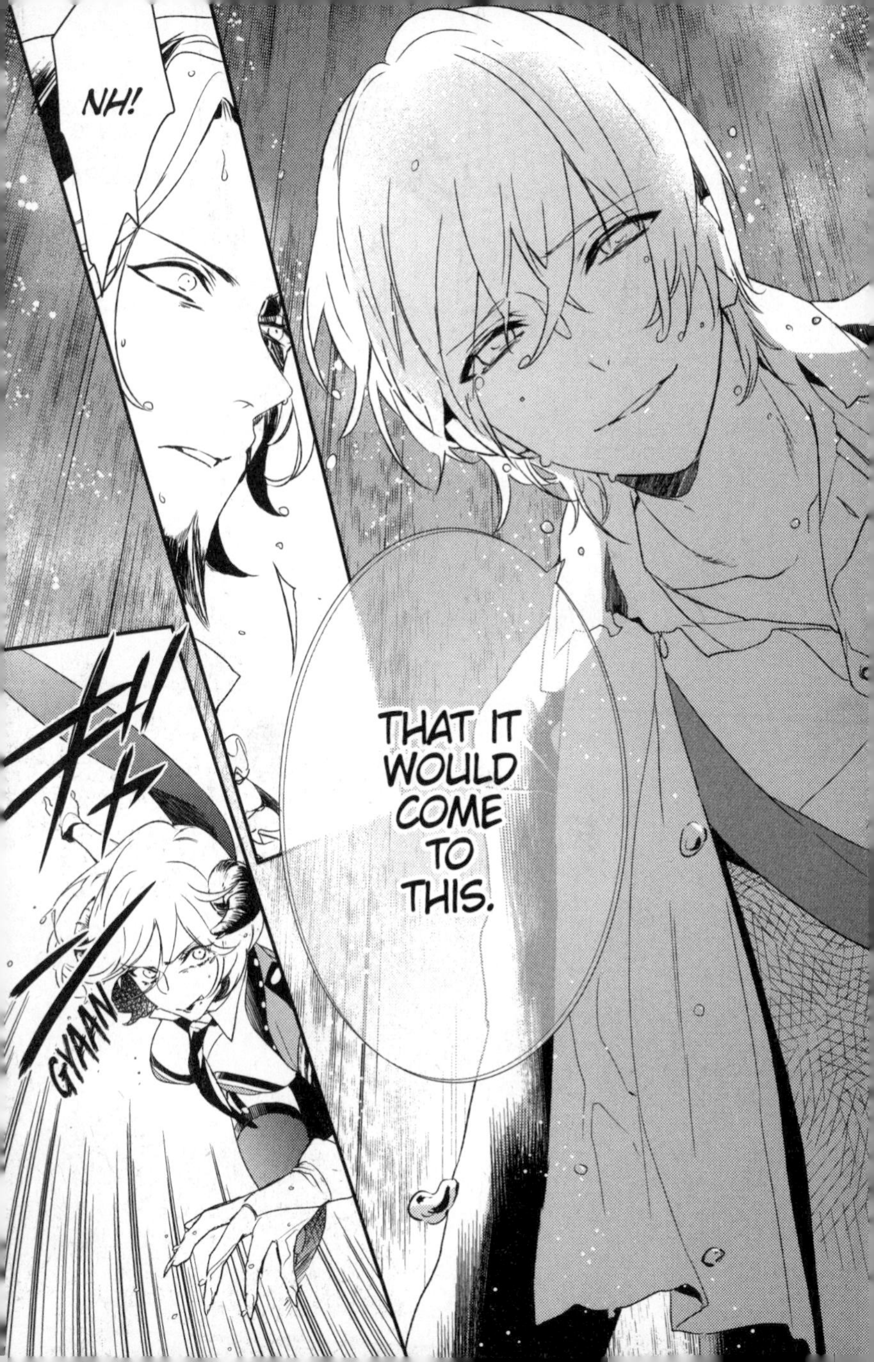
THAT IT WOULD COME TO THIS.
NH!
GYAAN

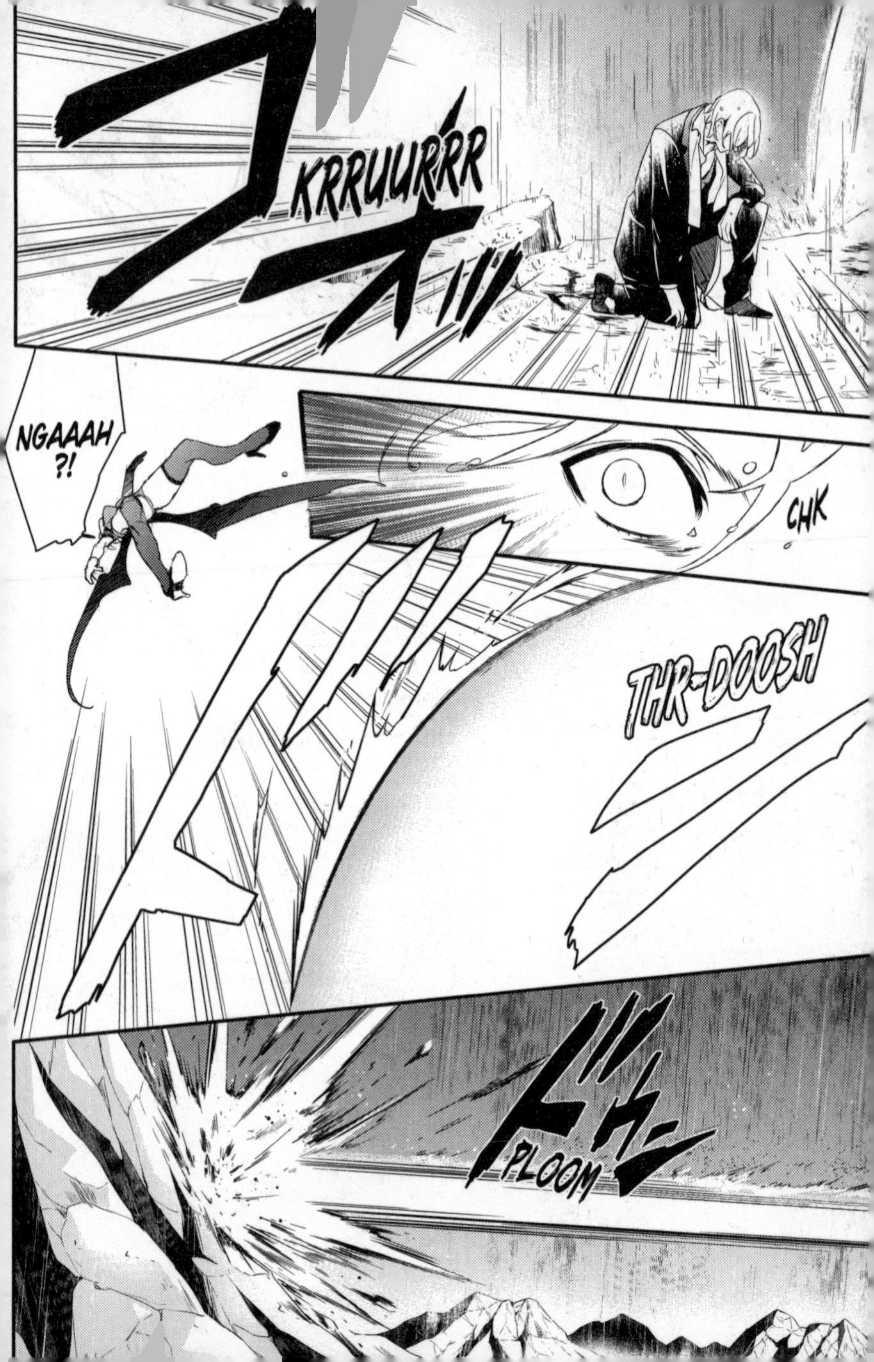
KRRUURRR
CHK
NGAAAH ?!
THR-DOOSH
PLOOM

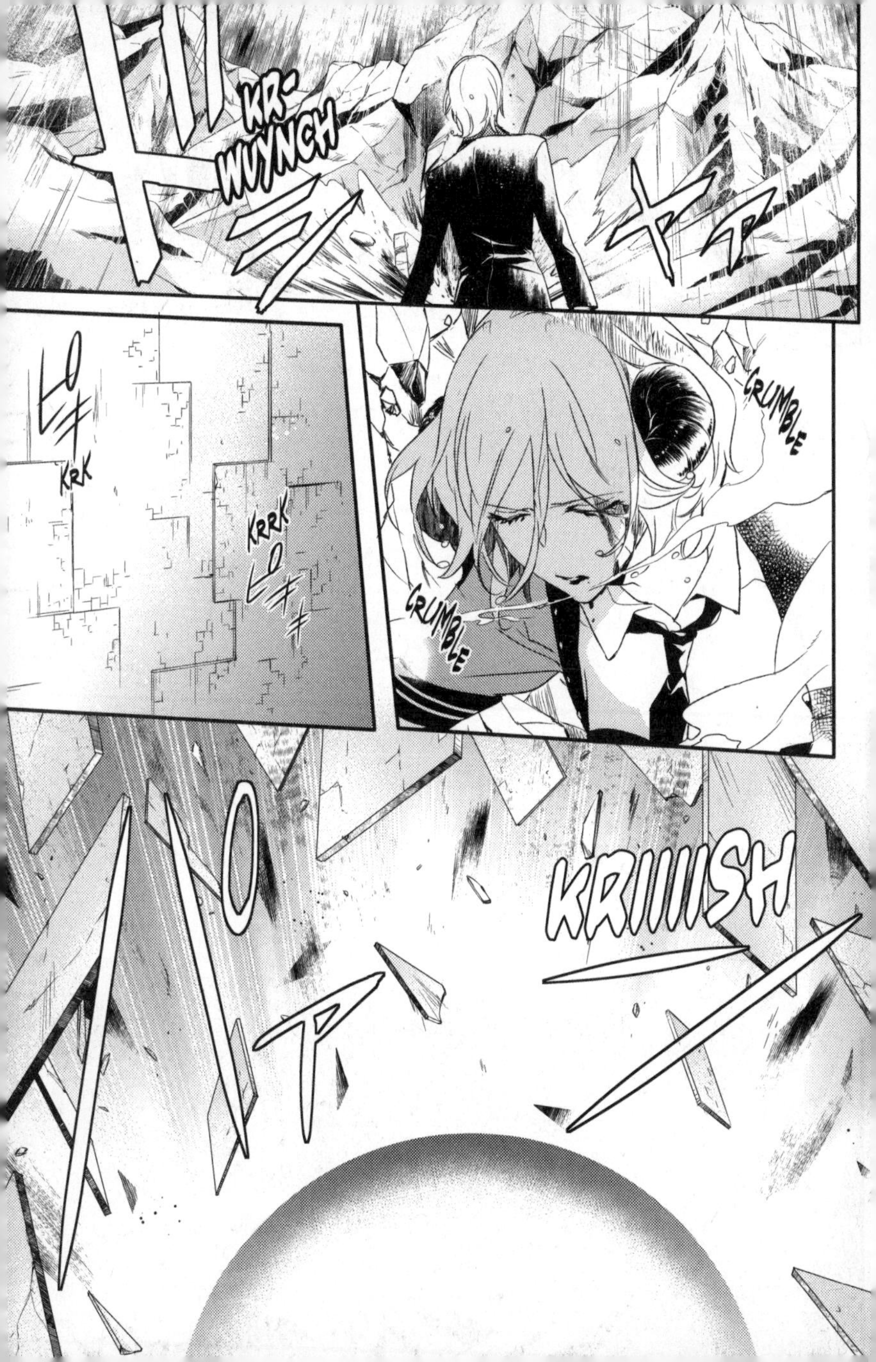
KR-WUYNCH
CRUMBLE
CRUMBLE
KRK
KRRK
KRIIIISH

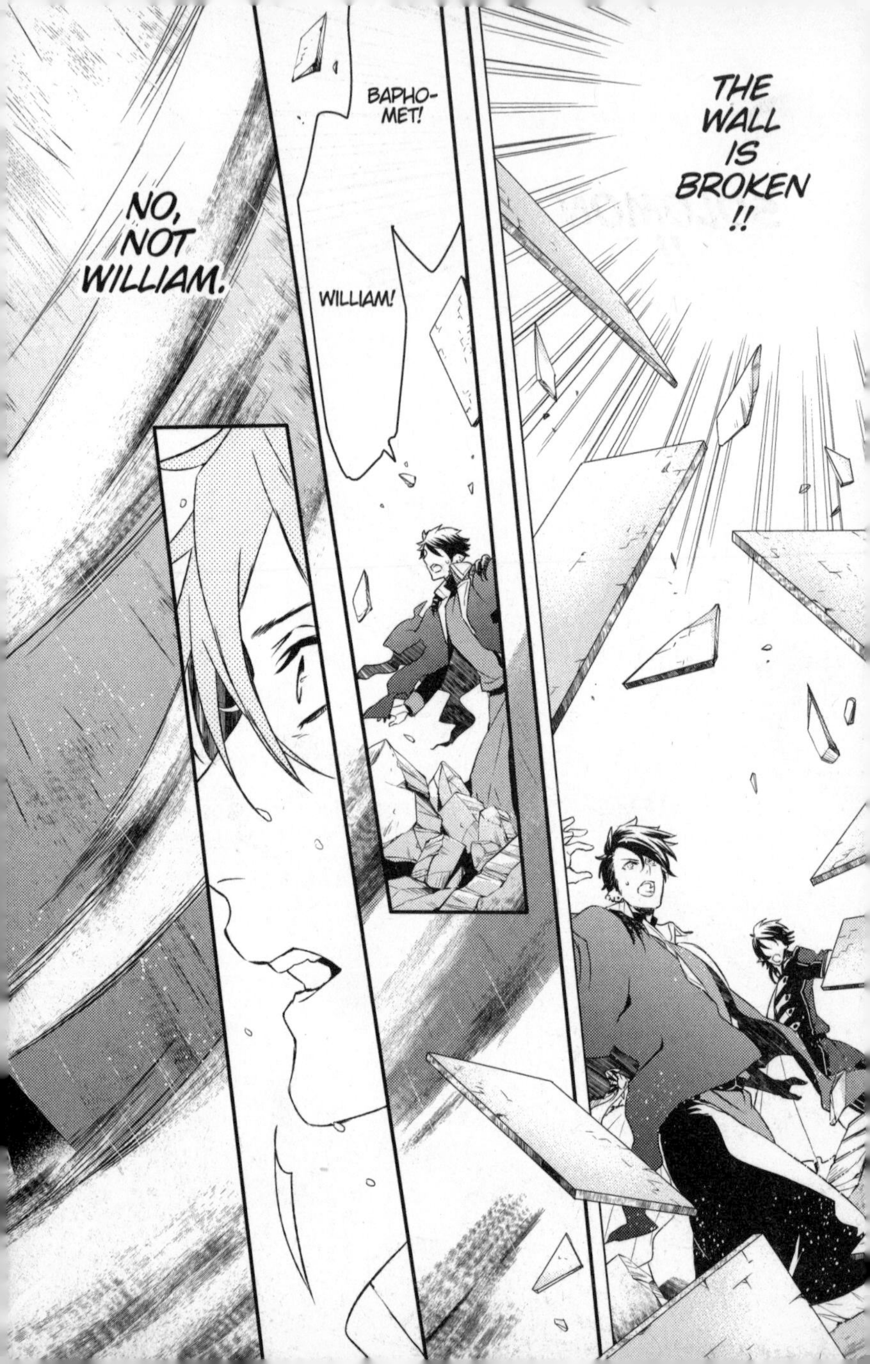
THE WALL IS BROKEN!!
BAPHO-MET!
WILLIAM!
NO, NOT WILLIAM.

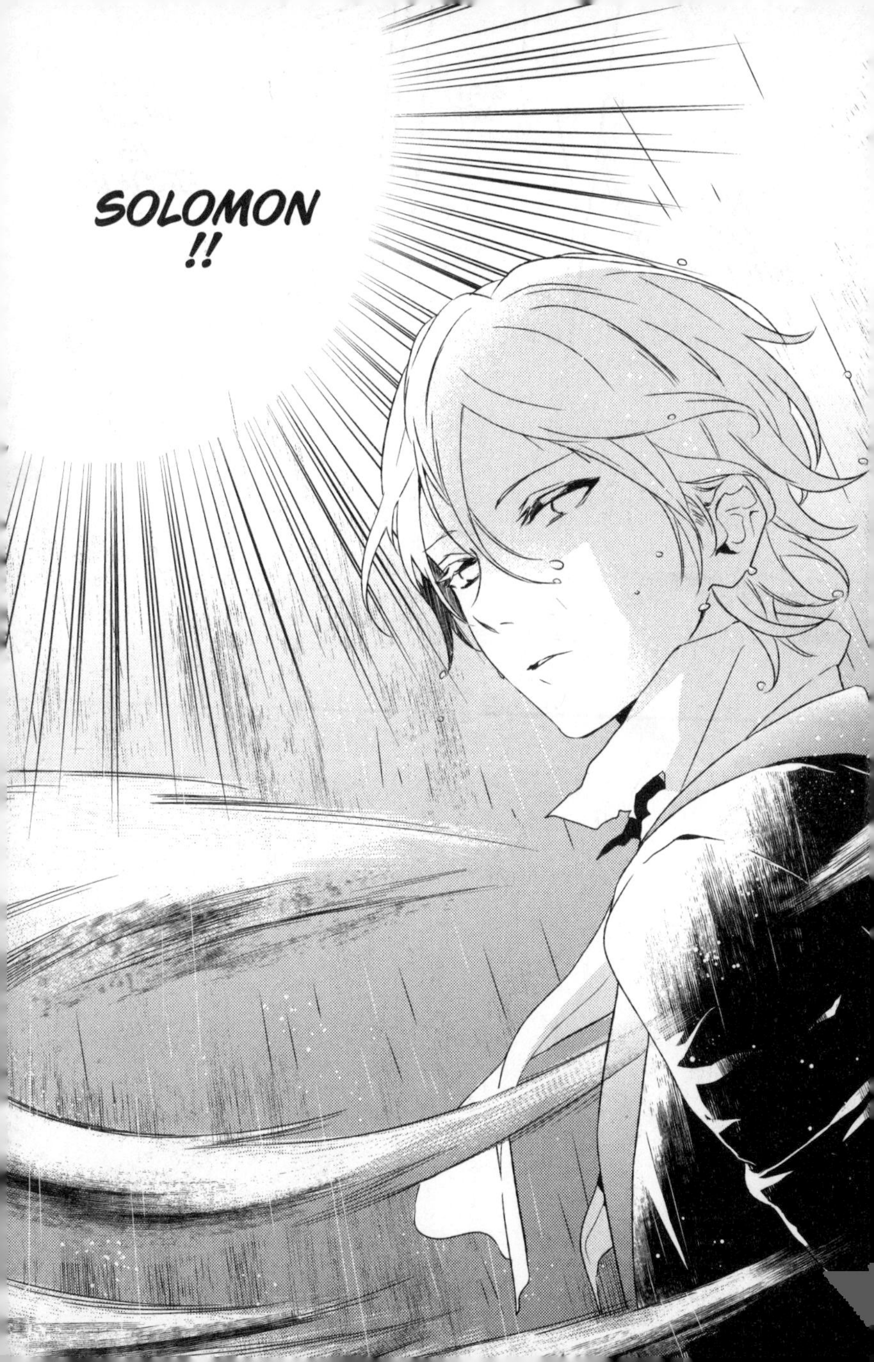
SOLOMON !!

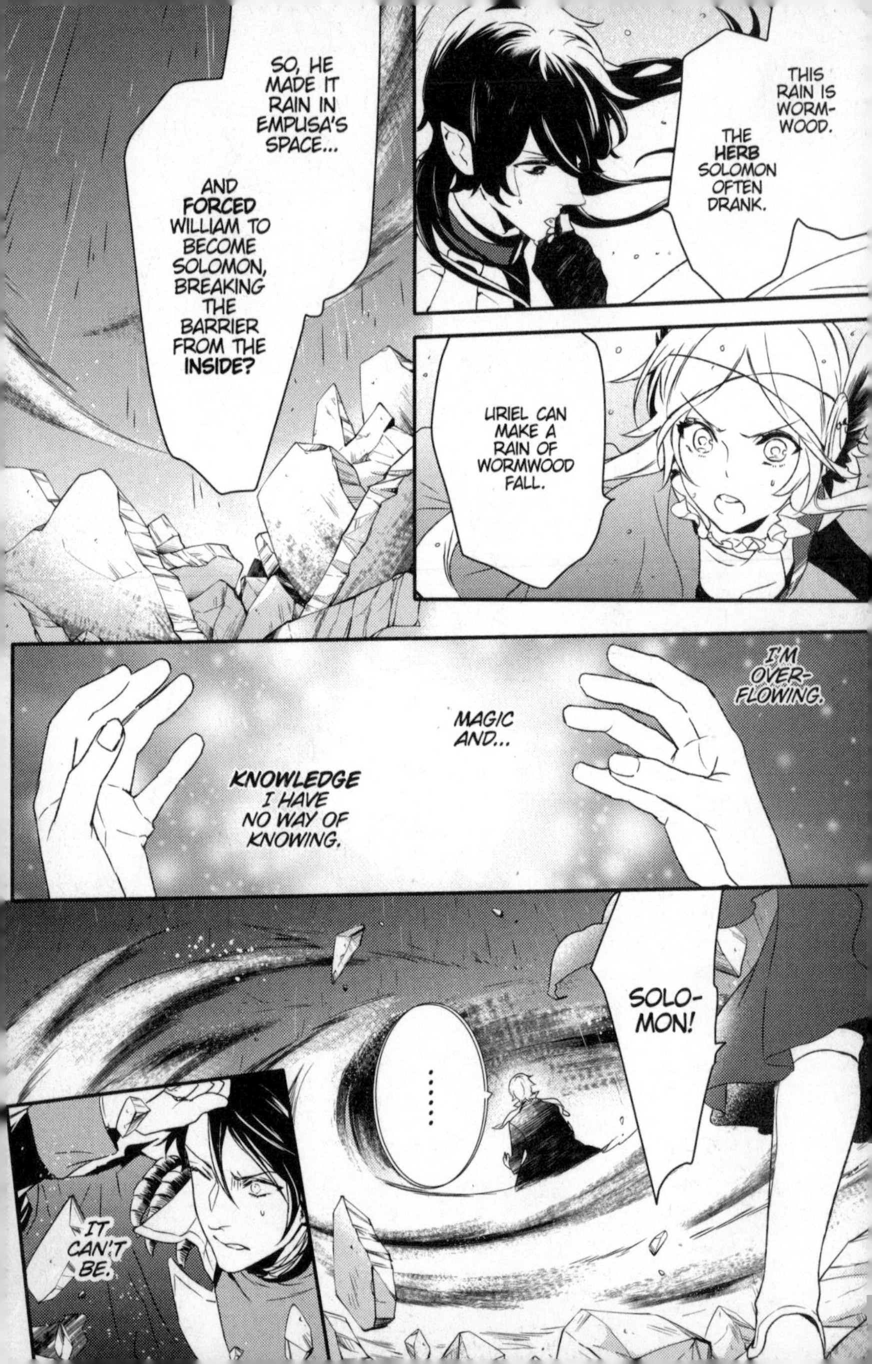
THIS RAIN IS WORM-WOOD.
THE HERB SOLOMON OFTEN DRANK.
URIEL CAN MAKE A RAIN OF WORMWOOD FALL.
SO, HE MADE IT RAIN IN EMPUSA'S SPACE...
AND FORCED WILLIAM TO BECOME SOLOMON, BREAKING THE BARRIER FROM THE INSIDE?
I'M OVER-FLOWING.
MAGIC AND...
KNOWLEDGE I HAVE NO WAY OF KNOWING.
SOLO-MON!
......
IT CAN'T BE.

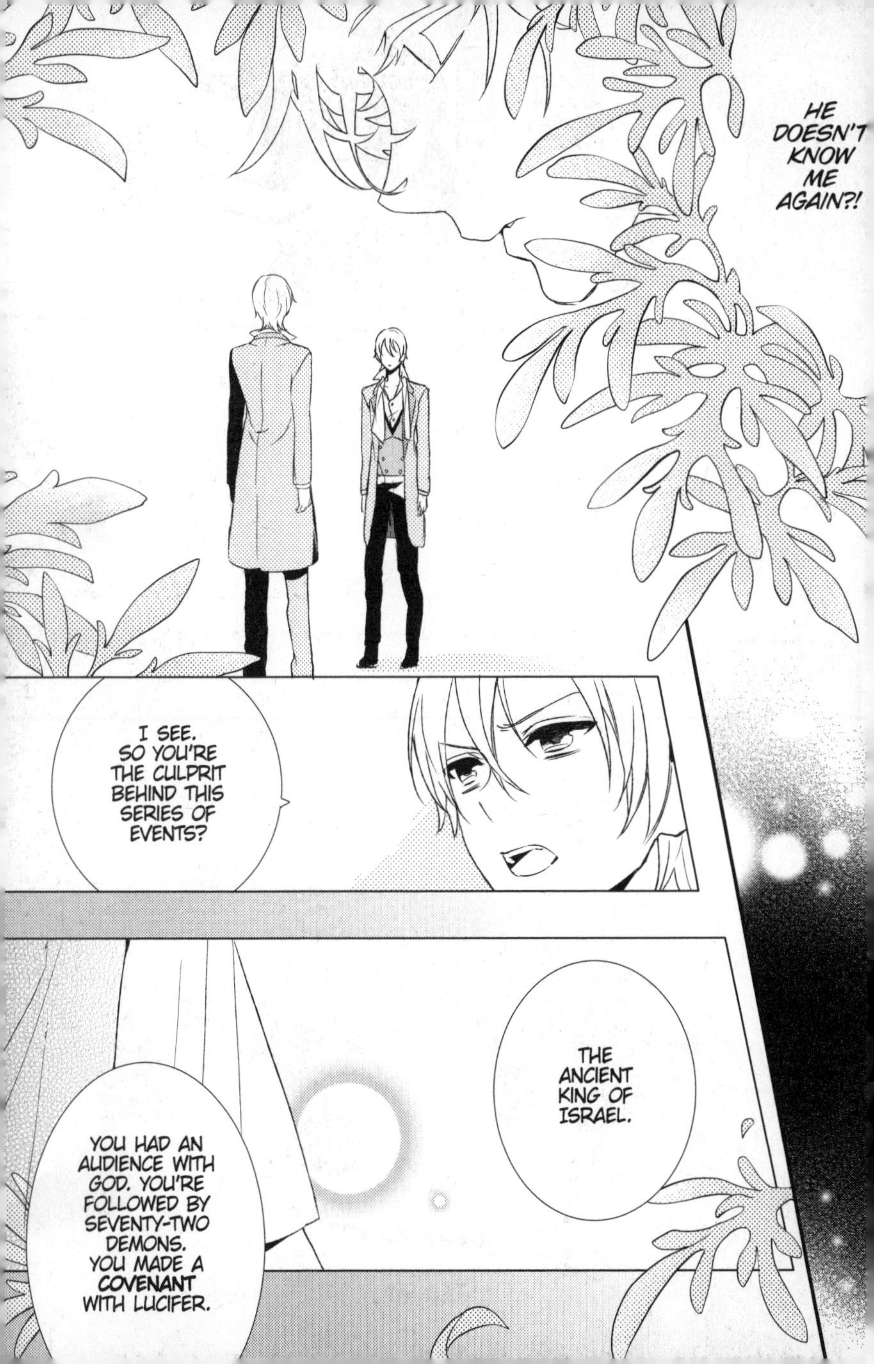
HE DOESN'T KNOW ME AGAIN?!
I SEE. SO YOU'RE THE CULPRIT BEHIND THIS SERIES OF EVENTS?
THE ANCIENT KING OF ISRAEL.
YOU HAD AN AUDIENCE WITH GOD. YOU'RE FOLLOWED BY SEVENTY-TWO DEMONS. YOU MADE A **COVENANT** WITH LUCIFER.

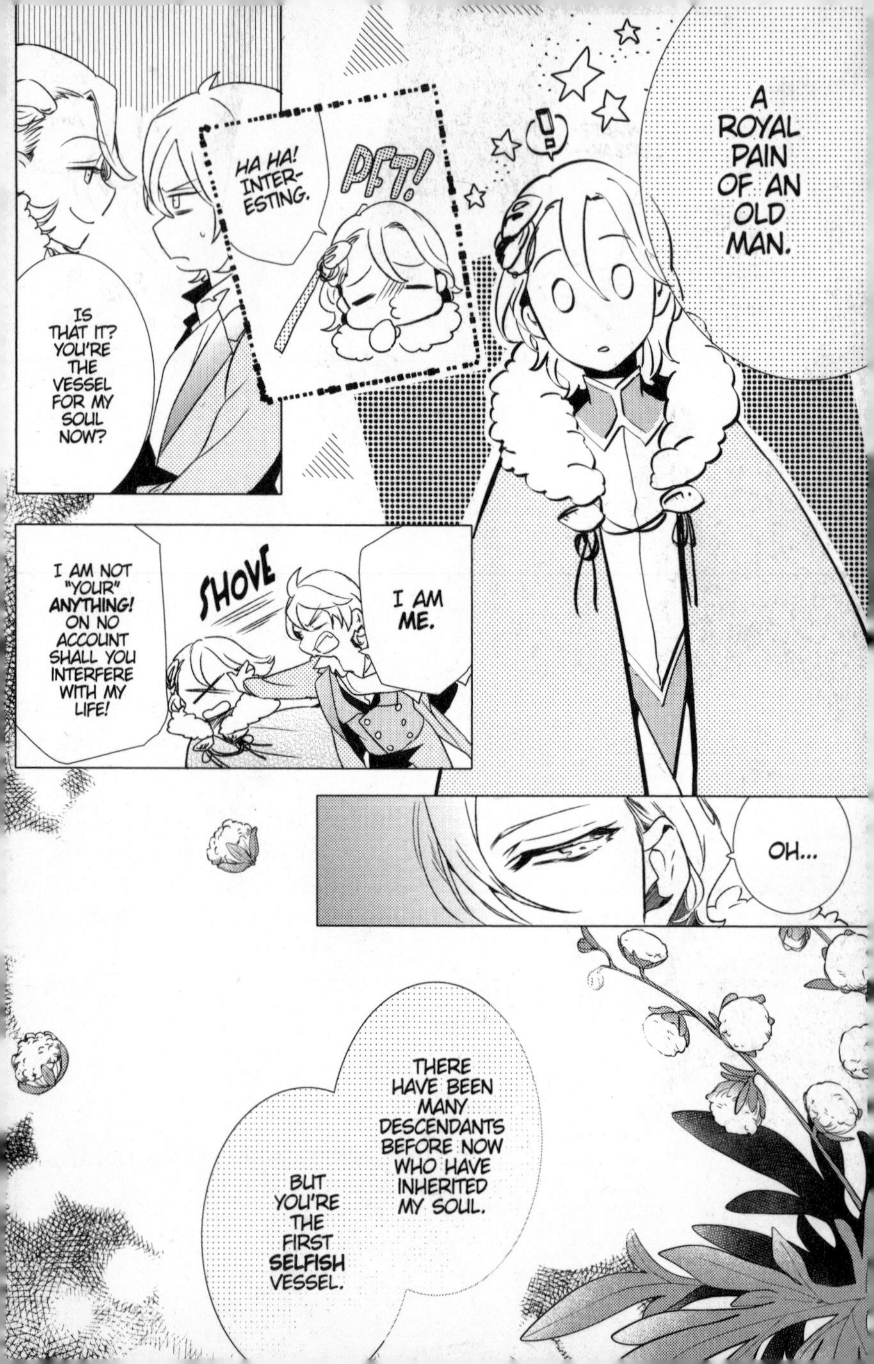
!
A ROYAL PAIN OF AN OLD MAN.
HA HA! INTERESTING.
PFT!
IS THAT IT? YOU'RE THE VESSEL FOR MY SOUL NOW?
I AM ME.
SHOVE
I AM NOT "YOUR" ANYTHING! ON NO ACCOUNT SHALL YOU INTERFERE WITH MY LIFE!
OH...
THERE HAVE BEEN MANY DESCENDANTS BEFORE NOW WHO HAVE INHERITED MY SOUL.
BUT YOU'RE THE FIRST SELFISH VESSEL.

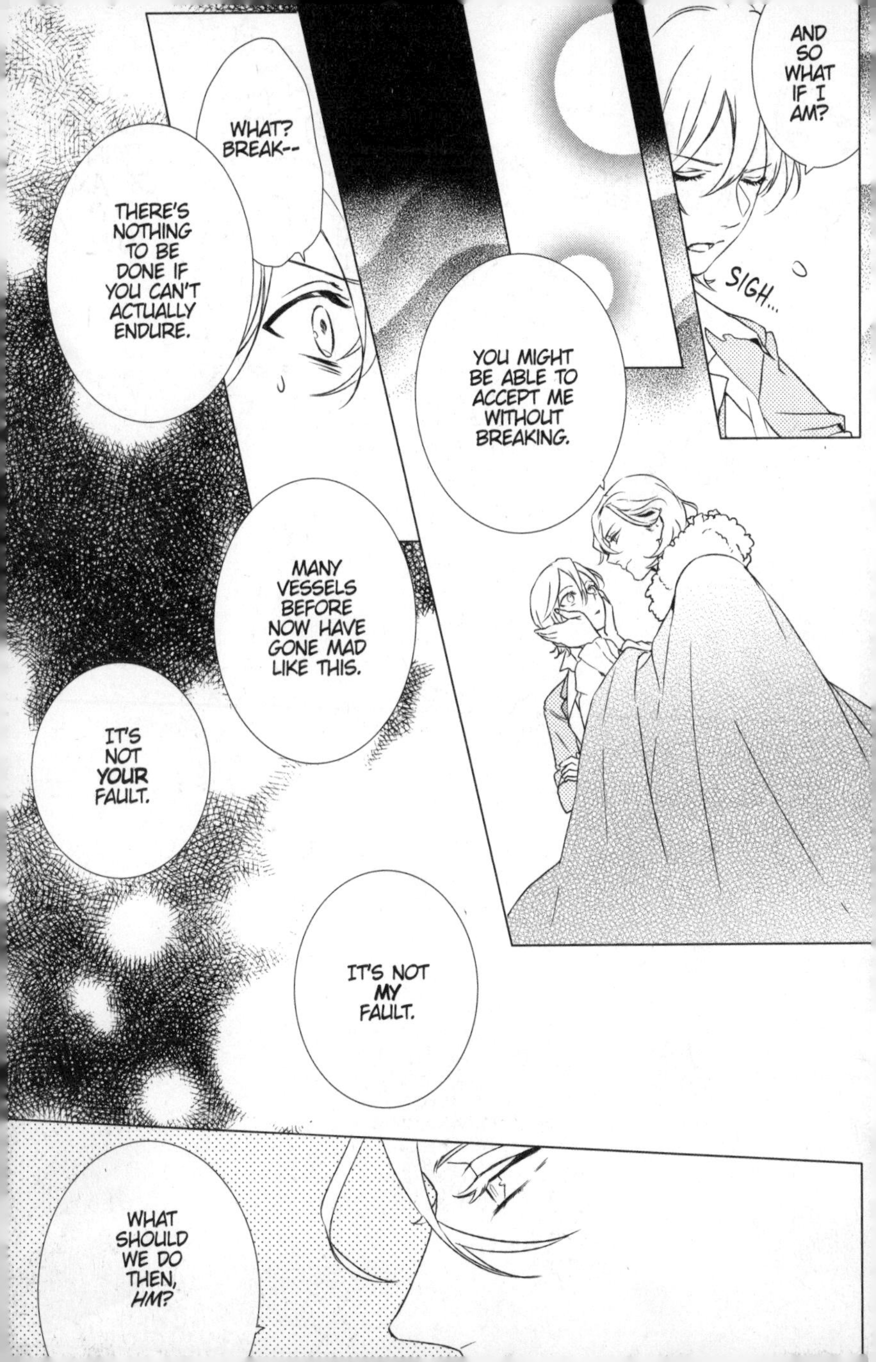
AND SO WHAT IF I AM?
SIGH...
YOU MIGHT BE ABLE TO ACCEPT ME WITHOUT BREAKING.
WHAT? BREAK--
THERE'S NOTHING TO BE DONE IF YOU CAN'T ACTUALLY ENDURE.
MANY VESSELS BEFORE NOW HAVE GONE MAD LIKE THIS.
IT'S NOT YOUR FAULT.
IT'S NOT MY FAULT.
WHAT SHOULD WE DO THEN, HM?

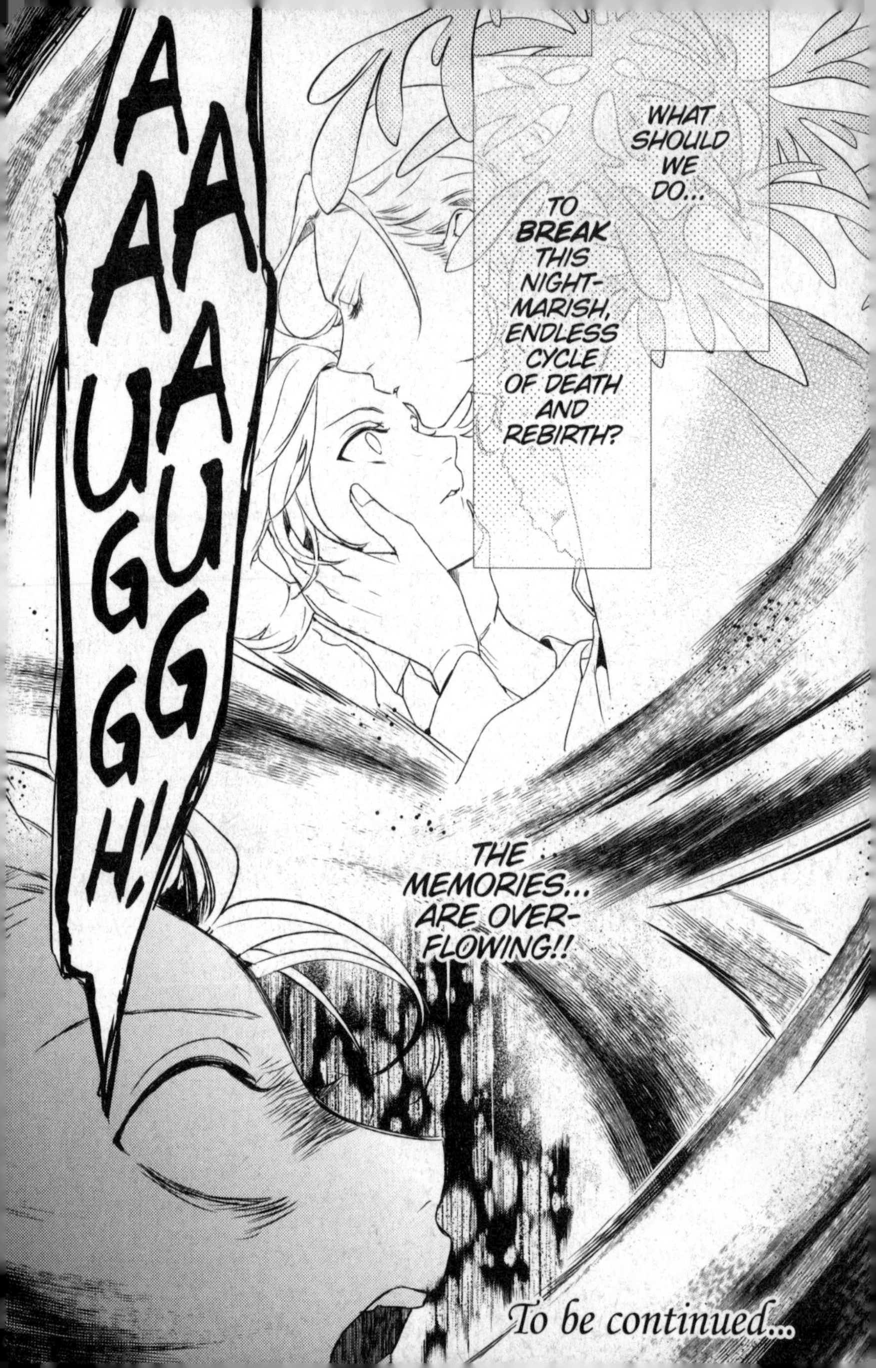
WHAT SHOULD WE DO...
TO BREAK THIS NIGHT-MARISH, ENDLESS CYCLE OF DEATH AND REBIRTH?
AAAAAUUGGGGH!!
THE MEMORIES... ARE OVER-FLOWING!!
To be continued...

魔界王子

devils and realist

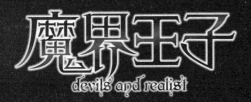

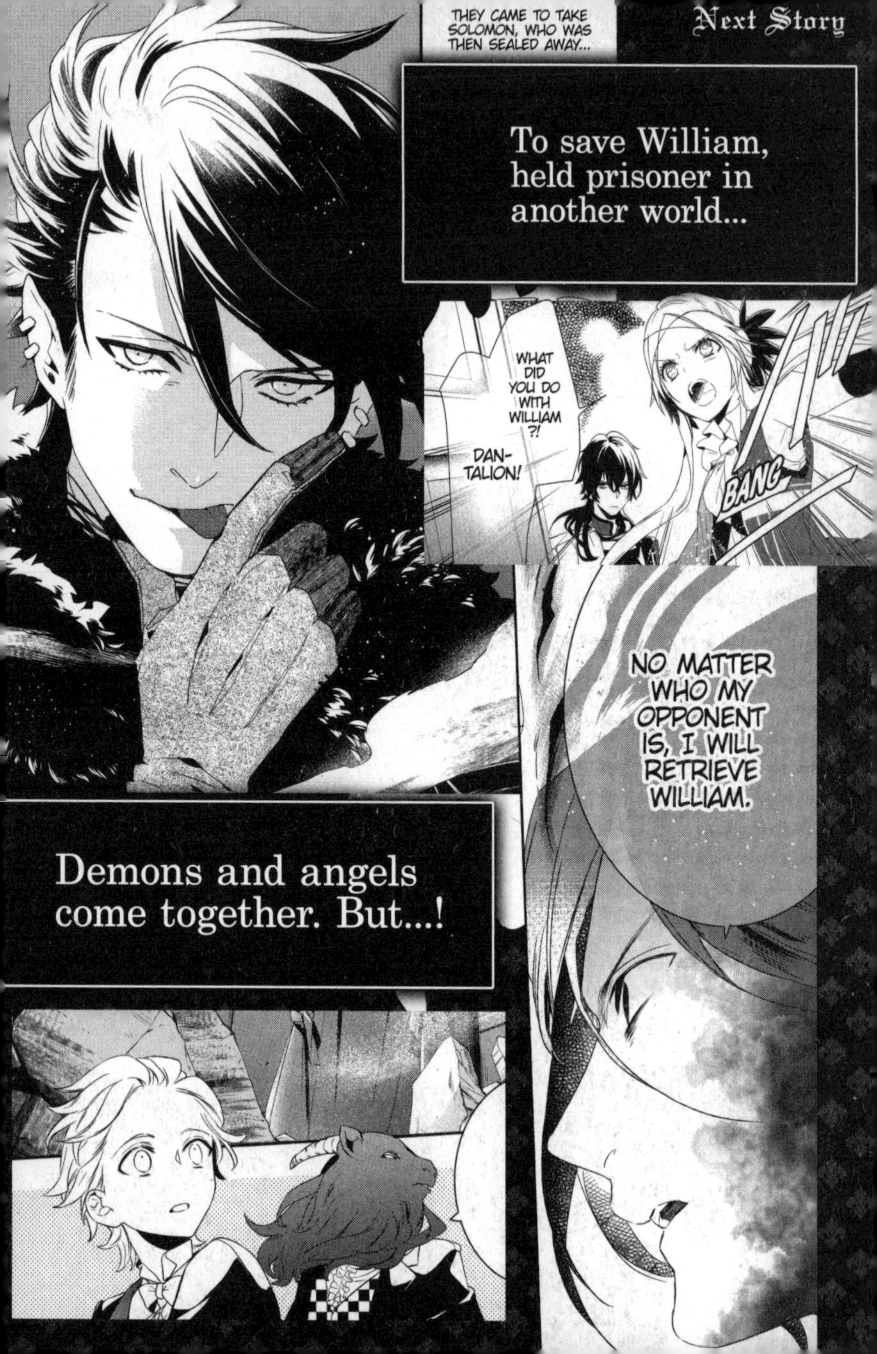
Next Story
THEY CAME TO TAKE SOLOMON, WHO WAS THEN SEALED AWAY...
To save William, held prisoner in another world...
WHAT DID YOU DO WITH WILLIAM ?!
DAN-TALION!
BANG
NO MATTER WHO MY OPPONENT IS, I WILL RETRIEVE WILLIAM.
Demons and angels come together. But...!

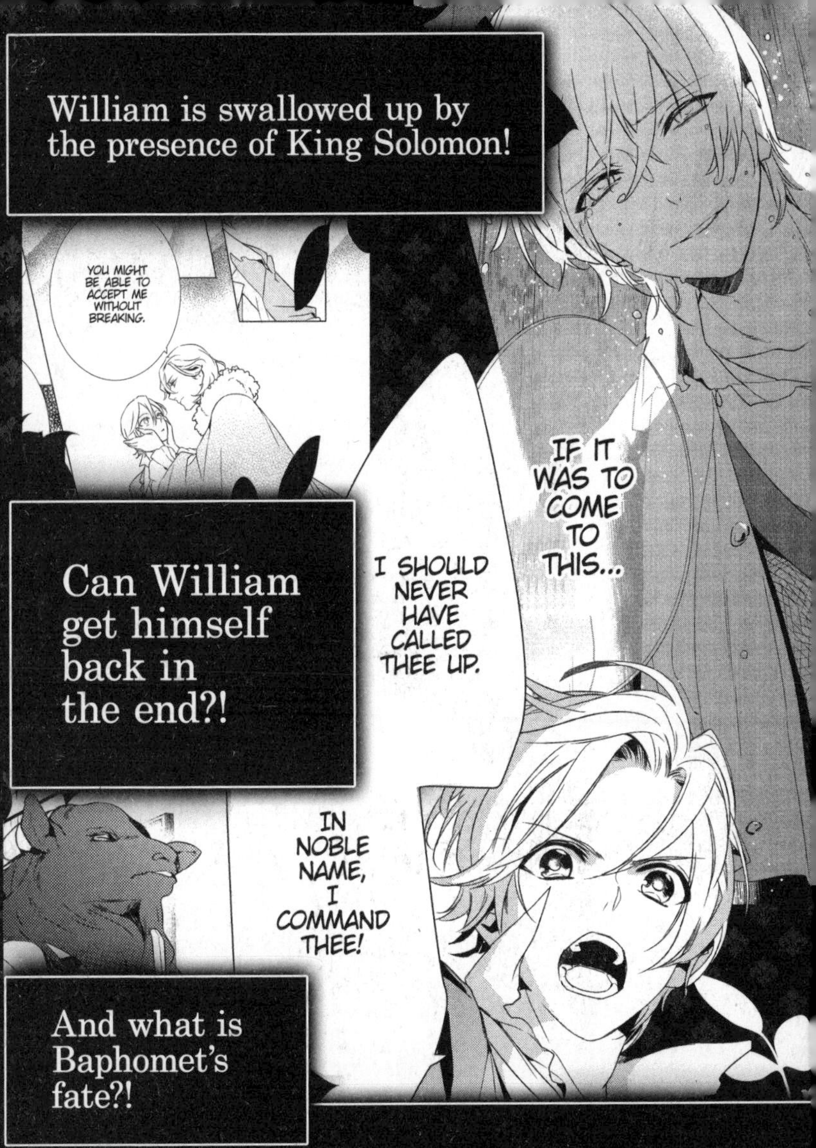
William is swallowed up by the presence of King Solomon!
IF IT WAS TO COME TO THIS...
I SHOULD NEVER HAVE CALLED THEE UP.
YOU MIGHT BE ABLE TO ACCEPT ME WITHOUT BREAKING.
Can William get himself back in the end?!
IN NOBLE NAME, I COMMAND THEE!
And what is Baphomet's fate?!

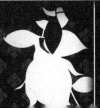

The fleeting changes of the world!
Volume 11, coming soon!

SEVEN SEAS ENTERTAINMENT PRESENTS

Devils and Realist

art by UTAKO YUKIHIRO / story by MADOKA TAKADONO   VOLUME 10

...AI OUJI: DEVILS AND REALIST VOL. 10
...ko Yukihiro/Madoka Takadono 2015
...ublished in Japan in 2015 by ICHIJINSHA Inc., Tokyo.
...sh translation rights arranged with ICHIJINSHA Inc., Tokyo, Japan.

...n Seas books may be purchased in bulk for educational, business, or
...ptional use. For information on bulk purchases, please contact Macmillan
...rate & Premium Sales Department at 1-800-221-7945 (ext 5442)
...te specialmarkets@macmillan.com.

...n Seas and the Seven Seas logo are trademarks of
...n Seas Entertainment, LLC. All rights reserved.

...: 978-1-626922-94-5

...ed in Canada

...Printing: August 2016

...8 7 6 5 4 3 2 1

FOLLOW US ONLINE: *www.gomanga.com*

READING DIRECTIONS

This book reads from ***right to left***, Japanese style. If this is your first time reading manga, you start reading from the top right panel on each page and take it from there. If you get lost, just follow the numbered diagram here. It may seem backwards at first, but you'll get the hang of it! Have fun!!

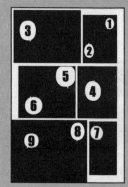